Modern Egyptian Drama

STUDIES IN MIDDLE EASTERN LITERATURE — NUMBER THREE

Farouk Abdel Wahab

MODERN EGYPTIAN DRAMA

An Anthology

Bibliotheca Islamica, Inc.
MINNEAPOLIS & CHICAGO
1974

Copyright © 1974 by Farouk Abdel Wahab
Manufactured in the United States of America
Library of Congress Catalog Card Number: 72-94939
ISBN: 0-88297-005-4

BIBLIOTHECA ISLAMICA, INC./Booksellers & Publishers
Box 14174 University Station
Minneapolis, Mn. 55403/U.S.A.

To my first love

EGYPT

Contents

INTRODUCTION

The Egyptian theatre has roots that go back more than
five thousand years, but its growth, if we can use such
a word to describe its sporadic shoots, has been extremely uneven. Like almost all the other aspects of intellectual and creative life in ancient Egypt (and indeed
throughout the ancient world) art was closely related
to and in the service of religion and the state – two
sectors that, in the case of Egypt, were almost inex-
tricably inter-related. One of the oldest theological
documents so far uncovered, namely *The Memphite Theology*
(which was published by the German Egyptologist, Kurt
Sethe, under the title *Dramatische Texte* in 1928), is both
an account of creation and an explanation, in short dramatic scenes, of the concept of kingship. It relates
how Horus got his inheritance and lays down the pattern that each new king is Horus succeeding his father
Osiris who was unjustly slain and dismembered by his
wicked brother Seth the "god of confusion." Horus's
succession is thus an act of retribution that brings
an end to chaos. Most of the works identified as dramas
or dramatic fragments by Egyptologists, particularly
Etienne Drioton to whom must go the credit for the
first serious and so far most thorough investigation of
the genre in ancient Egypt, focus on this issue and/or
on the part played by Isis, the wife of Osiris, in pro-
tecting Horus and preparing him for his rightful place
on his father's throne. One of the most important plays

or "cycles" (vaguely resembling medieval European Mystery and Passion Plays) is "The Passion Play of Osiris" which seems to have been performed regularly at Abydos, and which recounts the dismemberment of Osiris and his ultimate triumph. It is in this sense that ancient Egyptian drama was essentially religious. Some "productions," however, were more religious than others, in that they were presented in temples before select audiences of initiates. Those are often referred to as "mysteries" and there is abundant evidence that very sophisticated and lavish theatrical effects and properties were used in the production thereof. Other productions, those that are sometimes called "succession and jubilee dramas," for instance, were performed in halls built specifically for such purposes with miniature replicas of various edifices symbolizing different locations in Egypt. In those performances, the new king himself would play the leading role and would, in front of his subjects, be "transformed" into Horus.

In addition to such highly ceremonial performances as coronation and jubilee plays (the latter known as Heb Sed plays), there seems to have existed a less formal variety of drama in ancient Egypt. Herodotus, who admittedly testifies to less ancient practices than those offered by archaeological finds, claims that his people imported Bacchic festivals among other things from Egypt. A more ancient testimony was left behind by what some Egyptologists believe to be the commemorative stela of a wandering actor by the name of Emheb. Whether Emheb was a professional actor in a "commercial" company or simply an amateur is not readily ascertainable. He tells us, for instance, that he spent three years playing the tom-tom all the time. "I it was," the actor brags, "who accompanied his master on all his journeyings and who didn't grow tired of the declamations which he recited," and "I was the partner of my master in all his declamations. When he was a god, I was a prince; when he killed, I brought back to life." Emheb lists the places where he and his master had been and these lie over the country.

Although there is still much to be known about the

ancient Egyptian theatre, it is possible here to make
some remarks about its basic features. The most strik-
ing feature is, of course, the religious nature of most
performances. This is mainly so because of the *dramatis
personae*, who were gods and goddesses for the most part
(although in certain cases they were presented in human
forms) and because most probably the "plays" were performed in temples or at consecrated spots on lakes or on
the Nile. Under the circumstances the ritual element
is bound to have had a strong presence, especially in
cases where plays did not stop at imitating reality but
actually changed it (coronations, for instance). In this
sense these dramas were not simply means by which religion was commented upon, but were themselves the religion, and it is here that similarity with medieval European mystery and miracle plays ends. Unlike such genres
as lyrical poetry or stories, there was very little room
for the Egyptian plays to turn completely secular because of the collective nature of the art, and because
of the sway the priests had at the time over what we
consider secular.

It is also likely that religion was responsible for
the absence of tragedy in ancient Egypt. To begin with,
gods do not die but, at worst, suffer transformations.
Osiris, for instance, although slain and mutilated, is
transformed into the god of the nether world; and Seth
keeps reappearing in different guises after being completely vanquished. Besides, death, even for mortals,
was more of a new beginning than an end.

Whether or not the ancient Egyptian theatre might have
developed along the same lines as the Greek theatre is
purely conjectural and need not concern us here. Historians of drama tend to forget that even in Greece, and
specifically Athens, the magnificent flourishing of
tragedy and comedy was short-lived. Furthermore, Greek
drama developed under the influence of a host of cultural, political, economic and social factors, and in
an environment of intense intellectual ferment and not
under that of religion and ritual alone. At any rate,
the Egyptian theatre retained its gods and goddesses,
continually wrestled with succession to the throne, and
invariably had Horus succeed Osiris. Occasionally, this

drama was used to protest against foreign rulers, especially the Persians, who showed little respect for local
religious beliefs, and even the Greeks. Thus in the text
of the drama inscribed on the walls of the temple at
Edfu, namely "The Triumph of Horus over his Enemies,"
there are indications that Queen Cleopatra took part in
the play. She is referred to as "The Queen and Mistress
of the Two Lands, God's Mother of the Son of Ra (Ptole-
maeus-may-he-live-forever-Beloved-of-Ptah)."

In the meantime, the Greeks, and later the Romans, in
their closed communities in Egypt not only performed
their plays but taught them to school children. Several
papyri containing Greek plays or fragments of plays
have been found, and less than ten years ago, a Roman
theatre was unearthed in Alexandria. It has been re-
stored and plays are now performed in it every summer.

For a long time after the Egyptians lost their political independence, their culture continued side by side
with that of the invaders. However, in the year 392 A.D.,
Theodosius banned all forms of the pagan cult, and
those who disobeyed were charged with treason. The ban
dealt a fatal blow to all theatrical activities since
these could not be performed in secret. Egyptians who
converted to Christianity enriched their new religion
with parallelisms and commentaries which echoed the old
rituals. Those who did not convert right away, or did
so only formally, turned to magic and kept their traditions alive in a clandestine manner. A great number of
these traditions, with continual modifications, have
found their way into folklore and are today very much
alive, especially in the countryside.

Early Christianity in Egypt was too marred by tension
and conflict to develop its own mystery or miracle plays
although an abundant hagiographical literature arose.
With the Arab invasion in 641 A.D., the subsequent
settlements of Arabian, Persian, Turkish and North Af-
rican Muslims, the conversion of a considerable number
of Copts to Islam and the rapid Arabization of the
state, the indigenous cultural foundations of Egypt gave
way. Whatever survived of them did so within the closed
Christian communities, and the popular environment in
which the drama thrived ceased to exist. The new settlers

did not bring with them their own dramatic or theatrical forms, and it would be hard to imagine that they or the new Egyptian Muslims would have tolerated any theatrical activity. The turmoil attending such a transitional period and the inevitable loss of identity for the indigenous population as well as the new settlers caused Egypt to lose the social homogeneity necessary for a thriving popular theatre and led to a gap in the theatre's history.

Arabic literature in its classical and medieval periods, for all its richness and diversity and despite the abundance of dramatic elements in it, did not produce anything resembling drama as we know it today or as the Greeks knew it. We need not concern ourselves here with the various explanations given for this absence. It is sufficient to bear in mind that early Arabic literature was a product of the desert and of a basically nomadic way of life. And since the "ancients" did not produce or recognize drama as a legitimate genre, and an attitude of classicism came to dominate Arabic letters, drama did not have a chance to develop. Whatever dramatic forms appeared either locally or after prolonged association with other people had to content themselves with a peripheral existence for many centuries. It is amazing to note that Arab men of letters were familiar with Aristotle's *Poetics* and his *Rhetoric* in Arabic translation at an early stage, but that no evidence of familiarity with Greek drama has so far been discovered. It is also interesting that the early translators rendered "tragedy" as "panygeric" and "comedy" as "satire," having been misled by Aristotle's statement that tragedy and comedy, respectively, represent men better and lower than ourselves.

Of the popular theatrical forms which developed locally in Egypt, the *zar* seems to have been the oldest if only for its obvious affinity to both magic and pagan ritual. The *zar*, which one can still occasionally come across at the present day, involves magical chants and a dance for exorcising the demons possessing a person's soul. Although obviously psychotherapeutic in origin and nature, *zars* are quite elaborate productions. A variant of this collective art found its way into certain

Muslim groups, the so-called "dervishes" or sufi orders, the magical formulas being replaced by religious chants.

Other forms of popular theatrical phenomena which developed locally, but which also were enriched by Arabian lore, include crude mimicry, in Arabic called the art of the *muqallid*, and dramatic storytelling to the accompaniment of a one-string instrument called *rababa*. This latter form is usually referred to as the art of the *haki* or *hakawati*, an art which kept alive folk epics of considerable magnitude and charm. The storytelling here was not a one-sided activity but responded to the audiences' own preferences among the heroes of the story. Quite often the destiny of a particular hero would be decided according to the wishes of the most powerful faction in the audience and a wise storyteller would usually be alert enough to sense the audiences' reactions and weigh his chances in choosing the faction that he could safely please.

A more elaborate art of medieval Egypt, though considered still crude in comparison with formal theatre, was that of the *maddah*, (he who chants praises). These probably started out as religious choruses chanting crudely versified biographies of Muhammad and other prophets, but must have gradually developed a repertory of "plays" that were only remotely religious. A group of *maddahun** (between four and twelve members judging by present-day standards) chanted the narrative parts in chorus, and one or more singers did the solo parts, using very simple properties and costumes (a headdress, a stick, a veil, etc.) to change roles. Although the roles of performer and audience were clearly defined, the audience would usually respond spontaneously in an audible manner, sometimes joining in the singing or loudly cursing the villain.

Two forms of puppet theatre, namely, "shadow plays" and *qaragöz* were also developed in medieval Egypt, and at least one of these is believed to have been introduced from the eastern part of the Muslim world. China and Java are usually specifically mentioned as possible

*plural of *maddah*.

sources of this art. Whatever the case, we come across cryptic references to "shadow plays" in the works of historians, anthologists and poets around the end of the tenth century. It seems that at least the shadow play (Khayal al-zill) variety was quite popular not only with laymen but even more so with some theologians who saw an analogy between the shadow play master who moved all the figures, and God as the sole mover of creation.

Khayal al-zill involved using colored figures both of characters and sets or properties cut out of leather or paper and scraped so thin as to be almost transparent, and placing those figures behind a tightly stretched linen screen, with lamps behind the figures. The figures would then be manipulated by means of pins or short pieces of wire to simulate motions relevant to the action being depicted. This form must have preceded the other form called aragoz, which might have been borrowed from Turkey but had developed into something distinctly different. Hence I prefer to use aragoz rather than qaragoz when referring to the Egyptian variety.

The aragoz uses hand puppets above a screen just high enough to conceal the player and his hands. While the shadow play lends itself easily to lengthy speeches and elaborate situations, the aragoz, because of the muscular strain it involves, limits itself necessarily to very quick exchanges and slapstick routines. Working more or less within a crudely thought-out scenario, the aragoz player improvises both the dialogue and the action to suit his particular audience; hence, the texts that we occasionally come across are outlines rather than complete plays.

Although the Arabs were familiar with shadow plays towards the end of the tenth century, the earliest extant texts of such plays in Arabic date from thirteenth century Egypt. The three plays, sometimes erroneously referred to by the title of the first one, Tayf al-khayal, were composed partly in prose and partly in verse by the Egyptian oculist, Muhammad ibn Daniyal, who died in 1311 A.D. From the dedicatory epistle prefacing the text we learn that Ibn Daniyal came to what was a very well-established tradition. The shadow play, he wrote, "has become burden some for the hearer and...men's minds have turned from it because of its repetitions." The dedicatory epistle also contains stage directions and instructions on the melodies to be used with the songs.

The shadow plays of Ibn Daniyal are very lively and colorful pieces, with a lot of uninhibited bawdiness and, for their time, rather daring social and political satire. The characters are drawn from the different classes of the time, yet mostly living a sort of "holiday" existence, a "night" life. Apart from the obvious contradictions seized upon by caricaturists and puppeteers everywhere, the plays of Ibn Daniyal (particularly *Ajib wa Gharib, The Wonderful and the Strange*) strike an amazingly realistic tone and reveal a fascination with simple marketplace types on the part of the oculist-dramatist.

Action in the shadow plays is loosely centered around the main characters, and consists in following their exploits and changes in fortune. Like the *maqamah*, the literary genre from which the present writer believes Ibn Daniyal's plays to have developed, it is the different situations in which we encounter the protagonist rather than his "character" that keeps our interest alive. In the first and third plays, *Tayf al-khayal* and *al-Mutayyam* (the second being simply a gallery of type-portraits), the protagonists are seen as they indulge in one form of profligacy after another, yet they change in the end. The change, however, is not accomplished by moralizing as might be expected, but is brought about by compelling external circumstances. In the first play, the protagonist, Prince Wisal (the prince of pleasure, as he is appointed in a mock-ceremony), gives up the life of sin because, due to the strict government, sin has become almost impossible. The situation has caused even Satan to lose interest in life and die. A very touching elegy of the old devil forms part of the play, and in the end, Wisal goes on a pilgrimage to Mecca.

In the third play during a sort of orgy which is the culminating point in the protagonist's impassioned chase after a handsome Turkish lad (the fact that the love depicted in the play is homosexual love is seldom recognized by the scholars who have commented on the play), the Angel of Death appears. In a scene that bears close resemblance to that depicted in *Everyman*, the guests run away, leaving al-Mutayyam to face his destiny alone. He asks for and gets a very short respite, just enough to turn himself towards the *Qiblah* (the direction of Mecca), and to pray for forgiveness; then he dies. The possibility of such endings being mere lip-service to religion is not to be excluded of course, but strangely enough, in these irreverent and sometimes quite obscene plays, one is struck by a profoundly pervasive religious feeling.

Although no other texts of such an early origin have been discovered yet, it can be assumed with certainty that the shadow play tradition in Egypt continued with only very brief interruptions (when performances were occasionally banned by the rulers for being too politi-cal).

European travelers who visited Egypt since the middle of the eighteenth century have given accounts of crude farces presented by live actors. One of the earliest accounts is that of the Danish traveler, C. Niebuhr, who visited Egypt in January, 1761, and stayed there for over a year. Among the other travelers who recorded their observations about theatrical productions are Belzoni, Didier, Gerard de Nerval, and Edward W. Lane. Lane's account is extremely important not only because it gives a detailed description of the farce, which, despite Lane's obvious contempt, is a wonderful piece of social satire, but mainly because he has preserved for us the term used at his time (early nineteenth cen-tury) to refer to actors. The term is `"mohabbazeen"` which is significant, because it appears in the work of the Egyptian historian Ibn Iyas (d. 1524) in connection with the Mamluk princes and sultans. The Mamluks, we are told, were fond of the shows of *mohabbazeen*.* It is, of course, possible that the word is here used in a dif-ferent sense from Lane's, but to my knowledge, nobody

---

*Cited by Dr. Muhammad Zaghlul Sallam in *al-adab fi al asr al-mamluki* (Cairo: Dar al-Maarif, 1971) V.1, p. 285.

yet has investigated the issue or even pointed it out. If
it does turn out that the two of them use that word to
designate the same class of performers, this would sub-
stantiate to a great extent the contention that a form
of folk drama existed in Egypt for quite a long time--
perhaps even a survival of ancient Egyptian practices.
This, however, remains mere speculation until we have
more solid evidence.

In 1798 the cultural foundations of Egypt were once
again shaken, this time by Napoleon's cannonballs and
by the wonders he introduced. In addition to scientists
with their gadgets and equipment, the Comédie Francaise
was brought to Cairo to entertain the invading army and
possibly to dazzle the Egyptians. A theatre was built
on the edge of downtown Cairo. Even after the departure
of the French troops, French and Italian plays continued
to be shown in Cairo by amateur groups; but although an
increasing number of Egyptians saw those European plays,
their effect on potential native dramatists was slow in
coming.

In 1848 a young man from Beirut by the name of Marun
al-Naqqash brought the French (and to some extent also
the Italian) theatre closer to home by writing and producing the first Arabic play on a European model, *al-
Bakhil, (The Miser)* a musical comedy influenced only
in a remote way by Molière play of the same name.
Marun wrote two other plays before his untimely death
in 1855 and several members of his family, notably his
brother and cousin, continued the work he started. For
various cultural, religious and political reasons,
their troupe and another one formed in Damascus by
Ahmad Abu Khalil al-Qabbani moved to Egypt and started
presenting regular seasons.

Meanwhile, in Egypt a young schoolmaster named Ya'
qub Sanu' had been watching and occasionally acting in
French and Italian plays shown in Cairo. Through some
connections with the palace, Sanu' asked for permission
to form his own theatrical troupe and present his own
plays and translations in the colloquial dialect of
Egypt. The Viceroy of Egypt at the time, Khedive Ismail,
anxious to make Egypt '"part of Europe" readily granted
the permission and for two years enthusiastically sup-

ported the budding company. He even conferred upon Sanu'
the title "Egypt's Molière" and everything went well until the plays began to touch upon sensitive social and
political issues, whereupon the Khedive disbanded the
company and banned its performances. A few years later,
Sanu' himself was exiled to Paris.

Of the thirty-two plays that Sanu' reportedly wrote,
only seven complete texts and one fragment have so far
been published, and those only ten years ago. It was
understandable that scholars, before the publication of
the plays, should have depended in their evaluation of
Sanu's contribution on his expository writings on the
subject and on the one play published in 1912, *The
Trials of Egypt's Molière*. Now that we have the primary
sources, however, we should be able to reconsider the
question of the influence of the French and Italian
theatre on his work. That they did have an influence on
his drama one cannot deny. It should also be recognized,
however, that that influence in most cases did not go
beyond the most basic formal aspects of playwriting,
such as the division of the play into scenes, etc. In
fact, the plays are almost direct descendants of the
local forms of theatre, using the facilities of a more
formal stage, directed towards a more sophisticated kind
of audience, but retaining most of the characteristics
of their antecedents in the shadow plays, the *aragoz*,
and the farces referred to earlier. To this must be add-
ed the clever political use to which Sanu' put his medi-
um. This last trait reaches its peak, however, in the
political playlets that he published constantly in the
newspaper issued from his exile, namely *Abu Naddarah*,
a name which later on was applied to the man himself.
These playlets which he described as *muhawarah*
(dialogue) and *li'bah tiyatriyyah* (theatrical play or
game) were brutal satires attacking the repressive
practices of Ismail and his successor, Tawfiq, whom he
nicknamed the "Idiot Boy" among other, less flattering,
names. And although the playlets were not performed (to
the best of my knowledge) they can be viewed as early
equivalents of guerrilla theatre.

With Ya'qub Sanu's theatre closed down, the theatrical scene in Egypt in the last decades of the nine-

teenth century consisted of the visiting or local
troupes performing in European languages and the Syrian
companies. The latter offered musical comedies for the
most part based on European plays, or drawn from *The
Arabian Nights* and similar works, and performed in classical Arabic. Colloquial was thought to be too vulgar
and unliterary, an attitude which continued to plague
the Arabic theatre everywhere until quite recently.

The term "musical comedy" as used here is at best an
approximation for the sake of convenience only, and has
to be qualified. The plays, starting from Marun al-
Naqqash's until roughly around World War I, whether in
verse or a heavily-rhymed prose, contained a varying
number of songs that sometimes were only vaguely related
to the situations depicted. Each of the songs, as one
can tell from the "Index to the Tunes" appended to Marun
al-Naqqash's plays, for instance, was treated independ-
ently as a separate unit and set to music in a manner
suiting it alone, with little regard for an overall
musical effect. Although the songs in those musicals
were incidental, the public came to attend the theatre
mainly to listen to a favorite singer, and the artistic
quality of the plays fell. Roles were tailored in such
a way as to give the star singer the longest presence
on stage, "lyrics" were forced on parts of a play that
did not call for them, performances were interrupted by
applause, and shouts for encores destroyed whatever
"suspension of disbelief" the company might have
achieved. Given such conditions, the "formal" Egyptian
theatre during those years of the newly-introduced
European model was trapped in its box-office success,
and with it were trapped or strangled the few artists
who might have saved it.

Translations and adaptations from European drama kept
the theatres going. Translators took liberties with the
texts to make them fit the prevailing taste and norms,
however unsophisticated those were and regarded a play
by Molière, Racine or Corneille as little more than a
"dramatic source" (just as *The Arabian Nights*, for instance, was a fictional source). This might have been
a healthy attitude had the Egyptian theatre been suffi-
ciently mature at the time to cope with these sources,

but such was not the case. The finished products for
the most part were merely simplistic reductions of the
originals.

The choice of plays to be translated or adapted re-
veals the cultural mood of the times. At the beginning
French dramatists generally were favored over other
European authors. Thus, besides Molière and Corneille,
Racine was quite popular, but it was a highly romanti-
cized Racine. Victor Hugo made the scene both in the
novel and on stage, and Walter Scott provided several
plots for plays.

Like the few "original" plays contributed by local
talent and based on European models, the translations,
adaptations and Egyptianizations (shifting the whole
scene, and the *dramatis personae*, to an Egyptian environment) were, for the most part, rendered in a highly
ornate rhyming classical Arabic--a factor which had a
damaging effect on the development of the genre. Being
removed to a great extent from the everyday life of the
majority of the people, this classicism delayed the appearance of realism in the Arabic theatre, except for a few scat-
tered attempts. It also is probably wholly responsible
for the schism in the theatre between the popular or
"boulevard" variety and a kind of artificial "elite"
theatre divorced from the actual lives of the audiences.
The popularity of the "boulevard" variety encouraged it
to fall deeper and deeper into vulgarity, while the
high-brow character of the elite type was simply bad
drama and failed to attract any but the most perversely
obstinate elitists. For this, however, we should not
blame the use of classical Arabic as such, since some
authors later used it for the stage quite successfully
on the popular level, but rather the mental attitude
which encouraged the belief that literary excellence
consists of abundant figures of speech, purity of dic-
tion and imitation of style patterns more than a thousand years old.

One name that stands out as an exception in the field
of translation for the theatre is Muhammad Uthman Galal
who rendered four Molière and three Racine plays in
colloquial verse *(zajal)*. While Galal did change the
names of the characters (in Molière's works), and shift-

ed the scenes to Egypt, the plays retained most of the
qualities of their originals. The comedies were quite
popular and *al-Shaykh Matluf (Tartuffe)* in particular
is probably the only "Egyptian" play from that period
(1873) that can still be successfully played today without requiring drastic changes. Unfortunately Galal's
work remained an isolated phenomenon.

For this picture of the theatrical situation prior to
World War I to be complete, one should also mention
another contribution from Syria, a type of improvised
farce that came to be known as *fasl mudhik* or "funny
act." While it is true that farces had been performed
in Egypt since a much earlier date, as Niebuhr, Lane
and other travellers tell us, it was the Syrian-born
George Dakhul who did most to solidify farce as a tradition. The *fasl mudhik* has much in common with the Italian
commedia dell'arte, although direct borrowing seems
highly unlikely. Both used a limited number of character-
types whose behavior was highly predictable, simple stories or scenarios that were again limited in number and
familiar to the audience. There were no written texts,
at best only outlines with some jokes and routines that
were tested and proven before earlier audiences. In most
of the plays for which scenarios or outlines exist, the
events depicted do not seem to follow any rational or
logical sequence; things simply happen. In several in-
stances the melodramas which were beginning to innundate
the commercial theatre were consciously parodied and the
results were often hilarious. Farce and melodrama,
brought to "perfection" by the actors Nagib al-Rihani
and Yusuf Wahbi, respectively, quickly came to dominate the popular theatre in Egypt. During those formative
years and except for a few cases, well into the thirties,
no systematic training for actors was available. Actors
(and actresses since Sanu' introduced them on the stage)
were mainly amateurs with pleasant voices. The utmost
they could do by way of training consisted in watching
other amateurs act. The first actor to receive systematic and specialized training was George Abyad, who was
sent by the Egyptian government to study at the *Conserva-
toire* in Paris. There he studied under the French actor,
Sylvain. On his return in 1910, Abyad started to produce

plays in French, but was soon convinced to present them in Arabic. In transplanting the French theatre (in everything but language) to Egypt, Abyad introduced a note of professional sophistication hitherto unknown in the Egyptian theatre. An indirect result of his work, which perhaps outweighs the more obvious ones, was the appearance of translations that showed less tampering with the originals. The embellishments and the tendency towards overstatement, however, were slower to disappear because of Abyad's predilection for the heroic stance.

Abyad's example was soon followed by a number of young men who went to Paris to study acting and theatrics. Of these, Zaki Tulaymat was to play an important role in the Arab theatre by establishing the Higher Institute for Theatrical Art, and Fattuh Nashati was to become one of the ablest theatrical directors in Egypt. By the end of the first half of this century, a considerable number of actors, directors and scene designers had either graduated from the Institute or returned from their missions in Europe where they had received training.

Of the playwrights during the formative years, very few are of more than historical interest to us. Among these, three names deserve to be mentioned, if only for introducing what could be described as "melodramatic naturalism" to the Egyptian theatre. These are Anton Yazbak, 'Abbas 'Allam, and Muhammad Taymur. *Al-Dhaba'ih (The Victims)* by Yazbak deals with, among other things, the tragic results of East-West marriage (an Egyptian army general and a European woman), and young love conquered by conventions. Equally episodic in structure is 'Allam's *Malak wa Shaytan (An Angel and a Devil)* which deals with the conflict between two women whose behavior corresponds more or less to that of those suggested by the title. Muhammad Taymur, who died prematurely in 1921, wrote a melodrama, two comedies of manners and a number of dramatic monologues, and collaborated on an adaptation of *Bluebeard*, set in Mamluk Egypt. His musical, *al-'Asharah al-Tayyibah (The Ten of Diamonds)*, the score for which was composed by Sayyid Darwish, remains in the view of many scholars and critics the best of its kind in the Egyptian theatre.

In 1927 Ahmad Shawqi, acclaimed throughout the Arabic-

speaking world that very year as the "Prince of Poets,"
composed *Masra' Cleopatra (The Death of Cleopatra)*, a
tragedy in verse. Verse plays had been written before,
but this was the first to be written by a poet of
Shawqi's stature and is considered by a number of
Egyptian critics and scholars to be the first truly
Egyptian play in modern times. Advocates of such a view
naturally refer to it in terms of drama as a literary
genre, with little or no regard for any specific theatrical production. The play, they argue, can be read
and enjoyed on its own merits and for its poetry. And
despite the obvious echoes in the play from earlier
European versions, for example, Shakespeare's, it was
hailed as the expression of the spirit of a resurrected
Egypt.

Fresh praise began to pour on Shawqi from all quarters for what was considered to be a pioneering effort
in Arabic poetry, and in the last four years of his
life he wrote five more plays and rewrote a sixth,
'Ali Bek al-Kabir, which he had originally written in
1893 while studying law in France. The plays have often
been grouped into two major categories: *Masra' Cleopatra,
Cambysis*, and *'Ali Bek* are based on Egyptian history;
Majnun Laylah, *'Antarah*, and his only prose play, *Amirat
al-Andalus (The Princess of Andalus)* are based on Arab
history and tradition. *Al-Sitt Huda*, his only comedy,
takes place in Cairo in 1890. With the exception of
Majnun Laylah, his most popular play, Shawqi's work did
not have a long life on the stage because of the inap-
propriateness of classical Arabic prosody to the theatre; and now the plays lie securely buried in small
editions, revived occasionally for school use.

During the twenties and the early thirties of this
century, the theatre enjoyed a boom on several levels;
commercial companies mushroomed and rivalry among them
led to the production of an unprecedented number of plays.
Some companies even announced that they would present a
different play every evening, according to ads and hand
bills from that period. French and English farces were
adapted at a stupendous rate and very soon the hack
writers learned the recipe for the well-made play and
started to write on their own. Companies began to

present largely improvised parodies of each other's works. Melodrama also had its heyday and Yusuf Wahbi nearly monopolized the market with his impersonations of insane, criminal and diabolical characters, portraying the poor but honest people heartlessly victimized by the all-powerful but inevitably corrupt rich.

It was in such an atmosphere that the government decided to subsidize a theatre company to present serious masterpieces and thus was born what is today called the National Theatre Company. It chose Tawfiq al-Hakim's *Ahl al-Kahf (The People of the Cave)* for its debut in 1935, and the production, as al-Hakim recalled a few years later, convinced him that his dramas were best played inside the mind rather than on the stage. Since then the company has had an uneven history, resulting from the inability of the government to cope with the special nature of such an undertaking. Yet, in spite of such difficulties, the National Theatre served as the nucleus for the more serious aspects of the theatrical movement, until the early fifties when a group of graduates from the Institute of Theatrical Arts formed the Free Theatre.

Like its earlier counterparts in France and Germany, the Free Theatre *(al-Masrah al-Hurr)* espoused the cause of realism and naturalism and before long became the center of the theatrical movement. Its box-office returns compared favorably with the state-owned National Theatre despite the fact that the latter had more "stars" and better facilities. The National Theatre, however, augmented its ranks, and to some extent outgrew the predilection for "masterpieces" and classics and merged with The Modern Theatre Company, formed by Zaki Tulaymat in 1951. The competition between the National and the Free Theatre dominated the theatrical scene throughout the fifties. The return of some theatre directors from their study leaves in Europe (mainly England, France and Italy) infused new blood into the National Theatre, which began to produce the works of modern and contemporary European and American playwrights besides works of Shawqi, 'Aziz Abazah, and al-Hakim. The Free Theatre, on the other hand, presented successful adaptations of Egyptian novels (Mahfuz's, specifically), and their success encouraged a number of new Egyptian dramatists to present their works. These, for the most part, were in colloquial Arabic which slowly took over as the predominant language of the serious or literary theatre. The commercial companies meanwhile continued to present farces.

The early sixties witnessed a tremendous upsurge in theatrical activity. To begin with, a new wave of directors and men of the theatre who had been studying in Europe returned to Egypt in 1962 and 1963 and a group of them fostered a project for a "Pocket Theatre" to present avant garde and experimental plays from all over the world. In its first season, for instance, the Pocket Theatre presented Beckett's *Endgame*, Ionesco's *The Chairs* and a dramatic "lecture" made of extracts from Chekov's plays. These plays, particularly the first two, triggered a heated controversy among critics and intellectuals generally, some of whom questioned the relevance of these "absurd" plays coming from the "sick" culture of the West. Others defended the plays on artistic grounds and as being the logical domain of the Pocket Theatre. The debate was never resolved, but it did create an atmosphere of lively interest in the theatre.

A more important development was the decision, made by television authorities, to create special theatre companies to provide the network with televised plays. In 1962, four companies were formed by recruiting graduates of the Institute and former members of university theatre groups. Cinema actors were given renewable fortnightly contracts and were paid quite handsomely. The shortage of plays led to a rather heavy reliance on adapted novels at the beginning, but very soon a number of new authors were attracted to the theatre, which had now become the most lucrative literary enterprise. Each play was performed for two or three weeks in the course of which it would be televised and then would be succeeded by a new play. And contrary to the prediction that television would take people away from the theatre, the number of theatre-goers multiplied tremendously. Within two years the number of television theatre companies grew to ten. Members of the Free

Theatre Company were now mostly employed by the various
television theatre groups, and rivalry between these
companies on the one hand and the National and Pocket
Theatres, on the other, replaced that between the National and the Free Theatre.

The sixties in the Egyptian theatre were characterized by an intense search for identity and direction and
an abundance of political plays, sometimes trying to
hide their obvious meanings behind a symbolism which was
often quite transparent. These plays were described by
some critics, in a tongue-in-cheek manner, as works of
the "symbolic realism" movement. An offshoot of these
tendencies was the development in the press and other
information media of a kind of dramatic criticism that
rated plays according to their social and political
messages, and which was quite liberal in applying la-
bels to works and authors. While this is a legitimate
area of criticism, some opportunistic critics often
indulged in a sort of blackmail that does not belong
in discussions of either art or ideology. In spite of
some cheap accusations--in one instance a "critic" in
an evening newspaper called for the prosecution of a
dramatist for what he described as "making insinuations
about the regime,"--the Egyptian theatre during the sixties continued both to reflect the people's thinking on
most issues and to help mold it.

This period was also characterized by a search for
what was sometimes described is a "genuinely Egyptian
theatre," and this led to a lot of experimentation and
theoretical inquiry on the part of writers and artists
of the theatre. In article after article there were
calls for a return to those theatrical forms that developed naturally from the people's gatherings for
harvests or for "saints" anniversaries. Tawfiq al-
Hakim contributed a book to an exploration of these
possibilities. In *Qalibuna al-Masrahi (Our Theatrical
Form)* he called for a form that would combine the art
of the storyteller *(al-haki)* and that of the mimic
(al-muqallid), and gave several illustrations of how
this was to be accomplished. A related experiment, put
to the test quite successfully by the Pocket Theatre,
was a long dramatic poem by Nagib Surur, *Yasin wa
Bahiyah.*

The post-1967 years have been characterized by new
features reflecting various responses to the new situation in Egypt after the humiliation of defeat in the
1967 war. The works written immediately after the war
are full of anger against those responsible for the
defeat, and an equally angry self-criticism. In some
of these there is no attempt to hide behind symbolism
or disguise the anger. In other plays, however, the
situation has been transposed to another era and viewed
from the perspective of history, a trick that quite often
worked. The reaction in the case of at least one commercial company, the Tahiyah Karioka Company, came in
the form of daring satirical revues. More recently, a
wave of sex comedies and cheap farces seems to have
innundated the private theatre, and in certain in-
stances, the state-owned companies, which are currently enjoying their biggest boom ever. Competition among
the private companies is also at its fiercest, but unfortunately some of the finest talents are being wasted
on essentially trivial theatrical enterprises.

* * *

I cannot claim that the four plays chosen for this
anthology represent all trends of modern Egyptian playwriting or even of the other works of their own authors;
but they do, I believe, represent significant facets of
the prose drama of the 1960s in Egypt. All four depict
a struggle against different manifestations of power.
Tawfiq al-Hakim's career is one of those rare in-
stances where the development of a certain genre or
body of literature is epitomized by one man. Born in
Alexandria in 1898 (although he himself claims 1902 as
the year of his birth) to an Egyptian father of peasant
stock and a mother of Turkish descent, al-Hakim seems a
symbol of the birth of the Egyptian middle-class formed
by the alliance of the declining Turkish aristocracy of
Egypt with those of the Egyptian peasant class who managed through education to escape the village. Such an
alliance predictably results in a very conservative outlook, the declining class desperately holding on to
whatever is left of its better days, and the rising one,

fearing that its arrival on the scene might be a bit too
late, grabbing in an equally desperate manner what it
fears might soon disappear. Thus, despite the literary
inclination which al-Hakim developed very early in his
youth, his family decided that he should study law. He
did that half-heartedly, and while in law school collaborated with a friend on a number of "musical comedies." Except for *The Modern Woman* (1923), his writings
of this period have little to distinguish them from
other works of the popular theatre of the time.

Tawfiq's fascination with the theatre during his law
school days almost caused him to fail, yet he somehow
managed to earn his degree. When he told his father that
he wanted to pursue a literary career, the family would
not hear of it and sent him to Paris to read for a doctorate in law. He left Egypt in 1924, and once in Paris,
gave himself up completely to the study of literature
and the arts. Three years later, without having earned
the doctorate, he returned to Egypt where he took a job
as a prosecutor. He did not remain long in this position
but took a job in the Ministry of Education in 1934.

In 1939 he was appointed Director of Social Guidance
in the newly-formed Ministry of Social Affairs where he
remained until he resigned in 1943 to join the staff of
the newspaper, *Akhbar al-Yawm*, in which he published
several short plays. In 1951 he became Director General
of *Dar al-Kutub* (The National Library) and stayed there
for five years after which he was appointed a full-time
member of the Higher Council for Arts and Letters, a
position that was interrupted for one year when in 1959
he was appointed the United Arab Republic's Permanent
Delegate to UNESCO in Paris. Two years later he was
also appointed a member of the board of directors of
the newspaper *al-Ahram*, a post which he still occupies.

During those years al-Hakim was writing plays, mem-
oirs, stories, novels and expository works about literature and art. He has written more than seventy plays
covering a broad range of forms and a variety of tech-
niques. His works have been translated into many languages, notably French, Russian, Spanish, Italian,
English, Hebrew and Swedish.

Al-Hikim's stay in France convinced him that the Arab

theatre had had a false start, or at least a terribly immature one at the hands of the Naqqashes. The tradition which they started in 1848, he felt, led to an almost complete divorce of the theatre from literature, so much so that even the poet Ahmad Shawqi gave very little thought to publishing his plays. Al-Hakim believed that only a return to "the source of drama," that is, the works of the ancient Greek masters could rectify the situation. Such a return could not be accomplished simply by translating their works into Arabic, but required assimilating the Greek experience in drama, without, in the meantime, shedding one's character completely or losing oneself in one's model. Writing in retrospect in the Introduction to his *Oedipus,* al-Hakim gives an illustration from his own experience with Sophocles's tragedy. Although on an intellectual level he could understand and appreciate the conflict in the play, when he started thinking of writing his own version, his sensibility, both as a Muslim and as an Òriental man, rejected the idea that the gods could plot something so mean. So, he changed the play around, making Tiresias the chief culprit in the tragedy.

By writing *Ahl al-Kahf* (The People of the Cave) shortly after his return from Paris, al-Hakim aimed at "introducing the element of tragedy to an Arabic-Islamic theme." In so doing, he says "my purpose was not merely to take a story from the Glorious Book and to cast it in dramatic form, (but) rather to look at our Islamic mythology with the eyes of Greek tragedy, (hence) bringing about a fusion of the two mentalities and literatures." *(al-Malik Udib,* Cairo, n.d., p. 39.)

The play was the first production by the National Theatre Company formed in 1935, but strangely had little success with the audience.

> Twenty years ago or so, I used to
> write for the theatre in the true
> sense of the word. This true sense
> of the word "playwriting" means
> ignorance of the existence of the
> press...

I still remember what the manager
of a theatre told me once. "Do you
know what I do before deciding
whether or not to take your play?
...I read it at home to my young
children; if they keep listening
and do not fall asleep, I take
it."

What is it then that happened
to me after all these years? How
did I reach this sorry state of
affairs? Why do I write plays
which induce adults to sleep? The
reason in simply enough; today I
set up my theatre within the mind.
I transform the actors into ideas
moving in the absolute, dressed
in nothing but symbols...True, I
have preserved the spirit of the
"coup de theatre," but that is no
longer in the action as much as it
is in the idea...That is how the
gap between me and the stage has
widened, and now I find no bridge
to carry these words across other
than the press.

Some people have wondered: is it
not possible for these works to
appear also on the real stage? As
for me, I admit that I never thought
of that when I wrote such plays as
*The People of the Cave or Shahrzad
or Pigmalyn.... (Pygmalyun,* Cairo,
n.d., p. 9-10.)

Whether or not one agrees with al-Hakim's rationale
for abstracting his characters and concentrating on
the ideas and the symbols as he claims, there is little disagreement among critics of his work that that
is what he achieves. Setting our preconceptions about
drama aside and granting him the premise that his plays
were written to be acted out in each reader's mind, one

begins to perceive the talent that he has for reducing
his characters, dehumanizing, and abstracting them.
This trait in most of his plays does not result from
his failure to make his characters live, for he has
created some that are quite alive. The tendency towards
abstraction is part and parcel of his almost mathemati-
cal vision of life. Even in his so-called "social"
plays, which some critics have accused of being mere
lip service to the post-1952 regime in Egypt, a sort of
ironic futility pervades his universe. In this respect,
we can gain a better insight into al-Hakim's work if we
think of it in terms of the absurd.

If we look closely at *The People of the Cave*, or
*Shahrzad or Pigmalyun or Rihlah ila al-Ghad (Journey in-
to the Future)*, or for that matter *Ya Tali' al-Shagarah
(The Tree Climber)*, it will be noticed that one basic
pattern is present in all of them: the characters end
where they start or, if there is any change, we are
made to see that it was pointless. Not all of al-Hakim's
plays belong to what he himself called "theatre of the
mind" or abstract theatre. His writings include a considerable number of plays that address themselves to
specific social issues. Twenty-one such plays, some of
them quite short, were published in one volume in 1950
under the title *Masrah al-Mujtama' (Theatre of Society)*.
Twenty others were published in a similar format in 1956
under the title *al-Masrah al-Munawwa' (Varied Theatre)*.
Both volumes include plays that he wrote at different
stages of his career. And although he himself encouraged
people to believe that he was a sort of "ivory tower"
artist (he actually wrote a book using the expression as
a title), several of his early pieces leave us with no
doubt that the ivory tower outlook, like his reputation
as a misogynist and a miser, are public poses behind
which he chooses to hide. In fact, throughout his career,
in both his dramatic and non-dramatic works, al-Hakim
shows a profound preoccupation with the pressing social
and political issues of his day.

Al-Hakim has never ceased experimenting with new
forms and has shown a high degree of flexibility in
adapting himself to changes in taste and sensibility.
Thus, the wave of "absurd theatre" of the fifties caused

him to re-examine the local tradition for possible similarities in *The Tree Climber* (1962); and in 1963 he
tried his hand at the play-within-the-play, in *al-Ta'am
li-kull Famm (Food for Everybody)*. Al-Hakim experimented
with combining narrative with drama. *Bank al Qalaq (Bank
of Anxiety)* of 1967 he called a *Masriwayah* which corresponds to "theâtroman" in French. Here narrative and
dramatic dialogue alternate in almost equal proportions.
In *Our Theatrical Form*, published in the same year, he
advocates a new form of theatre derived from the Egyptian theatrical tradition and consisting of the arts of
the storyteller *(al-haki)* and the mimic *(al-muqallid)*.

The Sultan's Dilemma, chosen for this anthology, was
written in Paris in the fall of 1959 while the author
was serving as the U.A.R. delegate to UNESCO. The play
was both a commercial and critical success. Some critics
believe it is the best play that al-Hakim has ever written. It uses the device of deliberately "distancing" a
familiar situation to persuade the audience to look at
it in a more detached manner and with a clearer perspective. Although al-Hakim makes use of a historical situation, *The Sultan's Dilemma* is less a historical play
than a parable created by an elaborate scheme of parallelisms and echoes, which bring out the significance of
the action not just for the immediate situation but all
times. By giving the whole play a fairy tale atmosphere, the author is enabling us to pronounce our judgement on the quality of justice in our own day and perhaps inviting us to conclude that justice is not to be
found in the real world.

* * *

Rashad Rushdy's career represents another trend in
modern Egyptian drama. Like al-Hakim, his love for the
theatre started early in life, but he went on to major
in English literature, and at an early stage in his
career, started writing about literature in a professional way. Apart from a dozen short stories that were
broadcast on the radio and published later in a collection, and five one-act plays that he wrote in English,
Rushdy's literary career up to the early forties

consisted of criticism rather than literary works. He later became one of the most active critics in Egypt and was responsible for popularizing the "New Criticism" there.

Rushdy's career took him to England where he earned a Ph.D. In 1952 he became Chairman of the Department of English at the University of Cairo. He has edited a number of magazines, including *The Arab Review, The Arab Observer* and *al-Masrah (The Theatre)*, the only monthly review of the theatre published in Arabic. He has also served as literary editor of *Akhir Sa'ah,* a popular illustrated weekly. In 1969 he became Dean of the Higher Institute of Theatrical Art and is currently editor of the periodical *al-Jadid (The New)*. He taught courses on playwriting at the American University in Cairo, and from 1964 till 1967, was Chairman of the Board of al-Hakim Theatre in Cairo. He has published more than thirty books in Arabic and English, including nine full-length plays.

Rushdy's real apprenticeship in playwriting started in the early forties when he translated or adapted a number of plays for a semi-professional company, *al-Tali'ah* (The Vanguard Theatre). These plays included, among others, Marlowe's *Dr. Faustus,* Gogol's *The Inspector General* and some of Chekhov's one-act plays. In 1959, his first full length play *al-Farashah (The Butterfly)* was performed by the Free Theatre and was hailed by a number of critics as "the first Egyptian tragedy in colloquial Arabic," but it was *Rihlah Kharig al-Sur (A Journey Outside The Wall)* of 1963 that convinced the public, and the literary establishment most of all, that he must be taken seriously.

The action of the play takes place in pre-1952 Egypt. This is one of the simple tricks that dramatists sometimes have had to resort to in order to avoid problems with the censors. It is a harmless trick, anyway, since nobody but the censor seems to have been fooled by it. The characters fall into three distinct categories corresponding to the three broad circles in which they move. The first category is that of the family and the servants; the second is that of the government, and the third that of the people. The opening lines set forth

the tone of the play and impress upon us the duality or
near schizophrenia characterizing the dwellers of the
world that is about to unfold before our eyes. This
duality will later be intensified by the symbol of the
bridge. The unity of the play is not that of action,
but rather a unity depending on a main theme, or a group
of related themes presented in different variations. It
is in this respect that *A Journey Outside the Wall* is
"difficult," and not because it deals with riddles or
profundities.

If we characterize Tawfiq al-Hakim's universe as being governed by an intrinsic futility, leading to cyni-
cism, Rushdy's universe, which is largely internal, is
governed by a built-in corruptibility that attracts
evil from outside--an evil which the tragic victims
refuse to believe exists. Al-Hakim's characters, being
aware of the futility, can appear as well-defined abstrac-
tions. However with Rushdy's characters, naivete and
ignorance of the corruption inside and the evil outside
robs them of any clarity of vision, hence the looseness
of the terms in which they are presented and their broad
symbolic impact.

Al-Hakim's rational approach dictates the straight-
forward progression of his plots, which generally are
easy to sum up. The "story" in Rushdy's plays, on the
other hand, follows a more circular and uneven pattern
of progression which renders the task of summarizing the
"plots," if we can use this word here at all, more difficult and invariably unfair to the plays.

* * *

Yusuf Idris, who was born in 1927, has been acclaimed throughout the Arabic-speaking world as its greatest short story writer, but his is not a story of in-
stant success. As a medical student at the University
of Cairo, he became involved in politics and student
activism during the late forties. Charged with "sub-
versive" activities, like many others of his generation,
he was arrested and imprisoned several times. His first
collection of short stories was published while he was

in jail, and like most of his early works, the stories
reflect the influence of social realism—particularly
that of Maxim Gorki—an influence which wore off gradually as the young writer developed his own style in
the large number of short stories and novels he wrote
later. In 1960, Yusuf Idris cut short his medical
career and joined the editorial staff of the daily *al-
Jumhuriyah,* where he published his stories and a weekly
column. Early in 1967, he became director of the Drama
Section at the state-owned Organization of Theatre Arts
and Music, and shortly thereafter joined the staff of
the Newspaper *al-Ahram.*

Yusuf Idris began his career as a dramatist in 1954
with a short play *Malik al-Qutn (The King of Cotton).*
Since that time he has written a number of plays, some
of which have been performed, and others not.

With *al-Farafir,* (the Farfoors) in 1964, Yusuf Idris
made a significant contribution to the Egyptian theatre's search for roots and identity. In a series of
three articles entitled "Towards an Egyptian Theatre,"
and in the introduction he wrote for the play two
years later, Yusuf Idris blasted those who recognized
only the European forms of drama or who believed that
those were the universal forms, and that for an Egyptian or a Kenyan or a Vietnamese to write a play, all
he had to do was to take the ready-made moulds fash-
ioned in Europe and pour into them an Egyptian or a
Kenyan or a Vietnamese content. All peoples, he argued,
have always had one dramatic form or another, and he
called for exploring those forms and experimenting with
them in order to arrive at a genuine national theatre.
Not only would such theatres stand side by side with
the European, but would help enrich drama all over the
world. In Egypt, Yusuf Idris called particularly for
exploring such popular forms of drama as mimicry,
aragoz, the shadow play, and dervish dances, which he
believed to be the genuine expression of the dramatic
impulse of the people.

Whether or not we agree with Idris's point of view,
there is no doubt whatsoever that *al-Farafir,* whether
it is the most apt illustration of his theoretical
speculations or not, represents a fantastic leap forward

from the type of drama he wrote prior to it. Ironically
enough, by turning away from the social realism of
his earlier years, Idris managed in *al-Farafir* to give
more edge to the ideas he wanted to communicate and to
reach a far greater number of people than he ever did
before.

The word "farfoor" itself was either made up by Yusuf
Idris or was part of his village's dialect, and the
play simply brought it into general currency. Yusuf
Idris prefaced the published text of the play with a
lengthy note on the character of Farfoor. From that
note and from his role in the play, Farfoor comes close
to some of Shakespeare's "fools" or clowns. However, he
is not a king's but rather a people's fool, or a person
who, in the gatherings of the people, would act as the
group's collective conscience in a manner that is candid
enough to cause resentment of him, but hilarious enough
to let him get away with it. *Farfoor* shares some basic
features with *Aragoz*,* especially in those places in the
first part where he acts in a saucy and quick-tempered
but still pliable manner. Later on, and this makes the
analogy even more apt, Farfoor behaves like an *Aragoz*
who rebels against his manipulator and who wants to
lead an independent existence.

In that same note prefacing the published text, and
in the author's "prologue," Yusuf Idris states his pre-
ference for a theatre-in-the-round arrangement or one
where the acting area is contiguous with the spectators'
seats. In the case of a proscenium type stage, for instance, he suggests extending the stage by covering the
orchestra pit with boards and by placing spectators'
seats on the other end of the stage so that spectators
seated in the auditorium would watch, not just the
players, but the players-being-watched. In short, the
author would have no "suspension of disbelief," and no
reduction of the audience to a bunch of "peeping Toms,"
because as such the audience would not be a collective

---

*The term is capitalized here to indicate I am refer-
ring to the character Aragoz and not the genre which
takes its name from him.

mass, but rather a number of individuals accidentally gathered there. And it is in this respect that Idris, at least theoretically, and without mentioning it explicitly, distinguishes between the kind of theatre he calls for and illustrates in *al-Farafir*, and Brecht's "epic" theatre.

The author in the play starts out as simply an author and comes in for quite a number of digs from Farfoor. As the play proceeds, however, the author steadily acquires additional proportions that identify him, first as a type of arbitrary authority, then as a creator, and finally, more or less explicitly, with God. This, ironically, becomes more apparent as both the role of the author and his "size" diminish.

The play moves along two main lines, broadly, but not exclusively, corresponding to the two-part division. These two lines could be identified as diagnosis and attempts at therapy or a critique of the status quo and the search for alternatives. Within the first may be seen Farfoor's comments on almost all aspects of life in modern Egypt--and by extension, everywhere. These comments point out in very quick strokes, the innumerable absurdities underlying our daily existence and human relations. Along the second occur the "analysis" of most existing systems both of government and social relations, and the realization that these too are equally absurd. So hopeless is the human condition that the only option open to Farfoor and his Master is to seek a *deus ex machina,* and even that does not work. It is probably only in this sense that *al-Farafir* comes very close to being a modern tragedy and not simply an abstract discussion of social and political issues or of the question of power.

In discussing the play, critics have pointed to several similarities between *al-Farafir* and certain trends in modern European drama. Yet, while it is true that there are echoes in it from a number of sources, such as Beckett's *Waiting for Godot,* or Aristophane's *The Frogs,* and several others, these similarities or echoes are marginal to the central situation depicted by the play, and though quite simple, the dramaturgy of the play is so entirely its own, that it cannot be used again.

Al-Farafir had a good reception both with the public
and with most critics, and it stirred quite an interest
in the older popular dramatic forms. The amount of pub-
licity the play received, which was tremendous by Egyptian standards, increased considerably when a dispute
arose between the author and the director over the right
of the latter to use the script for creating his own
work of art, and this triggered an on-going debate about
the role of the director. Meanwhile, several critics
attacked the play as being defeatist and for undermining
people's faith in the inevitable victory of the socialist
solution which will eliminate the Farfoor-Master relationship. The author was accused of falsifying the pre-
mises on which the outcome of the play was based.

* * *

Mikhail Roman (1925 or 27--) started writing for the
theatre "all of a sudden," in 1962, as he himself puts
it, although he had translated a number of plays for
the Second Program of Radio Cairo (a station devoted
to cultural programs) and some novels, before he suddenly decided to write a play. A graduate of the Faculty
of Sciences at the University of Cairo, to which he had
come from Southern Egypt, Mikhail Roman is a professor
at the Advanced Industrial Institute at Shibin al-Kim,
a small town in the Nile delta.

Mikhail Roman represents anger at its most violent in
the Egyptian theatre--a trait in his work that was quite
apparent from the very beginning. And his anger is often
contagious; readers and spectators, except those that
are entirely immune to feeling, cannot remain neutral
when reading or watching his plays; they either get
angry with him or at him. He is, as far as I know, the
first Egyptian dramatist to have his characters use
the expression *"ibn kalb"* (son of a dog) on the stage--
and this is one of his mildest curses. And although
Mikhail Roman is a rather shy and reservedly amiable
person, theatre people can always count on several
months of fighting, mostly verbal, whenever a play of

his is performed. Usually, the most sensational of these fights will be with the censor at the final dress rehearsal. However, in most cases either the censor bans it from the very beginning or the theatre company, anticipating such a ban, does not accept it. Thus, although he has written at least twelve plays, only five have been performed, and only seven, including four of those performed, have been published.

The play chosen for this anthology, *al-Wafid (The New Arrival)* of 1965, was performed by the Mersa Matrouh Theatre Company only after the censor's permission was granted for one night and before a special audience. With *The New Arrival,* Mikhail Roman seems to have found the kind of theatre in which he is most at home, namely, the single-act play (within two years he wrote six such plays). In this group of six plays, an ordinary, everyday life situation that appears quite insignificant is developed into a crisis where the protagonist finds himself pressed against a wall of odds over which he has very little control. In *The New Arrival,* he encounters a hugh "hotel" with its complex system of buttons and its hierachy of button-pushers. The hotel is not a symbol only of technological progress, but also of all the organizations and institutions which, in their zealous efforts to improve the lot of man, occasionally crush him.

On another level, from the reminiscences of *The New Arrival* and the numerous references to past struggles in the history of Egypt, the play makes a political statement about the slogans raised by certain elements of the ruling class there, and the way these slogans are put into effect. On this level, like the others (technology, the myopia of organizations), despite the local references, the play captures what is very rapidly becoming the universal experience of man in our time.

THE SULTAN'S DILEMMA

A Play in Three Acts

by

Tawfiq al-Hakim

Cast of Characters

Convict	Vizier
Executioner	Sultan
Tavern Keeper	Judge
Servant	Shoemaker
Belle	Slave-Merchant
Muezzin	Notables and common people of the town

Act 1

*(A city square, during the Mamluk era. It is al-
most dawn. The place is very quiet. A pole, to which
a convict is tied, stands there, with the Executioner
near by, trying hard to stay awake.)*

CONVICT:
> *(Looking fixedly at his Executioner)* Sleepy? Of
> course you are! Calm, carefree and very serene!
> Because you are not awaiting something which
> might disturb your peace of mind!

EXECUTIONER:
> Sh!

CONVICT:
> For the last time, when?

EXECUTIONER:
> I told you, sh!

CONVICT:
> *(Pleading)* Please tell me when? When?

EXECUTIONER:
> When will you **stop** bothering me?

CONVICT:
> Sorry, but it especially interests me! When will
> this event, a happy one, I should say, as far as
> you are concerned, when will it take place?

EXECUTIONER:
> At dawn...I told you more than ten times, at dawn
I execute you! Do you understand now? Leave me in

peace for a moment!

CONVICT:

Dawn? It's still a long way off, isn't it so, Mr. Executioner?

EXECUTIONER:

I don't know.

CONVICT:

You don't know?

EXECUTIONER:

The Muezzin is the one who knows. As soon as he has climbed up this minaret and called for the dawn prayer, I will rise and cut off your head with my sword. Those were the instructions! Are you satisfied now?

CONVICT:

Without a trial? I haven't been tried yet, nor have I been heard by a judge!

EXECUTIONER:

It is not my business.

CONVICT:

Really! All you are concerned about is executing me.

EXECUTIONER:

At dawn. By order of the Sultan.

CONVICT:

For what crime?

EXECUTIONER:

I don't care.

CONVICT:

Because I said...

EXECUTIONER:

Sh! Sh! Shut your mouth! I was instructed to cut off your head the moment you utter one syllable about your crime.

CONVICT:

Don't worry, I'll shut up.

EXECUTIONER:

That's the best thing you can do. Shut up and let me enjoy my sleep! It's in your interest that I should have a pleasant, quiet sleep.

CONVICT:

My interest?

EXECUTIONER:

Certainly. It's in your interest that I am perfectly rested and enjoying good health, physical-
ly and psychologically, because when I am tired,
nervous, or tense, my hands shake, and when my
hands shake I don't perform so well.

CONVICT:

What do I care about your performance?

EXECUTIONER:

You fool, my performance has to do with your neck.
A bad performance means that your neck will not
be cut cleanly, because a clean cut requires a
firm hand and a soul at peace, so that the head
may be cut off with one blow, and this means that
you would have no time to feel the pain. Do you
understand now?

CONVICT:

Really, that's true!

EXECUTIONER:

See? Are you convinced now that you must make
me comfortable, try to please me, and raise my
morale?

CONVICT:

Your morale? You?

EXECUTIONER:

Of course! If I were in your shoes...

CONVICT:

May God grant you that! May you be in my shoes!

EXECUTIONER:

What did you say?

CONVICT:

Go on, continue, what would you do if you had the
honor and bliss of being in my shoes?

EXECUTIONER:

I'll tell you what I'd have done. Do you have any
money?

CONVICT:

Ah, money! Yes, yes, yes, money! An excellent
idea! As for my money, my friend, there's no
worry there. The whole city, including you, knows
that I am one of the richest slave-merchants.

EXECUTIONER:

> No, you misunderstood, it isn't bribery. It's im-
> possible to bribe me! Not because of my honesty
> or integrity, but because I, quite frankly, can-
> not save you. All I wanted was to accept your in-
> vitation to have a drink, if you invite me. A
> glass of wine is not a bribe, and really it's bad
> manners to turn down an invitation. Look, there's
> a tavern just across...It's open all night be-
> cause some of its customers visit that whore liv-
> ing in the house opposite to it.

CONVICT:

> Only a drink?

EXECUTIONER:

> That's all.

CONVICT:

> I have a better idea. Let's both of us, you and
> I, go up to that pretty woman! I know her. Once
> we are up there we can pass a splendid night,
> one in a lifetime. A night that will please you
> and raise your morale. What do you say to that?

EXECUTIONER:

> No, generous Master.

CONVICT:

> You accept my invitation for a drink, yet turn
> down my invitation to drink in pleasant and
> charming surroundings?

EXECUTIONER:

> In that house? My dear Convict, no. I'd rather
> you stayed as you are, chained until dawn!

CONVICT:

> What a pity! Don't you trust me? Even if I prom-
> ised you that before the Muezzin calls for the
> dawn prayer I'll be back here in my chains as I
> was?

EXECUTIONER:

> A bird coming to the net, as it were?

CONVICT:

> Yes, and I swear upon my honor!

EXECUTIONER:

> Your honor? What an oath!

CONVICT:

> You don't believe me...

EXECUTIONER:

I believe you so long as you are here with your
hands in the chains.

CONVICT:

But how then could I invite you for a drink?

EXECUTIONER:

That's simple. I go to the tavern and ask the
keeper there to bring us two goblets of his
finest wine. When he brings them, we can drink
here, in this place. What do you say to that?

CONVICT:

But...

EXECUTIONER:

Agreed then. I'll go myself. You need not bother
or trouble yourself. Just a moment. By your
leave.
*(The Executioner goes to the tavern at the other
end of the square. He knocks at the door. The
Keeper comes out. He whispers some words to him
and goes back to the Convict.)*

EXECUTIONER:

It's done. I have carried out your orders. Very
soon, my dear Convict, you will see the happy
result.

CONVICT:

What happy result?

EXECUTIONER:

My well-done job! For if I drink, I do my job
very well, and if I don't, it'll be a poor show!
I'll tell you, for example, what happened one
day: I was asked to do a head-job on somebody,
but that day I hadn't drunk anything. Do you
know what I did? I struck that poor man's head
so violently and clumsily that his head flew
away and fell far off, not in this basket of
mine but in another, over there, the Shoemakers
basket, right there by the tavern door. God
knows what trouble we had to go through to get
that lost head from those piles on piles of shoes
and soles!

CONVICT:

The Shoemaker's basket! What a resting place. I

beg you, for God's sake, to spare my head such a
fate!

EXECUTIONER:

Have no fear. In your case it is different. The
other head belonged to a man who was stinking
stingy!

(The Tavern Keeper comes out of the tavern carrying two goblets.)

TAVERN KEEPER:

(Addressing the Convict) This, of course, is for
you, your last wish.

CONVICT:

No, it's for the Executioner. His precious wish!

EXECUTIONER:

(To the Tavern Keeper) To bring his heart serenity
and rest.

TAVERN KEEPER:

From whom do I get my money?

CONVICT:

From me, of course. To cheer his heart.

EXECUTIONER:

It is my duty to accept his cordial invitation.

CONVICT:

And it's my duty to raise his morale.

TAVERN KEEPER:

What friendship!

EXECUTIONER:

It is mutual affection!

CONVICT:

Until the dawn!

EXECUTIONER:

Let's forget the dawn. It is still a long way
off. Let's touch glasses! *(The Executioner takes
the two goblets in his hand and taps the one
against the other. He raises one of them, to
toast the Convict.)* Your health!

CONVICT:

Thank you!

EXECUTIONER:

*(After drinking his, brings the other goblet
close to the Convict's mouth.)* Now it's your
turn, dear friend!

CONVICT:
  (Takes one sip, then coughs.) Enough! You drink
  the rest for me.
EXECUTIONER:
  Is that your wish?
CONVICT:
  My last one!
EXECUTIONER:
  (Raising the second goblet) I drink this for...
CONVICT:
  Your well-done job!
EXECUTIONER:
  If God wills...Also for your generosity and kind-
  ness, my dear convicted friend.
TAVERN KEEPER:
  *(As he gets the two empty goblets from the Execu-
  tioner)* What did this old slave-merchant do? What
  is the charge? Everybody in the city knows him.
  He is neither a murderer, nor a thief.
CONVICT:
  And yet my head will be cut off at dawn, like a
  murderer or a thief!
TAVERN KEEPER:
  Why? What crime?
CONVICT:
  Nothing, except that I said...
EXECUTIONER:
  Sh! Don't say anthing. Shut your mouth!
CONVICT:
  I'm shutting my mouth.
EXECUTIONER:
  And now you *(To the Tavern Keeper)*, you've taken
  your goblets, go away!
TAVERN KEEPER:
  And my money?
EXECUTIONER:
  It was he who invited me. It would have been mean
  to turn down the invitation.
CONVICT:
  That's true. I invited him and he was good enough
  to accept. Your money, Tavern Keeper, is in a
  purse in my belt. Come and take what you want.

EXECUTIONER:

Allow me to do it for him. *(He takes money from the Convict's purse and pays the Tavern Keeper.)* Here's your money. We've paid more than we have to, so you know we are generous.

(The Tavern Keeper takes the money and goes back to the Tavern. The executioner starts to sing softly to himself.)

CONVICT:

(Anxious) And now...

EXECUTIONER:

Now we sing and be merry. Do you know, my dear Convict, that I am fond of good singing, music, and poetry. It fills the heart with bliss and jubilation, and joy of life, and pleasure. Sing something for me!

CONVICT:

Sing?

EXECUTIONER:

Yes, why not? What is preventing you? Your throat, God be praised, is absolutely free. All you have to do is go ahead and sing, and the lovely tunes will come forth. Go ahead, sing! Enchant my ears!

CONVICT:

May God be my witness!

EXECUTIONER:

Go ahead! Sing! Let me hear you...'

CONVICT:

Do you really think that in my present mood I could have the right voice?

EXECUTIONER:

Didn't you promise me a short while ago that you would cheer my heart and take away this gloom?

CONVICT:

So it is you who feels gloomy?

EXECUTIONER:

Yes, and please take away my gloom. Let me drown it in merriment...Fill me with the bliss of music, and the splendor of melody...Listen, I remember something now. I know a song which I composed my-self on one of those melancholy nights.

CONVICT:
> Sing it yourself then.

EXECUTIONER:
> My voice isn't too good.

CONVICT:
> Who told you that mine is beautiful?

EXECUTIONER:
> For me all other voices are beautiful, because I
> don't listen to them...especially if I am tipsy
> ...All I care about is to have singing all around
> me. Feeling the air filled with melody around me
> soothes my nerves. Sometimes I like to sing my-
> self, but there is a condition to that: to find
> somebody who will listen to me! If such a person
> is to be found, woe to him if he is not all
> admiration and appreciation, or else I become shy
> and ashamed and confused, then I get into a fury.
> Now that I have drawn your attention to the con-
> dition, shall I sing?

CONVICT:
> Sing?

EXECUTIONER:
> Are you going to like it and express your appreci-
> ation?

CONVICT:
> Yes!

EXECUTIONER:
> Do you promise for sure?

CONVICT:
> Sure!

EXECUTIONER:
> Then I'll sing that gentle song for you. Will
> you listen?

CONVICT:
> I'll listen and appreciate...

EXECUTIONER:
> Appreciation comes in the end. Now you only have
> to listen!

CONVICT:
> Only listen.

EXECUTIONER:
> Well, are you ready?

CONVICT:

Why? I thought you were going to sing?

EXECUTIONER:

Yes, but you must be ready to listen.

CONVICT:

Can I help it? You have left my ears free...for
this purpose no doubt.

EXECUTIONER:

Well, let's begin. This tender song is entitled
'The flower and the gardener.' I composed it myself. Yes, all by myself.

CONVICT:

I know.

EXECUTIONER:

Strange! Who told you?

CONVICT:

You, yourself, a moment ago.

EXECUTIONER:

Really? Really? Now, do you want me to begin?

CONVICT:

Begin.

EXECUTIONER:

Here, I am beginning. Listen! But you are not
listening!

CONVICT:

I am listening.

EXECUTIONER:

You must listen very attentively.

CONVICT:

Very attentively.

EXECUTIONER:

I warn you not to embarass me by being unatten-
tive or lacking interest!

CONVICT:

I am interested.

EXECUTIONER:

Are you ready?

CONVICT:

Yes.

EXECUTIONER:

I don't see that you are terribly enthusiastic.

CONVICT:

And how should I show that?

EXECUTIONER:

 I want you to burn with enthusiasm. Tell me that
 you insist on listening to my singing.

CONVICT:

 I insist!

EXECUTIONER:

 You say it in a lukewarm, even a cold manner.

CONVICT:

 Cold?

EXECUTIONER:

 Yes, I want your insistence to come from deep in
 your heart.

CONVICT:

 It is deep in my heart.

EXECUTIONER:

 I don't feel the warmth of sincerity in your
 voice.

CONVICT:

 Sincerity?

EXECUTIONER:

 Yes, it does not show in your voice. You must
 know that the tones of the voice betray real feelings. And your voice is lukewarm and cold.

CONVICT:

 Now for the last time, are you going to sing or
 not?

EXECUTIONER:

 I am not going to sing!

CONVICT:

 God be praised!

EXECUTIONER:

 You praise God because I am not going to sing?

CONVICT:

 No, I always praise God whether you sing or not.
 I don't think anybody would object to praising
 God in all cases.

EXECUTIONER:

 Deep in your heart you wish me not to sing!

CONVICT:

 Deep in my heart? Only God knows what's in the
 heart, don't you think?

EXECUTIONER:
> Then you want me to sing?

CONVICT:
> If you like.

EXECUTIONER:
> I will sing.

CONVICT: Sing.

EXECUTIONER:
> I have one condition. First, beg me to sing. Go ahead, beg me!

CONVICT:
> I beg you.

EXECUTIONER:
> Say it imploringly!

CONVICT:
> I beg you, I implore you, by your God, and the God of all creatures! I pray to God Almighty, the All-Powerful, to soften your cruel heart so that you may listen to my entreaties and favor me with your singing!

EXECUTIONER:
> Again!

CONVICT:
> What?

EXECUTIONER:
> Repeat this entreaty and prayer!

CONVICT:
> Oh my God, please have mercy on me. You are killing me with your coyness and playfulness. Sing, if you want to sing. If you don't, I implore you by God to leave me alone!

EXECUTIONER:
> Are you angry? I don't like to see you angry. I will sing to soothe you and dispell your gloom. Here, I begin.
> *(He coughs, then starts to warm up for singing.)*

CONVICT:
> At last.

EXECUTIONER:
> *(Stops suddenly.)* If you'd rather I did not sing, tell me frankly!

CONVICT:
> God in heaven, he's at it again.

EXECUTIONER:
> Are you at the end of your patience?

CONVICT:
> Beyond that.

EXECUTIONER:
> Am I tormenting you?

CONVICT:
> Immensely.

EXECUTIONER:
> Patience, my good friend, patience.

CONVICT:
> This Executioner is executing me over and over!

EXECUTIONER:
> What did you say?

CONVICT:
> I can't bear it any longer!

EXECUTIONER:
> You can't bear it any longer? Oh, what a poor soul, tortured by the burning desire to hear my singing! I am about to begin, I'll not make you wait long. I am ready, listen. Here is the tender song...*(He clears his throat, then sings drunkenly.)*
> Oh flower one day old,
> Peace to you from your lovers.
> At dawn tomorrow you will get plucked,
> Your robe of dew falls on your feet.
> Sleeping in your firewood basket,
> My melodies die off at your ears,
> And in the air the blade of fate
> Brightly gleams in the gardener's hand.
> Oh flower one day old,
> Peace to you, peace to you.
> *(Silence)*

EXECUTIONER:
> Why are you silent? Why don't you appreciate? This is the time to show your admiration and appreciation!

CONVICT:
> Is this your tender song, you evil-eyed Executioner?

EXECUTIONER:

I beg your pardon, I am not an Executioner.

CONVICT:

What are you then?

EXECUTIONER:

I am a gardener.

CONVICT:

Gardener?

EXECUTIONER:

Yes, gardener, dó you understand? *(Shouting
drunkenly)* G-A-R-D-E-N-E-R!
*(A window in the Belle's house opens. A servant
leans out.)*

SERVANT:

What's this noise? And at such a time! When people are asleep! My Mistress has a headache, and
she wants to have a quiet sleep.

EXECUTIONER:

(Sarcastically) Mistress, huh? *(Laughs derisive-
ly.)* Her Mistress!

SERVANT:

I told you to stop this noise!

EXECUTIONER:

Get out of my sight, you servant of lechery and
fornication!

SERVANT:

Don't insult my Mistress! If she wished, she
could have twenty sweepers like you, sweeping
the dust from under her shoes!

EXECUTIONER:

Shut up, you filthiest of the filthy!
*(The Belle appears in the window behind her
Servant.)*

BELLE:

What is happening?

SERVANT:

This drunken Executioner is making all this noise
and insulting us.

BELLE:

How dare he?

EXECUTIONER:

(Pointing to the window) Here she comes, her High-

ness, her notorious Mistress.

BELLE:

Show some respect, you there!

EXECUTIONER:

(Laughing sarcastically) Respect?

BELLE:

Yes, and don't force us to teach you how to respect ladies.

EXECUTIONER:

Ladies? *(Laughs)* Ladies? She says 'ladies'!
Listen to her...

BELLE:

(To her Servant) Go down and give him a lesson in manners.

SERVANT:

(To the Executioner) Wait for me, if you are a man!
(The two women disappear from the window.)

EXECUTIONER:

(To the convict. He is now sobering up.) What does this she-devil intend to do, do you know? She is capable of anything! Did you see how she threatened me?

SERVANT:

(Coming out of the house with a shoe in her hand) Come here!

EXECUTIONER:

What are you going to do with that shoe?

SERVANT:

This is the dirtiest and oldest one I could find, understand? I found nothing older or dirtier that could be suitable for your ugly, dirty mug.

EXECUTIONER:

There goes the wine! Did you hear her polite speech, Mr. Convict?

CONVICT:

Yes.

EXECUTIONER:

And you remain silent?

CONVICT:

I?

EXECUTIONER:

> And you do nothing?

CONVICT:

> How?

EXECUTIONER:

> You let her insult me, and remain silent?

CONVICT:

> What do you want me to do?

EXECUTIONER:

> Do something! At least, say something!

CONVICT:

> What do I have to do with it?

EXECUTIONER:

> Oh, what a lack of courage and meanness of purpose! You see her brandishing the shoe as one would brandish a sword or a sabre, and you don't rise to defend me? You stand there motionless, watching indifferently and nonchalantly listening to her insulting me, humiliating me, and calling me names! By God, this is far from being chivalrous!

CONVICT:

> Really?

SERVANT:

> *(Shaking the shoe in her hand)* Listen, you there, leave this poor man alone. Face me yourself, if you have the courage. Your account is with me. You have misbehaved, and now you must apologize and ask forgiveness, or else, by God, the King of the Heavenly Throne and the Giver of Might...

EXECUTIONER:

> *(Gently)* Easy, easy.

SERVANT:

> Speak! What's your answer?

EXECUTIONER:

> Conciliation.

SERVANT:

> Ask for forgiveness first!

EXECUTIONER:

> Whom should I ask? You?

SERVANT:

> My Mistress.

EXECUTIONER:
Where is she?
BELLE:
(Appearing at her door step) Here I am. Did he
apologize?
SERVANT:
He will, my Lady.
EXECUTIONER:
Yes, my Lady.
BELLE:
Well, I accept your apology.
EXECUTIONER:
Only, my Lady, don't you think things should re-
turn to normal?
BELLE:
They have.
EXECUTIONER:
But the wine should go back to my head.
BELLE:
What do you mean?
EXECUTIONER:
I mean that a damage has been done, and it needs
repair. Your energetic servant has emptied my
head of all the ecstasy. Who will fill the empti-
ness of my head?
BELLE:
I'll do that. Take all the drinks you like from
the Tavern Keeper at my expense.
EXECUTIONER:
Thank you, generous lady.
*(The Executioner beckons to the Tavern Keeper
standing at his door to get him a drink.)*
CONVICT:
(To the Belle) Don't you know me, beautiful one?
BELLE:
Of course I do. Since the moment they brought you
here early in the evening. I saw you from my win-
dow and recognized you, and it distressed me to
see you in chains. But...what crime have you
committed?
CONVICT:
Nothing much. All I did was say...

EXECUTIONER:

> *(Realizes what is going on and shouts.)* Beware!
> Beware! Shut your mouth!

CONVICT:

> I'm shutting my mouth.

BELLE:

> They tried you of course?

CONVICT:

> No.

BELLE:

> What did you say? You were not tried?

CONVICT:

> Nor was I even referred for trial. I sent a peti-
> tion to the Sultan asking for my right to appear
> before the Chief Judge, the fairest and most sin-
> cere defender of the law. But, here's the dawn
> approaching, and the Executioner has received
> orders to cut off my head immediately at the call
> for prayer.

BELLE:

> *(Looking at the sky)* Dawn? It is almost upon us,
> look at the sky.

EXECUTIONER:

> *(Holding a goblet which he got from the Tavern
> Keeper)* It is not the sky, my dear lady, which
> will decide the hour of this Convict, but the
> minaret of this mosque. I am waiting for the
> Muezzin.

BELLE:

> The Muezzin? No doubt he is on his way. I stay
> up until morning sometimes, and I see him at this
> hour heading for the mosque.

CONVICT:

> Then my time is up!

BELLE:

> No, since your petition was not decided upon yet.

CONVICT:

> This Executioner is not going to wait for the
> result of the petition. Is that not so, Execution-
> er?

EXECUTIONER:

> I will wait only for the Muezzin. Those were the
> orders.

BELLE:

Whose orders? The Sultan's?

EXECUTIONER:

Almost.

CONVICT:

Almost? Wasn't it the Sultan?

EXECUTIONER:

The Vizier. The orders of the Vizier are as good as the Sultan's.

CONVICT:

Then I am surely going to die.

EXECUTIONER:

That's right. As soon as the Muezzin's call for prayer goes up to the sky, so will your soul go up to heaven. This is very painfully sad for me, but business is business, and a profession is a profession!

BELLE:

(Looking towards the road) Woe! Here comes the Muezzin!

CONVICT:

It's all over!

(The Muezzin appears.)

EXECUTIONER:

Make haste, Muezzin, we are waiting for you!

MUEZZIN:

Waiting for me? Why?

EXECUTIONER:

To call for the dawn prayers.

MUEZZIN:

Do you want to pray?

EXECUTIONER:

I want to do my job.

MUEZZIN:

What have I to do with your job?

EXECUTIONER:

As your voice reaches the sky so will this man's soul go up!

MUEZZIN:

God forbid!

EXECUTIONER:

Those are the orders.

MUEZZIN:

    This man's life is hanging from my vocal chords?

EXECUTIONER:

    Yes.

MUEZZIN:

    Oh God Almighty!

EXECUTIONER:

    Make haste, Muezzin, so I can do my job.

BELLE:

    Why the haste, gentle Executioner? The Muezzin's
voice is affected by the night cold and he needs
a hot drink. Come up to my house, Muezzin, I'll
fix you something to clear your voice.

EXECUTIONER:

    And the dawn?

BELLE:

    The dawn is all right. And the Muezzin knows his
job better, anyway.

EXECUTIONER:

    And my job?

BELLE:

    Your job is all right, so long as the Muezzin has
not yet called for prayer.

EXECUTIONER:

    Do you agree, Muezzin?

BELLE:

    Yes, he accepts my little invitation for a short
while. He is one of my best acquaintances in
this neighborhood.

EXECUTIONER:

    What about those who want to pray in the mosque?

MUEZZIN:

    There are only two men in the mosque, one of whom
is a stranger who has taken shelter there, and
the other is a beggar who is there because it is
cold outside. And everybody is sound asleep now.
Besides, hardly anybody listens to the call for
the dawn prayer anyway, and none except those I
kick rise to perform the prayer.

BELLE:

    And most people in this neighborhood are rich and
sleep till noon.

EXECUTIONER:
>You mean there will be no call for the dawn prayer today?

BELLE:
>We mean there's no hurry, and that haste is the work of the devil. Don't worry. The call for the dawn prayer will be given on time, and anyway you are not responsible; the Muezzin alone is responsible for that. Come on, Muezzin! A cup of coffee will be very good for your voice.

MUEZZIN:
>There is no harm in a small cup and a short visit.
>*(The Belle goes home with the Muezzin.)*

EXECUTIONER:
>*(To the Convict)* Did you see? Instead of ascending the minaret, he went up to this...respectable woman's house. There's a Muezzin for you!

CONVICT:
>A valiant man, risking everything! As for you, you whom nobody will blame, you who are safe from any responsibility, you get furious and outraged and scared! Compose yourself a little my friend, and be patient. Leave it all to God. Listen, I have an idea, a good wise idea that will relieve you of your gloom and cheer your heart. Sing your tender song for me in your own heavenly voice, and I swear I will listen in great admiration and appreciation. Go ahead, sing, I am all ears.

EXECUTIONER:
>I no longer feel like it.

CONVICT:
>Why? What is making you melancholy? Is it because you didn't cut off my head?

EXECUTIONER:
>Because I deviated from my duty.

CONVICT:
>Your duty is to carry out the sentence upon hearing the call for the dawn prayer. But who calls for prayer? Is it you or the Muezzin?

EXECUTIONER:
>The Muezzin.

CONVICT:
 Did he?
EXECUTIONER:
 No.
CONVICT:
 Then where's your fault?
EXECUTIONER:
 True, I have done nothing wrong.
CONVICT:
 That's what we all say.
EXECUTIONER:
 You are trying to console me.
CONVICT:
 I am telling the truth.
EXECUTIONER:
 (Looks towards the road, then cries.) What's all
 this crowd? Oh my God, this is the Vizier's pro-
 cession! It's the Vizier!
CONVICT:
 Don't shake like that! Calm yourself!
EXECUTIONER:
 I have done nothing. I am covered, am I not?
CONVICT:
 Don't worry! You are covered by a thousand ex-
 cuses.
EXECUTIONER:
 It is that accursed Muezzin who will have to
 answer some tough questions.
 (The Vizier appears, surrounded by his guards.)
VIZIER:
 (Shouting) How on earth? Hasn't this criminal
 been executed?
EXECUTIONER:
 We are waiting for the dawn, your Highness,
 according to your orders.
VIZIER:
 Dawn? We have prayed the dawn prayers at the
 palace mosque in the presence of our Lord, the
 Sultan, and the Chief Judge.
EXECUTIONER:
 It is not my fault, my Lord, the Muezzin of this
 mosque has not yet climbed the minaret.

VIZIER:

>How come? This is impossible! Where is that Muezzin?
>
>*(The Muezzin comes out of the Belle's house stealthily, trying to hide behind the Belle and her servant.)*

EXECUTIONER:

>*(Sees him and shouts.)* Here he is! Here he is!

VIZIER:

>*(To the guards)* Bring him here! *(They do.)* Are you the Muezzin of this mosque?

MUEZZIN:

>Yes, my Lord.

VIZIER:

>Why haven't you called for the dawn prayer until now?

MUEZZIN:

>Who said that, your Highness? I called for the dawn prayer a while ago.

VIZIER:

>You called for the dawn prayer?

MUEZZIN:

>On time, as I do every day. And those that heard me heard me.

BELLE:

>True, we all heard him call for the dawn prayer from the top of the minaret.

SERVANT:

>Yes, today as he does every day!

VIZIER:

>But this Executioner claims...

BELLE:

>This Executioner was drunk and sleeping soundly.

SERVANT:

>His snoring reached us and woke us from our sweet sleep.

VIZIER:

>*(To the dumbfounded Executioner)* Is that how you carry out my orders?

EXECUTIONER:

>I swear...I swear, my Lord.

VIZIER:

    Enough!

CONVICT:

    Mr. Vizier, I implore you to listen to me. I have
sent to his Majesty, the Sultan, a petition...

EXECUTIONER:

    (Coming to and shouting) I swear, your Highness,
that I was wide awake!

VIZIER:

    Enough, I told you! (Addressing the Convict) Yes,
your petition came to the attention of his Majesty,
our Sultan, and he has ordered that you be tried
by the Chief Judge. His Majesty, the Sultan, is
going to attend the trial himself. This is his
wish and irrevocable order. Guards, clear this
square of people, and let everybody go to his
house. This trial has to be conducted in absolute
secrecy. *(Guards clear the square.)*

EXECUTIONER:

    Your Highness...*(He tries to explain, but the
Vizier waves him away.)*
    *(The Sultan enters in procession, accompanied by
the Chief Judge.)*

CONVICT:

    (Crying) Your Majesty, our Sultan! Justice, I beg
you for justice!

SULTAN:

    Is this the defendant?

CONVICT:

    Your Majesty! I have not committed a crime or
erred!

SULTAN:

    We will see.

CONVICT:

    And I have not been tried! I have not been tried!

SULTAN:

    You will receive a fair trial, according to your
wish. Your trial will be conducted by the Chief
Judge in our presence. *(The Sultan makes a gesture
to the Chief Judge to go ahead with the trial,
then sits in a seat prepared for him. The Vizier
stands by his side.)*

JUDGE:
>   *(Sitting on a seat)* Unchain the defendant! *(One of the guards does so.)* Come closer. What is your crime?

CONVICT:
>   I have committed no crime.

JUDGE:
>   What is the charge against you?

CONVICT:
>   Ask the Vizier.

JUDGE:
>   I am asking you.

CONVICT:
>   I did nothing at all except utter an innocent word that will harm nobody.

VIZIER:
>   It is a terrifying, sinful word!

JUDGE:
>   *(To the Convict)* What word?

CONVICT:
>   I don't like to repeat it.

VIZIER:
>   Now you don't, but in the market-place, in the midst of the mob...

JUDGE:
>   What is the word?

VIZIER:
>   He said that his Majesty, our Lord the Sultan, is nothing but a slave.

CONVICT:
>   Everybody knows it. It's no secret.

VIZIER:
>   Don't interrupt me. He claims to be the slave-merchant who sold our Sultan as a child to our late Sultan.

CONVICT:
>   This is true, and I swear by everything. It is a deal that will forever make me proud.

SULTAN:
>   *(To the Convict)* You sold me to the late Sultan?

CONVICT:
>   Yes.

SULTAN:
>   When was that?

CONVICT:

>Twenty five years ago, your Majesty. You were a boy of six, lost and left behind in a Circassian village invaded by the Mongols. You were extreme-ly intelligent, probably too much so for your age. So I was glad to get you and I carried you here to the Sultan, who paid me a thousand dinars for you.

SULTAN:

>(Sarcastically) Only a thousand dinars?

CONVICT:

>You were worth more, of course, but I had just started my trade. I was only twenty-six. That deal was my first, and it made my future!

SULTAN:

>Yours and mine!

CONVICT:

>God be praised!

SULTAN:

>Does this deserve death? To bring me to this country? To me, it should be the contrary.

VIZIER:

>He deserves death because he is a chatterbox who cannot hold his tongue.

SULTAN:

>I don't see the danger in his saying or spread-ing the word that I was a slave. The late Sultan himself was one. Is that not correct, Vizier?

VIZIER:

>It is correct, but...

SULTAN:

>Is that not correct, Chief Judge?

VIZIER:

>True, your Majesty!

SULTAN:

>The Mamluk Sultans are a whole dynasty of former slaves. Everybody was brought at an early age to the palaces where they were raised in a sound, strong way, later to become governors and commanders of armies and sultans. I am only one of those, no different.

CONVICT:
>No, you are one of the wisest, may God preserve
>you for your subjects.

SULTAN:
>And yet, I don't remember your face. I don't even
>remember my childhood in that Circassian village
>where you say you found me. All I remember is my
>childhood in the palace under the patronage of
>the late Sultan, who treated me as his own son,
>since he had none of his own. He raised me and
>taught me so I could become a ruler. I knew
>definitely all the time that he was not my father.

CONVICT:
>Your parents were killed by the Mongols.

SULTAN:
>Nobody ever talked to me about my parents. I only
>knew that I was brought to the palace at a tender
>age.

CONVICT:
>And it was I who brought you.

SULTAN:
>Maybe.

CONVICT:
>Then, your Majesty, what is my crime?

SULTAN:
>I do not know. Ask whoever has accused you.

VIZIER:
>This is not his real crime.

SULTAN:
>Is there a real crime?

VIZIER:
>Yes, your Majesty. Saying that you were a slave
>is nothing to cause shame or disgrace--all
>Mamluk Sultans were like that. The crime is not
>there. But the Mamluk Sultan was usually freed
>before ascending the throne...

SULTAN:
>And then?

VIZIER:
>And then, my Lord, this man claims that you have
>not been freed yet, that you are still a slave
>and that your status is that of a slave, and that

a slave cannot rule a free people...

SULTAN:

(To the Convict) Did you really say that?

CONVICT:

I did not say it all, but the people in the
marketplace like this kind of talk.

SULTAN:

How do you know I was not freed?

CONVICT:

It is not I who said it. They attribute to me
all kinds of idle talk.

SULTAN:

But they chatter anyway?

CONVICT:

Not me!

SULTAN:

You or somebody else. It is no longer important.
What matters now is for everybody everywhere to
know that this is a mere lie. Is that not so,
Chief Judge?

JUDGE:

Actually, my Lord...

SULTAN:

This is a mere lie, a fabrication that is illogi-
cal and unreasonable. Not freed yet? I...I who
was a commander of the armies, and the vanquisher
of the Mongols, the right arm of the late Sultan,
and the successor prepared to rule after him?
All this and the Sultan did not think of freeing
me before his death? Is this possible? Listen,
Judge! All you have to do now is send the town
criers to announce the official refutation, and
broadcast to all the people the text of the document emancipating me, a document which, no doubt,
is kept in your safe. Is that not so?

JUDGE:

(Combing his beard with his fingers) You say, my
Lord...

SULTAN:

Did you not hear what I said?

JUDGE:

No, I...

SULTAN:
> You were busy passing your finger through your beard.

JUDGE:
> Your Majesty!

SULTAN:
> What? His Majesty the Sultan speaks to you in a clear simple language that does not require a lot of thinking or profundity. All there is to it is that it has become necessary now to make this document known to the public. Understand?

JUDGE:
> Yes!

SULTAN:
> You are still playing with your beard? Would you leave it alone for a while?

VIZIER:
> *(Intervening)* My Lord, do you permit me to...

SULTAN:
> What is wrong? What is wrong with you?

VIZIER:
> May I ask our Lord, the Sultan, to...

SULTAN:
> What is all this confusion? Both you and him...

JUDGE:
> We should probably postpone this trial until some other time. Once we are by ourselves...

VIZIER:
> Yes, yes, that is better.

SULTAN:
> I begin to understand...
> *(The Vizier makes a gesture to everybody to move away and take the Convict.)*

SULTAN:
> Here we are, alone. What do you have to say? Although I can already read it on your faces.

JUDGE:
> Yes, my Lord...Your insight...Well, actually there is no document in my safe pertaining to your being freed.

SULTAN:
> Probably you haven't received it yet. It must be

here or there, is that not so, Vizier?

VIZIER:

Actually, my Lord...

SULTAN:

What?

VIZIER:

Actually...

SULTAN:

Speak!

VIZIER:

There is no document proving that you were freed, my Lord!

SULTAN:

What did you say?

VIZIER:

The late Sultan fell suddenly after a heart attack, and he died before freeing you.

SULTAN:

What is this you claim, you wretch?

VIZIER:

I am a wretch indeed, my Lord, and a sinful criminal. This is something I will not deny. I should have taken care of this affair in time, but it never occurred to me. My head was full of other grave matters. You, yourself, my Lord, were at the time far off in the thick of battle, and there was no one but me by the bedside of the dying Sultan. I had forgotten this matter under those trying circumstances. I was completely preoccupied at that time with being sworn in by the dying man to serve you, my Lord, in the same faithful manner I served him throughout his life.

SULTAN:

Indeed, that is how you serve me!

VIZIER:

I deserve death, I know it. This is an unpardonable sin. The late Sultan could not have thought of everything or remembered everything. It was my duty to think for him and remind him of grave matters. It was my duty, really, to put forth to him the matter of the emancipation, since it was of the utmost importance, and to prepare all the

legal requirements. But your high estate, my
Lord, and your influence and august position, and
the respect we all have for you, all these elevated
qualities have made us overlook the status of
slavery as far as you were concerned. It made me
forget the need for documents. I realized the
whole situation only when you ascended the throne,
my Lord, and I panicked and was on the point of
madness, but I controlled myself and thought this
point would never be raised one day.

SULTAN:
It has now been raised.

VIZIER:
Woe to me! I did not know that a man like this
would come to speak idly.

SULTAN:
Hence, you wanted to shut his mouth for good by
handing him over to the Executioner.

VIZIER:
Yes!

SULTAN:
And bury your mistake with his corpse.

VIZIER:
(Brooding) Yes.

SULTAN:
What good is that now, when everybody is talking?

VIZIER:
If this man's head is cut off and hung in the
square for everybody to see, no tongue would dare
speak afterwards.

SULTAN:
You think so?

VIZIER:
If the sword cannot cut off tongues, then what
could?

JUDGE:
Allow me a word, your Majesty.

SULTAN:
I am listening.

JUDGE:
The sword indeed can cut off tongues and heads,
but not problems and issues.

SULTAN:

What do you mean?

JUDGE:

I mean the issue will always remain. That is, that the Sultan is ruling without having been freed, and that he is a slave ruling a free people!

VIZIER:

Who dares to say that? Anybody who does will have his head cut off!

JUDGE:

That's another matter.

VIZIER:

It is not necessary for the ruler to go about carrying documents and justifications. We have a splendid example in the Fatimid dynasty: everybody remembers what al-Mu'izz li-Din Allah, the Fatimid, did when he came claiming that he was a descendant of the Prophet, and as such had the right to rule in the land of Egypt. When the people did not believe him, he brandished his sword and opened the chests containing his gold, saying, "This is my ancestry and this my family tree." The people stopped talking, and he and his progeny ruled happily for a long time.

SULTAN:

What do you say to this, Judge?

JUDGE:

I say that this is historically correct...but...

SULTAN:

But what?

JUDGE:

Do you want then, great Sultan, to solve your problem this way?

SULTAN:

Why not?

VIZIER:

Yes, why not? Nothing is easier than that, especially in this situation. It is enough to announce to the people that our Lord, the Sultan, was legally freed, freed by the late Sultan before his death, and that the documents were registered and kept by the Chief Judge. Anybody who dares to deny this dies.

JUDGE:

There is somebody who will deny this.

VIZIER:

Who?

JUDGE:

I.

SULTAN:

You?

JUDGE:

Yes, I, my Lord. I cannot take part in this plot.

VIZIER:

It is not a plot, it is a plan to save the situation.

JUDGE:

It is a plot against the law which I represent.

SULTAN:

Law?

JUDGE:

Yes, Sultan, law. As far as the law is concerned, you are nothing but a slave. Now a slave, according to the law, is a thing, a commodity, an object. And since the late Sultan, who owned you, did not free you before his death, you are still a thing, a commodity belonging to another. Hence, you are not qualified to conduct ordinary deals or contracts engaged in by free people.

SULTAN:

Is this the law?

VIZIER:

Just a moment, Chief Judge, we are not now interested in the law as such, but in finding a way to get rid of this law. And this way consists of the following: we suppose that the emancipation has actually taken place, and since this is a secret between the three of us, and nobody else knows the truth, it is easy to have everybody believe...

JUDGE:

The lie.

VIZIER:

The solution. That sounds better...more fitting.

JUDGE:

Solution by lying.

VIZIER:

What is wrong with that?

JUDGE:

For the two of you, there's nothing wrong.

VIZIER:

And for you?

JUDGE:

For me, it is different. I, for instance, cannot
lie to myself. I cannot bypass the law when I am
the representative of the law. I cannot forswear
an oath in which I pledged myself to be an
honest servant of the law!

SULTAN:

You pledged yourself before me!

JUDGE:

And before God and my conscience!

SULTAN:

This means you will not go along with us?

JUDGE:

On this path, no.

SULTAN:

And would not put your hand in ours?

JUDGE:

On this plan, no.

SULTAN:

Well, in that case, all you have to do is take
yourself aside and not interfere in anything,
leaving us to do what we will. That way you keep
your oath and satisfy your conscience.

JUDGE:

I am sorry, my Lord.

SULTAN:

Why?

JUDGE:

Because now that I have learned that according to
the law you are not qualified to conduct deals
and contracts, I find myself compelled to rule
that all your transactions are null and void.

SULTAN:

You are mad! It's impossible!

JUDGE:
> I can, unfortunately, do nothing else, unless...

SULTAN:
> Unless?

JUDGE:
> Unless you fire me from my job, banish me from the country, or cut off my head; that way I become absolved from my oath, and you can do whatever you like.

SULTAN:
> Is that a threat?

JUDGE:
> No, it's a solution.

VIZIER:
> You are complicating the whole thing for us, Chief Judge.

JUDGE:
> I am helping you out of the problem.

SULTAN:
> This man is beginning to bother me.

VIZIER:
> He knows that we are in his power, and that the least violence done to him will expose everything to the people.

SULTAN:
> *(To the Judge)* In short, you don't want to help us.

JUDGE:
> On the contrary, my Lord. I wish to be of help, but not in this manner.

SULTAN:
> What do you suggest, then?

JUDGE:
> Enforce the law.

SULTAN:
> If you enforce the law, I will lose my throne.

JUDGE:
> Not only that!

SULTAN:
> Worse?

JUDGE:
> Yes!

SULTAN:

What else is there?

JUDGE:

Being, according to the law, a commodity belonging to the late Sultan, you have become part of his legacy. And since he had no heirs, this legacy went to the public treasury. Hence, you are a commodity that belongs to the public treasury, a worthless commodity, since it brings no profit in. And since I am also the Treasurer, I will tell you this: customarily in such cases, we have always gotten rid of such worthless property by selling it at auction, so that the Treasury might not suffer loss, and so that we can use the incoming cash in public projects that benefit the people, especially the poor.

SULTAN:

Worthless commodity? Me?

JUDGE:

I am speaking, of course, from the legal point of view.

SULTAN:

Until now, you have offered no solution, only insults!

JUDGE:

Insults? I beg your pardon, great Sultan. You know full well how much I esteem and respect you, and how high I place you. You will, no doubt, remember that since the very first moment, I was the first one to declare allegiance to you and proclaim you a sultan. What I am giving now is a frank summation of the situation, from the point of view of the law.

SULTAN:

The situation, then, is that I am a thing, a commodity, and an object, and not a man or a human being?

JUDGE:

Yes!

SULTAN:

And that this thing or commodity belongs to the public treasury?

JUDGE:

Indeed!

SULTAN:

And that the public treasury gets rid of such
commodities that bring in no profit by offering
them at auction for the public good?

JUDGE:

Exactly!

SULTAN:

Chief Judge, don't you agree with me that this
is a little strange?

JUDGE:

Yes, but...

SULTAN:

And that it is too much, going too far?

JUDGE:

Maybe, but as a judge, what interests me is the
relationship of the facts to the letter of the
law.

SULTAN:

Listen, Judge, this law of yours brings me no
solution, whereas a very slight movement of my
sword could cut off the whole problem immediately!

JUDGE:

Do it, then!

SULTAN:

I will. What does a little blood matter for the
sake of good government?

JUDGE:

Then you must start with my blood.

SULTAN:

I will do all I deem necessary for the security
of the state. And I will, indeed, start with
you and throw you in jail. Vizier, arrest the
Judge!

VIZIER:

My Lord, the Sultan, you haven't yet heard his
answer to your question.

SULTAN:

What question?

VIZIER:

The question about his solution to the problem.

SULTAN:

    He has answered that question.

VIZIER:

    What he gave was not the solution, but a summation of the situation.

SULTAN:

    Is that true, Judge?

JUDGE:

    Yes.

SULTAN:

    You do have a solution, then?

JUDGE:

    (In the same tone) Yes.

SULTAN:

    Speak then. What is the solution?

JUDGE:

    There is only one solution.

SULTAN:

    Give it. What is it?

JUDGE:

    Enforce the law.

SULTAN:

    Again? Once again?

JUDGE:

    Yes, once again and always. I don't see any other way out.

SULTAN:

    Did you hear, Vizier? Do you still have the slightest hope of cooperating with this demented, senile man?

VIZIER:

    Allow me, my Lord, to interrogate him a little.

SULTAN:

    Do what you will.

VIZIER:

    Chief Judge, this is a rather delicate problem, and requires that you explain your point of view clearly and in detail.

JUDGE:

    My point of view is clear and simple. I could explain it in two words. There are two ways to solve this problem. The way of the sword and the way of the law. As for the sword, I have nothing

to do with it. The law I can and ought to explain
and give judgement on. The law says only the owner
of a slave can free that slave, nobody else. In
this present case, the owner died without leaving
an heir behind, hence, the ownership of the slave
is that of the public treasury. The public treasury
does not have the right to free the slave for
nothing, because nobody has the right to dispose
of state property without a monetary return. It
is, however, possible for the public treasury to
sell its property. In order for this sale to be
legal, it has to be done in a public auction. The
legal solution then is to offer our Lord, the
Sultan, in a public auction, and whoever purchases
him, frees him. In this way the public treasury
will suffer no loss, and the Sultan gets his
freedom under the law.

SULTAN:
(To the Vizier) Did you hear that?

VIZIER:
(To the Judge) Offer our great Lord, the Sultan,
in a public auction? But this is madness itself!

JUDGE:
This is the legal solution.

SULTAN:
(To the Vizier) Don't waste your time. The only
answer we can give this fool is to cut off his
head, come what may. And I will do it with my
own hand! *(He draws his sword.)*

JUDGE:
It is a great honor, my Lord, for me to die by
your hand, and for my soul to be sacrificed for
the sake of right and principle!

VIZIER:
Patience, my Lord, don't create a martyr of this
man. He couldn't hope for a more splendid death.
It will be said that you have destroyed the law,
and he will become the living symbol of the
spirit of right and principle. And a glorious
martyr will oftentimes have more influence and
effect on the people than the mightiest king.

SULTAN:

    (Under his breath) God damn it!

VIZIER:

    Don't give him this glory, my Lord, at the expense
of the situation.

SULTAN:

    What shall I do then? This man places us right in
the center of a dilemma. He is offering us two
alternatives, both unpleasant: the law, which
makes me look like a weakling and a laughing stock,
and the sword, which makes me look barbaric and
hateful!

VIZIER:

    (Moving towards the Chief Judge) Please, Chief
Judge, be lenient. Let's meet halfway, find a
compromise, a reasonable way out.

JUDGE:

    The only reasonable way out is the law.

VIZIER:

    Offer the Sultan at auction?

JUDGE:

    Yes.

VIZIER:

    And he who purchases him...?

JUDGE:

    Sets him free immediately, on the spot; this is
the condition...

VIZIER:

    And who is it that will agree to lose his money
this way?

JUDGE:

    Lots of people, those that would buy the Sultan's
freedom with their money.

VIZIER:

    Then why don't we perform this duty, you and I?
We can buy the Sultan's freedom with our own
money, secretly, and receive all the honor.
Isn't that a good idea?

JUDGE:

    Unfortunately, no. It could not be done secretly.
The law is very clear on this point: any public
treasury sale has to be made publicly, and at
an auction open to everybody.

SULTAN:

    (To the Vizier) Don't waste your time with him.
He insists on humiliating us.

VIZIER:

    (To the Judge) And now, for the last time, Chief
Judge, is there no trick or loophole that would
get us out of this dilemma?

JUDGE:

    Loophole? I am not the one to go to for loopholes!

SULTAN:

    Naturally; this man seeks only that which defies
and humiliates us!

JUDGE:

    Not I personally, my Lord. My humble person has
nothing to do with the whole thing. Had it been
in my hands, or depended on my wish, nothing
would have been more pleasant than to get you out
of this situation in the manner you like best.

SULTAN:

    Oh poor humble person! It is not in his hands.
In whose hands, then?

JUDGE:

    The law.

SULTAN:

    Yes, this ghost behind which you hide to subjugate
me, impose your will on me, and put me in this
humiliating, ridiculous situation.

JUDGE:

    No, to make you a glorious ruler!

SULTAN:

    Do you think that one of the signs of glory for
the Sultan is that he be treated as a commodity
and sold in the market-place?

JUDGE:

    It is indeed a sign of glory, my Lord, for the
Sultan to be subject to the law like everybody
else.

VIZIER:

    It is surely a beautiful sentiment, Chief Judge,
that the ruler should obey the law like the
subjects, but there is a great risk involved
here. The politics of government has its own

methods, and ruling the people requires other
methods.

JUDGE:

I understand nothing about politics, or about the
profession of ruling people.

SULTAN:

It is our profession. Let's do it in our own way,
then.

JUDGE:

I haven't prevented you, my Lord. You are absolutely free to rule as you like.

SULTAN:

Well...I see now what I must do.

VIZIER:

What are you going to do, my Lord?

SULTAN:

Look at this old man. Does he carry a sword? Of
course not...He has no weapons but his tongue,
which he puts to a very clever use. But I carry
this *(Pointing to his sword)*, and it is not made
of wood, nor is it a toy. It is a real sword,
and should be good for something, and must have
a reason for being there. Do you understand me?
Answer! why do I carry this? Is it for decoration
or for work?

VIZIER:

For work.

SULTAN:

And you, Judge, why don't you answer? Answer!
Is it for decoration or for work?

JUDGE:

For one or the other.

SULTAN:

What did you say?

JUDGE:

I said it is for this or that.

SULTAN:

What do you mean?

JUDGE:

I mean you, my Lord, have the choice. You can
make it for work, or you can make it an ornament.
I admit the virtues of the sword. It is strong,

swift, and decisive, but the sword gives right
to might. And who knows where might will be tomorrow? A mightier man than you may appear! As
for the law, it protects your rights against all
aggression, because it does not recognize that
which has more might, but that which has more
right. Now, my Lord, all you have to do is choose:
either the sword which imposes you, but also exposes you, or the law which defies but also protects you!

SULTAN:

(*Thinking for a moment*) The sword which imposes
me and exposes me, and the law which defies me
and protects me...

JUDGE:

Yes.

SULTAN:

What is this?

JUDGE:

The naked truth.

SULTAN:

(*Thinking while repeating*) The sword which imposes
and exposes, and the law which defies and protects.

JUDGE:

Yes, my Lord!

SULTAN:

Oh, this accursed man. He has a rare genius for
placing us in dilemmas.

JUDGE:

My Lord, all I did was to expound the two sides
of the issue. The choice is yours.

SULTAN:

The choice? The choice? What do you think,
Vizier?

VIZIER:

It is you who must decide, my Lord.

SULTAN:

I can see that you don't know either.

VIZIER:

Actually, my Lord, the...

SULTAN:

The choice is difficult.

VIZIER:

    Yes!

SULTAN:

    The sword which imposes me on everybody, but
    which also exposes me to danger...or the law
    which defies my wishes but protects my rights!

VIZIER:

    Yes!

SULTAN:

    You choose for me.

VIZIER:

    I? No, no, no, my Lord!

SULTAN:

    What are you afraid of?

VIZIER:

    The consequences. The consequences of this choice.
    If it turned out one of these days that I had
    chosen the wrong alternative, that would be a
    catastrophe.

SULTAN:

    You don't want the responsibility.

VIZIER:

    I dare not, and I have no right to.

SULTAN:

    Ultimately, we have to decide...

VIZIER:

    No one but you, my Lord, has the right to decide
    this issue.

SULTAN:

    True, no one but me. And I cannot shirk it. It
    is I who must choose and be responsible for the
    choice!

VIZIER:

    You are our Lord and ruler!

SULTAN:

    Yes, and this is my frightful hour, the fright-
    ful hour for every ruler, the moment he makes
    the final decision which changes things. The
    moment he utters this little word...the choice
    that determines the future...*(Thinks deeply as
    he goes to and fro. Everybody is waiting for him
    to speak. Silence for a moment. Then, still*

thinking) The sword or the law? The law or the
swoard?

VIZIER:

I appreciate the delicate situation, my Lord.

SULTAN:

Yet you don't want to help me with a choice?

VIZIER:

I cannot. In this situation, you alone must make
the choice.

SULTAN:

The sword or the law? The law or the sword?
*(Thinks for a moment, then raises his head
decisively.)* Well, I have decided.

VIZIER:

Your orders, my Lord?

SULTAN:

I have decided to choose...to choose...

VIZIER:

What, my Lord?

SULTAN:

(Loudly, in a firm voice) The law! I have chosen
the law!

Act II

(The same square. Guards are busy keeping order in the ranks of the people assembled around a platform erected in the square. The tavern is closed and the Keeper is standing, talking with the Shoemaker who is busy working at the entrance of his shop.)

TAVERN KEEPER:
> I wonder at you, Shoemaker! You open your shop and work while all other shops are closed as if it were a holiday!

SHOEMAKER:
> Why should I close down? Just because they are selling the Sultan?

TAVERN KEEPER:
> Don't be foolish! To watch the best spectacle on earth!

SHOEMAKER:
> I can watch everything from here while I work.

TAVERN KEEPER:
> It's up to you; as for me, I closed down my tavern so that I won't miss the slightest move in this fantastic spectacle.

SHOEMAKER:
> A big mistake, my friend. Today is the day to get customers. It is not as if you get such crowds every day at the door of your tavern! And take it from me, lots of them will be dying of

thirst and yearning for a drop of your drink!

TAVERN KEEPER:

Think so?

SHOEMAKER:

It goes without saying. Look, here I've displayed the best shoes I have. *(Points to the shoes on display at the entrance of the shop.)*

TAVERN KEEPER:

My dear Shoemaker, whoever comes out to buy today has come to buy the Sultan, not your shoes.

SHOEMAKER:

Why not? Among these people there are some that have more need for my shoes.

TAVERN KEEPER:

Sh! Don't say anything. It appears that you don't see what is so dazzling about this event. You don't realize how unique the thing is. They don't have a sultan on sale every day!

SHOEMAKER:

Listen, my friend, and I am not mincing my words: If I had enough money to buy the Sultan, I swear by God, I wouldn't buy him.

TAVERN KEEPER:

Wouldn't buy him?

SHOEMAKER:

Never!

TAVERN KEEPER:

Permit me to tell you, you are a fool!

SHOEMAKER:

On the contrary, I am very wise. Tell me, what do you want me to do with a sultan in my shop? Can I teach him my craft? Of course not. Can I ask him to do anything? Definitely not. Then it would be I who would work and double my work, in order to feed him, support him, and serve him. That, I swear by God, is what would happen. I would end up buying a burden, a luxurious commodity that I couldn't afford. My resources, friend, don't permit me to acquire antiques.

TAVERN KEEPER:

What idiocy!

SHOEMAKER:

And you? Would you buy him?

TAVERN KEEPER:

Is there any doubt?

SHOEMAKER:

What would you do with him?

TAVERN KEEPER:

Lots of things! Lots and lots of things! His mere
presence in my tavern would be enough to attract
the whole city. It would be enough to ask him to
tell my customers every night the story of his
exploits against the Mongols, his adventures,
travels and anecdotes, what countries he saw, or
homes he had been into, the deserts he crossed.
Isn't all this useful and enjoyable.

SHOEMAKER:

True, you could use him in that manner, but I...

TAVERN KEEPER:

You could also do the same.

SHOEMAKER:

How? He doesn't know a thing about sewing shoes
or making soles, so that he could speak about it.

TAVERN KEEPER:

With you he wouldn't have to speak.

SHOEMAKER:

What would he do then?

TAVERN KEEPER:

If I were in your place, I'd know how to use him.

SHOEMAKER:

How? Tell me!

TAVERN KEEPER:

I'd seat him in front of the shop on a comfortable
chair, give him a new pair of shoes to wear, and
put a poster over his head, saying,"Sultan's Shoes
Sold Here." Then you would see how the people
would come from all over in multitudes to buy your
merchandise!

SHOEMAKER:

What an idea!

TAVERN KEEPER:

Wouldn't you say?

SHOEMAKER:

I am beginning to like your mind.

TAVERN KEEPER:

> How would you like it then if we think of buying him together and sharing him? I give him to you by day, and you leave him to me at night?

SHOEMAKER:

> A beautiful dream! But all the money we have, the two of us, would hardly be enough .to buy one of his fingers.

TAVERN KEEPER:

> Really?

SHOEMAKER:

> Look at this crowd!
> *(Great numbers of people gather, speaking among themselves.)*

FIRST MAN:

> *(To another)* Is this where they sell the Sultan?

SECOND MAN:

> Yes, don't you see the guards?

FIRST MAN:

> If I had the money...

SECOND MAN:

> Sh! This is for rich people!

A CHILD:

> *(Pointing to a guard)* Mother, is this the Sultan?

MOTHER:

> *(To her son)* No, my Son, this is one of the guards.

CHILD:

> And where is the Sultan, then?

MOTHER:

> He hasn't come yet.

CHILD:

> Does the Sultan have a sword?

MOTHER:

> Yes, a big sword.

CHILD:

> Will they sell him here?

MOTHER:

> Yes, my Son.

CHILD:

> When, Mother?

MOTHER:

> In a little while.

CHILD:
>   Mother, buy him for me.

MOTHER:
>   What?

CHILD:
>   The Sultan, buy the Sultan for me!

MOTHER:
>   Quiet! He is not a toy you can play with!

CHILD:
>   You said they will sell him here. Buy him for me!

MOTHER:
>   Quiet, my Son! This is not for the likes of you.

CHILD:
>   For whom then? For adults?

MOTHER:
>   Yes, for adults?
>   *(The window of the Belle's house opens and the Servant looks out.)*

SERVANT:
>   *(Calling)* Keeper...Tavern Keeper, did you close your tavern today?

TAVERN KEEPER:
>   Yes! Wasn't that a good idea? Where is your mistress? Is she still in bed?

SERVANT:
>   No, she is getting dressed, after her bath.

TAVERN KEEPER:
>   She was clever and her trick on that Executioner worked.

SERVANT:
>   Sh! There he is, I see him in the crowd. He has seen us now!

EXECUTIONER:
>   *(Moving towards the Tavern Keeper)* God damn you and your wine!

TAVERN KEEPER:
>   Why? What sin did my wine commit to deserve your curse? Isn't it what made you so happy that night and enabled you to sing and see everything around you clear and neat?

EXECUTIONER:
>   *(In exasperation)* Clear and neat? Really! I saw

everything that night clear and neat?

TAVERN KEEPER:

Certainly! Do you doubt it?

EXECUTIONER:

Hold your tongue and don't remind me of that night.

TAVERN KEEPER:

I'll say no more about it. Tell me, are you off today?

EXECUTIONER:

Yes.

TAVERN KEEPER:

And your friend the Convict?

EXECUTIONER:

He was pardoned.

TAVERN KEEPER:

And of course, nobody asked you about the dawn story!

EXECUTIONER:

No.

TAVERN KEEPER:

Then everything has turned out for the best!

EXECUTIONER:

Yes, but I don't like anybody to make a fool of me.

SERVANT:

Even if this meant saving a man's life?

EXECUTIONER:

Shut up, you hag! You and your Mistress!

SERVANT:

Are you going to insult us again on such a day?

TAVERN KEEPER:

(To the Executioner) Don't upset yourself! This evening I'll offer you a big goblet of good wine for nothing.

EXECUTIONER:

For nothing?

TAVERN KEEPER:

Yes, a gift to drink to the health of...

EXECUTIONER:

Of whom?

TAVERN KEEPER:

    (Spots the Muezzin approach.) The health of the brave Muezzin!

EXECUTIONER:

    This bloody liar?

MUEZZIN:

    Liar? me?

EXECUTIONER:

    Yes, you claimed I was sound asleep at the time!

MUEZZIN:

    And you were drunk!

EXECUTIONER:

    I am absolutely sure that I was wide awake and did not sleep for one moment.

MUEZZIN:

    Well, if you are that sure...

EXECUTIONER:

    Yes, I was not asleep at all.

MUEZZIN:

    Well...

EXECUTIONER:

    You agree to this?

MUEZZIN:

    Yes.

EXECUTIONER:

    Then you were lying?

MUEZZIN:

    No.

EXECUTIONER:

    I was asleep then?

MUEZZIN:

    Yes.

EXECUTIONER:

    How can you say "yes"?

MUEZZIN:

    No.

EXECUTIONER:

    Stick to one thing! Is it yes or no?

MUEZZIN:

    What do you want?

EXECUTIONER:

    I want to know whether I was awake or asleep at that time.

MUEZZIN:
> Why should you bother? Everything has ended well.
> Your friend the Convict was pardoned, and nobody
> asked you anything. As for me, nobody broached
> the subject to me. Everything is over in the best
> possible way. Why dig up the past?

EXECUTIONER:
> Yes, but it hasn't ceased to trouble me since
> that day. I haven't yet seen the situation clear-
> ly. I would like to know: was I really asleep at
> that moment? Did you really call for the dawn
> prayer without my realizing it? You have to tell
> me ultimately, and no doubt you know the whole
> truth. Please tell me what happened exactly at
> that moment. I was a little tipsy at the time, it
> is true, but...

MUEZZIN:
> Since it troubles you that much, why should I
> satisfy you? I prefer to leave you like this, to
> the embers of doubt.

EXECUTIONER:
> May you roast in the embers of hell, you vile
> Muezzin!

MUEZZIN:
> *(Loudly)* Look, look! Here comes the Sultan's
> procession. *(The procession appears, led by the
> Sultan, followed by the Chief Judge, the Vizier
> and the Slave-Merchant. They all head for the plat-
> form. The Sultan sits in the center, surrounded by
> the others. The Slave-Merchant stands by his side
> facing the people.)*

TAVERN KEEPER:
> *(To the Executioner)* How strange! Here is your
> friend the Convict. What brought him here beside
> the Sultan?

EXECUTIONER:
> *(Looking at him)* Indeed, it is he himself!

MUEZZIN:
> No doubt he has been asked to perform as auction-
> eer. Isn't he one of the biggest slave-merchants?

TAVERN KEEPER:
> See, Executioner? His escape from your hands was

not in vain!

EXECUTIONER:

How strange! He sells the same Sultan twice, once
as a young boy and now another time as a man!

MUEZZIN:

Sh! He is getting ready to speak!

SLAVE-MERCHANT:

(Clapping his hands) Silence, people! I announce
that as a slave-merchant and an actioneer, I have
been asked to conduct this sale, at public auction, for the benefit of the public treasury. It
gives me great honor that the Chief Judge should
inaugurate the proceedings by a few words in
which he will clarify the conditions of this sale.
Our respected Chief Judge will now speak.

JUDGE:

Listen, everybody. The sale being conducted here
now is not like any other sale. It is a special
one, and you have already been told about it.
This sale has to be accompanied by another contract which is the emancipation contract, which
means that the purchaser is not permitted to keep
that which he has bought, but must conclude the
emancipation at this session. I need not remind
you of the text of the law stipulating that no
state employee shall take part in selling state
property. Now that I have spoken to you, the
Vizier has a word for you about the national
aspect of these proceedings.

SHOEMAKER:

(Whispering to the Tavern Keeper) Did you hear?
The purchaser is not permitted to keep that
which he has purchased! This is like throwing
your money into the sea.

TAVERN KEEPER:

(Whispering) We shall see now what idiot will
come forward.

SLAVE-MERCHANT:

(Shouting) Silence! Silence!

VIZIER:

Dear people, today you have the privilege of
witnessing a great, unique event, one of the most

significant in our history. A glorious sultan
seeks his freedom, so he goes to his people instead of resorting to his sword, a mighty sword
by which he achieved victory in the war with the
Mongols, and by which he also could have triumph-
ed in freeing himself. But our glorious and just
Sultan has chosen to be subject to the law, as
his weakest subject would. Here he is, seeking
his freedom according to the letter of the law.
Whoever wants to buy the freedom of his beloved
Sultan, let him bid in this auction. The highest
bidder will have performed a great service for
the nation, one that will be remembered for ever
and ever.
(Shouts from the people.)

A VOICE:

Long live the Sultan!

ANOTHER VOICE:

Long live the law!

SLAVE-MERCHANT:

Silence, everybody!

VIZIER:

(Resuming) Now, dear people, you have been informed about what sacrifice your country expects
of you for the sake of this most elevated aim,
which is the emancipation of your Sultan by your
money. The proceeds will go to the public treasury to help support the poor and the needy. Now
that your beloved Sultan has come to you so that
you may compete in appreciating and liberating
him, I hereby declare that the proceedings can
begin. *(He makes a gesture to the Slave-Merchant
to start. The masses shout.)*

SLAVE-MERCHANT:

Silence! Silence, people of this city. The auction is open. I will not resort to those descrip-
tions and epithets that people use in the market
place for purposes of beautification and persua-
sion, because the object offered for sale here
is above all description, epithets or comments.
I would not be exaggerating if I say that he is
worth his weight in gold. I should make it clear,

however, that it is far from our intention to make
it an impossible matter. On the contrary, we have
set our assessment within the bounds of the possible. Hence, I open this auction with a very small
sum considering that it's a sultan: ten thousand
dinars!
(Noises among the people.)

SHOEMAKER:

(To the Tavern Keeper) Ten thousand? Only? Oh what
a cheap price! Look at that huge sapphire in his
turban. That alone is worth a hundred thousand
dinars!

TAVERN KEEPER:

Really, its a sickly sum, especially since it is
to be paid for a noble national purpose. Ten
thousand dinars? This is unbecoming. I am a good
citizen and cannot accept this. *(Shouting)* Eleven
thousand dinars!

SLAVE-MERCHANT:

Eleven thousand dinars! Eleven thousand!

SHOEMAKER:

(To the Tavern Keeper) Eleven thousand dinars
only? Is that all you have? Then I will say it!
(Shouting) Twelve thousand dinars! Twelve!

TAVERN KEEPER:

(To the Shoemaker) So you want to outbid me, heh?
Thirteen thousand dinars!

SLAVE-MERCHANT:

Thirteen thousand dinars! Thirteen!
*(An unknown man advances suddenly, pushing his
way through the people.)*

UNKNOWN MAN:

Fifteen thousand dinars!

SHOEMAKER:

Oh boy, who is this man?

TAVERN KEEPER:

A frivolous man like you, no doubt.

SHOEMAKER:

And you, too.

SLAVE-MERCHANT:

Fifteen thousand dinars!...fifteen...fifteen...

SHOEMAKER:

   (Shouting) Sixteen thousand dinars!

UNKNOWN MAN:

   Eighteen thousand dinars!

SHOEMAKER:

   (To the Tavern Keeper) In a lump sum! This man
   has gone too far.

SLAVE-MERCHANT:

   Eighteen thousand dinars!...eighteen...

TAVERN KEEPER:

   (Looking closely at the Unknown Man) It seems to
   me I have seen this man somewhere. Oh yes, it's
   he! He is one of those rich men. He comes to my
   tavern every now and then for a drink before he
   goes up to the Belle.

SHOEMAKER:

   (Looking towards her window) Look, there she is
   in her window, shining and colorful as if she
   were a sugar doll. *(Shouting at her)* You beautiful one up there, aren't you a faithful citizen
   also?

BELLE:

   Shut up, Shoemaker! I am not one to be frivolous
   under such circumstances. I swear by God if you
   don't stop, I'll report you. Then they will put
   you in jail!

SLAVE-MERCHANT:

   (Repeating) Eighteen thousand dinars, for the sum
   of eighteen...
   (One of the notables advances to the platform.)

NOTABLE:

   (Shouting) Nineteen thousand dinars!

UNKNOWN MAN:

   Twenty thousand dinars!

SLAVE-MERCHANT:

   Twenty thousand dinars! Twenty thousand dinars!
   Twenty!

NOTABLE:

   Twenty-one thousand dinars!

UNKNOWN MAN:

   Twenty-two thousand dinars!
   (Another Notable advances.)

SECOND NOTABLE:

Twenty-three thousand dinars!

SLAVE-MERCHANT:

Twenty-three!...twenty-three...

UNKNOWN MAN:

Twenty-five!

SLAVE-MERCHANT:

Twenty-five thousand dinars!...twenty-five...

(A third Notable advances.)

THIRD NOTABLE:

Twenty-six!

SLAVE-MERCHANT:

Twenty-six thousand dinars!...twenty-six...

UNKNOWN MAN:

Twenty-eight!

SLAVE-MERCHANT:

Twenty-eight!...twenty-eight thousand dinars.

THIRD NOTABLE:

Twenty-nine!

SHOEMAKER:

(Whispering to the Tavern Keeper) Are they serious about all this? These...?

TAVERN KEEPER:

It seems so.

SLAVE-MERCHANT:

Twenty-nine...twenty-nine thousand dinars... twenty-nine!

UNKNOWN MAN:

Thirty...thirty thousand dinars!

SLAVE-MERCHANT:

Thirty! For the sum of thirty...thirty thousand dinars...

SHOEMAKER:

(Whispering) Thirty thousand dinars thrown into the sea. He must be crazy!

SLAVE-MERCHANT:

(Shouting at the top of his voice) Thirty thousand dinars! Thirty! Does anybody want to pay more? None? None to bid more than thirty thousand! Is this all you can offer as a price for our great Sultan?

SULTAN:

(To the Vizier) This is the limit of the noble

national appreciation!

VIZIER:

My Lord, those present now for the auction are mostly stingy merchants whose whole orientation is towards money and profit, and who would not want to spend any money for a lofty purpose.

SLAVE-MERCHANT:

(Shouting) Thirty thousand dinars! Once again, who says more? Who says more? Nobody? No? No? *(Slave-Merchant exchanges glances with the Vizier, then announces)* I will repeat it three times: One. Two. Three. Finished! The thirty-thousand-dinar bidder gets it.
(People cheer.)

TAVERN KEEPER:

(To the Shoemaker) It is my customer who got it.

SLAVE-MERCHANT:

You, the winner, come here and receive congratulations for your good luck!
(People cheer.)

VIZIER:

I congratulate you, good citizen, and I greet you.
(People cheer.)

SLAVE-MERCHANT:

(Shouting) Silence! Silence!

VIZIER:

(Continuing) On behalf of this nation and this faithful people out of which you arose to buy the freedom of our great Sultan, I greet you, good citizen! This noble deed of yours will be inscribed forever in the history of this great nation...

SLAVE-MERCHANT:

Silence, everybody! *(Looks towards the Unknown man)* The money is ready, good citizen, is it not?

UNKNOWN MAN:

No doubt about that. The gold sacks are only two steps away.

SLAVE-MERCHANT:

Well, wait then for the instructions of our respected Chief Judge.

JUDGE:

> *(Announcing)* The case is settled and the law has been enforced. The problem is solved. Come here, good citizen. Can you sign your name?

UNKNOWN MAN:

> Yes, your Honor!

JUDGE:

> Sign these documents then.

UNKNOWN MAN:

> Yes, your Honor!

JUDGE:

> *(Gives him a document.)* Here, sign here.

UNKNOWN MAN:

> *(Reading before he signs)* What is this? What is this?

JUDGE:

> This is the sale contract.

UNKNOWN MAN:

> Yes, I can sign that. *(He signs it.)*

JUDGE:

> And here too. *(Gives him the other document.)*

UNKNOWN MAN:

> Here? What is this?

JUDGE:

> This is the document freeing the Sultan.

UNKNOWN MAN:

> *(Withdraws one step.)* I am sorry!

JUDGE:

> *(Taken aback)* What did you say?

UNKNOWN MAN:

> I cannot sign this document.

JUDGE:

> How? What is this you are saying?

UNKNOWN MAN:

> I say it is not in my hands.

JUDGE:

> What is not in your hands?

UNKNOWN MAN:

> To sign the emancipation document.

JUDGE:

> *(Stunned)* Not in your hands to sign?

Neither in my hands nor in my authority.

JUDGE:

What is the meaning of this? What do you mean. You are crazy, no doubt about it. It is a specifically defined obligation to sign the emancipation document. This is the condition, the basic condition for this whole procedure.

UNKNOWN MAN:

I regret very much to say that I cannot do this; it is beyond my capacity.

VIZIER:

What is this man saying?

JUDGE:

I don't understand.

VIZIER:

Why do you refuse to sign the emancipation document?

UNKNOWN:

Because I was not authorized to do so.

VIZIER:

Not authorized?

UNKNOWN MAN:

(Nodding in confirmation of what he says) Not authorized. I was authorized only to bid and buy, beyond this I was not authorized.

JUDGE:

Authorized? Authorized by whom?

UNKNOWN MAN:

By the person whom I represent.

JUDGE:

You represent another person?

UNKNOWN MAN:

Yes, your Honor.

JUDGE:

Who is this person?

UNKNOWN MAN:

I can't answer.

JUDGE:

But you must answer.

UNKNOWN MAN:

No, I can't.

VIZIER:

    You are obliged to tell us the name of the person who authorized you to sign the purchase contract.

UNKNOWN MAN:

    I cannot disclose the name.

VIZIER:

    Why?

UNKNOWN MAN:

    Because I swore to keep the name a secret.

VIZIER:

    Why is the person you represent anxious to keep his name a secret?

UNKNOWN MAN:

    I don't know.

VIZIER:

    He has a lot of money, of course, since he can afford to spend this huge sum in cash.

UNKNOWN MAN:

    These thirty thousand dinars are all he saved in his entire life.

VIZIER:

    And he authorized you to spend it all in this auction?

UNKNOWN MAN:

    Yes.

VIZIER:

    This is very generous and very noble. But why does he keep his name a secret? Is it modesty? Is it the desire to keep this charitable work concealed?

UNKNOWN MAN:

    Maybe.

JUDGE:

    In this case he should have authorized his agent to sign the emancipation contract also.

UNKNOWN MAN:

    No, he authorized me to sign the purchase contract only.

JUDGE:

    This proves that he has an evil purpose.

VIZIER:

    Really!

SULTAN:

    (In a sarcastic tone) It seems the problem is

getting complicated!

JUDGE:

A little, my Lord.

VIZIER:

This man must speak, or else I will force him.

JUDGE:

Wait a little, Vizier...He will speak of his own
accord, and will gently answer my questions.
Listen, good man, this person you represent, what
does he do?

UNKNOWN MAN:

He does nothing.

JUDGE:

Doesn't he have a profession?

UNKNOWN MAN:

They claim he does.

JUDGE:

They claim he has a profession, yet he does nothing?

UNKNOWN MAN:

Right!

JUDGE:

He is an official, then?

UNKNOWN MAN:

No.

JUDGE:

He is rich?

UNKNOWN MAN:

Somewhat.

JUDGE:

And you are taking care of his affairs?

UNKNOWN MAN:

Almost!

JUDGE:

Is he one of the notables?

UNKNOWN MAN:

Better than that.

JUDGE:

How so?

UNKNOWN MAN:

The notables visit him, but he doesn't care to
visit them.

JUDGE:

    Is he a Vizier?

UNKNOWN MAN:

    No.

JUDGE:

    Does he have influence?

UNKNOWN MAN:

    Yes, on his acquaintances.

JUDGE:

    Does he have a lot of acquaintances?

UNKNOWN MAN:

    Yes, a lot!

JUDGE:

    (Thinking silently while combing his beard with his hand) Yes...yes.

SULTAN:

    And now, Judge, have you found a solution to these puzzles? Or are we going to spend all our time trying to solve them?

VIZIER:

    (Impatiently) We have to resort to violence, my Lord! We have nothing else. This mysterious person, who conceals his name and forces his way into the auction in this manner, must be planning something suspicious and dangerous. By your leave, my Lord, I'll handle this. *(Ordering the guards)* Take this man to the torture chambers, until he discloses the name of the person he represents and who is behind this action of his.

UNKNOWN MAN:

    (Loudly) No! No! No! Don't send me to the torture chambers. For the sake of God, no torture, I beg you...

VIZIER:

    Speak then!

UNKNOWN MAN:

    I swore...

VIZIER:

    (To the Guards) Take him!

    (The Guards surround him.)

UNKNOWN MAN:

    (Shouting in panic) No! No! No!

(The door of the Belle's house opens and she advances towards the platform, followed by her servants, and slaves carrying sacks.)

BELLE:

Leave him! Leave him! I am the person he represents, and here are the sacks of gold. Thirty thousand dinars in full.

(The people become noisy.)

SLAVE-MERCHANT:

(Shouting) Silence! Silence!

VIZIER:

Who is this woman?

SEVERAL VOICES:

(Shouting) The whore living over there.

VIZIER:

Whore?

SEVERAL VOICES:

Yes, a notorious whore living in this neighborhood!

SULTAN:

Well, well! A fine end!

VIZIER:

You, Woman! Are you the one?

BELLE:

Yes, it is I who authorized this man to bid on my behalf. *(Turning to the Unknown Man)* Isn't that so?

UNKNOWN MAN:

It is the truth, my Lady.

VIZIER:

You dare buy our Lord?

BELLE:

Why not? Am I not a citizen, and don't I have the money? Why shouldn't I have the same right as the others?

JUDGE:

Yes, you have this right. The law applies to everybody. Yet you also have to be aware of the conditions attached to this purchase.

BELLE:

That is natural. I know it is a sale...

JUDGE:
Of a special nature.

BELLE:
A public auction.

JUDGE:
Yes, but...

VIZIER:
Before everything, it is a national act, and you
are a citizen, so you must care for the good of
the nation, I believe...

BELLE:
Undoubtedly!

VIZIER:
Then sign this document!

BELLE:
What's in this document?

VIZIER:
The emancipation.

BELLE:
What does that mean?

VIZIER:
Don't you know what emancipation means?

BELLE:
Does it mean that I give up what I have?

VIZIER:
Yes.

BELLE:
Give up the goods I bought at the auction?

VIZIER:
Exactly.

BELLE:
No, I don't want to give it up.

SULTAN:
Beautiful!

VIZIER:
You will, Woman!

BELLE:
No.

VIZIER:
Don't make me use force. You know I could force
you.

BELLE:
How?

VIZIER:
(Pointing to his sword) With this!
SULTAN:
You resort to the sword now? It is too late.
VIZIER:
She must give in!
BELLE:
I will give in, Vizier, I will give in to the law.
Isn't it according to the law that I signed a pur-
chase contract with the state? Is this law re-
spected or not?
SULTAN:
Answer, Chief Judge!
JUDGE:
Indeed, Woman, you have signed a purchase con-
tract, but it is a conditional contract.
BELLE:
Which means?
JUDGE:
Which means that the purchase depends on a condi-
tion.
BELLE:
What condition?
JUDGE:
The emancipation, or else the sale itself becomes
null and void.
BELLE:
You mean, Judge, that for the sale to be valid,
I have to sign the emancipation?
JUDGE:
Yes.
BELLE:
You also mean that I have to sign the emancipation
document so that the purchase becomes valid?
JUDGE:
Exactly.
BELLE:
But your honor, what is a purchase? Is it not
taking possession of something in return for a
certain price?
JUDGE:
That's it.

BELLE:

>And what is an emancipation? Isn't it the opposite of possession? Giving up the possession?

JUDGE:

>Yes.

BELLE:

>Then, your Honor, you are making the emancipation a condition of possession, which means that for the possession of the purchased item to be valid, the purchaser has to give up that thing.

JUDGE:

>What? What?

BELLE:

>In other words, in order to have something you must give it away.

JUDGE:

>How do you say that to have is to give away?

BELLE:

>Or, if you will, to have you must have not.

JUDGE:

>What is she talking about?

BELLE:

>This is your condition: to buy I must emancipate, to have I must have not. Do you find this reasonable?

SULTAN:

>She is right. This is acceptable neither to reason nor to logic.

JUDGE:

>Who taught you this, Woman! No doubt a jurist, a devil of an expert in the law prompted her to say what she is saying.

SULTAN:

>What does it matter? This will change nothing. This is your law, Judge. Do you see? In the law there is always a counter-argument to an argument and both very logical.

JUDGE:

>But this is all play on words. It is sophistry. What this woman says is nothing but sophistry!

SULTAN:

>It is your condition that is sophistry. A sale

is a sale. This is self-evident. As for the rest,
it binds nobody!

JUDGE:

Yes, my Lord, but this woman came to the auction
with full knowledge of its nature and all the
implications involved and its whole purpose. Her
subsequent behavior, therefore, is nothing but
cheating and deception.

SULTAN:

If you want to give her a lesson in morality, that
is up to you. But as far as the law is concerned,
this is irrelevant, and you have to stop speaking on behalf of the law in this instance.

JUDGE:

On the contrary, my duty is to protect the law
from those creatures that abuse and ridicule it.

BELLE:

Please, your Honor, don't insult me.

JUDGE:

And you, Woman, are you not ashamed of yourself
and of what you are doing?

BELLE:

Ashamed of myself? Why? Is it because I bought
something sold by the state? Because I refused
to let that which I bought at a very high price
be stolen from me? Here is the gold. Count it
and take it.

JUDGE:

I reject your money, hence I rule this contract
null and void.

BELLE:

Why do you do that?

JUDGE:

Because you are a woman with a bad reputation,
and this money might have been sinfully gotten.
How can we accept it for the public treasury?

BELLE:

My money has already been accepted in taxes and
customs. Do taxes and customs go to the public
treasury and the state? If this is your judgement,
I will not pay one tax to the state ever.

SULTAN:

Accept her money, Judge. This is simpler and
safer.

JUDGE:

Then you insist on your stand, Woman?

BELLE:

Undoubtedly! I am not joking with these sacks of
gold. I pay to purchase and I purchase to pos-
sess and the law gives me this right. A sale is
a sale, and possession is possession. Take your
due and give me mine.

VIZIER:

How do you expect us to give you the Sultan of
this land, Woman?

BELLE:

Why then did you offer the Sultan of this land for
sale?

SULTAN:

She speaks very logically, this woman!

BELLE:

I'll answer, because the answer is simple. You
offered him for sale so that someone might buy
him. And here I have bought him in the public
auction before everybody, and here is the sum
agreed upon. All you have to do is give me the
goods.

SULTAN:

Goods?

BELLE:

Yes, and I want it delivered at home.

SULTAN:

Which home?

BELLE:

Mine, of course. That one. (Pointing) The one
right there.

SULTAN:

(To the Judge) You hear?

JUDGE:

There is no use having any discussion with such
a woman, my Lord; I wash my hands of this.

SULTAN:

A very good solution, Chief Judge. You get me
stuck in this quagmire and then you wash your

hands of it!

JUDGE:

I admit my failure. I didn't know I'd face this
type of person.

SULTAN:

And so?

JUDGE:

Punish me, my Lord. I deserve the most terrible
punishment for my short-sightedness and my mis-
guided advice. Order them to cut off my head!

SULTAN:

What use is cutting off your head? Your head has
placed us in this dilemma while on your shoulders.
Do you think that cutting it off will get us out
of this?

VIZIER:

Leave it to my, my Lord! I now see clearly what
I should do! *(He draws his sword.)*

SULTAN:

No!

VIZIER:

But, my Lord...

SULTAN:

I said, no! Put your sword away.

VIZIER:

Listen to me a little, my Lord...

SULTAN:

Put back your sword! We have accepted this situation. Let's continue.

VIZIER:

My Lord, since the Judge has failed and declared
his incompetancy, let's go back to our own de-
vices.

SULTAN:

No, I am not going back.

VIZIER:

With the sword everything could easily be over in
a second!

SULTAN:

No, I have chosen the law, and I will go through
whatever quagmire I have to go through.

VIZIER:

>The law?

SULTAN:

>Yes, and you yourself said it a short while ago
>in beautiful words: the Sultan has chosen to be
>subject to the law, as the weakest subject would
>be. These splendid words deserve every effort to
>realize them.

VIZIER:

>Do you think, my Lord, that your weakest subject
>would agree to stand where you are? Here are the
>poeple in front of us. If you permit me, I'll
>ask them and have them judge. Will you permit
>me?

SULTAN:

>Do, and show me.

VIZIER:

>(Addressing the crowd) Our people, you see how
>this insolent woman treats your glorious Sultan.
>Do you approve of what she does?

PEOPLE:

>(Shouting) No!

VIZIER:

>Are you satisfied with her humiliating behavior
>toward our august ruler?

PEOPLE:

>No!

VIZIER:

>Do you deem that she deserves punishment?

PEOPLE:

>(Shouting) Yes!

VIZIER:

>What punishment is right for her?

PEOPLE:

>(Shouting) Death!

VIZIER:

>(Looking towards the Sultan) Do you see, my Lord?
>The people have uttered the sentence!

BELLE:

>(Addressing the people) Death for me? Why should
>you people sentence me to death? What crime have
>I committed? Is purchasing an insult and a crime?
>Did I steal the money? It is all my savings! Did

I steal that which was offered for sale? I
bought it with my own money in a public acution
in front of everybody. What is my crime then?
Speak! On what charge do you ask for the blood of
a weak woman who bought something at an auction?

VOICES:

(Here and there among the people) Death to the
whore!

OTHER VOICES:

(Again, here and there) No! Don't kill her!

SULTAN:

(To the Vizier) Do you see?

VIZIER:

(To the people) You people! Do you think we
should carry out the sentence?

VOICES:

(Shouting) Yes!

OTHER VOICES:

(Shouting) No!

SULTAN:

The opinion is divided, Vizier.

VIZIER:

But the majority, my Lord, are on the side of
death!

SULTAN:

That is no justification to kill this woman. You
want to resort to a pseudolegal justification to
use the sword.

VIZIER:

The death of this woman is necessary to get us
out of this predicament.

SULTAN:

Now we need a corpse to save us?

VISIER:

Yes, my Lord.

SULTAN:

Between quagmire and bloodshed, I must choose
once again?

VIZIER:

There remains nothing but the sword to carve a
way out.

SULTAN:

> He who goes forward in a straight line will always find a way out.

VIZIER:

> You mean, my Lord...?

SULTAN:

> I mean there is no going back and no retreat, understand?

VIZIER:

> I understand, my Lord. You would like to go on following the law.

SULTAN:

> That is correct. I will not deviate from what I have chosen or go back on what I have decided.

VIZIER:

> But how do we proceed according to the law when the Judge himself declares his failure and incompetancy?

SULTAN:

> He is free to declare his incompetancy. As for me, I will not retreat. Let's pursue this to the end.

VIZIER:

> How about this woman who is blocking our way?

SULTAN:

> Leave her to me. *(Looking at the woman)* Come here, Woman, closer. Another step. Here before me. I would like to ask you some questions. Will you allow me?

BELLE:

> I obey, my Lord.

SULTAN:

> First of all, who am I?

BELLE:

> Who are you?

SULTAN:

> Yes, who am I?

BELLE:

> You are the Sultan!

SULTAN:

> You recognize me as the Sultan?

BELLE:

> Of course!

SULTAN:

Good, now what does a sultan do?

BELLE:

What does he do? He rules.

SULTAN:

Then you agree that he rules?

BELLE:

Without question.

SULTAN:

Very good. Now since you agree to all this, how then can you ask that the Sultan be delivered to you?

BELLE:

Because he has become my property.

SULTAN:

I am not contesting your right to your property. I am just wondering how it is possible to realize the possession. Since I am a ruling sultan, how can I assume the responsibilities of my office if I am delivered to you at home?

BELLE:

Nothing is simpler or easier. You are a sultan by day. I'll lend you to the state all day long; in the evening, you come back to my house.

SULTAN:

Unfortunately, you have an imperfect understanding of my job. The Sultan is not a keeper of a shop that he can open by day and close by night. He is at the disposal of the state every moment. And there are some urgent, grave matters that force him many times to meet with his statesmen at midnight.

BELLE:

That's very easy too. In my house there is a quiet, isolated room where you can work with your statesmen.

SULTAN:

Do you find such a situation acceptable?

BELLE:

More than acceptable. I think it is wonderful!

SULTAN:

It is wonderful, indeed! A sultan ruling his

state from the house of a woman who is said to be,
pardon me, a...pardon me!

BELLE:

Say it! Say it! The word no longer hurts me. I
have been stabbed so often that the new blades
break on the old ones. Yet I assure you, Sultan,
that you will find more joy at my place than
what you have at yours!

SULTAN:

Maybe, except that a ruler cannot do a good job
from other people's houses.

BELLE:

That is, if the ruler is free.

SULTAN:

You are right, I am not free. *(He lowers his
head. Pause.)*

BELLE:

What I like about you, Sultan, is your quiet,
collected attitude in this catastrophe!

SULTAN:

(Looking up at her) Do you admit that it is a
catastrophe?

BELLE:

Obviously! Such a great sultan as you being mal-
treated in this way!

SULTAN:

Is anybody else besides you maltreating me?

BELLE:

No, not really. And what pride and pleasure it
gives me to hear it from a great sultan. It's an
honor worth all the gold in the world! Nobody
in the whole city will ever dare despise me. I
maltreat sultans!

VISIER:

(Furious) Stop it, Woman, stop! This is beyond
all endurance! She has gone beyond all limits.
This insolent, impudent wretch must be executed!

SULTAN:

Calm yourself!

BELLE:

Yes, calm yourself, Vizier, and don't stick your
nose in other people's affairs.

VIZIER:

Can anyone bear all this? Patience! My God, give
me patience!

BELLE:

Yes, be patient, Vizier, and.let us talk it over,
the Sultan and I. This is our business alone.

SULTAN:

Right!

BELLE:

Where were we, your Majesty?

SULTAN:

I no longer know. You were talking.

BELLE:

Yes, I remember. We stopped when I said "It is a
great honor."

SULTAN:

To maltreat me.

BELLE:

No, but to have the privilege and the joy of
speaking with you. Really, my Lord, this is the
first time I ever saw you so closely. They have
often talked to me about you, but I didn't know
you were so nice.

SULTAN:

Thank you.

BELLE:

Really, it seems we are very old friends!

SULTAN:

Do you usually expose your friends to this
humiliation and ridicule?

BELLE:

No, never! On the contrary...

SULTAN:

Then, why did you make me an exception?

BELLE:

This indeed is what is beginning to cause me
pain. How I wish to cheer your heart and offer you
my respect! But how? How can I do it? What is the
way?

SULTAN:

There's a very simple way.

BELLE:

Sign the emancipation document?

SULTAN:

I think so!

BELLE:

No, I don't want to give you up or leave you.
You are mine, mine, mine!

SULTAN:

Yours and all other people's!

BELLE:

I want you to be mine alone.

SULTAN:

And my people?

BELLE:

Your people have not paid gold to get you.

SULTAN:

That is true, but you must know that it is impossible to be yours alone and remain a sultan.
There is only one formula by which I could be
yours alone.

BELLE:

What is that?

SULTAN:

Not to be a sultan, to abdicate the throne.

BELLE:

No, I don't want you to do that, I want you to
remain a sultan!

SULTAN:

In that case there must be a sacrifice.

BELLE:

On my part?

SULTAN:

Or on my part.

BELLE:

I should give you up?

SULTAN:

Or I should give up the throne.

BELLE:

And I must choose?

SULTAN:

Of course you must choose, because the whole
thing is in your hands!

BELLE:
Do I have all that importance and power?
SULTAN:
At this moment, yes.
BELLE:
This is wonderful!
SULTAN:
True!
BELLE:
This means that I have the last word now?
SULTAN:
Yes!
BELLE:
If I will it, the Sultan remains!
SULTAN:
Yes!
BELLE:
And one word from me and the Sultan is no longer a sultan?
SULTAN:
Yes.
BELLE:
This is really wonderful!
SULTAN:
No doubt.
BELLE:
What gives me all this authority? Money?
SULTAN:
The law.
BELLE:
One word can change your destiny, either to slavery or to liberty and sovereignty.
SULTAN:
And you are the one to choose.
BELLE:
(Thinking it over) Between the slavery that gives you to me and the freedom which keeps you for your throne and people!
SULTAN:
And you are the one to make the choice.
BELLE:
It's a difficult choice.

SULTAN:

> I know.

BELLE:

> It is painful to let you go, to leave you forever, yet it is equally painful to see you lose your throne, because our country will never have a sultan as just or brave as you are. No, don't abdicate. I want you to stay a sultan.

SULTAN:

> So...?

BELLE:

> I will sign!

SULTAN:

> The emancipation?

BELLE:

> Yes!

JUDGE:

> *(Hastens to proffer the document.)* Here's the document.

BELLE:

> I have one last wish.

SULTAN:

> What is it?

BELLE:

> To give me, my Lord, one night. Honor me by accepting my invitation and be my guest until dawn. The moment the Muezzin calls for the dawn prayer from this minaret, I will sign the document, and my Lord the Sultan will be free.

JUDGE:

> If the Muezzin calls for the dawn prayer!

BELLE:

> Yes, is that too much? To purchase with all this gold, not the Sultan himself, but one night as my guest?

SULTAN:

> I accept!

VIZIER:

> But, my Lord, who will guarantee for us a promise from such a woman?

SULTAN:

> I guarantee. I trust her.

JUDGE:
　　Do you swear to keep your promise, woman?
BELLE:
　　Yes, I swear by God to sign the emancipation docu-
　　ment at the call for the dawn prayer from this
　　minaret.
JUDGE:
　　May God be our witness, and we here, all of us,
　　are witnesses.
SULTAN:
　　As for me, I believe her without an oath.
BELLE:
　　And now my Lord, noble Sultan, will you conde-
　　scend and honor my humble house by your gracious
　　visit?
SULTAN:
　　With great pleasure.
　　*(The Sultan rises and follows the Belle to her
　　home. Music)*

Curtain

Act III

(The same square, in which part of the mosque with its minaret appears. Also seen is a part of the Belle's house, revealing the room with a window overlooking the square. Time: night.)

VIZIER:
> *(In the square, addressing the Guards loudly)*
> What are all these people doing here at midnight?
> Turn everybody away! Let them go home to bed.

GUARDS:
> *(Turning the people away)* Go home, go to your houses!

PEOPLE:
> *(Fiercely)* No! No!

SHOEMAKER:
> *(Shouting)* I want to stay here!

TAVERN KEEPER:
> I will not budge from here either!

VIZIER:
> *(To the Guards)* What do they say?

GUARDS:
> They refuse.

VIZIER:
> *(Shouting)* What? Refuse! What nonsense! Force them!

SHOEMAKER:
> I am at home here and this is my shop!

TAVERN KEEPER:

    My tavern also is right here in front of you!

GUARDS:

    So you don't obey orders? Well then! Well then!

    (Guards push them.)

SHOEMAKER:

    Please, no violence.

TAVERN KEEPER:

    Don't push me so hard!

VIZIER:

    (To the Guards) Get these two rioters!

    (The Guards arrest the Shoemaker and the Tavern
    Keeper and bring them to the Vizier.)

SHOEMAKER:

    I swear by God I've done nothing, your Highness.

VIZIER:

    Why do you refuse to go home?

SHOEMAKER:

    I don't want to go to bed! I have a very strong
    desire to stay here, my Lord, to watch.

VIZIER:

    Watch what?

SHOEMAKER:

    Watch our Lord the Sultan coming out of that
    house!

TAVERN KEEPER:

    Me too, my Lord, let me watch that.

VIZIER:

    This is really too much! Everybody is impudently
    daring today. Even you and your friend. How dare
    you use this language?

TAVERN KEEPER:

    It is not daring, my Lord Vizier, it's a...a
    petition.

VIZIER:

    Petition?

SHOEMAKER:

    Yes, my Lord, we petition you to allow us to
    watch.

VIZIER:

    What impudence! What have you to do with this?

SHOEMAKER:

Aren't we good citizens? The destiny of our
Sultan interests us, no doubt!

VIZIER:

That is no reason for disobedience!

SHOEMAKER:

We are not being disobedient. We are begging. How
can we sleep tonight when the destiny of our Lord
the Sultan is being decided?

VIZIER:

Decided?

SHOEMAKER:

Yes, my Lord, decided by whim!

VIZIER:

What do you mean?

SHOEMAKER:

I mean the prospects don't look very reassuring.

VIZIER:

How do you know?

SHOEMAKER:

With a woman like that, who can be sure of anything?

TAVERN KEEPER:

We have a bet going between us. He says this
woman is going to break her promise, and I say
she'll keep it!

VIZIER:

Very nice! Such a grave event as this is becoming
the object of a bet!

TAVERN KEEPER:

We are not alone, my Lord. Everybody is betting
tonight, even the Muezzin and the Executioner
have a bet going!

VIZIER:

The Executioner? Where is the Executioner?

TAVERN KEEPER:

(Pointing) There, my Lord. He is trying to hide
among the people!

VIZIER:

(To the guards) Bring him here!
(The guards bring the Executioner to the Vizier.)

EXECUTIONER:

(Afraid) It is not my fault, my Lord. It is the

Muezzin's fault. He is the one to blame. He did
not call for the dawn prayer!

VIZIER:

Dawn? What dawn? The dawn is still far off, you
fool. *(The Tavern Keeper and the Shoemaker laugh.)*
You dare to laugh in my presence? Go away immediately! Go away! *(The Tavern Keeper and the Shoemaker run away.)* And now you, Executioner, are you
busy betting?

EXECUTIONER:

Betting? Who said that, my Lord?

VIZIER:

I want a frank answer to my question.

EXECUTIONER:

But my Lord...

VIZIER:

Don't be scared; tell me.

EXECUTIONER:

But this bet, my Lord...

VIZIER:

I know, I know, and I am not going to punish you.
Answer this question frankly. Will this woman
break her promise or will she keep it?

EXECUTIONER:

But, my Lord...

VIZIER:

I told you not to be afraid. Say what you want.
Don't be embarassed. This is an order and you
have to obey!

EXECUTIONER:

Your orders are obeyed, my Lord. Actually, I don't
trust this woman.

VIZIER:

Why?

EXECUTIONER:

Because she is a liar, a trickster.

VIZIER:

Do you know her?

EXECUTIONER:

I came to know some of her tricks when I was here
last night, waiting until the dawn to execute the
Slave-Merchant.

VIZIER:

A liar and a trickster?

EXECUTIONER:

Yes!

VIZIER:

And what does a woman like this deserve?

EXECUTIONER:

Punishment, of course!

VIZIER:

And what punishment do you think is fitting if
she lied and deceived our glorious Sultan?

EXECUTIONER:

To be executed, no doubt.

VIZIER:

Well then, be ready to execute this sentence at
dawn!

EXECUTIONER:

(As if talking to himself) At dawn? Again?

VIZIER:

What did you say?

EXECUTIONER:

I was saying that at dawn I will be ready to carry
out the orders of my Lord, the Vizier.

VIZIER:

Yes...If the Muezzin calls for the dawn prayer and
our Sultan does not come out of this house a free
man...

EXECUTIONER:

I will cut off this woman's head!

VIZIER:

Yes, in punishment for...

EXECUTIONER:

Lying and deception?

VIZIER:

No.

EXECUTIONER:

(Not understanding) No?

VIZIER:

(As if talking to himself) No, that is not enough.
This is a crime that might not deserve death. And
this woman is sure to find in the law and logic
big words and statements that might justify her

deeds. No, there must be a terrible crime that cannot be justified or defended; a crime that can arouse the general indignation of the whole people. We can, for instance, say that she is a spy!

EXECUTIONER:

A spy?

VIZIER:

Yes, working for the Mongols. Then the whole people will rise up and ask for her head!

EXECUTIONER:

Yes, a just punishment!

VIZIER:

Don't you think?

EXECUTIONER:

And I will shout, "death to the traitress."

VIZIER:

Your voice alone will not be enough. There must be other voices besides yours shouting these words.

EXECUTIONER:

There will be other voices.

VIZIER:

Do you know them?

EXECUTIONER:

They are not difficult to produce.

VIZIER:

Yes, we must prepare the witnesses.

EXECUTIONER:

All this is easy, my Lord.

VIZIER:

I think this arrangement has every chance of success. I'll depend on you if matters go wrong.

EXECUTIONER:

I am your faithful servant, my Lord!

(Part of the room in the Belle's house is lighted.)

VIZIER:

Sh! The light in the window. Let's go a little nearer. *(The square darkens as the room now becomes fully lighted. The Sultan and the Belle appear, moving towards a comfortable chair.)*

SULTAN:

(As he sits down) Your house is very elegant, and

the furniture is luxurious!

BELLE:

> *(Sitting at his feet)* Yes, as I told you my Lord,
> my husband was a wealthy merchant with fine taste.
> He was fond of poetry and singing.

SULTAN:

> You were one of his slaves?

BELLE:

> Yes. He bought me when I was sixteen, then freed
> me and married me several years before his death.

SULTAN:

> You had better luck than me. At least nobody for-
> got to free you at the right time.

BELLE:

> My good luck really is your honoring my house to-
> night.

SULTAN:

> Here I am, in your house. What do you intend to
> do with me tonight?

BELLE:

> Nothing, just entertain you a little.

SULTAN:

> Is that all?

BELLE:

> Nothing more. I have told you already that the
> entertainment you will find here is something
> even you don't have. I have pretty slave girls
> that have mastered the arts of dancing, singing
> and playing all musical instruments. Rest assured
> that you will not be bored here tonight.

SULTAN:

> Until the break of dawn?

BELLE:

> Don't think of the dawn now. The dawn is still
> far off!

SULTAN:

> I'll do all you ask me to do until the break of
> dawn.

BELLE:

> I will ask nothing more of you than to talk, eat,
> and listen to song.

SULTAN:

Nothing but that?

BELLE:

What more do you want me to ask of you?

SULTAN:

I don't know. You know better.

BELLE:

Let's begin by talking. Talk to me.

SULTAN:

About myself?

BELLE:

Yes, about your life. Tell me your story.

SULTAN:

So you want me to tell you stories?

BELLE:

Yes, you really must have quite a few terribly interesting stories.

SULTAN:

So it is my turn to tell stories now?

BELLE:

Why not?

SULTAN:

That's how it should be, really! Since I am in Scheherazade's place. She also had to tell stories all night long, waiting for the dawn which would decide her fate.

BELLE:

(Laughing) And I the awsome, terrible Schahriar.

SULTAN:

Yes, isn't that strange? Everything is the other way around today!

BELLE:

No, you are always the Sultan. As for me, I am like Scheherazade, sitting forever at your feet.

SULTAN:

Scheherazade holding anxious Schahriar's throat until the morning overcomes him!

BELLE:

No, a Scheherazade who will cheer the heart of her Sultan, and give him joy and pleasure. You will see how I dispel your anxiety and doubt. (She claps. Soft music is heard from behind the curtains.)

SULTAN:

(After he listens) Beautiful music!

BELLE:

And I myself will dance for you! *(She gets up and dances.)*

SULTAN:

(After her dance is over) Beautiful! Everything is beautiful! Do you do this every night?

BELLE:

No, my Lord. This is an exception...for you. I haven't danced myself since my emancipation and marriage. The other nights the slave girls dance and sing.

SULTAN:

For your customers?

BELLE:

No, for my guests.

SULTAN:

As you will, your guests. These guests of yours must pay you very handsomely. I now realize why you are so rich.

BELLE:

I inherited my wealth from my husband. I sometimes spend more on these nights than I receive.

SULTAN:

Why, for the love of God?

BELLE:

For the love of art. I love art!

SULTAN:

(Sarcastically) High art, of course?

BELLE:

You don't believe, and you don't take what I say seriously! Well, let it be. Think ill of me as much as you like. It is not my habit to defend myself against the wrong ideas of others. In the eyes of the world, I am a woman with a bad reputation. I have come to accept this verdict. I find that quite a comfort, and am no longer interested in correcting people's opinion. When a human being goes beyond all the bounds of the bad, he becomes free...and I need my freedom.

SULTAN:
>You too?

BELLE:
>Yes, to do what I like.

SULTAN:
>What do you like?

BELLE:
>The company of men!

SULTAN:
>Obviously!

BELLE:
>No, you've misunderstood. It's not as you think.

SULTAN:
>How is it then?

BELLE:
>Do you want a lie or the truth?

SULTAN:
>The truth, of course.

BELLE:
>You will not believe the truth. What is the use
>of telling it then? A truth that nobody will be-
>lieve is a useless truth.

SULTAN:
>Tell it anyway.

BELLE:
>I'll tell it just to entertain you. I like the
>company of men for their souls, not for their
>bodies. Do you understand?

SULTAN:
>No, I do not at all understand!

BELLE:
>I'll explain. When I was a little slave-girl, the
>same age as the girls I have now, my master
>brought me up on the love of poetry, singing and
>music. He always made me attend his feasts and
>talk to his guests, who were poets and singers,
>and men of intellect. We used to stay up whole
>nights reciting poetry, singing, talking or ex-
>changing witticisms and laughing from our hearts.
>Those were splendid nights and they were also
>innocent and pure nights, and I wish you to be-
>lieve that, for my master was a good man, and had
>no pleasure in life aside from these nights, plea-

sure without sin or depravity. That was how I
was brought up. When I became his wife, he didn't
want to deprive me of the fantastic pleasure
these nights gave me, so he allowed me to attend
them, but from behind silk curtains. This is the
whole story.

SULTAN:

And after his death?

BELLE:

After his death I couldn't give up the habit, so
I went on inviting the guests of my husband. At
the beginning I used to receive them concealed
behind silk curtains, but when the people in the
neighborhood began to talk and spread rumors
about me because they saw men coming every night
to the home of a woman that had no husband, I
found no sense in continuing to conceal myself
behind curtains. I said to myself, since the people have already passed their verdict and con-
demned me, let me be my own judge.

SULTAN:

It really is very strange that your appearance
should declare so emphatically that which is not
your reality. The facade of your shop advertises
goods that are not sold inside!

BELLE:

It is up to you to believe or disbelieve what I
have told you.

SULTAN:

I prefer to believe. It is more reassuring to do
so.

BELLE:

Whatever happens, I don't intend to change my life
or habits at all. If my path has become full of
mire, I will go on walking through it.

SULTAN:

Mire! It is everywhere, be sure of that!

BELLE:

You reminded me now of what I did with you in
front of the crowd.

SULTAN:

Indeed, you smeared me all over with it!

BELLE:

I was intentionally insolent with you and deliberately impolite. Do you know why? Because I had visualized you differently. The arrogant, haughty Sultan swelling with the pride of his might, like most sultans, maybe even more so because of your wars and exploits. People have always talked about this legendary sapphire adorning your turban, the unique sapphire which, it is said, was snatched by you from the head of the Mongol leader. Yes, your deeds are wonderful and great. That is why I thought of you as being arrogant, hard and cruel. But as soon as you talked to me so gently and modestly I was perplexed and stunned.

SULTAN:

Don't be deceived. I am not always that gentle or modest. There are moments when I become more cruel and brutal than the worst sultan.

BELLE:

I don't believe it.

SULTAN:

Because you are under the influence of the present circumstances.

BELLE:

You mean you are particularly nice with me? That flatters me exceedingly, my dear Lord. Yet wait, probably I misunderstood. What could make you that gentle with me? Is it me or the decision you expect from me at dawn?

SULTAN:

I am pretending to be gentle with you so that you may have pity on me. Is that not so?

BELLE:

And as soon as you get your freedom, your original character comes back to the surface, and you become the cruel Sultan who seeks revenge for the hours of his humiliation. And then my hour will have come!

SULTAN:

So it is wise and farsighted to hold me in your clutches!

BELLE:

Don't you think so?

SULTAN:

This is the only logical thing to do, so long as
you are starting to have some doubts.

BELLE:

Don't I have the right to some doubts?

SULTAN:

I wouldn't blame you if you did. For it was I who,
without suspecting it, simply sowed the seeds of
suspicion in you by saying what I did about myself.

BELLE:

(Scrutinizing him) No!

SULTAN:

No, what?

BELLE:

I prefer to depend on the woman's instinct in me.
It never deceives me.

SULTAN:

What does your woman's instinct tell you?

BELLE:

It tells me that you are not that type of man, that
you are different, and that I should have realized
it the moment I saw you decide against using the
sword.

SULTAN:

If you knew how much easier things would have been
if I had used my sword!

BELLE:

Do you regret that now?

SULTAN:

I am talking about easiness, but true victory is
using clever fingers for untying a knot.

BELLE:

And this is what you are doing now?

SULTAN:

Yes, but I am not sure about the result.

BELLE:

Suppose the result disappoints you, what are you
going to do?

SULTAN:

I have already told you.

BELLE:

Abdicate the throne?

SULTAN:

Yes.

BELLE:

No, I don't believe you are really going to do
that. I am not stupid enough or naive enought to
believe it, or even to take it seriously. Even if
you wanted to do it, no one in the country would
accept or let you do such a thing. You will be
forced to accept the easier solution, and will
go back to the simple method.

SULTAN:

I have never once taken a backward step, not even
on the battlefield. I admit that this is wrong
from the military point of view, because there
are cases when retreat is inevitable. But I never
did, perhaps because luck was on my side. Anyway,
I got used to this bad habit.

BELLE:

You are wonderful!

SULTAN:

Actually, I am a man without imagination.

BELLE:

You?

SULTAN:

Because if I had an imagination and had visualized
what was waiting for me at the end of such a path,
I would have been shocked!

BELLE:

Nothing shocks you. You have self-control and self-
confidence, and an ability to do what you want to
do precisely and firmly. You are far from being
weak or deceptive. You are frank, natural, courage-
ous, and you respect the rules of the game honestly and sincerely. That's all there is to it!

SULTAN:

Are you flattering me? Which of us should flatter
the other? Things are the other way around again!

BELLE:

Will you permit me, my dear Sultan?

SULTAN:

What?

BELLE:

A personal question that I would like to ask you.

SULTAN:

Personal? Wasn't all this personal?

BELLE:

I would like to ask you about the heart...about love.

SULTAN:

Love? What love?

BELLE:

Love...of a woman.

SULTAN:

Do you think I have time for such things?

BELLE:

Strange! Has your heart never beaten with love for a woman?

SULTAN:

And why have you opened your eyes so widely in surprise? Is it such a grave matter?

BELLE:

But you certainly have known many women.

SULTAN:

By necessity. This is the nature of military life. The commander of the army, as you know, has one of the captured women brought to him each night. Sometimes some of them are pretty. That's all.

BELLE:

And not one of them in particular succeeded in attracting your eyes?

SULTAN:

My eyes? You must know that at the end of the day I always go back to my tent with eyes filled with the dust of battle.

BELLE:

And on the next day? Don't you remember any of the pretty ones?

SULTAN:

On the next day I mount my horse again and think of something else.

BELLE:

But now...You are the Sultan and you have enough

leisure for love.

SULTAN:

Do you think so?

BELLE:

What prevents you?

SULTAN:

Problems of government. And this is one of them, which fell on me today unexpectedly, and placed me in this dilemma. Do you think with such a problem one could be in the right mood for love?

BELLE:

(Laughing) Really!

SULTAN:

You laugh?

BELLE:

One last question. Be sure of this! A very serious one this time, because it has to do with me.

SULTAN:

With you?

BELLE:

Yes. Let's suppose you are freed at dawn. You will go back to your palace, of course?

SULTAN:

Of course, there are things to be done awaiting me there.

BELLE:

And I?

SULTAN:

And you what?

BELLE:

Won't you think of me after this?

SULTAN:

I don't understand.

BELLE:

You really do not understand what I mean?

SULTAN:

You know that women's language is sometimes too subtle and vague for me.

BELLE:

You understand me quite well, because you are intelligent and wise, and also very tender, despite your appearance, or what you like to pretend. And yet I will explain my words to you. Here's what I want to know: Are you going to forget me completely and erase me from your memory as soon as you leave here?

SULTAN:

I don't think it will be possible to erase you completely from my memory.

BELLE:

Are you going to retain a fond memory of me?

SULTAN:

Undoubtedly!

BELLE:

That's all? That is how everything ends, as far as I am concerned?

SULTAN:

Are we going back to what we previously...?

BELLE:

No, I just want to ask you, is this our last night together?

SULTAN:

This is a difficult question to answer.

BELLE:

Don't answer it now then.
(The Servant appears.)

SERVANT:

Supper is ready, my Lady.

BELLE:

(Rising) Please, my Lord.

SULTAN:

(Rising) You are very generous and hospitable.

BELLE:

It is you who are generous to me. *(She leads him inside the house, to the accompaniment of music. The lights in the room go out. The square is lighted slightly.)*

SHOEMAKER:

(With the Tavern Keeper in a corner of the square) Look! They put out the light.

TAVERN KEEPER:

(Looking at the window) That's a good sign!

SHOEMAKER:

How?

TAVERN KEEPER:

Putting out the light means going to bed!

SHOEMAKER:

Then?

TAVERN KEEPER:

Then agreement is complete!

SHOEMAKER:

On what?

TAVERN KEEPER:

On everything!

SHOEMAKER:

You mean she'll accept giving him up at dawn?

TAVERN KEEPER:

Yes!

SHOEMAKER:

And thus you win?

TAVERN KEEPER:

Without the least doubt!

SHOEMAKER:

You are too optimistic, my friend. Does a woman like this accept throwing her money into the sea that easily?

TAVERN KEEPER:

Who knows? I say yes.

SHOEMAKER:

And I say no!

TAVERN KEEPER:

Well, we'll wait until dawn.

SHOEMAKER:

What time is it?

TAVERN KEEPER:

(Looking at the sky) According to the stars, it is almost midnight.

SHOEMAKER:

The dawn is still far off, and I am beginning to be sleepy.

TAVERN KEEPER:

Go to bed!

SHOEMAKER:

Me? Impossible! Everybody is staying up tonight, and you want me to sleep? If anybody should stay up until dawn it should be me, so I can watch your defeat.

TAVERN KEEPER:

My defeat?

SHOEMAKER:

Without the slightest doubt.

TAVERN KEEPER:

We will see whose defeat...

SHOEMAKER:

(Looking to one side of the square) Look! There!

TAVERN KEEPER:

What?

SHOEMAKER:

(Whispering) The Vizier and the Executioner...
They look like they are conspiring.

TAVERN KEEPER:

Sh!
(Vizier goes to and fro, cross-examining the Executioner.)

VIZIER:

What exactly did you hear the Guards saying?

EXECUTIONER:

I heard them saying it is impossible to keep the people back or force them to sleep tonight. The crowds are still standing or sitting in the lanes and alleys, everybody whispering and buzzing.

VIZIER:

Buzzing?

EXECUTIONER:

Yes!

VIZIER:

And what are they whispering and buzzing about?

EXECUTIONER:

About the Sultan, of course, and...and what he is doing tonight at that house.

VIZIER:

And what is he, in your opinion, doing in that house?

EXECUTIONER:

Are you asking me, my Lord?

VIZIER:

Yes, I am asking you. Are you not one of the people, and your opinion part of public opinion?

Answer me! What do you imagine the Sultan is doing in that house?

EXECUTIONER:

Actually, he definitely is not praying there.

VIZIER:

Are you joking? Do you dare?

EXECUTIONER:

Pardon, my Lord. I just wanted to say that this
house is...is not a holy shrine.

VIZIER:

Then this is what the buzzing is about? That the
Sultan is spending the night in a house...

EXECUTIONER:

A whorehouse!

VIZIER:

What did you say?

EXECUTINER:

That's what they say, my Lord. I am just repeating what I heard.

VIZIER:

Is that all they remember about this grave business? They forget the noble purpose and the lofty
aim and the national significance. Even you, as
far as I can see, have forgotten all this.

EXECUTIONER:

No, my Lord, I have forgotten nothing.

VIZIER:

We will see! Tell me then, why did the Sultan
agree to enter this house?

EXECUTIONER:

To...to satisfy the whore!

VIZIER:

Is that all? What baseness!

EXECUTIONER:

My Lord, I was there and I saw and heard everything right from the beginning.

VIZIER:

And you understood nothing of the whole thing except this trivial, base aspect of the problem?
Are there many like you among the people?

EXECUTIONER:

Everybody was present like myself.

VIZIER:
> And they all understood what you understood, I believe. They are not talking about the profound reason and the lofty significance of all that happened. They talk about what you say: The Sultan is spending his night in a whorehouse! What a catastrophe! It's a real disaster!
> *(The Chief Judge appears.)*

JUDGE:
> I couldn't sleep at all.

VIZIER:
> You too?

JUDGE:
> What do you mean, me too?

VIZIER:
> The whole city hasn't slept tonight.

JUDGE:
> I know.

VIZIER:
> And everybody is whispering and buzzing.

JUDGE:
> I know that too.

VIZIER:
> And you know what they are saying?

JUDGE:
> The worse that could be said. The only interesting part for the people is the scandal aspect in the whole thing.

VIZIER:
> Unfortunately!

JUDGE:
> It's my fault!

VIZIER:
> And mine too. I should have been more firm in defending my opinion.

JUDGE:
> But, on the other hand, how could we have anticipated this interference on the part of the woman?

VIZIER:
> We should have anticpated everything.

JUDGE:
> Right!

VIZIER:
>   Now it is over and we can do nothing.

JUDGE:
>   But we can extricate him from this house.

VIZIER:
>   We have to wait until dawn.

JUDGE:
>   No, now, at once!

VIZIER:
>   But the dawn is still far off.

JUDGE:
>   It has to be brought now and at once!

VIZIER:
>   Who? What?

JUDGE:
>   Dawn.

VIZIER:
>   Pardon me, I don't understand!

JUDGE:
>   You will very shortly. Where is the Muezzin of
>   this mosque?

VIZIER:
>   *(Looking towards the Executioner)* This Executioner
>   must know.

EXECUTIONER:
>   He is there among the people.

JUDGE:
>   Go get him!
>   *(The Executioner hurries obediently.)*

VIZIER:
>   *(To the Judge)* It seems you have a plan!

JUDGE:
>   Yes!

VIZIER:
>   May I know what it is?

JUDGE:
>   Shortly!
>   *(The Muezzin appears, panting.)*

MUEZZIN:
>   Here I am, my Lord.

JUDGE:
>   Come closer. I would like to talk to you about dawn.

MUEZZIN:

> Dawn? I assure you my Lord that I haven't done
> anything wrong. This Executioner accuses me
> falsely that...

JUDGE:

> Listen to me carefully...

MUEZZIN:

> I swear to you, my Lord, that on that day...

JUDGE:

> Won't you stop this nonsense? I told you to listen
> to me carefully! I want you to do exactly as I
> tell you, understand?

MUEZZIN:

> Yes!

JUDGE:

> Go climb your minaret and call for the dawn pray-
> er.

MUEZZIN:

> When?

JUDGE:

> Now!

MUEZZIN:

> *(Surprised)* Now?

JUDGE:

> Yes, immediately.

MUEZZIN:

> Dawn?

JUDGE:

> Yes, dawn. Go and call for the dawn prayer! Is
> what I say clear or isn't it?

MUEZZIN:

> Clear, but it is almost midnight!

JUDGE:

> So what?

MUEZZIN:

> Dawn at midnight?

JUDGE:

> Yes, and be quick!

MUEZZIN:

> Is that not a little too early?

JUDGE:

>No!

MUEZZIN:

>*(Whispering to himself)* I am puzzled by this dawn. Once I am asked to postpone it and another time to bring it early!

JUDGE:

>What did you say?

MUEZZIN:

>Nothing, my Lord. I will go immediately to carry out your order!

JUDGE:

>Listen, don't ever tell anybody that it was the judge who gave you this order.

MUEZZIN:

>You mean, my Lord...?

JUDGE:

>Yes, you are doing this of your own accord.

MUEZZIN:

>Of my own accord? I go to the minaret and call for the dawn prayer at midnight of my own accord? A man who does such a thing must be a crazy idiot!

JUDGE:

>Leave it to me to explain your behavior at the right time.

MUEZZIN:

>But my Lord, by doing this I am exposing myself to the people's anger, and they will demand punishing me.

JUDGE:

>Before whom are you going to have your trial? Isn't it me, the Chief Judge?

MUEZZIN:

>What if you denied me and let me down?

JUDGE:

>Don't be afraid. This will never happen.

MUEZZIN:

>How can I be sure?

JUDGE:

>I promise you. Don't you trust my promise?

MUEZZIN:

>*(Whispering to himself)* Promises are many tonight, and nobody is sure of anything.

JUDGE:

What did you say?

MUEZZIN:

Nothing. I am just wondering why I should take all
this risk.

JUDGE:

It's a service you are rendering the state.

MUEZZIN:

(Surprised) The state?

JUDGE:

Yes. And I will explain the whole thing to you so
that you may be at rest. Listen, if you call for
the dawn prayer now, the Sultan will come out of
this house free, immediately. That's the whole
story, briefly. Do you understand now?

MUEZZIN:

This is a patriotic deed!

JUDGE:

Indeed it is. What do you say to it then?

MUEZZIN:

I will do it immediately! And I will be proud of
it all my life. Besides, by your leave, my Lord,
I will also disclose a little thing to you. But
keep it between us. I have already told a little
lie like this one to save a convict's life, so why
shouldn't I do it to save our beloved Sultan's freedom?

JUDGE:

Very good! But I warn you to keep it to yourself.
Don't start talking. Keep your pride to yourself,
because if you start to boast of it in our present circumstances, you'll spoil everything. Keep
your mouth shut completely if you want your work
to bear fruit and be appreciated.

MUEZZIN:

I will keep my mouth shut!

JUDGE:

Good. Now go and do it at once!

MUEZZIN:

In no time. (The Muezzin hurries away.)

JUDGE:

(To the Vizier) What do you think?

VIZIER:

Do you think such a trick can work?

JUDGE:
>Yes, and in the best possible way. I have been examining the issue very closely tonight. I no longer believe that I have failed. I, or actually the law, still has a lot of tricks.

VIZIER:
>Let's pray that one of your tricks works this time. Your dignity is at stake!

JUDGE:
>You will see.
>*(The Muezzin's voice is heard:*
>>*God is most great. God is most great.*
>>*Come to prayer. Come to prayer.*
>>*Come to security. Come to security.*
>*The crowds appear, infuriated, and noisily protest.)*

VOICES:
>*(Shouting)* Dawn now? In the middle of the night? It's midnight. He is crazy! Crazy! Arrest him! Bring him down! Get him! Bring him down from the minaret. Get him...

VIZIER:
>*(To the Judge)* The mob will tear this poor man to pieces!

JUDGE:
>Order your Guards to disperse them!

VIZIER:
>*(Shouting to the Guards)* Clear the square, clear everybody from the square.
>*(The Guards disperse the people and clear the square. The Muezzin continues to call for prayer. The light in the Belle's room is turned on and she appears in the window, followed by the Sultan.)*

BELLE:
>Is it really dawn?

JUDGE:
>It is the call for the dawn prayer! Come down here immediately!

BELLE:
>This is impossible! Look at the stars...

SULTAN:
>*(Looking up)* Indeed, it is rather strange.

JUDGE:

I told you to come down immediately, Woman!

SULTAN:

(To the Belle) Let's go down together to look into the matter.

BELLE:

Let's go, my Lord.
(They leave the room and put out the light, then appear coming out of the house.)

SULTAN:

(Looking at the sky) Dawn? At this hour?

VIZIER:

Yes, my Lord the Sultan.

SULTAN:

This is really strange! What do you think, Judge?

JUDGE:

No, my Lord the Sultan, it is not yet dawn.

VIZIER:

(Taken aback) How...?

JUDGE:

This is quite obvious. It is still night.

VIZIER:

(To the Judge, surprised) But...

JUDGE:

But we have all heard the Muezzin calling for the dawn prayer. Did you hear that, Woman?

BELLE:

Yes, I heard.

JUDGE:

You admit then that you heard the voice of the Muezzin calling for the dawn prayer?

BELLE:

Yes...but...

JUDGE:

Say nothing more! Since you admit that, nothing remains but for you to keep your promise. Here is the emancipation document; all you have to do is sign. *(He presents the document to her.)*

BELLE:

I promised to sign at dawn. And here you admit, your honor, that it is still night!

JUDGE:
> Wait, Woman. Your promise is inscribed word by
> word in my head. You said literally: "Upon hear-
> ing the voice of the Muezzin calling for the dawn
> prayer..." The whole question now becomes, did
> you or did you not hear the voice of the Muezzin?

BELLE:
> I heard, but since dawn is still far off...

JUDGE:
> Dawn itself was not the issue. The promise had to
> do with the voice of the Muezzin calling for the
> dawn prayer. If the Muezzin miscalculated or mis-
> behaved, he is responsible for his mistake. This
> is his business, not ours! Understand?

BELLE:
> Yes, I understand. It is not a bad trick!

JUDGE:
> The Muezzin will, of course, be tried for his
> mistake. But this does not change the fact, which
> is, that we have all heard the Muezzin calling
> for the dawn prayer from his minaret. Hence, all
> legal consequences must follow, and that immedi-
> ately. Come and sign then.

BELLE:
> Is that the way you interpret my condition?

JUDGE:
> As you interpreted our condition!

VIZIER:
> You have fallen into the same kind of trap. Yield
> and sign.

BELLE:
> But this is not honest; it is cheating.

VIZIER:
> Cheating for cheating, and you are the one who
> started it. The one who begins is more culpable,
> and you are the last person to object or protest.

SULTAN:
> *(Shouting)* Fie on you! Enough! Enough! Stop this
> nonsense and childishness. She shall not sign!
> I absolutely refuse that she sign in this manner!
> And you, Chief Judge, aren't you ashamed to turn
> the law into a plaything?

JUDGE:

My Lord!

SULTAN:

I am disappointed. You disappointed me, Chief
Judge. Is this the law, in your opinion? Nothing
but sophistry and play on words and cheating.

JUDGE:

I only wanted, my Lord, to...

SULTAN:

To save me, I know, but do you think I could
accept being saved in this manner?

JUDGE:

With a woman like this, my Lord, we have every
right...

SULTAN:

No, you don't have the right at all. It is not
your right. This woman might have the right to
play with words or cheat and nobody will blame
her if she does; she might be forgiven for her
intelligence and cleverness. But the Chief Judge,
the representative of justice, the protector of
the law and its faithful servant has as his main
obligation to protect the purity and sacredness
of the law, whatever the price. It was you, yourself, who showed me in the beginning the merit of
the law and the respect due it, telling me that
it's a master to be obeyed, and that I have to
bow in front of it. And I have bowed very sub-
missively till the very end. But...did I ever
dream to see you in the end looking upon the law
in such a manner, divesting it of all sacredness,
so much so that in your hands it is nothing more
than tricks, sentences, words, and twists?

JUDGE:

Let me explain, my Lord.

SULTAN:

No, don't explain a thing. Go now! It is better
to go back home and to sleep until morning. As
for me, I will respect this lady's condition in
its true sense, which we all understand. Let's
go, my Lady. We both will go back to your house.
I am at your disposal.

BELLE:
>No, your Majesty.

SULTAN:
>No?

BELLE:
>Your Chief Judge wanted to save you and I don't
>like to be less faithful to you than he is. You
>are now free, your Majesty.

SULTAN:
>Free?

BELLE:
>Yes. Chief Judge, give me the document to sign.

JUDGE:
>You will sign now?

BELLE:
>Yes, now!

JUDGE:
>*(Presents the document to her)* May God make her
>true to her word!

BELLE:
>*(Signing the document)* Believe me this time. Here's
>my signature!

JUDGE:
>*(Examining the signature)* Yes, despite everything,
>you are a good woman!

SULTAN:
>She is one of the best women. And the whole city
>must respect her. This is an order, Vizier.

VIZIER:
>Your orders are obeyed, your Majesty.

JUDGE:
>*(Folding the document)* Everything has turned out
>for the best, your Majesty.

SULTAN:
>And without a drop of blood being shed. That is
>more important!

VIZIER:
>That is thanks to your courage, your Majesty. Who
>would have imagined that pursuing this path till
>the end required more courage than that of the
>sword?

JUDGE:

True.

SULTAN:

We should praise the generosity of this noble lady. Permit me, my Lady, to thank you, and I hope you will accept the return of your money, since there is no longer a reason why you should lose it. Vizier, let her be paid from my own money a sum equal to that which she spent.

BELLE:

No, no, your majesty. Don't take this honor away from me. All the riches of the world could not be equal to this beautiful memory with which I will live all my life! I have contributed a negligible thing towards one of the greatest events...

SULTAN:

Well, since you cherish memories so much, then keep this souvenir. *(He takes the huge sapphire from his turban.)*

VIZIER:

(Whispering) The unique sapphire?

SULTAN:

Compared to her graciousness, it is nothing.
(Offers her the sapphire.)

BELLE:

No, my dear Sultan, I don't deserve...I really don't deserve all this...this...

SULTAN:

(Starting to leave) Goodbye, good Lady.

BELLE:

(With tears in her eyes) Goodbye, dear Sultan.

SULTAN:

(Sees her tears) Crying?

BELLE:

From joy!

SULTAN:

I will never forget that I was your slave!

BELLE:

For the sake of principle and the law, your majesty!
(She bends down to hide her tears.)
(Music. The Sultan's procession moves.)

Curtain

THE NEW ARRIVAL

A comedy in One Act

by

Mikhail Roman

Cast of Characters

The New Arrival   The Agent

The Waiter

The Expert   The Supervisor

The Set:

The place is shiny and polished, possessing that
kind of sterilized and disquieting cleanliness that
characterizes hospital rooms, with stark white walls
and strong lighting. A broad glass window is at the
back of the stage. On the walls are several gadgets,
such as thermometers, thermographs, barometers and a
huge chart which might express anything. Also a beautiful oil painting of a heavily-muscled worker, another
of a ballet dancer or a vase of roses or the face of a
young peasant woman with a headdress. However, the place
lacks beauty and proportion, as if all these objects
have to be in the room, somehow. In the background, beyond the glass window, a mountain composed of several
small hills, to be lighted by scores of small lamps.
Part of this mountain could be lighted by a glaring red
light. Ventian blinds on the window.

The set might also be unrealistic; it could simply
be a huge emptiness, and the greater the space, the
better and the more effectively expressive of the
psychological condition of the New Arrival, the hero of
the play. In the middle of the set is a table covered
with a white tablecloth and very shiny, elegant place
settings. Close to this table is another that has
neither place settings nor tablecloth. There is only one
chair.

*At the time the curtain rises, the New Arrival is
discovered sitting at the first table in the posture of
one who is getting ready, in a very enthusiastic manner,
to eat.*

Time: Now.

AGENT:
(Coming from a distance) Hello...*(Rushing toward
him)* Let me hug you! How do you do? Oh, it's been
so long!

NEW ARRIVAL:
(Coldly) Hello...welcome. *(A word about the New
Arrival: He is a man between thirty and forty,
handsome, well-off and well-dressed. His outfit,
however, betrays an unusual, almost feminine taste,
and hence, he is prone to go from sudden severity
to extreme tenderness.)*

AGENT:
(While sitting down) I am sorry I didn't come on
time.

NEW ARRIVAL:
When?

AGENT:
Thursday.

NEW ARRIVAL:
Which Thursday?

AGENT:
Last week.

NEW ARRIVAL:
Last week?

AGENT:
Of course, have you forgotten?

NEW ARRIVAL:
No, of course not...so many things to think about...

AGENT:
How are things?

NEW ARRIVAL:
Fine.

AGENT:
The season is slow.

NEW ARRIVAL:
> Well...

AGENT:
> Nimrud says the season is slow; not like last year.
> Last year there was quite a boom.

NEW ARRIVAL:
> Maybe...

AGENT:
> And you? How is work?

NEW ARRIVAL:
> Not bad.

AGENT:
> Busy?

NEW ARRIVAL:
> So-so.

AGENT:
> Hotel full?

NEW ARRIVAL:
> *(Completely surprised)* Hotel?

AGENT:
> Palace, your hotel.

NEW ARRIVAL:
> *(Laughing awkwardly and a bit embarrassed)* So-so.

AGENT:
> What's wrong with you?

NEW ARRIVAL:
> Nothing. Do you care for a cold drink or tea or
> coffee?

AGENT:
> Nothing. I have to go in fifteen minutes. I'll
> take the nine o'clock train. Mikhail Roman sent me
> the tickets and travel allowance. They say there
> is a festival, and the train is air conditioned.
> So, I said to myself, I should go watch the festi-
> val and enjoy the air conditioning. Mikhail Bey
> sends his greetings.

NEW ARRIVAL:
> Who is Mikhail?

AGENT:
> Mikhail, your friend. What's the matter? I don't
> understand what's happening to you.

NEW ARRIVAL:

Nothing! *(With sudden severity)* There are hundreds of Mikhails in town; which Mikhail?

AGENT:

For God's sake! Mikhail, your friend. You are together day and night.

NEW ARRIVAL:

(Laughing awkwardly) My memory is terrible. I forget names. *(With affected nonchalance)* By the way, his name is Mikhail what?

AGENT:

Mikhail Roman

NEW ARRIVAL:

Of course, Mikhail Roman. Who else could it be but Mikhail Roman. It must be Mikhail Roman. Shall I get you a cold drink?

AGENT:

(Cutting him with an icy look) How come, then, you had forgotten his name?

NEW ARRIVAL:

(Sharply) Because there are a hundred or even a thousand Mikhails in town. Is it a crime, or what?

AGENT:

Never mind.

NEW ARRIVAL:

Why should I mind? Besides, why should I know his father's name? What is his father to me? What is his father even to him? The significance of his father cannot go beyond him at the very utmost. And even there, just for the identification card only...

AGENT:

(Offering him a cigarette, while looking coldly at him) Have a cigarette.

NEW ARRIVAL:

(Sharply) I don't want one!

AGENT:

Are you upset?

NEW ARRIVAL:

Oh God, why should I be upset? Do you know my father's name?

AGENT:

    (Immediately) Of course. I know your name, your father's and your mother's. I know your address, number of children, your wife's name and why and wherefore and how and when you married her, I know ...

NEW ARRIVAL:

    (Interrupting) You are a genius!

AGENT:

    No, I am an amateur. Listen, would you like to come and work with us?

NEW ARRIVAL:

    Where?

AGENT:

    Where do you think? In the hotel, of course.

NEW ARRIVAL:

    (Awkwardly) But, I see, you think...is it...? The problem...

AGENT:

    (Coldly) What?

NEW ARRIVAL:

    I don't know.

AGENT:

    What is it you don't know?

NEW ARRIVAL:

    It requires some thinking.

AGENT:

    So it requires thinking? It is one chance in a lifetime!

NEW ARRIVAL:

    I don't know.

AGENT:

    What is the matter with you? Have a cigarette.

NEW ARRIVAL:

    (Looking at him coldly and defiantly) I do not know Mikhail Roman.

AGENT:

    (Screaming) Oh my God!

NEW ARRIVAL:

    I do not know Mikhail Roman!

AGENT:

    Sh! Is there any person who does not know Mikhail

Roman? Say that you don't know anyone but Mikhail
Roman! Show me one single creature who does not
know Mikhail Roman!

NEW ARRIVAL:

Me!

AGENT:

You are drunk.

NEW ARRIVAL:

No, I've had only black coffee. Call my wife on
the telephone and ask her...five O's, one (000001).

AGENT:

(Eagerly) Is that your home phone number?

NEW ARRIVAL:

Did you think it was the cattle shed? *(The Agent
writes the number in a little notebook.)* Why are
you taking down the number?

AGENT:

I am completing the data. Besides, we are old
friends, and I might need you. *(He comes very
close to him.)*

NEW ARRIVAL:

What are you doing?

AGENT:

Just smelling your mouth.

NEW ARRIVAL:

(Sarcastically) Smells good?

AGENT:

Smells of hunger.

NEW ARRIVAL:

True, I haven't eaten for two days.

AGENT:

Why?

NEW ARRIVAL:

(Sarcastically) Don't like the food.

AGENT:

(Sarcastically) Do you swear to that?

NEW ARRIVAL:

Oh yes, by God, I am serious!

AGENT:

Listen, a bit of free advice, and all for the
love of God. The Mikhail Roman Hotel is the best
hotel. Food, drink, sleep with all the extras,

and anything that your heart desires. *(Standing)*
I have to leave you.

NEW ARRIVAL:

(Very coldly) Why don't you stay a little longer.

AGENT:

No, the train is already in.

NEW ARRIVAL:

(Coldly) Goodbye.

AGENT:

Listen, do get in touch some time.

NEW ARRIVAL:

Certainly.

AGENT:

You have my telephone number?

NEW ARRIVAL:

Of course, goodbye.

AGENT:

Here's the waiter coming. Eat well, so you can
sleep.

NEW ARRIVAL:

Thank you very much. *(To the waiter who is coming
closer to him)* How do you do?

WAITER:

(Sharply) Come with me!

NEW ARRIVAL:

(Sudden panic) Where should I go?

WAITER:

Come with me.

NEW ARRIVAL:

(Scared) But why? Why? I came here to eat. Where
do you want to take me?

WAITER:

I'll seat you in a better place.

NEW ARRIVAL:

No, it's O.K. here. I'm comfortable like this.

WAITER:

It's crowded here.

NEW ARRIVAL:

(Interrupting) No, no, I'm happy here like this.
This is fine.

WAITER:

Listen, you want to sit alone at a table by yourself, right?

NEW ARRIVAL:

Of course.

WAITER:

Here it's impossible, with four or five or six at one table, and even then sometimes someone will sit on top of it. Would you like that?

NEW ARRIVAL:

No, that would be anarchy.

WAITER:

Then come with me, or would you rather go get your food yourself, and eat while you are standing? Do you want plain or gourmet food?

NEW ARRIVAL:

Gourmet food, of course. *(Apologetically)* I'm... hungry.

WAITER:

Here there is no gourmet food. Everybody eats like the other: the first like the second like the third like the fourth. What did you say?

NEW ARRIVAL:

I don't know.

WAITER:

But I know. Come with me before the shift is over and the men rush in by the thousands. Come.

NEW ARRIVAL:

Where are you going to seat me?

WAITER:

(Coaxingly) What should you care? There is a racket here that won't appeal to you. I know what you like. Come. Come. I'll seat you in a place that you will find extremely pleasing. And I'll put roses on the table for you. *(In a whisper)* You might also find somebody who will sit with you and keep you company. That's besides the music, the merriment, and all you desire. The food will have a taste then. You want extra excellent food. Special, heh?

NEW ARRIVAL:

Indeed...

WAITER:

All right, then, come.

NEW ARRIVAL:

    I don't know...what if...say...one sat here with
them...company...you know?

WAITER:

    It's up to you.

NEW ARRIVAL:

    Eh, what do you think?

WAITER:

    It's up to you.

NEW ARRIVAL:

    But you say that the menu here is fixed?

WAITER:

    And served in shifts.

NEW ARRIVAL:

    (Severely) No, anything but shifts. I'm hungry.
Where are you going to seat me? *(He stands up;
both move two steps, then the New Arrival sits at
another table with no table cloth, no plates or
silverware. It also looks older.)*

WAITER:

    See! Which do you like better, here or there?

NEW ARRIVAL:

    No, it's better here. Here one can eat leisurely,
with nobody telling him to get up so they can sit
in his place. Here one can clap, and a thousand
persons will come to wait on him. *(Contemplating
the view)* The view is splendid. *(Relaxing)* Ah...
*(Waiter offers him an open packet of cigarettes.
He takes one. The Waiter lights it for him. He
inhales deeply.)* Ah...What do you have?

WAITER:

    Everything

NEW ARRIVAL:

    Everything?

WAITER:

    Everything.

NEW ARRIVAL:

    Good. Hunger be accursed. Well, then, take this.
Write it down on a piece of paper lest you forget.

WAITER:

    My memory is good. Go ahead, please.

NEW ARRIVAL:

>What do you have? Huh? I swear by God, after hun-
ger, after the crushing, painful awareness of the
existence of the abdomen, the stomach and the in-
testines, I swear by God, I'll have the food that
a man would order before being executed, when they
tell him, "You have an hour in this world, what do
you crave?" He would sit back, cross his legs, and
would order, choose, select, and turn his nose up
while the warden stood before him, a dog and a
bastard, a kitchen boy, a servant, and a son of a
slave, and would have to tell him "Yes sir." Do
you understand? The man walking up the steps of
the gallows does not care whether he digests or
not, whether he gets a stomachache, or diarrhea,
or constipation, or even poisoning. He doesn't care
about anything. Pleasure! He will satisfy his
pleasure and, for the first time in his life, get
away without paying the price. He will take the
pleasure for free and escape with it. The whole
world can go hang; it will not be able to do anything to him. Right? *(Pause)* Why don't you answer?
(Laughing) You don't want to commit yourself?
What I say is true, though. It doesn't matter. Take
this. Write it down on a piece of paper.

WAITER:

>My memory is better than a book. Go ahead, please.

NEW ARRIVAL:

>Take this. *(Suddenly bitter)* A beast of a man,
whom I have never seen or spoken to before comes
and hugs me. I don't even know him. And "how do
you do?" and "how are the kids?" and I have never
met him before. What made it worse is that friend
of mine, Mikhail Roman, and that story about a
hotel. The bastard thinks I work in a hotel. Me!
And I must by law know somebody whose name is
Mikhail Roman. I have never seen a man with such
a name. I swear by God Almighty that if I see him,
I'll spit in his face! Disgusting! And he has paint-
ed a smile on his face, the beast, and speaks with
such confidence as only the insane and the stupid
can afford. *(Accusingly)* You saw him, and he told

you something while he was leaving. Do you know
him? What is his name? *(Pause)* What's the story?
Why don't you want to talk?

WAITER:

If I don't get your order, I will leave immediately.

NEW ARRIVAL:

But you know him. You certainly know him. You spoke
to him and he smiled at you, did he not?

WAITER:

If I don't get your order, I will leave immediately.

NEW ARRIVAL:

(Astonished, sad) What happened? What is wrong
with people? *(Pause)* It doesn't matter. *(He speaks
the words slowly, with great pleasure.)* Chicken?
Pigeons stuffed with hazel nuts? No...No...That
isn't my order. I'm just working myself up. Stir-
ring the latent animal desires...Pleasure and
appetite; Freud says the lips and the anus. Wait!
The lips. My God! The lips of any woman are not
like the lips of any other woman. How I wish that
the lips of all the world's women were rolled into one pair, so I could kiss them once and satisfy
this insatiable hunger. *(The Waiter moves. Firmly)*
Wait! *(To himself)* He took my telephone number,
and he looks ugly, and...Mikhail Roman? Later...
Later, I'll think of it at my leisure. Let's
attend to the important matter at hand *(Rubbing
his hands together, affecting gaiety)*, which means
that we will have a respectable, solid supper,
then light a cigarette, cross our legs, drink a
cup of strong, black tea, and sleep till the morning. Good, it's been a long time since I ate a
self-respecting meal. There is plenty, isn't there?
(Waiter nods his head.) Good, let's begin...What
should you bring me? Don't bring soup, aperitif
or appetizer. My appetite is wide open. I want to
put in my stomach only the most valuable stuff.
Bring me neither bread nor salad, but get me some
hot pepper so that my mouth will burn in flames
that nothing but more food can put out. Don't bring
any water, so my pleasure may be spiced with a
little pain. *(Shouting)* Wait! *(Eagerly)* I have to

hurry up before the food is all gone. The good
things go fast. All right, pay attention to what I
tell you. Listen very carefully to what I say. *(As
if his tongue speaks against his will)* Mikhail
Roman...? *(Shaking his head, as if commanding himself)* Later...later. I should think of it at leisure. *(Bitterly)* Who did I see first this morning?
It doesn't matter. A turkey...get me a turkey that
has reached the age of maturity, stuffed with al-
monds, hazel nuts, nuts of all sorts, and cracked
wheat. Be sure to warn the cook. I once ordered a
turkey, and the turkey came stuffed with paper.
Do you understand? Newspapers, books, and magazines!
I swear, by God, I found the Communist Manifesto
inside it. The whole Communist Manifesto! I shriek-
ed and the food shot from my stomach to my mouth
like a cannon ball. Panic reached my stomach, then
diarrhea, like a fire hose working full force. I
could not reach the sewage system in time. I re-
ported him, but to no avail. And although I was
innocent, they put me behind bars in an iron cell.
For three years, my God, for three years I did
not see God's light, what with the investigations,
the cross examinations, the beatings, the humiliation, and the insults. You hear me? Warn the cook
or else I'll get him into real trouble! I want a
turkey stuffed with rice, liver and kidneys, not
paper and ink and nonsense. *(Suddenly exclaiming
very sadly)* By the head of my father in his grave,
I will get no supper tonight. *(Laughing)* A turkey,
like I told you. On second thought, let him get
me an absolutely unstuffed turkey, perfectly empty.
I don't want any problems, O.K.? Agreed? An absolutely unstuffed turkey, did you take that down?

WAITER:
My memory is better than a book.

NEW ARRIVAL:
Bring me two pairs of pigeons, too, grilled over a
very low fire, or, listen...about the turkey, have
him cut it up in four quarters. Have it brought
here cut up on a platter with absolutely nothing
under it, no vegetables, rice, potatoes or anything

whatsoever. It is better to sacrifice an aesthetic
value for the time being. A whole turkey is a sight
that is full of dignity and greatness, but cut up,
it is ugly, like a corpse. Yet, it doesn't matter.
One is far better off sacrificing an aesthetic
value than one's own self. Are we agreed concerning the turkey? Don't forget, if, for any reason,
the turkey should arrive here whole, I will not
accept it. I will not permit it to be placed before
me or even come close to me. Even if you cut my
hand off, I will not touch it or reach out for it.
Yes, he is wise who learns from past experience.
(Suddenly) You know the man who was sitting with
me. He spoke to you, and you smiled at him. *(The
Waiter does not seem to have heard him.)* It doesn't
matter. Ultimately, I will know who he is. Let's
stick to what is important...the pigeons.

WAITER:

(Interrupting for the first time) Does this mean,
sir, that you will not eat what is on the regular
menu?

NEW ARRIVAL:

Regular menu? What does that mean?

WAITER:

It means four huge pots, each as tall as a high-
rise. And one serving from each pot...vegetables,
rice, salad, fruit and a piece of meat. Thousands
eat this way. Each one eats like the other: the
first like the second like the third like the fourth...
Or would you rather place a special order? Those who
are excellent...

NEW ARRIVAL:

Most definitely a special order; I have a wild
hunger.

WAITER:

Pigeons?

NEW ARRIVAL:

Pigeons? No, I don't want any pigeons. A leg of lamb
grilled over a very low fire. A leg of lamb buried
to a great depth in the sand, with the fire above it
blazing sky high, outshining Vesuvius, which destroyed Pompeii the beautiful. Heat slowly creeping

downwards, the most difficult direction for fire to move, because fire is the daughter of the sky, offspring of planets and stars...And so am I... On top of the lamb, roses and flowers. Sprinkle it with jasmine, Arabian and the other variety, and mint. No, leave the jasmine for the water with which I wash my hands. *Ya Salaam!* That is how a man should eat, like the emperors of Rome when Rome was dying, when the Germanic tribes and the Christians destroyed it.

WAITER:

And the dessert?

NEW ARRIVAL:

The dessert is still a long way off. But, before I forget, wild honey...They say it is good for one. I have T.B. *(Coughs)*.

WAITER:

Take streptomycin shots.

NEW ARRIVAL:

(Coughing) I don't believe in antibiotics. I am anti-antibiotics. I am committed to that, because I am bioticity itself. *(Laughing. The other does not smile.)* Do you have any swallows?

WAITER:

Everything!

NEW ARRIVAL:

Everything?

WAITER:

Yes, everything.

NEW ARRIVAL:

But why bother with swallows? Swallows are for widows, spinsters and whores! Do you have any gazelles?

WAITER:

Everything.

NEW ARRIVAL:

Bring me a piece of the leg of a gazelle.

WAITER:

And the wild honey?

NEW ARRIVAL:

No *(Coughing)* I don't want honey. All right, my good man, don't keep me waiting too long *(The*

Waiter does not seem to have any intention of moving.), O.K.?

WAITER:

   (After a pause) But...I beg your pardon, are you with us in the hotel, sir?

As this scene, which should be played very fast, proceeds, lighting slowly dims all over the stage until a blackout is reached, except for a very strong spotlight over the New Arrival alone. The Waiter remains in the dark.

NEW ARRIVAL:

   Yes?

WAITER:

   Are you with us in the hotel, sir?

NEW ARRIVAL:

   (Eagerly) Of course.

WAITER:

   What number?

NEW ARRIVAL:

   (Eagerly) I don't know, perhaps 66.

WAITER:

   When did you arrive?

NEW ARRIVAL:

   An hour ago.

WAITER:

   Exactly?

NEW ARRIVAL:

   I don't know.

WAITER:

   By plane?

NEW ARRIVAL:

   No.

WAITER:

   Then how did you arrive, sir?

NEW ARRIVAL:

   By train.

WAITER:

   The train arrived at nine; it is now ten after one, and you said...

NEW ARRIVAL:
(Interrupting) No...no...I probably arrived two
hours ago, perhaps even earlier.
WAITER:
Two and a half hours?
NEW ARRIVAL:
Almost.
WAITER:
Nobody informed us.
NEW ARRIVAL:
Does it really matter?
WAITER:
So we could make arrangements for you, sir.
NEW ARRIVAL:
I came straight from the train.
WAITER:
Impossible, sir.
NEW ARRIVAL:
(Beginning to get tense) Why? Why is it impossible?
WAITER:
Because it is 223 meters from the train to here,
sir.
NEW ARRIVAL:
(With obvious hostility) Measured it to the centi-
meter, huh? I took a horse cab.
WAITER:
What number was it, sir?
NEW ARRIVAL:
I don't know. I didn't take it down.
WAITER:
Impossible, sir!
NEW ARRIVAL:
That is what happened.
WAITER:
Then it would have taken you ten minutes, sir.
NEW ARRIVAL:
No...no...the horse was tired.
WAITER:
Twenty minutes.
NEW ARRIVAL:
No, the horse fell on the way, and the cab driver
and I together had to pull it up.

WAITER:

>Impossible, sir.

NEW ARRIVAL:

>No, that is what happened. The horse fell.

WAITER:

>Impossible, sir!

NEW ARRIVAL:

>*(Loudly)* It fell! The horse fell down! And the cab driver and I together had to pull it up, and the cab driver told me the story of the horse. It used to be a race horse, and always won. It was handsome and charming, and beautiful women fed it chocolate and sugar from their hands. People came from the fields and mountain tops to greet it and watch it, until time ate it up. It fell out with one of those native horses that belong to the peasant paupers. Its leg was broken. Ever since then it has been a day up and a year down. Because its downfall was exactly the day of the quarrel. He told me about it. You must know him, because he is an old, unsteady man and must tell the story to whomever is ready to listen. You must know him! You certainly know the cab driver's name! You know his name! You know his name!

WAITER:

>*(As if hearing nothing)* What does he look like, the cab driver?

NEW ARRIVAL:

>He is dark and old.

WAITER:

>Is his hair white?

NEW ARRIVAL:

>I don't know.

WAITER:

>You must know! Dark and old, then his hair, of necessity, must be white. An unforgettable sight.

NEW ARRIVAL:

>*(Severely)* I did not look at the cab driver at all. Of what importance is the cab driver to me? Of what importance is anybody in this world to me? I was preoccupied.

WAITER:
> With what?

NEW ARRIVAL:
> I don't remember. *(Pleading)* Of what importance is all this. I am here, with you, with you...

WAITER:
> *(Interrupting)* Please...

NEW ARRIVAL:
> *(Pleading)* I'm hungry.

WAITER:
> The food we have is prepared precisely to meet the requirements of our customers only. We must feed them.

NEW ARRIVAL:
> *(Scared)* And me?

WAITER:
> I must know exactly when you arrived, on what train, and the number of the train. I want to help you. What time did you say you arrived?

NEW ARRIVAL:
> *(Now exhausted, despairing)* I don't have a watch. Never had a watch. It is not important for me to have a watch. I came directly from the train to the hotel.

WAITER:
> Which train?
> *(The New Arrival rushes violently from his place to forestage right, but stops as a very bright spotlight covers his face. He covers his face with his hands.)*

NEW ARRIVAL:
> *(Shouting)* Put out the light! I am being blinded.

WAITER:
> Go back to your place.

NEW ARRIVAL:
> Put out the light...put out the light.

WAITER:
> Which train? *(The New Arrival goes back to his place, covering his eyes with his hands.)*

NEW ARRIVAL:
> I don't know.

WAITER:
>The number?

NEW ARRIVAL:
>I don't know.

WAITER:
>There is a train every half hour. There is one at
>ten, one at ten thirty, one at eleven, one at eleven
>thirty, one...

NEW ARRIVAL:
>(Interrupting) I don't know. I don't know at all.

WAITER:
>The first one?

NEW ARRIVAL:
>Perhaps. Perhaps the second, or perhaps the third
>(Quite hopelessly), or perhaps I never arrived at
>all.

WAITER:
>(Without any feeling) If it was the first, then you
>must have arrived here at nine twenty five on foot,
>in a horse cab at nine ten, in a taxi cab at nine
>five. And if it was the second, on foot you would
>have arrived at nine fifty five, in a horse cab at
>nine forty, in a taxi cab at nine thirty five. And
>if it was the third, on foot at ten twenty five,
>in a horse cab...

NEW ARRIVAL:
>My head! My head will burst!

WAITER:
>(Immediately) Where is the ticket?

NEW ARRIVAL:
>I threw it away.

WAITER:
>(Without any feeling) The ticket has the number of
>the train, time of departure and time of arrival.

NEW ARRIVAL:
>(Rising suddenly) Impossible! (Searches his pockets
>madly for the ticket.) I threw it away. I certainly
>threw it away. (Sits down, collapsing.) I threw the
>ticket away. (Eagerly) Listen, give me the food,
>and then we can talk as much as you like.

WAITER:
>Impossible!

NEW ARRIVAL:

    Impossible?

WAITER:

    Of course...Everybody knows that. Your name is not in the books.

NEW ARRIVAL:

    No! My name is in the books! I am sure my name is in the books.

WAITER:

    Impossible.

NEW ARRIVAL:

    (As if talking to himself) Why? Why is it not in the books? All my life, my name has always been in the books. *(Eagerly)* We'll write it down! You can solve the problem.

WAITER:

    I am very sorry. You are taking an unobjective attitude, sir. Everybody here is very carefully arranged for, and all services must be rendered. Please come with me.

NEW ARRIVAL:

    I am hungry.

WAITER:

    Please come with me.

NEW ARRIVAL:

    I am hungry, and you, where do you want to take me?

WAITER:

    A mere formality.

NEW ARRIVAL:

    (With sudden panic) You will kill me! *(Rushes to the door.)* You will kill me!

WAITER:

    (Without moving) A mere formality. We must know how, when, and why you entered here.

NEW ARRIVAL:

    (Collapsing) Please. I don't want any problems. In any investigation, an innocent man can easily become a defendant and end up with capital punishment. Please, I renounce my order for food!

WAITER:

    I am very sorry, a mere formal procedure...

NEW ARRIVAL:

Actually, I am quite full. Even if you place the
food before me, I will not be able to touch it,
really. Listen, please consider my order as if it
were never placed...Consider my whole existence as
if it never were.

WAITER:

I am very sorry.

NEW ARRIVAL:

No, no, no, please, consider me nonexistent alto-
gether. Do me a favor.

WAITER:

I am very sorry.

NEW ARRIVAL:

Please, I am tired after my trip. Later.

WAITER:

No, I am sorry. Please come with me. A problem has
developed.

NEW ARRIVAL:

What? What's happening? Did I commit a crime? I
really came on the train. I paid for the ticket,
and all my life I have thrown the tickets away.
This is not the first time. All my life long I
never had a watch, and never cared about time. It
is not a mere coincidence. I hate chains, all kinds
of chains, and a ticket is a chain, a watch is a
chain, a suitcase is a chain. I do not have a
suitcase because everything around me shackles me,
and all my life I've hated chains. Even time; I hate
time.

WAITER:

(With no feeling at all) I advise you to spare your
words a little.

NEW ARRIVAL:

(Shocked) Spare my words a little?

WAITER:

Unless it is to some purpose.

NEW ARRIVAL:

But I am expressing my opinion.

WAITER:

Perhaps someone here or there might hear you. Time
is very important here. Everything has to be done

exactly on time, not before or after. If the opera-
tors of the dredges or the trucks or the big rock-
ets heard what you are saying. If the cooks in the
restaurant...

NEW ARRIVAL:
    (Scared) No, anyone but the cooks!

WAITER:
    Please come with me, I beg you.

NEW ARRIVAL:
    Where am I going?

WAITER:
    Just a little errand, and then we will come back
    immediately.

NEW ARRIVAL:
    Is it far?

WAITER:
    No.

NEW ARRIVAL:
    I haven't eaten anything since yesterday.

WAITER:
    Please come with me.

NEW ARRIVAL:
    Nor slept.

WAITER:
    Please come with me.

NEW ARRIVAL:
    And I would love to have a cup of coffee.

WAITER:
    Please come with me.

NEW ARRIVAL:
    My clothes are filthy, filthy, filthy. The perspira-
    tion has mixed with mud, and the dirt is layer upon
    layer on my skin. *(Standing up)* The most terrible
    smell on earth is that of a human being. Who could
    give me a clean change of clothes? *(He walks two
    steps, his back bent. The Waiter points to the only
    chair, and he sits in it. The Waiter exits unnoticed.
    The Supervisor enters.)* I..., it seems I have seen
    you before.

SUPERVISOR:
    I have the same feeling.

NEW ARRIVAL:

We come from the same part of the country, your
accent...You are from Lower Egypt.

SUPERVISOR:

No, Upper.

NEW ARRIVAL:

I mean Upper, Upper! Hunger does things to one. We
come from the same part of the country.

SUPERVISOR:

(Smiling) Yes, and a good one too.

NEW ARRIVAL:

Certainly. Everyone in our part of the country is
generous, be he son or father, and everyone a man.
I remember you. Yes, you are the son of Sheikh Abdel
Ghaffar, son of Hagg Mahmoud. Your cousin is
Hassanein the Martyr.

SUPERVISOR:

(Responding to the praise) May paradise be his
abode.

NEW ARRIVAL:

Exactly! I remember you perfectly. Both of us were
raised under the palm trees there, near the railway
bridge.

SUPERVISOR:

I am from Kalabsha.

NEW ARRIVAL:

So am I! The granite above and beneath us the tombs,
thousands stretched side by side, with their eyes
open, living with us, watching us. And the rocks
were smooth as alabaster. There were lions in the
wilderness, and we were the fierce giants. Where,
where is he who can scare us?

SUPERVISOR:

(Moved) Not yet created.

NEW ARRIVAL:

(Vehemently) Who is it that can make us go hungry?

SUPERVISOR:

(Shouting) Not yet created!

NEW ARRIVAL:

I have no fear of the red devil.

SUPERVISOR:

Nor do I.

NEW ARRIVAL:

>You are a hero. You are the cousin of Hassanein the Martyr.

SUPERVISOR:

>*(Shouting)* May paradise be his abode!

NEW ARRIVAL:

>His blood is your blood, his flesh your flesh.

SUPERVISOR:

>And my sword is for danger and the battlefield!

NEW ARRIVAL:

>And the blood goes back to the seventh grandfather. You are from the Abdel Abeeds; in your family there was a martyr who died at el-Tell el-Kebir with the hero of heroes, Urabi...

SUPERVISOR:

>May paradise be his abode. *(Shouting)* My sword is for danger and the battlefield!

NEW ARRIVAL:

>*(Shouting as if in a battle)* Forward! Forward!

SUPERVISOR:

>*(Shouting. They are back to back now.)* Bring the tractors and the plows and blow up the iron mountain! Block the way before the knave and teach him how to behave...

NEW ARRIVAL:

>With dynamite, guns and the bodies of men...

SUPERVISOR:

>Toss the grenades, blow him up!

NEW ARRIVAL:

>Forward, men!

SUPERVISOR:

>Freedom or death!

NEW ARRIVAL:

>Death to imperialism, death to the cowards!

SUPERVISOR:

>Forward, men!

NEW ARRIVAL:

>Three hundred thousand in the streets...to the barracks...to the barracks!

SUPERVISOR:

>Qasr el-Nil! Qasr el-Nil!

NEW ARRIVAL:
Remove the two lions, break them, and drown them
in the Nile!

SUPERVISOR:
With fire and sulphur! Not one step backward! Each
man stand in place!

NEW ARRIVAL:
Die in your places, men! Death to the cowards!

SUPERVISOR:
Eighty years of struggle, crown them with victory!

NEW ARRIVAL:
For peace, for the sake of all peoples! Forward!

SUPERVISOR:
(With mad hate) The bastard Ali Khonfis betrayed
us!

NEW ARRIVAL:
The bastard Ismail Sidki betrayed us!

SUPERVISOR:
The bastard Wilson betrayed us!

NEW ARRIVAL:
The bastard Mohammed Mahmoud betrayed us!

SUPERVISOR:
The bastard Sultan betrayed us!

NEW ARRIVAL:
The bastard Ahmad Fouad betrayed us!

SUPERVISOR:
The bastard Gamal Gamal Eddin betrayed us!

NEW ARRIVAL:
(In terror) They are shooting to kill!

SUPERVISOR:
Wrap the martyr in flags and lay him to rest in
the bosom of the valley.

NEW ARRIVAL:
(In a wailing-like tune) In a bed of roses and a
coffin of sycamore.

SUPERVISOR:
(Wailing-like tune) Oh...and I, sleeping in the bosom
of my beloved.

NEW ARRIVAL:
(Wailing-like tune) In a sea of perfume, and the
locks of hair like musk covering me.

SUPERVISOR:

> *(Singing as in a mawwāl)*
>
> A black hair from the beloved's head they took as
> a gift from me.
> Hung between two banks, over the buildings, near the
> moon, touching the stars,
> A black hair from the beloved's night between the
> bridges.
> And I, hanging to the hair, swimming and walking in
> the sea of space.
> I, and the iron, and the men, in a beautiful ship
> between the banks watching,
> And the hair neither breaks nor relaxes, as a river
> of blood,
> Beneath, the mountains of light singing from the
> heart a greeting,
> To the wilderness, the fields, the factories and
> the houses.
> And Egypt enters victorious.
> Egypt, the mother of cities, was built first by a
> candyman.

NEW ARRIVAL:

> *(Shouting)* Egypt, a thousand cheers!

SUPERVISOR:

> *(His enthusiasm growing lukewarm)* A thousand cheers.
> *(Looking at his watch)* I have to go; the time for
> changing the shifts is approaching. The men will be
> coming by the thousands, and they must eat at once.
> Excuse me.

NEW ARRIVAL:

> *(Trying to appeal to his emotions)* None from our
> part of the country heard someone crying for help
> and did not help him. None from our part of the
> country closed his door in the face of guests, none
> closed his door at all.

SUPERVISOR:

> Impossible!

NEW ARRIVAL:

> Then why didn't you embrace me in the room when
> you saw me. We are relatives.

SUPERVISOR:

> *(Hugging him)* Welcome.

NEW ARRIVAL:

   Welcome. How do you do?

SUPERVISOR:

   (Without enthusiasm) A thousand greetings.

NEW ARRIVAL:

   To you! To you!

SUPERVISOR:

   That is what a reunion should be like.

NEW ARRIVAL:

   (Hugging him again) It is good to see you, friend.

SUPERVISOR:

   (Coldly) God preserve you.

NEW ARRIVAL:

   (With profound doubt) You really know me?

SUPERVISOR:

   (Politely) Of course, of course.

NEW ARRIVAL:

   Who amongst us can let a brother go hungry? He who
   does that is a bastard.

SUPERVISOR:

   Of course.

NEW ARRIVAL:

   A thousand times. *(Very tenderly)* I am hungry,
   friend. I haven't eaten for two days.

SUPERVISOR:

   (Impulsively) At once! At once! From the flesh of
   my shoulders if there's no food in the kitchen.

NEW ARRIVAL:

   Make haste, make haste, please!

SUPERVISOR:

   Immediately! *(Quickly produces a pen and a writing
   pad.)* Are you with us in the hotel? *(Everything
   collapses: the New Arrival's head falls down on his
   chest very slowly; he has exhausted all his energy.)*
   Are you with us in the hotel? *(The New Arrival's
   whole body relaxes in utter despair.)* Are you with
   us in the hotel? *(The Supervisor reaches out his
   hand, touches the New Arrival's chin, and raises it
   very slowly. The latter is completely passive, and
   lets his head go back. The New Arrival's eyes are
   closed; he does not resist at all. His head goes
   as far back as possible.)* Do you shave with a blade

or a razor? *(The New Arrival does not hear.)* Do
you shave with a blade or a razor? *(He regains con-
sciousness slowly, listlessly, looking around like
an animal captive in a cage.)* Razor or blade?

NEW ARRIVAL:

(Shakes his head questioningly.) With what?

SUPERVISOR:

A blade is a very sharp razor that you put in a
shaver, and after you shave you throw it away.

NEW ARRIVAL:

(Shakes his head several times.) Yes, that's it,
that's it.

SUPERVISOR:

Yes, indeed, you look it.

NEW ARRIVAL:

What is it that I look?

SUPERVISOR:

Your face...It will suffer a little.

NEW ARRIVAL:

(Pointing to his own chest) Me?

SUPERVISOR:

There is a difference between a razor and a blade.
A razor is delicate, and whenever it becomes dull
we rub it on a strap until it becomes sharp again.
But the blade is different. You will get used to it.

NEW ARRIVAL:

Do you think I have understood any of this?

SUPERVISOR:

It doesn't matter. But if you find that your chin
is a little stubbly, don't be upset. *(The New
Arrival laughs bitterly, then hysterically, finally
almost crying.)* Some people like their faces to be
extremely smooth.

NEW ARRIVAL:

(Sarcastically) Never mind, I don't even care if I
don't shave at all.

SUPERVISOR:

(Immediately) But we care!

NEW ARRIVAL:

You?

SUPERVISOR:

Of course, we make sure that all faces are smooth

and shaved as close as possible. An indispensable hygienic procedure.

NEW ARRIVAL:

(Shrugs his shoulders indifferently.) Have you got a cigarette?

SUPERVISOR:

Help yourself.

NEW ARRIVAL:

Could you light it for me, please?

SUPERVISOR:

(Seriously) With a match or a lighter?

NEW ARRIVAL:

(Laughing) You think I...

SUPERVISOR:

No, it is essential that I should ask. There are some people, a few, it is true, but with very sophisticated tastes--very sensitive people who grew up in palaces--who would never light a cigarette from a lighter. They must have matches; wooden ones too, you know, the gasoline smell...

NEW ARRIVAL:

No, I am not one of those! I probably was until I came here, but now, no. I don't care if you light it for me with a lighter or matches or a bamboo stick. What matters is that you light it for me. *(He does not light it for him.)*

SUPERVISOR:

Did you order dinner, sir?

NEW ARRIVAL:

(Having given up hope that his cigarette will be lighted) Your colleague who sent you, didn't he tell you? *(He looks at him suddenly, and stands up. Now he has some suspicion that this might be a different man. He points at him with a shaking hand, and is about to ask him, but doesn't. His hands fall slowly to his sides.)*

SUPERVISOR:

I would like to complete the procedure.

NEW ARRIVAL:

Thank you, I am not going to eat. Gandhi once fasted exactly forty days. I would like to undergo the experience.

SUPERVISOR:
    Here? Impossible!
NEW ARRIVAL:
    (Completely surprised) Why?
SUPERVISOR:
    Eating is compulsory.
NEW ARRIVAL:
    (Shouting) Here?
SUPERVISOR:
    Of course, eating is compulsory here.
NEW ARRIVAL:
    (With an almost insane surprise) Here?
SUPERVISOR:
    Of course.
NEW ARRIVAL:
    Well then, I abstain; I am not eating!
SUPERVISOR:
    A doctor must see you, and you must sign a statement
    to be co-signed by two witnesses, who must be adults.
    Then it has to have an official stamp, which must
    be canceled. The statement must be in nine copies,
    one of which is to be deposited and registered in
    the Civil Affairs Department, and posted for thirty
    days, and published in at least two daily newspapers,
    or one daily newspaper and two weekly magazines or...
NEW ARRIVAL:
    I must?
SUPERVISOR:
    Of course, or else I will be in endless trouble.
NEW ARRIVAL:
    And if I refuse to sign?
SUPERVISOR:
    We feed you against your will.
NEW ARRIVAL:
    All right, go get the food.
SUPERVISOR:
    At once. *(Produces a pen and writing pad very
    quickly.)* Are you with us in the hotel, sir?
NEW ARRIVAL:
    (In disgust) How much do they give you for this
    job?

SUPERVISOR:
> What job?

NEW ARRIVAL:
> The job you are doing with me now.

SUPERVISOR:
> This is not my job.

NEW ARRIVAL:
> Then what do you do?

SUPERVISOR:
> I press a button.

NEW ARRIVAL:
> (*Sarcastically*) And this is a great responsibility!

SUPERVISOR:
> Yes, indeed. I am one of the first men who came
> here.

NEW ARRIVAL:
> And how much do they give you?

SUPERVISOR:
> For what?

NEW ARRIVAL:
> For pressing the button.

SUPERVISOR:
> Nothing.

NEW ARRIVAL:
> Nothing?

SUPERVISOR:
> The honor of the responsibility for pressing the
> button is enough for me.

NEW ARRIVAL:
> Indeed! Which finger do you press it with?

SUPERVISOR:
> This one.

NEW ARRIVAL:
> Make a statue of it.

SUPERVISOR:
> That would be a great idea. What would I do with-
> out it?

NEW ARRIVAL:
> Press with another finger. You have ten.

SUPERVISOR:
> Of course, I meant the button.

NEW ARRIVAL:

What could you do without the button?

SUPERVISOR:

Yes?

NEW ARRIVAL:

You'd be like me. You'd sit down, order dinner and end up not eating.

SUPERVISOR:

Heaven forbid!

NEW ARRIVAL:

Indeed, now you can choose to press the button, or not to press it.

SUPERVISOR:

No, that's not true.

NEW ARRIVAL:

Do you want to know what I think of you?

SUPERVISOR:

No.

NEW ARRIVAL:

Wouldn't you like to hear?

SUPERVISOR:

It doesn't interest me.

NEW ARRIVAL:

But if I said it, you would hear it against your will.

SUPERVISOR:

It's all the same to me.

NEW ARRIVAL:

Then I'll tell you what I think of you, so long as I am not going to eat.

SUPERVISOR:

I can't prevent you. The use of violence is forbidden.

NEW ARRIVAL:

You are a bastard!

SUPERVISOR:

I have instructions not to respond to any provocation, especially coming from somebody whose presence in the hotel is doubtful and one hundred percent temporary.

NEW ARRIVAL:

Me?

SUPERVISOR:
> Yes, you!

NEW ARRIVAL:
> *(Rushing at him)* Who told you that?

SUPERVISOR:
> Nobody did. Look around you and you'll know. Nothing
> belongs to you, and you belong to nothing.

NEW ARRIVAL:
> Me? I was here before you. You yourself and those
> who employ you are here because of me, me alone. I
> was here before them, before they were born, before
> all the machines and the gadgets. My roots run very,
> very deep into the earth. My history is long. I was
> here before the world, before the ax and the sail
> and the plow; before Judas, Brutus, Franco, Musso-
> lini and Hitler; before Cortez or Rhodes or Nietz-
> sche the ingenious. I am a struggling desert plant
> that is impossible to destroy or exterminate. I...
> a drop of water is enough for me because my roots
> have struck deep into the earth, into the rocks,
> into the burning center of the earth. Yes, into the
> burning center of the earth!

SUPERVISOR:
> Please, spare your words a little.

NEW ARRIVAL:
> For the second time, for the second time, spare my
> words?

SUPERVISOR:
> It's of no use.

NEW ARRIVAL:
> It's of no use! *(To himself)* A strange feeling of
> smallness, a terrifying feeling of loneliness, a
> great game, but my legs are paralyzed. I cannot
> run, and must stand on the line, my eyes blind; I
> can neither look nor see. How? How did all this
> happen? When? Where was I?

SUPERVISOR:
> *(Tenderly, as he approaches him.)* Do you want to
> press a button?

NEW ARRIVAL:
> Me? Impossible!

SUPERVISOR:

    I must leave you without completing the procedures.
I have things to do.

NEW ARRIVAL:

    (With utter contempt) What things? Won't they find
somebody else to press the button. Anybody can
press the button. *(Sarcastically)* I, for instance,
can press ten buttons.

SUPERVISOR:

    Those big words are not going to be of any use. Are
you with us in...

NEW ARRIVAL:

    I don't feel like doing anything.

SUPERVISOR:

    Then I have to proceed with the measures.

NEW ARRIVAL:

    Shut up! It is a beautiful day; don't spoil it by
your buzzing. A bee hive! Accursed lines of bees
that never heard of fatigue or suffering or pain...
And the mountain is silent, crimson, red like
blood...The color of turquoise, chrysolite and all
gems. And the procession of history above it, and
the lines of the dead in hearses underneath, and
beautiful, smooth lizards, brilliant with red and
blue eyes, and a solitary fig tree on the mount of
fire, with silence all around.

SUPERVISOR:

    I have to...

NEW ARRIVAL:

    Shut up! The food be damned! On the mountain and
underneath it is inspiration enough for a million
historians and a thousand million poets.

SUPERVISOR:

    As for poetry, we have a definite view about that.

NEW ARRIVAL:

    Shut up! Even if the price should be that I starve
to death!

SUPERVISOR:

    What is certain is that I won't press the button.

NEW ARRIVAL:

    (Laughing sarcastically) Very worried about your

button, as if there is nothing in the world but
your button.

SUPERVISOR:

The world is made up of millions of buttons, and
this is one of them.

NEW ARRIVAL:

May they all be damned until the Day of Judgment!

SUPERVISOR:

It is obvious that I will not...

NEW ARRIVAL:

Press the button. Allow me to go and press it.

SUPERVISOR:

No, you are the last person fit for that job.

NEW ARRIVAL:

(Sarcastically) Really!

SUPERVISOR:

Absolutely!

NEW ARRIVAL:

I will give you ten years of my life if you tell
me why.

SUPERVISOR:

*(Suddenly jumps on the other chair, produces a piece
of paper from his pocket and holds an imaginary
microphone in his hand. He reads in a voice which is
too loud.)* Genus number four, species number two,
group seven: referred to in dictionaries under the
name...under the name...*(stammering)*, it doesn't
matter. Has lost its time-space relationships. Lost
contact with the inevitable historical development
which determines the relationship between a body
in motion, and the speed and time between them.
Suffers from several ailments, all of which can be
treated only in sanitoriums for incurable diseases.
It is a dull static body, the potential energy
within which cannot be converted into dynamic
energy. The high electric tension in it, which
amounts to one hundred fifty thousand volts, is exhausted within centripetal circles and random cur-
rents revolving around essential axes which represent thought and action, a matter which makes it
impossible to convert thought into power without

first converting it into motion. *(He folds the paper and speaks directly to him.)* Because anybody could convince you to press the button. Because you might press the button out of humanitarian motives or pity, which in the final analysis are nothing but individual hostile attitudes. Because, motivated by a lack of conviction, which in fact is a failure to submit to any system or commitment, you might break the laws, disregard the rules, and press the button. Because at all times you have an inflated awareness of your own ego, an illusion that you are above the multitudes, that you are rare, that you are extremely important...*(Folds the paper, puts it away and gets down from the chair.)* I have heard the likes of you shouting as they were going up to the gallows, "I am the State."

NEW ARRIVAL:

(Now seriously worried) Louis XIV used to say, "I am the State."

SUPERVISOR:

Louis XIV was revolutionary and progressive when compared to the historical circumstances around him.

NEW ARRIVAL:

Couldn't I also be revolutionary and progressive when compared to the historical circumstances around me?

SUPERVISOR:

I have received no instructions concerning this subject.

NEW ARRIVAL:

Does that mean if you receive instructions, I could be revolutionary?

SUPERVISOR:

Of course.

NEW ARRIVAL:

And progressive.

SUPERVISOR:

Of course.

NEW ARRIVAL:

And great and glorious and immortal?

SUPERVISOR:

>Of course.

NEW ARRIVAL:

>Disregarding the historical circumstances surround-
>ing me?

SUPERVISOR:

>It is obvious you are not hungry.

NEW ARRIVAL:

>No, I have a ravenous hunger. Upon your father's
>honor, I have eaten nothing for the last two days.
>Yet, it seems the problem here is much greater and
>much more profound than hunger.

SUPERVISOR:

>See?

NEW ARRIVAL:

>See what?

SUPERVISOR:

>As I told you! My diagnoisis was correct. You are
>incapable of concentrating on and solving even a
>simple problem such as that of hunger. Imagine
>that you are responsible for feeding others! You
>had to complicate it and get yourself into problems
>that you don't need!

NEW ARRIVAL:

>No, that was just talk.

SUPERVISOR:

>My memory is better than a book.

NEW ARRIVAL:

>I didn't say anything to displease anybody.

SUPERVISOR:

>And you didn't say anthing to please anybody.

NEW ARRIVAL:

>I don't know.

SUPERVISOR:

>But I believe that what you said will please some-
>body! What is certain is that this somebody is not
>here!

NEW ARRIVAL:

>(Laughs, then realizes part of the grave meaning.)
>Me? No...

SUPERVISOR:

>Because I have learned from personal experience

that anything that is said must ultimately please
somebody.

NEW ARRIVAL:

(Scared) No, impossible, I am above suspicion!
I am known!

SUPERVISOR:

I don't know . . .

NEW ARRIVAL:

No, anyone but me. Anyone but me.

SUPERVISOR:

Is this a law of physics?

NEW ARRIVAL:

(Trying to take the edge off it) It is just talk
between you and me.

SUPERVISOR:

No, look at the mountain.

NEW ARRIVAL:

Oh, the trucks are coming down by the thousands.

SUPERVISOR:

Loaded with men.

NEW ARRIVAL:

Coming to eat!

SUPERVISOR:

And you are delaying them. Look behind this curtain!

NEW ARRIVAL:

All those people sitting there, waiting. They are
all looking at me, with exasperation and anger in
their eyes.

SUPERVISOR:

Because you are delaying them. They take turns
eating here, and here I am standing with you, for
I don't know how long.

NEW ARRIVAL:

I didn't know.

SUPERVISOR:

Had it not been for the security measures . . .

NEW ARRIVAL:

(Interrupting) I didn't know. Why didn't you draw
it to my attention. Go to them before they do something because of their hunger!

SUPERVISOR:

No, they have never done anything like that.

NEW ARRIVAL:

But I don't want them to have any wrong ideas
about me, or imagine that I am their enemy. It is
very important that they have a good opinion of me,
that they know I am not responsible for...

SUPERVISOR:

You are responsible.

NEW ARRIVAL:

I didn't know.

SUPERVISOR:

That does not relieve you of the responsibility.

NEW ARRIVAL:

Responsibility! Responsibility! For an hour now you
have been standing here talking like a machine,
saying nothing to cheer a man's heart, and with
not one particle of humanity in your face. You
neither smiled nor got mad, nor did your face show
any feeling. Oh my God! It would have been impossible for my mother when she gave birth to me
to imagine that I would be...that I would be...
(As if talking to himself) Nor is this the way for
dreams to come true, nor the words, spoken or
written, to be interpreted. No, not this at all.
*(From outside voices of men singing loudly and
clearly. With obvious anxiety)* Give me a cigarette.

SUPERVISOR:

The packet is right in front of you.

NEW ARRIVAL:

I should take a cigarette before the cigarette
becomes part of the machine. *(He listens to the
signing and his sense of isolation increases.
He smokes quickly and frequently. The hand holding
his cigarette shakes.)*

SUPERVISOR:

You most definitely are not with us in the hotel!

NEW ARRIVAL:

I am! I most definitely am, whether you like it
or not.

SUPERVISOR:

The ticket?

NEW ARRIVAL:

The conductor saw me, and the driver. All the

thousands of people on the train noticed me. My
face is unforgettable. I am different in every way
from them, in my dress, my manner of speaking,
my words...

SUPERVISOR:

We don't take people's testimony.

NEW ARRIVAL:

No, a lot of people saw me. In Rosetta, Alexandria,
el-Tell el-Kebir, Imbaba, everywhere. In Port
Said, Ismailia, the people at al-Azhar, Husseinia,
Megharbleen, every one of them.

SUPERVISOR:

The ticket?

NEW ARRIVAL:

I told you I threw it away.

SUPERVISOR:

I am very sorry.

NEW ARRIVAL:

I can go and look for it.

SUPERVISOR:

Sorry.

NEW ARRIVAL:

Why? Why shouldn't I go and look for it?

SUPERVISOR:

Because it is impossible for you to find it. The
red iron mountain and all the equipment on it
throw dust and particles on the ground, the
streets, the houses, and the sands in the desert
at the rate of 00.001 mm per hour, and you have
been here for three hours. The ticket has been
covered over and it is impossible for you or anyone else to find it. It has disappeared for good.

NEW ARRIVAL:

(With hatred) Everything is measured to the last
millimeter and gram! He cannot give you an atom
of hope.

SUPERVISOR:

These statistics are compiled as the result of
scientific experiments.

NEW ARRIVAL:

He cannot give you one atom of hope! Let me go
and look for it.

SUPERVISOR:

    It's no use.

NEW ARRIVAL:

    Perhaps one in a million.

SUPERVISOR:

    Impossible!

NEW ARRIVAL:

    What? You mean I can't get out of here?

SUPERVISOR:

    I don't know...but...

NEW ARRIVAL:

    You mean I...

SUPERVISOR:

    (Interrupting) Regrettably!

NEW ARRIVAL:

    What is the charge?

SUPERVISOR:

    I either fill out the form completely and press
the button or...

NEW ARRIVAL:

    Does that mean no food and no going out?

SUPERVISOR:

    It is not that definite.

NEW ARRIVAL:

    Then let's talk about the razor and the blade.

SUPERVISOR:

    I'll have to consult somebody. I'll call the
Expert.

NEW ARRIVAL:

    No, no, don't call the Expert! Not because I am
afraid of him, may his father be damned a thousand
times! I don't want him to come, although I don't
know him, because at this moment I have an insane desire for silence; because I want to look
at the night and feel the beauty and the quiet
and the peace, even if the price is my life; because I want to look at the distant white horizon
and the sky and the sun. And the sun is a mad
animal burning and throwing fire on the earth.

SUPERVISOR:

    I advise you to spare your words a little.

NEW ARRIVAL:

Because what is the value of man? Where is the essence? Where is the reason for existence, if the price of his life is a ticket that he threw from a train window? *(He bursts out crying. The Supervisor withdraws backstage. Lighting dims out until there is a complete blackout. The stage is lighted after a few moments. The New Arrival raises his eyes; he is now terribly exhausted.)* Oh, it seems I am very important.

EXPERT:

How do you do?

NEW ARRIVAL:

I threw my ticket away, and you don't take testimony of...

EXPERT:

(Very politely interrupting) Excuse me?

NEW ARRIVAL:

I am sorry. I am supposed to speak only when I am asked to.

EXPERT:

No, no, who said that?

NEW ARRIVAL:

And if I answer, then my answer should be precisely to the point.

EXPERT:

Allow me...

NEW ARRIVAL:

And laughter for no reason is bad manners. It is all written on the back of the Arabic composition themebook. I got six out of ten. A vile teacher. The boy who was first in our class wrote on a trip to Switzerland, and I wrote on the second theme, a plough's discussion with a tractor. I proved that the tractor was a thousand times better than a plough. I got six out of ten, the bastard! The other boy wrote about a trip to Switzerland, and said that minarets are covered with clouds and fog. The ass thought there were minarets in Switzerland, and the teacher gave him ten out of ten. He himself didn't know. I told him and he beat me. *(Laughs sadly, then turns his back to the Expert and walks off.)*

EXPERT:

> (*Seriously*) In Geneva there is one minaret at least, and maybe two.

NEW ARRIVAL:

> (*Turns toward him as soon as he hears him.*) You are Hassan.

EXPERT:

> And you are Hamdy! (*They rush towards each other and hug.*)

NEW ARRIVAL:

> (*On the point of tears*) You are here and yet you did not come to see me! They tormented me terribly. They would like me to pay for a morsel of bread with my life. Where were you? Where were you, man?

EXPERT:

> How are you, Hamdy?

NEW ARRIVAL:

> (*Eagerly*) Listen, Hassan, before you open your mouth with one word, I'll ask you one question which you must answer, and then we can talk at leisure, as much as we like. Ever since I arrived, the people here have been using a language that I have never heard before, nor ever imagined that anyone spoke. (*The Expert tries to speak.*) No, no, wait. "Are you with us in the hotel? Are you with us in the hotel? Are you with us in the hotel?" No, no, no, don't explain anything, because one can explain anything on earth. Wait, I'll ask you one question and everything after that will depend on your answer. You are Hassan. Do you work with a button?

EXPERT:

> (*Immediately and simply*) Of course!

NEW ARRIVAL:

> (*Collapses on the chair and puts his head between his hands.*)

EXPERT

> (*Puts his hand on the New Arrival's shoulder and speaks very tenderly.*) Hamdy.

NEW ARRIVAL:

> Leave me, leave me a while. (*The Expert presses a button. Ringing of bell is heard.*) No, don't call anyone,

a doctor or anyone at all. I am not sick. Let's be alone and talk for five minutes only like everybody else. We are old friends. But leave me a while until I come to.

EXPERT:

As you wish. *(He presses another button which gives a different sound. Hamdy laughs and soon the Expert joins in with him. They laugh for a while and then hug.)* How are you, man, haven't seen you in years.

NEW ARRIVAL:

Nor I. Ten years or more! Damn all the buttons and machines. How are you? Where have you been hiding?

EXPERT:

Here.

NEW ARRIVAL:

Here? Doing what?

EXPERT:

(Laughs) As you see.

NEW ARRIVAL:

In the mountain? It's been a long time.

EXPERT:

What about you? What do you do? I haven't seen you for twenty years. Yes, twenty years now! What do you do now? Where do you work? With whom?

NEW ARRIVAL:

Eh...Twenty years, and thousands upon thousands of men as rapacious as lions, and I in front on their shoulders facing the guns. *(With great sorrow)* Eh...

EXPERT:

Yes, you feared nothing! By the way, my sister Hosnia used to like you a lot.

NEW ARRIVAL:

Hosnia? Where is Hosnia now, by the way?

EXPERT:

Here.

NEW ARRIVAL:

Honestly? Working?

EXPERT:

Of course, do you think she came as a tourist?

NEW ARRIVAL:
> *(Sadly)* Hosnia, *(Self-pitying)* she was like a
> flower, tender and beautiful.

EXPERT:
> To this very day. Today she may be more beautiful,
> and she certainly is more tender.

NEW ARRIVAL:
> Is she married?

EXPERT:
> Of course. *(Pause)* Hamdy, what's wrong? What hap-
> pened? What did you do all these years?

NEW ARRIVAL:
> *(Walks away, laughing.)* Whenever I start walking
> in an avenue, I find it crowded, so I have to keep
> looking for a side lane in order to arrive...

EXPERT:
> You know something, you are a poet. We have a
> shortage of poets.

NEW ARRIVAL:
> I don't think you care much about poets.

EXPERT:
> No, no, you are mistaken. By the way I discovered
> a strange thing. Whenever a situation calls for
> a song, a song just happens. One day after the
> other you find people singing it. Where did it
> come from? Who wrote it? Nobody knows, not even
> those who sing it. How are you, Hamdy?

NEW ARRIVAL:
> I am fine. How are you Hassan? Do you have a
> good position now?

EXPERT:
> *(Laughing)* I drop asleep like a corpse. You are
> with us in the hotel, of course?

NEW ARRIVAL:
> Hassan, dear friend, if you respect our old friend-
> ship, please postpone the questions for a while.

EXPERT:
> Impossible! I have to do this, because when I
> press the button...

NEW ARRIVAL:
> *(Shouting excitedly)* Button?

EXPERT:
> Of course!

NEW ARRIVAL:
    Machine?
EXPERT:
    (Relatively exasperated) Of course!
NEW ARRIVAL:
    A machine. The only means of communication is the
    button.
EXPERT:
    Of course.
NEW ARRIVAL:
    (Savagely) It's an infernal machine, the work of
    the devil. Destroy it, man, and get me the food!
    I am Hamdy, your mate and comrade throughout the
    years of struggle, and I am hungry. I can't go
    hungry for the sake of a filthy machine invented
    by a bastard of a man. Destroy it and all the
    chains it has created.
EXPERT:
    (Smiling as if listening to a child) Is that
    possible?
NEW ARRIVAL:
    Destroy the machine and don't worry. You are
    Hassan; you yourself overturned a truck loaded
    with those dogs of Englishmen at Qasr el-Nil.
    Hassan, you are a hero. Destroy the machine and
    get me the food.
EXPERT:
    And when we destroy the machine, who will set us
    to work?
NEW ARRIVAL:
    The machine sets you to work? You?
EXPERT:
    Of course, it does everything, organization,
    distribution...
NEW ARRIVAL:
    (Interrupting) And you? What do you do? What is
    your role?
EXPERT:
    I press a button.
NEW ARRIVAL:
    You? You press a button?

EXPERT:

> And the whole mountain is made up of a number of
> buttons.

NEW ARRIVAL:

> It is a mean and trivial job when a man's whole
> function in life is to press a button!

EXPERT:

> No, there is no such thing as a mean and trivial
> job, or an exalted one. Any work done by man is
> noble. No kind of work is better than another. An
> astronaut is no better than a man who plants two
> stalks of mulukhiyya, and the world cannot do
> without either. Work is an honor!

NEW ARRIVAL:

> Stop! Slogans, slogans, slogans!

EXPERT:

> That is a fact, Hamdy.

NEW ARRIVAL:

> Please stop! Your words give me a stomachache!

EXPERT:

> No, you are mistaken. I have to feed all the data
> about you to the machine. In order for it to give
> me the food, I have to tell it everything, your
> life history, your position, and the job you do...

NEW ARRIVAL:

> I am your brother. We grew up, both of us, in the
> same house.

EXPERT:

> I am very sorry. I have to give the complete
> data, and the work you do, to the machine...

NEW ARRIVAL:

> (*Exasperated to the point of madness*) And without
> these data, my whole existence becomes doubtful?
> I become non-existent altogether?

EXPERT:

> Here, at least.

NEW ARRIVAL:

> I become nonexistent altogether, unborn, my mother
> did not give birth to me, my name is not Hamdy,
> and I am neither speaking to you, nor are you
> answering me?

EXPERT:

> Here, at least. You know how I feel towards you.

NEW ARRIVAL:
  How much is the worth of what you feel towards me
  in the slave market?
EXPERT:
  You know my feeling towards you.
NEW ARRIVAL:
  And I spit on your feeling towards me. My blood has
  mixed with yours in the years of struggle.
EXPERT:
  All these things have no meaning. When will you
  realize that?
NEW ARRIVAL:
  I spit on every word coming out of your mouth.
EXPERT:
  (With annoyance) You must stop these bombastic words!
NEW ARRIVAL:
  These bombastic words are me.
EXPERT:
  No, you used to be far greater than all the bombastic
  words in the world.
NEW ARRIVAL:
  I still am. I still am. I wish a thousand times I had
  died before seeing you. You with your whole life and
  livlihood, and that of your children, depending on a
  button. Your finger your only capital, your only means
  of making a living! And your mind? Your mind is a
  garbage can!
EXPERT:
  Listen, I would like to give you some advice.
NEW ARRIVAL:
  I spit on every bit of advice coming out of your
  mouth!
EXPERT:
  Spit if it makes you feel better.
NEW ARRIVAL:
  Shut up! I don't want to hear one word from you!
EXPERT:
  Hamdy!
NEW ARRIVAL:
  Shut up! Every word coming from your mouth will bury
  one virtue. Every word out of your mouth is a dagger
  directed...

EXPERT:

> (*Interrupting*) What crime has been commited against you?

NEW ARRIVAL:

> What ARE the crimes committed against me?

EXPERT:

> What are the crimes committed against you?

NEW ARRIVAL:

> Your name, the train, the ticket, the horse-cab, the time--as if I were a nonentity.

EXPERT:

> You are a nonentity.

NEW ARRIVAL:

> No, I am not a nonentity. I am not a nonentity at all. Ask about me...

EXPERT:

> (*Interrupting*) Ask the tens of thousands here, ask them one by one, see who will know you.

NEW ARRIVAL:

> To hell with them! I·know myself, and that is enough, and anyone who asks to see my I.D. is a bastard, and a bastard is anyone who asks me, "Are you with us in the hotel?" A bastard and three times a bastard! (*He collapses on the chair. The Expert runs to him. Feebly*) I am tired...very tired.

EXPERT:

> Shall I get you some coffee?

NEW ARRIVAL:

> (*Feebly*) No, it is too serious to be solved by coffee.

EXPERT:

> Have a cigarette. (*The mountain is lighted in the background.*)

NEW ARRIVAL:

> No. Between the problem of food and that of existence itself, there is no opportunity for a choice, and every problem conceals other problems that appear to be simple, but which are more terrible.

EXPERT:

> I will appeal to the bosses to issue you some food.

NEW ARRIVAL:

> No, no, no, not in this manner. I either am or am

not. I am here and I exist in this hotel, and there
is no power on earth that can nullify my existence.
It is impossible, even in hell itself,. that my existence can be determined by a ticket that i threw
away, and which was buried under the dust blowing
from the iron mountain. No. It is impossible. Not
even if I lose an identification card with my name,
my father's name, my mother's name, my address, job,
position, and all that nonsense. It is impossible
that this should make me nonexistent. I am! I am!
I am here. *(The Agent appears as if called by the
shouting of the New Arrival. He stops, holding his
briefcase and with a cigarette dangling from his
lips. The New Arrival sees him, rushes at him and
grabs him violently by his jacket, pulling him to
the center of the stage.)* You! Tell them who I am!
Tell them at what hour you met me and when and
where you were going. Tell them you know me, my
name, my father's name, my mother's name, my grandfather and great grandfather, my wife's name, when
and how and why I married her, and my telephone number. Open your notebook and you will find my telephone number, which you wrote down as you were leaving. You couldn't have forgotten. We talked about
work, and just to remind you, you advised me to
work in Mikhail Roman's hotel.

AGENT:

This is Mikhail Roman's hotel.

NEW ARRIVAL:

I don't care. Tell them we met, and that we are old
friends, and that you had come by invitation--the
ticket and the air conditioning. *(The Agent does not
seem to be affected. He does not speak.)* No, it is
impossible that you should have forgotten. *(To the
Expert)* I am not a liar. I am not a liar at all.
The first waiter saw me sitting with him, and he
knows him. Call him and he will testify for me. He
recommended me to him. *(Points to the Agent.)* He
knows which train I took. *(Nobody moves or speaks;
he backs away from both, looking at them at the
same time.)* No! No! No! The world must have changed
while I was not looking. The world has become full

of bastards, everybody a bastard. *(The Waiter, the Supervisor, and a number of people arrive on the scene. Lights brighten the background behind the window, and the side curtains of the stage. The center of the stage remains dim.)*
You, one by one, I despise you! You are all slaves, nonentities, creatures that have no talents or ambitions or dreams; herds that want to live any kind of life with bigger herds in any unknown place, lost from history. *(In a state of panic)* I am free! I am free! I have broken all my chains, and I am free of the ticket, the I.D., and the suitcase. I couldn't care less for all you do, nor does it move a single hair on my head. Greater than all you can do is a line in a poem, or a song sung by a virgin, or a wild rose in the wilderness. And you and all the machines, the buttons, the gadgets, and the equipment are nothing but symptoms of the degeneration of this age, the age of fingers, buttons, and machines of steel. *(Pause)* There is nothing more beautiful than a plough in the hands of an ancient Egyptian peasant, or sweeter than a spindle of wool in the hands of a white-haired old man. All beauty may be found in the weeping waterwheels and sad palm trees in narrow lanes, where the old women wear black as if they were in an ancient Egyptian tomb of the days of Ramses. And I am alone! Ah? I hear somebody saying "What do you crave?" Somebody is saying "What do you crave?" *(Everybody looks on without moving. His panic and violence have now reached their extreme.)*

Somebody is saying "What do you crave?" No, I don't want to die...I don't want to die...No, no, no, no, nobody ask me "What do you crave?" I don't want anybody to ask me "What do you crave?" No! No! No! No!

Curtain

A JOURNEY OUTSIDE THE WALL

A play in three acts

by

Rashad Rushdy

Cast of Characters

Uncle Kamel.........A lawyer who has retired early be-
    cause of "family circumstances."
Mahassen...........Kamel's daughter. She is engaged to
    Farid.
Said...............Kamel's son.
Karima.............Said's wife.
Shahira............Kamel's deceased wife. In the play
    she "appears" only to Abul Uyun.
Abul Uyun..........Shahira's cousin and a relative of
    Kamel's. His name literally means "the one who has
    eyes." He is blind.
Farid..............Kamel's nephew who is engaged to
    Mahassen. He is a young engineer.
Hamed..............Farid's younger brother, a school-
    teacher and writer.
Zakya..............A servant girl in Uncle Kamel's house.
Sundus.............A servant boy in Uncle Kamel's house.
Youssef............A friend of Farid's.
Selim..............A journalist.
Kharboutli.........Senior engineer
Mumtaz.............Senior engineer
Senior engineers and members of the Engineers' Council:
Agib...Labib...Muhib...Gharib...Hasib...Shakib...Mugib...
Munib...Habib...Naqib.
Nasib..............Clerk to the Engineers' Council.
People of the town: Dr. Lam'i...Sha'lan...Sarhan...Sheikh
Tannir...Halawa...Zaki...Others (chorus).

Act I

(A hall in Uncle Kamel's home in a small town. Time:
11 a.m. Abul Uyun is sitting in his chair wearing a
striped galabiya and a cap. It looks as if he is asleep.
He has on a large pair of sunglasses. At the end of the
hall is a parlor which opens to the garden in which various trees and two tall palm trees appear. The parlor has
two entrances leading to the garden and also to the
upper floor. The hall has three doors for the rooms of
Shahira, Kamel and Abul Uyun. At the rear of the stage,
near the parlor, Zakya is playing with a small ball.)

ZAKYA:
 (Playing with the ball and speaking with a childish
 lisp) One red and one green, and one green and one
 red...
 (The door to Shahira's room opens and she comes out
 with her hair down and wearing a white night gown.)
SHAHIRA:
 (To Abul Uyun) Do you see this ring? So is our love
 ...
ZAKYA:
 One red and one green...
SHAHIRA:
 It has no beginning and no end...
 (The door to Uncle Kamel's room to the left opens
 and he comes out wearing a white galabiya and a cap.)
KAMEL:
 (Calling) Zakya! Zakya! (He sees her.) It's no use!

She's having her fit. *(He enters his room and slams the door shut.)*

ZAKYA:

(Approaching Abul Uyun) One red and one green...

SHAHIRA:

Don't look at me like that. I can't! *(Going back to her room)* I can't! *(She enters her room and closes the door.)*

ZAKYA:

One green... *(The ball falls into Abul Uyun's lap. She reaches out her hand to pick it up from his lap, unaware of his existence. He grabs her hand. She tries to release it.)* Let go of me! Let go of my arm!

ABUL UYUN:

Come to your sense, Zakya, won't you?

ZAKYA:

Give me the ball. It's my ball.

ABUL UYUN:

Girl!

ZAKYA:

(With childish nervousness) Let go of my hand! The ball...*(She stamps the ground with her feet, trying to get away from him.)* The ball... *(Louder)* My ball...

ABUL UYUN:

(Lets go of her hand and throws the ball on the floor.) You and your ball can go to hell! Go to hell!

ZAKYA:

(Picks up the ball and starts to walk in the direction of the exit while playing.) One red and one green...one red... *(The shrill neighing of a horse is heard. On hearing this Zakya stands in the center of the stage then turns to face Abul Uyun and addresses him without any trace of her earlier childish lisp, but rather slut-like.)* What could this horse be wanting now, Master Abul Uyun? Since the first day they brought it here, it hasn't stopped neighing. *(Approaching Abul Uyun, and speaking in a rather friendly tone.)* Could it be that something is bothering it? Or perhaps it craves something or other? *(Standing in front of him)* What did

you say, Master Abul Uyun? *(She stands so close to him now that she almost touches him. Playfully)* You are so silent today. You are not talking... *(The neighing of the horse is heard again, louder.)*

KAMEL:

(From his room) Sundus! Sundus! Abul Uyun! Sundus! *(Sundus comes in.)*

ZAKYA:

(As soon as she sees Sundus she rushes towards him. Seductively) Sundus! Sundus! Sundus! *(Approaching him)* Oh my!

SUNDUS:

Contain yourself, Girl! Contain yourself! *(The horse neighs. Sundus exits hurriedly to the garden. Zakya hurries back to Abul Uyun.)*

KAMEL:

(From his room) Sundus! Sundus!

ABUL UYUN:

Give me your hand.

ZAKYA:

(Gives him her hand. He leans on it to stand up, then walks by her side, leaning on her. She leads him out.) Did you hear, Master Abul Uyun? Did you hear what Sundus said?

ABUL UYUN:

What did he say?

ZAKYA:

He says that Shihab, the horse, is neighing so wildly because it wants to jump over the fence, but can't do it. *(Laughs with obvious playfulness.)* And how could it? The fence is high. Could anybody jump the fence? *(Horse neighs.)* What a silly horse!

ABUL UYUN:

(As they go out) Don't bother about it. It's a jackass of a horse!

KAMEL:

(As he comes out of his room) Abul Uyun. *(He looks at Abul Uyun's chair.)* Where did that man go? Well, he must have gone to see about the horse. *(He sees Zakya's ball and picks it up.)* Are you here? Then he didn't go to see about the horse. This horse is driving me crazy. All the other horses are quiet. *(He looks at the ball in his hand.)* Aha...she must

have come to her senses. Ha...*(Changes his tone
suddenly)* But what is so strange? Yes, what is so
strange, your Honors? Isn't murder death, and is
death not murder? Either we punish nobody at all
or we punish everybody! This is justice indeed!
(Shouting loudly) Acquitted! Acquitted! Ha, ha, ha...
(Hamed and Karima enter talking.)

HAMED:

Is Capri beautiful?

KARIMA:

It's wonderful! The sea there is blue and vast. Why
isn't the world as open as the sea, Hamed? And the
songs of the Italians, the joy and the love...

HAMED:

Love? How did you know they were love songs?

KARIMA:

The way they sang.

HAMED:

Erotic?

KARIMA:

I don't mean love in that sense.

HAMED:

What's wrong with love in that sense?

KAMEL:

(Approaching her) When did you go to Capri, Karima?

KARIMA:

I went a lot of places. I've been to India, China,
France and Japan. I've been everywhere.

KAMEL:

How come? Your father, may God have mercy on his
soul, was employed by the Cairo court and not by
the diplomatic service. With whom then did you tour
the world?

KARIMA:

Alone, Uncle Kamel. *(Dreamily)* Alone.

KAMEL:

Alone? When?

HAMED:

(Laughing) She dreams it, Uncle, dreams. She tours
the world without moving one step.

KARIMA:

(Approaching Kamel tenderly) You know, Uncle, you
should do like me.

KAMEL:

    (Roughly) Do like you?

KARIMA:

    (Gently again) Yes, tour the world instead of sitting there all day doing nothing.

KAMEL:

    (Laughing sarcastically and self-pityingly) May God forgive you, Karima! I toured the world before you were born and in reality, not in dreams.

KARIMA:

    (Teasing) When was that?

KAMEL:

    A long time ago. When the world was still good.

KARIMA:

    (Gently) When you were Kamel Bey Abdel Geleel, the big lawyer--before you were pensioned off--my father used to talk to us about you all the time.

KAMEL:

    (Interrupting) I was not pensioned off, Karima.

HAMED:

    (Trying to change the subject) There you are, Karima. Uncle Kamel can tell you what he saw instead of...

KARIMA:

    Tell me, Uncle, did you go on that tour as I did on mine, alone?

KAMEL:

    Why this question?

KARIMA:

    Because I always travel alone. Tell me, really, with whom did you travel?

KAMEL:

    (Looking at Shahira's room) With her.

KARIMA:

    (In surprise) Really?

KAMEL:

    She loved travelling!

KARIMA:

    (Trying to overcome her surprise) And you?

KAMEL:

    I loved it for her sake.

KARIMA:

    (Absently) Impossible!

KAMEL:

What is impossible?

KARIMA:

Impossible...that Said should agree to travel for my sake. He refuses to take me with him anywhere. Why does he travel so much, Uncle?

KAMEL:

Doesn't he tell you?

HAMED:

Business, it must be for business.

KARIMA:

He's been away for the last twenty-five days. Where does he go, Uncle?

KAMEL:

I don't know.

KARIMA:

He said he'd be away for one week only. Why do you think he is taking so long?

KAMEL:

(Roughly) I told you I don't know. I don't know anything about him. Didn't I? *(He goes to his room sulking.)*

HAMED:

(Trying to change the subject) Tell me, where is the next trip going to be?

KARIMA:

You know, Hamed, the one place I really long to see is the other side. I'd love so much to see it!

HAMED:

So you've toured the whole world and still haven't seen the other bank? You must be...
(Enter Farid. Karima rises quickly to meet him.)

KARIMA:

Hello, Farid. You stayed a long time in Cairo.
(Enter Abul Uyun)

Hamed:

Well! How did it go?

FARID:

(Calmly) Didn't I tell you?

HAMED:

What did you tell me? It was I who told you.

FARID:

(Disapprovingly) What did you tell me? On the con-

trary, it was I who told you.

HAMED:

Didn't I tell you it was no use?

FARID:

Who told you it was no use?

HAMED:

Impossible! Do you mean to tell me that your efforts resulted in something?

KARIMA:

What happened, Farid?

FARID:

The committee came with me.

HAMED:

Committee?

FARID:

An investigative committee composed of two directors...

HAMED:

Wonderful! You're a smart one, my Brother. How come I don't take after you? (Almost to himself) But It's a miracle! Where are they now?

FARID:

They are inspecting the piers. I thought I'd leave them alone so they wouldn't think I was trying to influence them.

KARIMA:

I was sure you'd win. Didn't I tell you, Hamed?

HAMED:

I don't believe it. I swear I don't believe it. But why did you leave them alone? Nobody can tell what...

FARID:

I'll join them shortly so we can write the report.

HAMED:

You said we?

FARID:

Yes, of course. The ministry has appointed me to the investigation committee.

KARIMA:

Bravo, Farid.

HAMED:

You must've pulled some strings, and very good ones at that!

FARID:

Absolutely nothing of the sort. It's quite natural.

HAMED:

Natural? How is it natural?

FARID:

To begin with, I have no personal interest in removing the piers. Secondly, the piers are sitting
there for anybody who cares to see and know immediately that they are defective, no good. Besides,
there is nothing between me and Sherif Sami, the
engineer who built the piers. I never saw him or
even heard his name before I was transferred here
to take over the bridge project.
(Kamel enters and walks over to Abul Uyun.)

HAMED:

Right, but who can tell what is right from what is
wrong?

KAMEL

(To Abul Uyun) Did you come, my Friend?

KARIMA:

And after you write your report, Farid, what
happens?

ABUL UYUN:

(To Kamel) Do you know who's in town?

FARID:

They'll remove the existing piers and then we'll
build good, new ones.

KAMEL:

Who?

KARIMA:

And you'll build the bridge?

ABUL UYUN:

Abdel Salem Bey...

FARID:

And I'll build the bridge.

KAMEL:

Abdel Salam who?

KARIMA:

And take us to the other side?

ABUL UYUN:

Abdel Salam Mashhoor, my cousin. Shahira's brother.

FARID:

(Simply) Yes , of course!

KAMEL:
>What's he doing in town?

KARIMA:
>You mean I will go to the other side, Farid?

ABUL UYUN:
>He's selling the last thirty acres of Shahira's land.

FARID:
>Why shouldn't you go to the other side? All you have to do is cross the bridge.

HAMED:
>Miracle worker!

ABUL UYUN:
>It was wrong of you to give up your share...but anyway, it was the price for the acquittal.

KAMEL:
>Price of the acquittal? Have you taken their side now?

KARIMA:
>The other side is beautiful, isn't it, Farid?

ABUL UYUN:
>What's come over you, Kamel? Have you forgotten, or what?

FARID:
>Much more beautiful than here. You know what you could do? Build yourselves a little house there where you and Said could live.

KAMEL:
>(Feebly) No, I haven't forgotten. I haven't forgotten, my Friend. How could I forget?

KARIMA:
>(Dreamily, melancholic) Said and I!

HAMED:
>I tell you, you're a miracle worker!

KAMEL:
>Could I forget that your father disinherited you because you stood by me?

FARID:
>What miracles? Is it a miracle to build a bridge?

HAMED:
>Of course! Because the foundation of the bridge is rotten, as good as non-existent.

FARID:
>Didn't I tell you we will change the foundation. Do

you want to write a story or something? By the way,
I dropped in at the magazine in Cairo, and they
said they had read your novel and would send you a
letter. Didn't you receive it?

HAMED:

They sent it a year ago, but it didn't arrive yet!
(*Zakya enters in a state of madness again. She
spots the ball in Kamel's hand. She takes it and
goes out.*)

ABUL UYUN:

Said is in town. He's been here for a week.

KARIMA:

And Said, Farid, didn't you see him in Cairo?

KAMEL:

Is he back?

FARID:

You never gave me his address.

ABUL UYUN:

Yes, he's back...to that woman, Sabra.

KARIMA:

I don't know his address.

KAMEL:

And her husband?

FARID:

And Mahassen, hasn't she come back?

ABUL UYUN:

Oh, he divorced her.

KARIMA:

Up until yesterday, her room was dark.

KAMEL:

Because of Said?

FARID:

Any news of her?

ABUL UYUN:

God knows.

HAMED:

They say she sent a letter to Uncle Kamel.
(*Zakya enters.*)

ZAKYA:

One white and one black...

FARID:

What is Zakya doing?

KAMEL:

Does anybody know the reason?

KARIMA:

Haven't you seen her like this before?

SHAHIRA:

(Coming out of her room, addressing Abul Uyun)
Our love has no beginning and no end.

FARID:

(Staring at Zakya) No.

KARIMA:

Oh yes, she hasn't had a fit for quite some time.

ZAKYA:

One yellow and one green.

KAMEL

Say, does nobody know why?

FARID:

Strange.

HAMED:

A case of schizophrenia.

SHAHIRA:

It has no beginning and no end. *(She enters her
room and closes the door.)*

KAMEL:

Have you fallen asleep, my Friend? I'll go too, and
rest for a while. *(Goes to his room and closes the
door.)*

KARIMA:

Ever since her daughter died...

ZAKYA:

One red and one green.

HAMED:

When she has her fits, she changes completely, becomes very innocent...

KARIMA:

Exactly like a child!

HAMED:

A miracle, don't you think?

FARID:

An escape. An escape from reality.

HAMED:

Still, a miracle!

FARID:

I leave you to your miracles. I'll go up, leave my

suitcase and go to the committee meeting. Excuse me.
(He walks over to the door at the right.)

KARIMA:
(As Farid reaches the door) Farid, you told me there
are beautiful roses on the other side, didn't you?

FARID:
The most beautiful you can imagine. Tomorrow, when
I build the bridge you can go and pick as many as
you like.

ZAKYA:
One white and one red...

KARIMA:
(Joyfully) Wonderful! *(Dejectedly)* But Said...!

FARID:
What about Said?

KARIMA:
He doesn't like roses.

FARID:
(Indifferently) Strange! *(He goes out.)*

HAMED:
Oh you should see the roses in Hagg Bassiouni's
garden. Tomorrow, on my way back from school, I'll
get you some.

KARIMA:
Really! *(Frightened)* No, no need!

ZAKYA:
One red and one green...

KARIMA:
Could we go to look at the roses? Just to look.

HAMED:
(As they go out) Look at them, pick them, whatever
you like. *(They go out. The neighing of the horse
is heard, louder than before and continues while
Zakya speaks.)*

ZAKYA:
(Very fast, as if counting) One green and one red
and one green and one red and one red and one
green...

KAMEL:
(Suddenly opening his door and calling) Sundus!
Sundus! (Enter Sundus)

KAMEL:
Do something about that horse, Boy! What's the

matter with you? *(Exit Sundus. Shahira's door opens
and Mahassen, in a night gown, enters.)*

KAMEL:

(Vehemently) How did you enter that room?

MAHASSEN:

(Yawning) What's all this noise you're making so
early in the morning?

KAMEL:

I am asking you, why did you enter that room?

MAHASSEN:

You haven't even asked me where I was or when I
came back. As if I weren't your daughter. Only
(Mimicking his voice), "why did you enter that
room?"

KAMEL:

(More furiously) Why did you enter that room?

MAHASSEN:

(Returning to Shahira's room) Shall I show you
what I brought with me?

KAMEL:

(In a rage) I want to know why you entered that
room!

ZAKYA:

(Approaching him) Shall I get you a cup of tea or
some bread and cheese?

KAMEL:

Go away.

ZAKYA:

I made you a cap. I'll go get it for you. *(Exits)*

MAHASSEN:

*(Comes back from the room holding a gazelle hide
and a beach bucket full of shells.)* Do you see this
gazelle hide? I'll make a purse and a pair of shoes
out of it. It's enough for two pairs. Do you see
these shells? Fantastic, aren't they? *(She puts
some shells on her extended palm. Kamel turns away.)*
I sent you a letter. Did you get it?

KAMEL:

*(Puts his hand in his galabiya picket, produces a
sealed envelope and throws it to her.)* Here's your
letter!

MAHASSEN:
>You didn't open it. *(Matter-of-factly)* Are you afraid to open it? I wasn't asking for anything. I just wanted you to know where I was so that if I died you could bury me. I got you some fantastic rocks. Don't you like rocks? I'll go get you the rocks. *(Walking towards Shahira's room)* My pants' pockets are full of them. *(Horse neighs.)*

ZAKYA:
>*(Dropping the ball and returning to her normal condition. Playfully)* The horse wants to jump. It wants to jump the fence. *(She runs playfully to the parlor.)*

KAMEL:
>Sundus! Sundus!

ABUL UYUN:
>*(Same tone)* Sundus! Sundus!
>*(Zakya enters holding a cap in her hand. When she sees Mahassen, she hides it behind her back and stands watching.)*

KAMEL:
>*(Furious)* Come here!
>*(Mahassen stops and turns to him.)*

KAMEL:
>Did you sleep in that room?

MAHASSEN:
>There he goes again!

KAMEL:
>Answer me! Did you sleep in that room?

MAHASSEN:
>*(Matter-of-factly)* Yes, I slept in that room.

KAMEL:
>Where did you get the key?

MAHASSEN:
>I know where you hide it. You think you're smart?

KAMEL:
>And you slept...in her bed?

MAHASSEN:
>Yes, I slept in her bed. The bed she died in.
>*(Wickedly)* You know it.

KAMEL:
>Shut up!

MAHASSEN:
>   *(Advancing towards him)* Oh, you're being bad today.
>   I know what will reconcile you. *(Moving closer)* Do
>   you see this gazelle hide? I'll make you a cap from
>   it. It'll be fantastic on you. Show me. *(She tries
>   to put the gazelle hide on his forehead.)*

KAMEL:
>   *(Jumping back, scared)* Go away!

MAHASSEN:
>   Are you afraid? Afraid of the gazelle? It's dead.
>   They killed it. The hunters killed it. *(She advances
>   suddenly and tries to touch his head.)* Show me.

KAMEL:
>   *(Pushing her away in a fury)* Go away!

MAHASSEN:
>   *(Calmly, slowly and gently)* Then you must be afraid
>   ...because I slept in her bed? Are you afraid of
>   her? But she's dead, dead, finished. She can do
>   nothing to you.

KAMEL:
>   *(Attacking her)* Go away. Out! Out! Out! *(He
>   collapses. Mahassen runs into Shahira's room and
>   closes the door.)*

ZAKYA:
>   Master Kamel, look at this pretty cap.
>   *(Kamel opens his eyes and holds Zakya's hand as if
>   asking for help. Suddenly the horse neighs. Kamel
>   violently withdraws his hand from Zakya's and calls
>   furiously.)*

KAMEL:
>   Sundus! Sundus!
>   *(Enter Sundus)*

KAMEL:
>   Get the whip, Boy. I'll teach that horse how to be
>   quiet. Why can't it stay quiet. *(Walks out behind
>   Sundus, Zakya waving her hands.)*

ABUL UYUN:
>   Sundus! Sundus! Have they said, Boy?[*] They didn't
>   say yet? They didn't?
>   *(Enter Farid from the house door right. At the same*

[*]This line is in a peasant dialect and, as becomes clear
later, is a line Abul Uyun remembers from a play.

time, Mahassen enters from Shahira's room.)

MAHASSEN:
    Here are the rocks...Farid! *(She runs toward him.
    The rocks fall to the floor. She and Farid hold
    hands longingly. Suddenly she starts to cry.)*

FARID:
    Why are you crying? Why are you crying, Mahassen?

MAHASSEN:
    *(Raises her head and dries her tears. Her face
    brightens.)* I don't know, Farid. Maybe it's seeing
    you after all this time.

FARID:
    (Mildly rebuking) Does that mean you missed me? Why
    did you do that, Mahassen?

MAHASSEN:
    (Moving away from him) Did you see what I brought
    back? *(She shows him the gazelle hide.)* Fantastic,
    isn't it? I'll make a purse and a pair of shoes.
    It's even enough for two pairs. Shall I make you
    some slippers out of it? It will be fantastic, won't
    it, darling?

FARID:
    Mahassen, why did you do that?

MAHASSEN:
    Oh Farid, I had such a nice time! I never spent a
    nicer time in my life. Don't be cross like that and
    look as serious as a school teacher. *(Mimicking him)*
    "Why did you do that?" How should I know why I did
    that? Come here and sit down. *(They sit down.)* I
    was bored and it was hot. So I decided to go to
    the seashore for a couple of days. And so I went
    and I came back. Nothing happened to me. Or are you
    angry because I came back?

FARID:
    With whom did you go?

MAHASSEN:
    Stop these questions and don't be a bad boy. If
    you sit very quietly I'll tell you everything.

FARID:
    Tell me.

MAHASSEN:
    Do you still love me or have you already forgotten me?

FARID:

Did you forget that we are going to get married, Mahassen?

MAHASSEN:

So?

FARID:

What do you mean "so"? I love you and I am serious about it, and for this reason we are getting married.

MAHASSEN:

Not necessarily. My father, for instance, was married to my mother. It doesn't matter. The important thing is that you still love me.

FARID:

And you?

MAHASSEN:

(Kissing him on the cheek) I told you to stop asking me questions. *(Looking at him)* You've slimmed down a little and it suits you. Stand up, Farid. *(She takes his hand and makes him stand up and looks at him.)* What a pity! If you were only three or four inches taller. Even two would be enough! Sit down. *(She makes him sit.)*

FARID:

Are you crazy?

MAHASSEN:

Maybe. *(She laughs.)* You can't imagine how splendid the sea is there. I've never seen such a beautiful sea in my life.

FARID:

Where?

MAHASSEN:

In Mersa Matrouh. Didn't I tell you? Munira called me up and told me they were going to stay there only three days. Her husband doesn't have a vacation this year. Do you understand?

FARID:

But you stayed there sixteen days, not just three.

MAHASSEN:

My God, he counted them! Wait until I finish. Adel went to Cairo and I stayed with Munira. There, I've told you everything. Are you happy now?

FARID:

I have just one question. It's not even a question. I don't mind that you have a good time. On the contrary, I like you to be happy. What annoyed me was your leaving without telling me. You know when I came back from work and they told me that Mahassen had left, I felt that my whole life fell apart, collapsed before my eyes. Why, Mahassen? Why didn't you tell me?

MAHASSEN:

It wasn't possible, my Love...

FARID:

Why?

MAHASSEN:

I don't know. When Munira called me up I suddenly felt that I wanted to escape, escape from here. And I escaped.

FARID:

But you could've...

MAHASSEN:

It wasn't possible, Farid. I told you. You asked to be transferred here so we could be together all the time. It was impossible that you would have agreed.

FARID:

If you'd insisted...

MAHASSEN:

I wouldn't have insisted. The minute you'd have told me to stay, I'd have stayed.

FARID:

Why?

MAHASSEN:

Because I love you, Farid.

FARID:

Perhaps.

MAHASSEN:

Don't you believe me? Then listen to this, when I was going out to meet Munira I was scared to death that I would see you, but I was also dying to see you before I left. Yet I knew that if I met you I wouldn't leave.

FARID:

Then you still love me?

MAHASSEN:

You're a bad boy today. Of course, I love you. In Mersa Matrouh I thought of you every day, and I looked it, you know. Once I was sitting there thinking of you and a young man came and told me "Mademoiselle, you must be in love." I told him "yes, indeed, I am in love." He said "whom do you love?"

FARID:

Very nice! He was flirting with you.

MAHASSEN:

No, he was serious and he was so refined, educated in Europe. Imagine, he had a Cadillac. He seemed to be quite rich.

FARID:

It seems you know him well.

MAHASSEN:

Everybody in Mersa Matrouh knows everybody else. But he was so gentle...like a movie star, the way he looked, of course...tall and dark...

FARID:

What does he do?

MAHASSEN:

I don't think he does anything. They have a farm near Alexandria, but he lives in Glim.* His mother died and his father has no other children.

FARID:

What's his name?

MAHASSEN:

Ismail Hassanin. Oh, my darling Farid. Are you jealous of him? Don't be silly! I have nobody on earth but you, Farid. Although I had great fun in Mersa Matrouh with Munira, I never feel happy except when I am with you. I feel at ease, say what I want to say, and do what I want to do. We were created for each other, Farid. Isn't that so, Darling?

FARID:

Yes, Oh the last few days were so difficult--troubles and problems, and then you were not there and I did not even know where you were. But thank God every-

*A residential quarter in Alexandria.

thing is all right now. *(Looks at his watch.)* I should go see what the Committee has done.

MAHASSEN:
What committee, Darling?

FARID:
An investigation committee inspecting the bridge. *(He stands up.)* I won't be long. *(Playfully)* But I hope you won't go before I come back.

MAHASSEN:
(As if in a dream) Go before you come back? *(When Farid reaches the door she calls.)* Farid.

FARID:
Yes?

MAHASSEN:
Come here. I want to tell you something.

FARID:
(Comes back) Yes, Mahassen.

MAHASSEN:
Sit down for just one minute.

FARID:
(Sitting down) Yes?

MAHASSEN:
(Childishly crafty) You didn't ask me with whom I came back.

FARID:
You must have come back with Munira.

MAHASSEN:
No, Munira is still there. Adel is going there tomorrow to get her.

FARID:
Then you came by train.

MAHASSEN:
What train is it that would arrive here at midnight?

FARID:
Then how did you come back?

MAHASSEN:
Do you want to know? I'll tell you, but don't be angry. I came back with Ismail in his car.

FARID:
He gave you a ride to this place? Here?

MAHASSEN:
Yes, of course.

FARID:

Were the two of you alone in the car?

MAHASSEN:

Yes, of course.

FARID:

And then where did he go?

MAHASSEN:

He said he'd spend the night at a friend's house.
The liar, he must have gone to a hotel.

FARID:

Why didn't you wait to come back with Munira?

MAHASSEN:

I found out that Ismail was driving back, so I
decided to come with him. I'd missed you so. How
come you say you missed me?

FARID:

You won't see him again?

MAHASSEN:

Maybe.

FARID:

What does this "maybe" mean?

MAHASSEN:

We didn't agree to meet.

FARID:

Then why "maybe?"

MAHASSEN:

He took my telephone number.

FARID:

And you, did you take his telephone number?

MAHASSEN:

How could you say such a thing? Me calling him!

FARID:

But he will call you?

MAHASSEN:

He said maybe he would.

FARID:

What will he say to you if he calls you?

MAHASSEN:

Invite me to go out with him.

FARID:

Where? Didn't you say he lives in Alexandria?

MAHASSEN:

Oh well, he has invited me to Alexandria. Not really invited me. He said if I go to Alexandria he will drop in and we could go out together.

FARID:

And you, did you agree?

MAHASSEN:

Agree to what? It's just talk.

FARID:

Yes, but suppose he did call you up and ask you to go out, would you do it?

MAHASSEN:

I don't know, Farid.

FARID:

(Stunned) You don't know? That means you could go out with him! (He thinks a little, then says, in pain) Mahassen, do you like him?

MAHASSEN:

I don't know. He's nice and handsome, unbelievably handsome, tall and dark, and his eyes...

FARID:

(Now impatient) All that doesn't matter.

MAHASSEN:

(Matter-of-factly) What do you mean it doesn't matter? That is what matters. Ismail is the man I've been dreaming of all my life.

FARID:

Then you are in love with him.

MAHASSEN:

If I had known him before you, I'd have loved him. And yet...and yet, Farid, you're something else. With you I feel happy. Ismail isn't my man, Farid, I feel it.

FARID:

So, if he asked you to go out with him you'd refuse?

MAHASSEN:

Don't be silly, Farid. He must have forgotten me. He refused to write down my number. He has a good memory, he said. He must have forgotten it.

FARID:

Suppose he didn't forget it! Suppose he called you up and asked you to meet him! Would you meet him?

MAHASSEN:

    If you don't want me to meet him, I won't.

FARID:

    Leave me out of it now. I want to know what you would do by yourself.

MAHASSEN:

    What do you mean "by myself?" I don't understand.

FARID:

    (Furious) Suppose I didn't exist! How would you go about it?

MAHASSEN:

    All right, Farid. Don't upset yourself. I know that you don't want me to meet Ismail. O.K., it's over. *(She begins to cry.)* I won't meet him.

FARID:

    (Scared) Why are you crying? Mahassen, why are you crying?

MAHASSEN:

    (In tears) Go to your committee! Go, you're late!

FARID:

    (Stands up) Just tell me why. *(Puzzled)* Why are you crying?

MAHASSEN:

    I don't know, honestly I don't. You should go now.

FARID:

    (He holds her hand and kisses it.) Did I offend you? I'm sorry. *(He walks to the door, then goes back.)* If you imagine that I don't trust you, you're mistaken. Mahassen, for me, you are the purest woman on earth.

    (Hamed and Karima enter from the garden. Hamed carries a bunch of roses.)

MAHASSEN:

    I know. I know.

KARIMA:

    Are you still here, Farid? We thought that perhaps you'd...

FARID:

    (Embarrassed) Oh, I actually am late. *(He goes out quickly.)*

MAHASSEN:

    (Calling) Zakya!

KARIMA:
>How are you, Mahassen? When did you come back?

MAHASSEN:
>Last night.

HAMED:
>You're so tanned, my cousin! What happened? Did you stay in the sea all the time or what?

MAHASSEN:
>*(In a suppressed voice)* It's because the sea is so beautiful in Mersa Matrouh.

HAMED:
>Where did you go, Alexandria or Ras el-Barr?*

KARIMA:
>Didn't she just say Mersa Matrouh?

HAMED:
>Wait! I'm confusing her!

MAHASSEN:
>Buzz off! *(Calling)* Zakya!

HAMED:
>You didn't tell me, where were you?

MAHASSEN:
>I told you Mersa Matrouh.

HAMED:
>Only there? I thought you'd gone to Capri or the Riviera.

MAHASSEN:
>*(To Zakya)* Find a key that will open my room and go clean it.

ZAKYA:
>The key to this room *(Pointing to Shahira's room)* opens yours.

MAHASSEN:
>Come with me. *(Both exit.)*

KARIMA:
>*(To Hamed)* So Mahassen was in Capri? Are you making fun of me, Hamed? Well, it doesn't matter.

HAMED:
>I make fun of you? That would be the last day of my life. It's because she stayed for such a long time, and then came back to tell us that she was in Mersa Matrouh. Well, I guess it's as far as she can go.

KARIMA:
>Is Capri too far for her?

*Another Mediterranean summer resort town.

HAMED:

>Of course it is. Do you think she's like you, cap-
able of going any place, opening all doors? No, Karima, you have that thing which makes illusion a reality and reality an illusion. You're an artist, Karima,
and no one but an artist can understand you.

KARIMA:

>*(Without a sign of interest)* All this about me?

HAMED:

>*(Trying to change the subject)* Did you like Hagg
Bassiouni's garden? Did you see how beautiful the
roses were?

KARIMA:

>I liked the jasmine covering the whole house.

HAMED:

>Take one. *(He offers her a rose.)*

KARIMA:

>No, *merci*. Once when travelling with papa, about
ten years ago, the train stopped in a small station.
I looked out of the window and saw a small house,
with jasmine covering all the windows and walls. I
imagined that if I went down there and entered it
I'd find myself sitting with my husband. Did anything like that ever happen to you?

HAMED:

>Once in a movie there was a small house on the sea-
shore, with the waves breaking on its walls day and
night, and nothing else whatsoever around it. Do
you know what I imagined?

KARIMA:

>What?

HAMED:

>That you were living in that house.

KARIMA:

>Me?

HAMED:

>That you were the wife of an artist who was writing
or composing music all the time. And you were sitting by his side talking gently to him, joining him
in his imaginings. *(Suddenly enthusiastic)* Drawing
forth the things stored inside him for years, breaking the bottle imprisoning the jinni...

*(Enter Said from outside, carrying a small suitcase.
He stands near the veranda door watching Karima and
Hamed, in a theatrical pose as if inspecting or
waiting for something.)*

KARIMA:

Said! *(She rises to meet him. He kisses her on the
cheek and gives her the suitcase. All Said's move-
ments are short and rather mechanical. Karima takes
the suitcase inside with Said walking by her side.)*
You stayed away very long this time, Said.

SAID:

I had work to do.

KARIMA:

You said you'd stay a week...

SAID:

(Interrupting) I told you I had work to do. *(He
spots the roses that Hamed has put in a glass filled
with water. He advances towards the roses quietly
and steadily.)* Bonjour, Monsieur Hamed. *(He takes
the glass and throws it on the floor. It breaks.
He goes to the roses and squashes them with his
foot. Kamel enters from the garden. He stands watching Said squashing the roses with his shoe.)*

KARIMA:

These roses belong to Hamed, Said.

SAID:

(Still squashing them) I said I didn't want any
roses in this house.

HAMED:

Is there anyone who doesn't like roses?

SAID:

Me!

KAMEL:

Where have you been, Boy?

SAID:

In Cairo.

KAMEL:

What were you doing in Cairo?

SAID:

Taking my exams.

KAMEL:
> Where did you take your exams?

SAID:
> At the university, of course. Where else can I take exams?

KAMEL:
> The university has expelled you. Here. *(Throws him a letter from his pocket.)* Here's your expulsion letter from the university.

SAID:
> I know.

KAMEL:
> You were expelled because you don't attend exams. You didn't take exams for the last two years.

SAID:
> I know.

KARIMA:
> I don't believe it, Said!

SAID:
> You stay out of it!

KAMEL:
> Where did you go each time you said you were going to Cairo? And this time, where did you go this time?

SAID:
> I was in Cairo, I told you.

KAMEL:
> You're lying. You were here in town.

SAID:
> I told you I was in Cairo.

KAMEL:
> Well, what were you doing in Cairo?

SAID:
> I was doing what I was doing. I'm free.

KAMEL:
> No, you are not free.

SAID:
> Not free?

KAMEL:
> No, you're not. You are not free. When a man does wrong, he doesn't get himself alone into a mess, he gets everybody around him into a mess. This girl

(Pointing to Karima), what did she do? What wrong
has she done to deserve what you're doing to her,
killing her with your hands.

SAID:

(Sarcastically) Me? I kill my own wife with my hands?
Me?

KAMEL:

(Assulting him) You dog! Oh, you dog! I knew you were
on their side.

SAID:

Well, did they make anything up? Isn't it the truth?

KAMEL:

The truth? The truth has to come out so that everybody should know where he's going. You were at Sabra's,
not in Cairo.

SAID:

(Sarcastically) Is that the truth?

KAMEL:

Speak, Coward, speak. You've come now from Sabra's
place, haven't you?

SAID:

I've come from Sabra's and I'm going back to Sabra!

KARIMA:

Said!

SAID:

Immediately. Give me my suitcase. *(He snatches the
suitcase and walks hurriedly towards the garden gate.)*

KARIMA:

Said!

SAID:

What do you want?

KARIMA:

I can't believe it! I can't believe it!

SAID:

You can't believe it? Come with me, I'll let you see
with your own eyes. *(He goes out.)*

KAMEL:

(Going to his room) Go, die, kill yourself. The
problem is, nothing will happen to you. *(He enters
his room.)*

KARIMA:

Why, Said, why?

HAMED:
> *(Goes to her and leads her out.)* Come, Karima, go
> to your room. Get some rest.

ABUL UYUN:
> Sundus! Sundus!
> *(Enter Sundus)*

SUNDUS:
> Do you want something?

ABUL UYUN:
> Did they say, Boy?

SUNDUS:
> *(Not understanding)* Who is it that said what?

ABUL UYUN:
> Don't you want to act, Boy?

SUNDUS:
> Oh, act. No. Yes, let's act!

ABUL UYUN:
> Did they say, Boy? Did they say yet or not?

SUNDUS:
> *(Acts, laughing)* No, they didn't say!
> *(Shahira enters from outside wearing a red dress.)*

SHAHIRA:
> You're my love.

SUNDUS:
> They didn't say.

ABUL UYUN:
> Cut it out, Boy.

SUNDUS:
> I said...

ABUL UYUN:
> Cut it out, I said.
> *(Sundus walks towards the door. Zakya meets him at
> the other end of the stage.)*

ZAKYA:
> Show me.

SUNDUS:
> Show you what?

ZAKYA:
> Show me the cap on your head.

SUNDUS:
> What for?

ZAKYA:
> It's not your business, just show me!

SHAHIRA:
> Show me your face, my Love. You've lost a lot of weight.
>
> *(She approaches Abul Uyun and touches his face.)*

SUNDUS:
> No, I won't show you.

SHAHIRA:
> You're again like you were when you were young.

ZAKYA:
> What's the matter, Boy? Are you a kid?

SUNDUS:
> Kid or no kid, you've got plenty of men.

SHAHIRA:
> I like no man on earth as I like you.

ZAKYA:
> Which men, Boy? Where are they?

SHAHIRA:
> Do you remember the trip we both went on? *(She sits next to Abul Uyun.)*

SUNDUS:
> Do you think I'm stupid? .

SHAHIRA:
> The full moon and the white sea...

ZAKYA:
> Would you like some fish, Boy?

SHAHIRA:
> You had a blue shirt on. It was beautiful on you.

ZAKYA:
> This cap is not beautiful on you.

SUNDUS:
> I like it.

SHAHIRA:
> I didn't take my eyes off of you for a second...

ZAKYA:
> Show me, Boy.

SHAHIRA:
> You said you'd come and ask for my hand from my uncle the next day...

SUNDUS:
> Go away.

SHAHIRA:
> The days passed and I waited...

ZAKYA:
> *(Approaching him)* Show me, Boy.

SUNDUS:
> Cool down, Woman.

SHAHIRA:
> And then they told me you had left for Europe...

ZAKYA:
> Give it! *(She snatches the cap from Sundus's head and runs.)*

SUNDUS:
> *(Running after her)* Give me the cap, Woman! Zakya!

ZAKYA:
> *(Running inside)* Come and get it. *(Exits)*

SHAHIRA:
> That night I couldn't sleep, and after that my heart knew no joy...

SUNDUS:
> *(Running after Zakya)* It's the only one I have, Woman. *(Exits. Shahira goes into her room as Farid enters with Kharboutli Bey and Mumtaz Bey.)*

KHARBOUTLI:
> Of course we've seen everything for ourselves. Yet it is customary that before we write the report... Did you ever serve on committees before?

FARID:
> This is the first time, sir.

KHARBOUTLI:
> That's why.

MUMTAZ:
> Exactly!

KHARBOUTLI:
> What was I saying? Yes, customarily, the junior member of the committee would write a summary and present it to the committee. What rank are you, Engineer?

FARID:
> Fifth.

MUMTAZ:
> Well, then you'd be the junior member, in years that is, of course. His Excellency Kharboutli Bey is a Bey of the first class, and I am a Bey of the

second class. His Excellency *(Pointing to Kharboutli)* is a Director General A, and on his way to becoming an Assistant Under-secretary. I am a Director General B, and on my way to becoming a Director General A. Don't you have a cold drink or something, young man?

FARID:

Immediately, sir. *(Calling)* Sundus! *(Enter Sundus)* Get us some cold drinks, quick!

KHARBOUTLI:

What did you say, young man?

FARID:

I am ready, sir. Since public interest...

KHARBOUTLI:

(Addressing Mumtaz) I like young men who have a sense of responsibility. Are you married, Engineer?

FARID:

No, sir. Engaged.

KHARBOUTLI:

Oh, let's go back to public interest.

MUMTAZ:

To whom are you engaged, Engineer?

KHARBOUTLI:

No need, Mumtaz Bey.

MUMTAZ:

Your Excellency, we should know what family the engineer is marring into.

FARID:

I'm engaged to my cousin, daughter of Mr. Kamel Abdel Geleel.

MUMTAZ:

Oh, Mr. Kamel Abdel Geleel...the name is familiar. He's a Wafdist, right?

FARID:

No, sir.

MUMTAZ:

Free Constitutionalist? Sa'dist?

FARID:

He doesn't belong to any political party, sir.

MUMTAZ:

Oh. Then he has connections...

FARID:
Connections with whom, sir?

MUMTAZ:
Connections with whom? With the palace, of course.

FARID:
My uncle has no connections.

MUMTAZ:
Strange. What does he do?

FARID:
He was a lawyer.

MUMTAZ:
Oh, then he made his fortune in the law and then died.

FARID:
My uncle is alive, sir. He retired from his practice some time ago...family circumstances.

MUMTAZ:
Family circumstances? What are...

KHARBOUTLI:
I think it's time to go back to the public interest, Mumtaz Bey.

MUMTAZ:
Well, your Excellency, what else are we seeking but the public interest? What else but the public interest would bring us all the way from Cairo in this horrid heat? By the way, I got the travel allowance forms. All that remains is the signature. Of course, we've stayed here for five days to finish our inspection. (He looks at his watch.) We have half an hour to catch the train.

FARID:
There are other trains, sir.

MUMTAZ:
Yes, but this is an express that takes only an hour and a half to Cairo.

KHARBOUTLI:
All right, Junior Engineer, give us the summary orally.

FARID:
It's a very simple matter, sir. This bridge was begun by Engineer Sherif Sami and then he was transferred to Cairo and I replaced him here.

KHARBOUTLI:

Exactly. And then?

FARID:

And then I found out that the piers built by Engineer Sherif Sami were defective because instead of using reinforced ferro-concrete, he used bricks and rocks, which means that if we built the bridge on top of them the bridge would fall down.

KHARBOUTLI:

Exactly.

MUMTAZ:

And this is what you mentioned in your report, word for word. I have it with me.

FARID:

And your Excellency *(Addressing Kharboutli)* and his Excellency, Mumtaz Bey, inspected the piers today and found out that they were made of bricks and rocks. Isn't that right, sir?

KHARBOUTLI:

Right! Right!

FARID:

Which means that if the piers were able to support the bridge for one day, they won't the next.

KHARBOUTLI:

Certainly! It will fall down in the Nile as if it were a bridge of paper.

MUMTAZ:

With all the people, the vehicles and the cattle and everything. The damage would be colossal!

KHARBOUTLI:

A very dangerous prospect.

FARID:

Exactly, sir.

KHARBOUTLI:

So?

FARID:

So, sir?

KHARBOUTLI:

You still didn't tell us what to write down in the report?

FARID:

What to write down in the report?

KHARBOUTLI:

Yes, what do we write down in the report?

FARID:

(Simply) We write down what you've just said.

KHARBOUTLI:

(Taken aback) In the report?

FARID:

Yes, in the report.

KHARBOUTLI:

Tell me, haven't you served on committees before?

FARID:

This is the first time, as I told your Excellency.

MUMTAZ:

Right! Right!

KHARBOUTLI:

(To himself) No, not right at all!

MUMTAZ:

Right! Not right at all!

KHARBOUTLI:

(Almost to himself) I might have misunderstood.
Tell me, Junior Engineer, do you want us to write
down in the report that the piers are defective,
and that if the bridge is built on top of them it
would fall down?

FARID:

Yes, of course!

KHARBOUTLI:

(Exasperated) But this is not possible!

FARID:

Why isn't it possible? Isn't it the truth?

KHARBOUTLI:

Listen, didn't you write this down in a report and
submit it to the Ministry?

FARID:

Yes.

KHARBOUTLI:

And the government received your report, which means
that the government learned the truth.

FARID:

Yes.

KHARBOUTLI:

Then could you tell me why the government appointed

this Committee?

FARID:

To make sure.

KHARBOUTLI:

And after it makes sure, what does it do?

FARID:

It writes a report?

KHARBOUTLI: .

Great. What does it say in the report?

FARID:

It says the truth.

KHARBOUTLI:

The same truth that you've told in your report.
That means the government is playing.

FARID:

Playing?

KHARBOUTLI:

Of course, playing! It appoints a committee which
costs travel allowances, etc., and the Committee
travels over from Cairo and wastes its time--the
committee of two Directors General, one a first
class Bey and the other a second class Bey. All
this, and in the end the Committee comes to write
a report which is a replica of the report you wrote.
You, Engineer Farid Ezzat of the fifth rank. Is this
reasonable, Young Man?

MUMTAZ:

No, it isn't reasonable, not reasonable!

FARID:

Not reasonable? Then what is reasonable?

KHARBOUTLI:

That we do what is proper. *(Pause)* Have you served
on committees before?

MUMTAZ:

It seems he hasn't.

FARID:

I told you, this is the first time.

KHARBOUTLI:

You haven't served on committees before, but I
have. I've served on innumerable committees, and
nothing in any of the committees I served on went
bad...

FARID:

>Even wrong things?

KHARBOUTLI:

>What's wrong and what's right? There's something
>called propriety.

FARID:

>Is it proper to let the wrongs go unchallenged?

KHARBOUTLI:

>*(Resentful)* We are not waiting for you to come
>and tell us what we should do!

MUMTAZ:

>Do you want to change the world, young man?

KHARBOUTLI:

>Tell him, Mumtaz Bey. Explain to him.

MUMTAZ:

>I'll explain to him, your Excellency. I'll explain.

FARID:

>What are you going to explain? It's very obvious.

MUMTAZ:

>All right, then...

FARID:

>*(Continuing)* Didn't you see the piers yourselves,
>Sirs?

KHARBOUTLI:

>Of course.

FARID:

>*(Continuing)* Haven't you established for yourselves
>that they are bad?

MUMTAZ:

>Of course they're bad!

FARID:

>*(Continuing)* And that no bridge can be built with-
>out a foundation?

MUMTAZ:

>Of course it's impossible!

FARID:

>And that this is the truth?

MUMTAZ:

>Exactly!

FARID:

>Then why don't we tell the truth?

KHARBOUTLI:
   I told you it's impossible. Personally, I am not
   ready to take such a responsibility upon myself.
MUMTAZ:
   Nor am I. It's a very serious responsibility!
FARID:
   A very serious responsibility to tell the truth?
KHARBOUTLI:
   It seems you're irresponsible.
FARID:
   Me?
KHARBOUTLI:
   Of course! Because you cannot...understand...you
   cannot take into consideration...
FARID:
   Take what into consideration?
KHARBOUTLI:
   Take into consideration that this is not the only
   bridge built without foundations, nor are these
   the only piers that are defective, nor is Sherif
   Sami the only engineer who cheats and steals. The
   whole country is like that.
FAIRID:
   So, defective piers are a natural thing?
KHARBOUTLI:
   Of course they're natural, hence, we...
FARID:
   Hence, we must shut up and never say they're de-
   fective.
KHARBOUTLI:
   Look here, Young Man. I don't want any problems,
   understand? No headaches. I think I should write
   the report, Mumtaz Bey.
FARID:
   Impossible!
MUMTAZ:
   (Takes out a piece of paper and a pen.) Go ahead,
   your Excellency.
FARID:
   I'll write a separate report.
MUMTAZ:
   Oh! What shall we do, your Excellency? A separate
   report will create a problem.

KHARBOUTLI:

    Yes.

MUMTAZ:

    Especially since it's so easy to prove that the piers are defective.

KHARBOUTLI:

    And the solution?

MUMTAZ:

    I have an idea. We say that had Sherif Sami increased the amount of rock a little, the piers would've been all right!

KHARBOUTLI:

    But this isn't true, because no matter how much he might have increased the amount of rock...I have an idea. We say that the piers are defective.

MUMTAZ:

    They are defective indeed!

KHARBOUTLI:

    But not defective.

MUMTAZ:

    Then they are not defective!

KHARBOUTLI:

    This way we would've reached a good compromise.

MUMTAZ:

    Exactly. *(Pause)* But how?

KHARBOUTLI:

    This is the idea that occurred to me. You carry it out.

MUMTAZ:

    (Thinking) The piers are defective but they are not defective. It's possible. *(Writing)* "The piers are weak but they are not weak." No, that won't do. Well, how about *(Writing)* "The piers are bad but..." No, not good enough. Oh, I've found it. *(Writing)* "The piers are defective but they'll do." I think this is best. It's a great idea, your Excellency!

KHARBOUTLI:

    Yes, it's a good idea.

MUMTAZ:

    Only good? It's ingenious. They are defective because they are in fact defective, but will do in our opinion, and our opinion is an expert opinion that nobody can dispute. *(Overjoyed)* Here, we've said the truth, Junior Engineer. Sign!

FARID:
> What do I sign? A decision that acknowledges cor-
> ruption, that misleads the people, that tells them
> that stealing and murder are acceptable? No, thank
> you.

MUMTAZ:
> Are you accusing us of corruption, you...

KHARBOUTLI:
> No need, Mumtaz Bey.

FARID:
> This decision of yours is more rotten than the
> piers themselves. It's a crime, a real crime!

KHARBOUTLI:
> *(Stands up furiously.)* You forget yourself, Farid
> Effendi. Let's go, Mumtaz Bey. *(He walks out.)*

MUMTAZ:
> *(Stands up and follows him.)* Exactly! Exactly!
> *(Both exit. Farid walks after them seeing them off
> silently. As soon as they go out and he is on his
> way back, Mahassen enters.)*

MAHASSEN:
> Farid, Ismail called me up.

FARID:
> And he asked you to go out with him?

MAHASSEN:
> *(Crying)* Yes.

FARID:
> And you're crying because you turned him down? You
> wanted to go?

MAHASSEN:
> *(Raises her face gently.)* I'm crying because you
> won't love me. I know.

FARID:
> I won't love you?

MAHASSEN:
> I didn't refuse to go out with Ismail.

FARID:
> You agreed to go out with him?

MAHASSEN:
> Yes.

FARID:

>When?

MAHASSEN:

>I was going out now, then I found you so I decided
>to tell you.

FARID:

>Why did you do that, Mahassen? Didn't we agree?
>Why did you do it?

MAHASSEN:

>I don't know, Farid. I don't know.

FARID:

>Did he plead with you, beg you over the telephone
>so you couldn't bring yourself to say no?

MAHASSEN:

>I didn't believe it. I thought he'd forgotten the
>number. I was going mad.

FARID:

>You wanted him to call you up?

MAHASSEN:

>Very much so, Farid. And when he said, "Let's
>go out," I said, "at once." I didn't think.

FARID:

>And where are you going?

MAHASSEN:

>I don't know. He says we might go to Alexandria.

FARID:

>Go to Alexandria with him?

MAHASSEN:

>*(Nods and puts her head on Farid's shoulder and
>bursts into tears.)*

FARID:

>Why are you crying?
>*(Mahassen continues to cry.)*

FARID:

>Mahassen, why are you crying?

MAHASSEN:

>I don't want to go.

FARID:

>You don't want to go?

MAHASSEN:

>*(Still crying)* I don't want to go out with Ismail.
>*(A pause, during which she stops crying.)*

FARID:
> Is he going to call for you here?

MAHASSEN:
> No

FARID:
> Where are you going to meet, then?

MAHASSEN:
> He's waiting for me at the hotel now.

FARID:
> Well, then, let him wait!

MAHASSEN:
> And then?

FARID:
> Don't go!

MAHASSEN:
> Don't go?

FARID:
> Yes, since you don't want to.

MAHASSEN:
> I can't, Farid. I can't.

FARID:
> Then go! Go to Ismail! Go!

MAHASSEN:
> Are you asking me to leave, Farid? Is it over?
> Don't you want me anymore. But I want you, Farid.

FARID:
> Mahassen, I...

MAHASSEN:
> Whenever I am with you, Farid, I'm happy. I love
> you, Farid. *(She suddenly starts to cry. The
> horse neighs. Mahassen raises her head and stops
> crying immediately.)*

MAHASSEN:
> With Ismail I am frightened. I fear him especially
> when he looks at me with his eyes. If you could
> see his eyes, Farid. Small and black and shining,
> like the eyes of the insane. *(She laughs.)*

FARID:
> What are you laughing about?

MAHASSEN:
> *(Continuing)* Because he always says that I'm in-
> sane. And he is also insane. That's why we fit

each other. *(She stands up suddenly and walks away briskly.)* Bye, bye, Farid.

(The neighing of the horse is very loud.)

KAMEL:

(From his room) Sundus. Silence that horse, Boy!

SUNDUS:

(From inside) It wants to jump. It wants to jump the fence.

KAMEL:

(From his room) Tie his feet, Boy. Tie his feet.

FARID:

(To Mahassen as she walks to the door) Mahassen!

KAMEL:

(From his room) The bastard! So it wants to jump?

MAHASSEN:

(Looking towards Farid.) Yes, Farid?

FARID:

Take care of yourself, Mahassen.

MAHASSEN:

(Advancing towards Farid.) Farid, my Love, my Love, Farid...my Love...I can't...I can't leave you...I can't *(Throws herself into his arms)* I can't...

ABUL UYUN:

Sundus! Sundus! Have they said, Boy?

MAHASSEN:

(Still in Farid's arms.) I can't. I can't. I can't, Farid. *(Loudly)* I can't. *(She extricates herself from Farid's arms. Feverishly)* I can't. *(She runs out.)*

ABUL UYUN:

Are you sure they haven't said, Boy?

ZAKYA:

(Enters, playing with the ball.) One red and one...

Quick Curtain

Act II   Scene I

(The scene is the same as that of Act One at Uncle Kamel's house. Time: 11 a.m.)

KARIMA:
> Don't you believe me? Then what if I tell you that
> I woke up today to find myself in India--Farid,
> why don't you sit down--in the palace of a big
> maharaja married to an English woman and they have
> a daughter called Shamim.

HAMED:
> You know her name, too?

KARIMA:
> Isn't she my friend? Shamim is married to a very
> nice young man and they love each other.

HAMED:
> What's his name?

KARIMA:
> I don't remember. Her husband was on a trip. Shamim
> said to me, "Let's go to the swimming pool," so
> we took the car and went. When we went in we saw
> her husband before us, swimming with an Indian danc-
> ing girl...

HAMED:
> How very nice, and...

KARIMA:
> When Shamim saw this she held my hand and squeezed
> it hard.

HAMED:

(Gently) Did it hurt?

KARIMA:

(Continuing) I looked around to find myself here
and the maharaja became Uncle Kamel.

HAMED:

And the swimming pool turned into a stable.

FARID:

(Interested) And where did Shamim go?

KARIMA:

She disappeared as if she'd never been there. *(To
Hamed)* Didn't I tell you? I'm no good anymore.
Whenever I go any place I find it transformed into
Uncle Kamel's house with its walls and doors and
windows that are locked.

HAMED:

Imprisoned!

KARIMA:

Yes, imprisoned indeed!

FARID:

How long has it been like that?

KARIMA:

Almost a month now. Since Said left the house.

HAMED:

What a strange coincidence. Since the day of the
committee meeting Farid has been suspended from
work, and so has Karima.

KARIMA:

How true, Hamed. I really think of the bridge all
the time. That's why whenever I go any place I
find myself back where I started as if I am tied
by a rope around my waist. It seems to me, Farid,
that when you build the bridge and when I see it
in front of me, I will have peace of mind, and I
will come out of my prison.

FARID:

(Matter-of-factly) Then you will stay in prison
all your life.

KARIMA:

Impossible, Farid. I'd suffocate and die.

HAMED:

Do you think that to live in reality is to die?
How about us? We're living.

FARID:

Like flies stuck on a fly-paper.

HAMED:

What poetry!

FARID:

When I was notified that I'd been suspended from
work, I went to Cairo. What do you think I did?

KARIMA:

You must have gone to the ministry.

KARID:

Nothing of the sort. I didn't even think of going
anywhere near it. Before leaving I opened my desk
drawer and found thirty pounds. I put the money in
my pocket, bought my ticket and left. I wanted to
go to any nightclub in Cairo and get drunk.

HAMED:

For thirty pounds? Why, did you think you'd drink
the whole bar?

FARID:

And then take any woman from the nightclub and go
with her all over town so that everybody would see
me and know I'd been defiled.

HAMED:

Defiled? All the pashas and beys in the country
do that and worse every night.

FARID:

I wanted to be like them.

HAMED:

Do you want to be a pasha for thirty pounds?

FARID:

I wanted to humiliate myself, eliminate my being.

HAMED:

That's nothing to pay money for.

KARIMA:

And what did you do then, Farid?

FARID:

I slept.

HAMED:

Slept? Where did you sleep?

FARID:

In my apartment in Cairo. Before I left here I'd
taken a tranquilizer, so when I went to change my
clothes I stretched out on the bed. I didn't wake

up until the following morning. I took the train
and came back.

KARIMA:

God loves you, Farid.

HAMED:

And the following day, what made you come back?
Why didn't you stay in Cairo and do what you
wanted to do?

FARID:

I didn't feel like it.

KARIMA:

It was a passing thing and it passed, Hamed.

FARID:

I don't think so.

HAMED:

You still want to go to Cairo? Let's go.

FARID:

No, Hamed, I don't want to go to Cairo, but...

HAMED:

But what?

FARID:

I want to walk in the mire.

KARIMA:

Why, Farid? What for?

FARID:

In order to arrive...

HAMED:

Arrive? Do you want to become a director general?
An undersecretary?

FARID:

I want to arrive at where the people are...

HAMED:

Those who are stuck on the fly-paper? A beautiful
sight!
(Sundus enters.)

SUNDUS:

There are some people outside who want to see
Master Farid.

FARID:

Ask them to come in.
(Sundus goes out.)

KARIMA:

I should go up.

(Enter Agib, Nasib, Selim and Labib.)

SELIM:

My brother-in-law had just come back from Europe. When I told him the story he said, "Do you know what I feel like doing? I feel like throwing myself from this balcony? And I live..."

HAMED:

On the ninth floor. Quite a distance.

AGIB:

No morals. This is the problem. I don't care about learning or efficiency, only morals.

SELIM:

(To Farid) And why didn't you see the Minister?

AGIB:

Morals are everything. How many employees do I have in the Irrigation Engineering Department?

FARID:

Why should I see him?

AGIB:

(To Nasib) How many, Nasib Effendi?

NASIB:

Thirty-five.

AGIB:

None of them is immoral.

HAMED:

They are all hand-picked!

AGIB:

Nothing can be accomplished without morals.

SELIM:

The Engineers' Council meeting is tonight, they say.

AGIB:

When I was appointed a director, I met with the Undersecretary and told him, "I don't want engineers!"

HAMED:

Your Excellency is enough.

AGIB:

I want morals. Give me morals and I'll give you work.

HAMED:

Give me engineers and I won't give you work.

AGIB:
Exactly. Engineers without morals are useless.
SELIM:
How about Sherif Sami's morals?
AGIB:
I should be going. When I learned they were coming to see you, I decided to come along.
LABIB:
Did your Excellency see the piers?
AGIB:
Yes, of course I saw them.
LABIB:
What do you think of them?
AGIB:
They can't support a straw bridge.
LABIB:
How come Kharboutli Bey wrote such a report. We must come up with a solution tonight.
AGIB:
I told him, "If you don't mend your manners..."
SELIM:
(To Agib) Your Excellency told Kharboutli Bey that?
AGIB:
To Sherif. Sherif Sami.
LABIB:
In the Council tonight, we...
AGIB:
Is there a Council meeting tonight?
LABIB:
Of course, didn't you get an invitation?
AGIB:
Yes, yes. He told me, "My morals are good."
SELIM:
Sherif Sami?
AGIB:
Yes, I told him...
SELIM:
But he's a thief!
AGIB:
Morals are everything. Without morals, I told him, you can't get any work done.
SELIM:
Your Excellency was aware of this piers business for a long time?

AGIB:

>What piers? I was talking to him about something much worse than the piers. Imagine, he'd taken all the blotting paper in the office and locked it up in his cabinet!

HAMED:

>*(Sarcastically)* And he locked up the ink and the red and green pencils?

AGIB:

>No, only the blotting paper.

HAMED:

>*(Continuing)* The paper, the erasers and the rulers? He's a criminal.

AGIB:

>When I threatened to transfer him, he opened his drawer and distributed the blotting paper among his colleagues.

SELIM:

>And he straightened out after that?

AGIB:

>To perfection!

HAMED:

>His morals were straightened then?

AGIB:

>Very much so. Anything but...

HAMED:

>Blotting paper!

AGIB:

>*(Correcting him)* Morals!

SELIM:

>Tell me, Agib Bey, is Sherif well connected?

AGIB:

>I don't know.

NASIB:

>He has no connections whatsoever.

SELIM:

>Does he usually pay bribes?

AGIB:

>What do you mean, Mr. Selim?

SELIM:

>I don't mean... Does Kharboutli Bey, for instance, take bribes?

AGIB:

    The new Undersecretary?

SELIM:

    Kharboutli Bey.

AGIB:

    His Excellency, Kharboutli Bey, is a very honest
    man. He's notorious for his honesty.

HAMED:

    Kharboutli Bey is indeed honest. Farid asked
    about him at the Ministry.

AGIB:

    I assure you that Kharboutli Bey's name is well-
    known and his morals...

HAMED:

    (Sarcastically) Great!

AGIB:

    Yes, indeed, great.

HAMED:

    How about the report that he wrote?

AGIB:

    What's the report to us? We are talking about his
    morals. He's a very sweet man. Never annoyed any-
    body, nor did anyone ever complain about him. I
    should be going.

SELIM:

    I told the story to the editor-in-chief. He's going
    to write it himself. He told me literally (In a
    deep voice) "This is a scandal. A scoop. A scoop."
    He has hopes to topple the Cabinet.

LABIB:

    What has the Cabinet to do with it?

SELIM:

    Do you belong to the party?

LABIB:

    The Cabinet has nothing to do with it.

SELIM:

    The Cabinet has nothing to do with it! The party
    has nothing to do with it! Colonialism has nothing
    to do with it! Then who is responsible? Who is
    the culprit? Who is responsible for all these
    scandals? For all the crimes committed every day?

AGIB:

    In the name of morals...

SELIM:

For the ignorance, the poverty and the disease in which this country has been living for years? Who is responsible for all that? Me?

AGIB:

Morals.

SELIM:

(Continuing) Who is responsible for this backward mentality that we have?

LABIB:

Did you say backward?

SELIM:

Yes, backward. Do you think I'm afraid to say it? Who is responsible for feudalism and the Middle Ages and the class-system, for the passivity, the partisanship and the bourgeoisie? The whole system is no good. And it is necessary...

AGIB:

Morals, without morals...

SELIM:

(Furiously) Look here. To hell with your morals!

AGIB:

My morals? *(He stands up.)* I'm leaving!

SELIM:

(Continuing) I know that morals are rotten. But as a result of what? The system! Change the system and morals will change. Why do you think I'm inter-ested in the bridge story? Because I know the cul-prit. Yes, I know Sherif Sami well. We were friends and then we disagreed. All his life he's been a crook and a thief, going from one office to the other, kissing asses and wronging people. And he is getting on very well. Why? Ask me why? Because he is a legitimate son...

HAMED:

And we are the bastards?

SELIM:

A legitimate son of the rotten system under which we are living.

HAMED:

(Clapping. Sarcastically) Bravo! Bravo!
(Youssef enters in a hurry.)

YOUSSEF:
    Hello. I have important news. First of all...
SELIM:
    First of all, the system must...
AGIB:
    First of all, morals must...
YOUSSEF:
    (*Loudly to silence them.*) First of all, Farid is
    going to attend the Engineers' Council meeting
    tonight. These instructions were given over the
    phone just now.
FARID:
    Why should I attend the Council?
YOUSSEF:
    To make the presentation.
AGIB:
    Congratulations, Farid. Be sure the truth comes out.
HAMED:
    (*Sarcastically*) As the day from the night.
YOUSSEF:
    (*As if announcing something*) Second, Sherif Sami
    is here. He's been in town for the last two days.
NASIB:
    Four days.
AGIB:
    How do you know, Nasib Effendi? Did you see him?
NASIB:
    Did your Excellency not see him?
AGIB:
    Where would I have seen him?
NASIB:
    At the Irrigation Engineering Department. He went
    from the train straight to your office. It was he
    who told me. Your Excellency probably was away or
    in the bathroom.
AGIB:
    No. Now I remember. I met him, indeed. But that
    was Wednesday.
NASIB:
    And today is Saturday. Exactly.
SELIM:
    And what did he tell you, Agib Bey?

AGIB:

    I told him, "Listen, if your morals are good, fear nothing."

HAMED:

    His morals good? Haven't you seen the piers?

AGIB:

    Of course, I saw them.

HAMED:

    Bad, aren't they?

AGIB:

    Very bad. They can't support a straw bridge. Why do you ask?

HAMED:

    Oh, nothing.

AGIB:

    I should be going. *(He stands up.)* Aren't you coming, Labib Bey?

LABIB:

    I'll go with you.

ALL:

    We'll all go. *(They walk towards the door.)*

YOUSSEF:

    The Council meeting is at eight o'clock, Farid. Don't be late.

    (While they are going out:)

AGIB:

    Nations are nothing but morals...

SELIM:

    Poverty, ignorance and disease...

NASIB:

    How can the office work with one ruler?

LABIB:

    There must be a reason.

    (Farid goes out with them. Hamed sees them to the door and then returns.)

HAMED:

    (Calling) Karima! The sixth class period is in a quarter of an hour. *(He opens a book and reads.)* Oh, if the miracle should happen!

KARIMA:

    (Entering) Do you still insist?

HAMED:

    (Hurrying to her) The Council meeting is tonight and Farid is going to attend!

KARIMA:

    Really!

HAMED:

    (Accompanying her out) I won't be late. As soon
as the bell rings you'll find me with you, in the
midst of the roses. Oh, if the miracle should
happen! *(They go out.)*
    (Enter Zakya and Abul Uyun.)

ABUL UYUN:

    Where did he go?

ZAKYA:

    I don't know.

ABUL UYUN:

    Strange. *(Feeling his way with his hands as he
sits down)* Did you bring the candy?

ZAKYA:

    He hasn't slept for the last two days.

ABUL UYUN:

    And how do you know?

ZAKYA:

    I see him.

ABUL UYUN:

    Where's the candy, Girl? *(He feels his pockets.)*
Where do you see him?

ZAKYA:

    In the garden. What candy?

ABUL UYUN:

    My candy. What does he do in the garden?

ZAKYA:

    He walks all night.

ABUL UYUN:

    Did you eat the candy? What does he do all night?

ZAKYA:

    He walks, I told you.

ABUL UYUN:

    And you, do you watch him? Go now. *(He pushes her.)*

ZAKYA:

    Go where?

ABUL UYUN:

    Go get the candy.

ZAKYA:

    It's all gone.

ABUL UYUN:

    You ate it? You'll die, Girl!

ZAKYA:
>You ate it.

ABUL UYUN:
>*(Singing)* "I thought your love would make me sweeter." Go get the candy.

ZAKYA:
>Don't push.

ABUL UYUN:
>*(Singing again)* "You disappointed me."
>*(Shahira's door opens and Mahassen comes out.)*

ZAKYA:
>In the name of God... When did you come back, Miss Mahassen?

MAHASSEN:
>Go make me some tea.

ZAKYA:
>Why did you sleep in that room. Master Kamel doesn't like that.

ABUL UYUN:
>Where were you all that time, Mahassen?

MAHASSEN:
>Are you still awake? *(She sees Farid entering from the garden. She rushes towards him, extending her hand towards him.)* Farid, my love!

ABUL UYUN:
>Sundus! Sundus!
>*(Enter Sundus)*

FARID:
>*(Turns his face away from her.)*

MAHASSEN:
>You don't want to see me, Farid? Look in my eyes. Show me your eyes. *(She looks closely into his eyes while holding his face in her hands.)*

ABUL UYUN:
>Sundus! Why is the horse silent, Boy?

MAHASSEN:
>Your eyes are beautiful and they say a lot of things.

SUNDUS:
>Yes, it's silent.

MAHASSEN:
>Do you love me, Farid?

FARID:
>   *(Pointing to those present)* Don't...

MAHASSEN:
>   What do you care?

ABUL UYUN:
>   Did they say, Boy? *(He seems about to fall asleep.)*

MAHASSEN:
>   Our love is like the moon...

ABUL UYUN:
>   Did they say or...

MAHASSEN:
>   It appears for a while and disappears for a while.

ABUL UYUN:
>   Not yet? *(He snores.)*

MAHASSEN:
>   Do you know what your eyes say?

ZAKYA:
>   *(Holding Sundus's hand)* Come.

SUNDUS:
>   Let go of my hand, Woman.

MAHASSEN:
>   They say that you love me.

ZAKYA:
>   Let's go to the other side of the river.

SUNDUS:
>   That was in the past.

MAHASSEN:
>   Like in the past.

ZAKYA:
>   Do you remember when you used to sing to me?

MAHASSEN:
>   You are still my love.

ZAKYA:
>   And say to me, "Your dark eyes..."

MAHASSEN:
>   And I love nobody else but you.
>   *(Sundus turns his face away from Zakya.)*

ZAKYA:
>   Look at me, Sundus. Am I not Zakya, old Zakya.
>   Zakya, who...

MAHASSEN:
>   What are you thinking of, Farid?

SUNDUS:
> *(Violently)* Zakya is dead and buried.

FARID:
> I had a dream.

MAHASSEN:
> What did you dream about?

ZAKYA:
> Buried? *(Understanding)* She's dead...dead. *(She cries as she goes out.)* And buried. *(She goes out.)*

FARID:
> That I died.

SUNDUS:
> *(Almost to himself as he goes out the opposite door.)* Yes, dead. Long ago, long, long, ago.

FARID:
> That I'm dying. Someone came and took the money in my pocket. Someone else cut my hair and took it, and another one with a huge knife in his hand came and said, "Give me your arm so I can suck your blood." I told him, "Why the hurry? I'll be dead in a while." He said, "What good is your blood to me after you're dead? Give me your arm." He put the knife on my arm, then I heard a sound like a lion roaring. The knife fell on the floor and he ran away. They all ran away. I closed my eyes and said to myself, "Thank God this monster is going to finish me off and spare me the pain." I felt its breath on my face, on my arm, on the wound. I opened my eyes and saw a cat, a little white cat.

MAHASSEN:
> It's I, Farid. I am the cat who loves you and that you love.

FARID:
> And Ismail?

MAHASSEN:
> He's mad and I am also mad. But I love you. Love me as I love you, Farid. Both of us... *(Farid puts his hand on her mouth and holds her hands and kisses them.)*

FARID:
> Tell me, what did you do?

MAHASSEN:

    Let's go to the garden. This man pretends to be asleep, but he hears everything. *(Points to Abul Uyun.)* Come. *(She takes his hand and they walk out.)* *(Enter Zakya, playing with an imaginary ball.)*

ZAKYA:

    One red and one green, one red and one green and one red...

    (Shahira enters from her room.)

SHAHIRA:

    (To Abul Uyun) You haven't changed, my Love, and you've come back to me after twelve years. Who'd have believed it?

ZAKYA:

    And one green, and one...

    (Kamel enters.)

KAMEL

    Go play somewhere else.

    (Zakya goes out.)

ABUL UYUN:

    Did you come, my Friend? Come, sit beside me.

KAMEL

    (Sitting beside him) Are you awake?

ABUL UYUN:

    What's the matter with you, why don't you sleep? Zakya told me.

KAMEL:

    Whenever I sleep, I see her in my dreams.

ABUL UYUN:

    What's the matter with her? What does she want?

KAMEL:

    She cries and is anxious.

SHAHIRA:

    For twelve years we were together, every day.

ABUL UYUN:

    What's she anxious about?

KAMEL:

    Her father is sick. She's afraid he may die.

ABUL UYUN:

    She loved her father very much.

SHAHIRA:

    Only you, when Papa died it was only you I wanted.

KAMEL:

> She must be anxious about Said. I heard he's in smuggling now.

ABUL UYUN:

> Mahassen is back. What smuggling?

KAMEL:

> I don't know.

SHAHIRA:

> And the way out? There's no way out. We'll go on whirling like that...whirling. *(She enters her room and closes the door.)*

ABUL UYUN:

> Where's he now?

KAMEL:

> I don't know. And the way out? I don't know the way out.

ABUL UYUN:

> *(Yawning)* The way out? *(He falls asleep)* The w...

KAMEL:

> Are you asleep, my Friend. *(He walks to his room. At the same time, Karima and Hamed enter. Karima holds a rose in her hand.)*

HAMED:

> What do I teach them? "I am. She is. He is." I am what? Nothing.

KARIMA:

> You're a respectable school-teacher. You have something to live for.

HAMED:

> Live on, yes. I wasn't born a teacher. I was born a human being, a man who has the right to live as he wants, do what he wants to do.

KARIMA:

> You'll soon write and realize all that you want to realize.

HAMED:

> Sometimes I think I should gather all the cats and dogs in the whole country...

KARIMA:

> What would you do with them, Hamed?

HAMED:

> Feed them, play with them, kiss them.

KARIMA:

    Kiss them?

HAMED:

    Yes, give them some of the love stored in my heart.
    My heart's full of love, Karima.

KARIMA:

    That's a very beautiful thing.

HAMED:

    Beautiful? May your heart never be imprisoned
    like mine. And so long as my heart is imprisoned,
    my thoughts will also remain imprisoned until they
    are forgotten and die and are buried with me, and
    also be just another handful of dust.

KARIMA:

    This is the second time you have spoken of death
    today, Hamed. The doctor told you the troubles you
    had were in the stomach, not the heart.

HAMED:

    Do you think I'm afraid of death? Then what if I
    tell you that I died?

KARIMA:

    Died?

HAMED:

    Yesterday I dreamt that I died. But it was a
    beautiful death. I wish it would come true!

KARIMA:

    That means you'll live long, so don't be silly!

HAMED:

    Why silly? I'll tell you what I dreamt. I dreamt
    that I was on a trip with a lot of people, as if
    we were crossing the sea in a big ferry. When they
    reached the land, they stood in a line one after
    the other in a narrow path leading to a cave be-
    hind which were tall trees. All the time, drums
    were beating. In the line, in front of me, was a
    girl, tall and pretty. Without seeing her face, I
    knew she was pretty. Suddenly the drums stopped.
    She turned and faced me, removing her veil. I
    knew her and screamed, "It's she, it's she." The
    drums started beating again, loud, louder than be-
    fore. She took my hand in hers and we left the
    line and in a second, less than a second, our
    bodies were blown up and the pieces flew into the

air as if we had been hit by a bomb. I died. When
I woke up I was happy. I felt I had become complete.

KARIMA:

(Dreamily) It's a strange dream.

HAMED:

Did you ever have such a dream?

KARIMA:

While you were telling it, I saw before me a
beautiful vision.

HAMED:

(Enthusiastically) The sea and the ferry and the
cave. Then you were with me.

KARIMA:

(As if having a vision) I see the sea, but there's
no ferry. There's a bridge. I see it right in
front of me, a long, broad bridge. On the sides
there are trees and in the trees lots of singing
birds. The dawn is breaking and the people are
starting to walk on the bridge. Lots of people.
There's a light coming from afar, from the other
side, far away. *(In her ordinary voice)* The light's
gone, Hamed. I don't see a thing.

HAMED:

(Enthusiastically, still in his dream) Do you know
who she was? The girl I saw? The one...

KARIMA:

(Suddenly joyful) The light's back. I see everything. A lot of people walking on the bridge. I
am walking in their midst and I see the other
side. There he is. Someone is standing on the
other side, waving to me. Farid. Yes it is Farid.

HAMED:

(With similar enthusiasm. Anxiously) And me? Me,
Karima?

KARIMA:

(Now completely awake) You? What about you, Hamed?

HAMED:

(Same enthusiasm and anxiety) Me? Don't you see me?

KARIMA:

(Simply, half-dreamily) You are here, in front of me.

HAMED:

(Same enthusiasm and anxiety) Where? Where?

KARIMA:

(Surprised. Simply) Here. At Uncle Kamel's house.

Curtain

Act II   Scene II

*(The Council of Engineers. It is 8 p.m. the same
day. A rectangular room with one window and one door.
In the middle, taking almost all the space is a U-
shaped table with an old-fashioned chandelier hanging
over it. The table has a green broadcloth cover and
sheets of paper. Around the table, the members of the
Council of Engineers sit in the following order: at
the head of the table the chairman, Muhib; to his right
sit Gharib, Agib, Labib, Hasib and Shakib; to the left
of the chairman sits the secretary, Nasib, then Mugib,
Munib, Habib and Naqib. On a single chair facing the
table sits Farid. As the curtain rises, Farid stands
next to his chair. The Council is in a state of commotion. Two waiters are offering the members tea, coffee,
coke, etc. The chairman has an unlit cigarette dangling
from his lips. He is listening to a joke being told
privately to him by Mugib. The chairman is leaning in
his chair towards Mugib in such a way that he is on the
point of falling down.)*

MUGIB:
> A man told his wife, "Pack a suitcase for me." She
> asked, "Why?" He said, "I want to go to Alexandria."
> She asked him why, and he said...*(Whispers in-
> audibly.)*

LABIB:
> *(To Hasib while taking some banknotes from him)*
> Where do you get this new money from, Hasib Bey?
> I put it in front of me and keep watching it. Do
> you have change for another five-pound note?

CHAIRMAN:
> *(Laughs loudly and takes a sip of tea rather audibly, lights the cigarette, then taps with his pen on the table.)* All right, everybody, go ahead. Speak.

SHAKIB:
> *(Rather loudly to the member next to him)* Three women went to the market looking for a mute man. A man heard them and pretended to be mute, so he stood there and started stammering and saying *(Mimicks a mute man.)* "Ta mma ma...ma...ah..." and then... *(He whispers.)*

CHAIRMAN:
> Go ahead and speak, everybody. We want to get it over with. Enough now, enough. *(He taps with his pen. Farid sits down.)*

NASIB:
> The defendant sat down.

CHAIRMAN:
> What defendant, Nasib Effendi? Do you think you are still a court clerk? You're the secretary of the Council.

SHAKIB:
> Nasib Effendi is right. I think Engineer Farid is a defendant. *(Surprised buzzing sounds from the Council members.)*

LABIB:
> Defendant?

SHAKIB:
> Patience. I personally accuse Farid. I accuse him of accusing a colleague of his who had done him no harm. And he accuses him of such a deed as would jeopardize his livelihood, one that could even put him in jail.

FARID:
> Shakib Bey...

SHAKIB:
> Please, don't interrupt me.

CHAIRMAN:
> Mr. Farid, ask permission before you speak. Go ahead please, Shakib Bey.

SHAKIB:
> Now what do those defective piers mean? The meaning is that Engineer Sherif Sami is a thief. Yes, that's the only significance.

FARID:
>I didn't say that Sherif Sami was a thief.

SHAKIB:
>*(To Farid)* Yes, but it's obvious. Now, he's charged the government for reinforced ferro-concrete piers, yet he made the piers of mud and rock.

FARID:
>That is the truth.

SHAKIB:
>Which means that he pocketed some ten thousand pounds.

LABIB:
>Much more than that.

SHAKIB:
>*(To Farid)* Have some fear of God, Man. Did you see him steal? Did you see him with your own eyes? Let's suppose that he's a thief. I agree with you that he is a thief. What business is that of yours? Did he put his hand in your pocket to steal your wallet? Are these the morals of the new generation?

AGIB:
>There are no morals any more!

FARID:
>Sir, in my report I didn't say that Sherif is a thief.

SHAKIB:
>Yes, but anyone who reads the report can infer that Sherif is a thief.

MUNIB:
>In the Ministry of Education there is a high-ranking official who is notorious for taking bribes. O.K.? Now, an elementary school teacher had some business there, but he refused to pay a bribe so nothing was done for him. So this teacher thought he was a man of letters and wrote a story in which the main character was a donkey who stole food from other donkeys. When that big shot heard of the story he complained. The Undersecretary of Education called the teacher in and said to him, "How dare you write a story about a high-ranking official of the ministry?" The teacher said, "Your Excellency, I wrote a story about a donkey." The

Undersecretary said, "True, but anyone who reads
the story can easily see that the donkey is so
and so Bey, especially since you say that that
donkey is a thief. Young man, you're fined fifteen days' pay."

SHAKIB:

The same thing. I don't want to punish Farid. I'm
just reprimanding him.

FARID:

You're reprimanding me for telling the truth?

NAQIB:

The truth! The truth! Mr. Engineer, where is the
truth? Who are you to tell the truth? The truth,
as philosophers defined it, does not exist. The
truth is that there is no truth!

MUNIB:

True!

NAQIB:

(Encouraged) Most distinguished Sirs, the truth
is too great to be told. Most distinguished Sirs,
there is...there is only one truth: Let's die for
the homeland. Let's die for the homeland. Say
with me, my Brethren "Let's die for the homeland."
(With the enthusiasm of students in demonstra-
tions) Let's die for the homeland! (Some of those
present repeat after him.)

CHAIRMAN:

Thank you, Naqib Bey.

NAQIB:

Don't mention it. (In the same demonstration-like
tone) Let's die for the homeland!

CHAIRMAN:

Please, be seated.

NAQIB:

Pardon me. Let's die...

CHAIRMAN:

Please!

NAQIB:

(Sitting down)...for the homeland.

HASIB:

(To Farid) Mr. Farid, what is there between you
and Sherif Sami? Why do you want to do him harm?

HABIB:

Sherif is a nice guy. He's good.

FARID:

    (Calmly and simply) I would like to tell the Council that the problem is far more serious than Sherif Sami's being a thief, far graver than his stealing ten thousand pounds or whatever. It's a matter on which the life of this town depends. A bridge on which people will walk cannot be built on defective piers. It will fall down. They will die.

GHARIB:

    Didn't you write this in your report? Why do you say it now?

SHAKIB:

    Tell him, Gharib Bey. Tell him.

FARID:

    I am saying it because it is my duty to say it.

GHARIB:

    You did what you could. Leave everything in the hands of those responsible.

FARID:

    Who are?

GHARIB:

    We, Sir. We are responsible.

FARID:

    (Interrupting) And I am responsible. Everyone in the country is responsible. Responsible for the life of the country, for its future...

NAQIB:

    The future? The future is in the hands of God. And by the way, Mr. Engineer, who are you? Who are you to speak of the future? *(He takes out his handkerchief and blows his nose.)*

MUNIB:

    (To Agib) I see, said the blind man.* Haha.

NAQIB:

    The future awaiting this great country is blooming full of roses and flowers...

---

*This, in the original, is an untranslatable play on words. My rendering tries to preserve the irrelevance and tastelessness of the interjection.

SHAKIB:

> *(To Habib)* They say the prime-minister will join
> the king in Capri.

NAQIB:

> *(Continuing)* At the hands of the majority party
> government, the wise government, the government
> that watches over the interests of the people, the
> government that never sleeps. Did you ever see a
> government that doesn't sleep? It's this one.
> *(He shouts.)* Say with me. "Long live the government!"
> Long live the government!

CHAIRMAN:

> Naqib Bey, please!

NAQIB:

> Your pardon, long live the government!

CHAIRMAN:

> Listen!

NAQIB:

> *(Coming to)* Yes, Mr. Chairman.

CHAIRMAN:

> We are speaking of the piers!

NAQIB:

> What are the piers, if you don't mind? What's the
> worth of the piers, if you please? Compared to
> Egypt and the glory awaiting Egypt? What does it
> matter if the bridge falls down? But Egypt will
> not fall down! She will not fall down a victim to
> traitors! She will not fall down a victim to
> colonialism! She will not fall down a victim to
> the wolves! She will not fall down a victim to the
> dogs! Let the bridge fall down! Let all the bridges
> fall down! Yet Egypt will never fall down! Never!
> Never! Never! *(Almost chanting)* "Dear Egypt is my
> motherland, it is my shield and my abode and every-
> thing in it is good." Says with me, "Dear Egypt is
> my motherland..."

CHAIRMAN:

> Naqib Bey, please! Please!

NAQIB:

> With your permission, Sir. Egypt is our country!
> Egypt is our fatherland! Egypt is our mother! Do
> you think that because a bridge may fall down, the
> future of the country is lost? Leave it to God,

man! Say with me, "Long live Egypt free!" Long
live Egypt free!"

CHAIRMAN:

O.K., sit down, please.

NAQIB:

(In a trance) Long live Egypt free.

CHAIRMAN:

Please sit down now and let's do our job. Sit down,
I tell you!

NAQIB:

(Sitting down, murmuring as if still in a trance)
Long live Egypt free!

LABIB:

What he says is very reasonable. Does it follow
that if the bridge falls down...? What could
happen?

SHAKIB:

(Suddenly sings) ""There was a woman who had twelve
daughters." Shall I give you her address?

MUNIB:

The papers are writing about defective weapons. As
if that were a scandal! When I was at Oxford...

CHAIRMAN:

Please, we are meeting here to discuss the bridge.
Please don't get off the subject. Understand?

MUNIB:

Are there such things as defective weapons and good
weapons? It's slanderous! It's a slander against
the state!

HASIB:

(Raising his finger to speak) Excuse me, Munib Bey?

CHAIRMAN:

Go ahead, Hasib Bey.

HASIB:

It's my opinion that we should speak about the
bridge.

CHAIRMAN:

Go ahead, speak.

HASIB:

I have nothing to say.

---

*A popular nursery rhyme.

MUNIB:
    It is either that there are weapons or that there are no weapons. But defective weapons and good weapons--that's nonsense.

LABIB:
    I'd like to ask Engineer Farid an important question.

CHAIRMAN:
    Go ahead.

LABIB:
    Those piers that you don't like, did an effort go into making them?

FARID:
    Yes, of course.

LABIB:
    Then why don't you like them?

FARID:
    Because they are bad, rotten and cannot support a straw bridge, as Agib Bey put it.

CHAIRMAN:
    Did you say so, Agib Bey?

AGIB:
    Without morals...

NAQIB:
    There could be no bridge. Nothing like morals. What's that about piers and bridges? Nations are nothing but morals.

AGIB:
    And so long as morals are good, the country is good. This, Mr. Chairman, is what I said.

SHAKIB:
    (Singing like a voracious animal) "There was a woman who had twenty daughters."

LABIB:
    See? You are persecuting Sherif Sami.

FARID:
    Persecuting him?

LABIB:
    Yes, of course! You're denying the effort that he exerted.

MUNIB:
    In stealing...

LABIB:

It's an effort, anyway.

SHAKIB:

And why do you persecute him? Did he do anything to you? Did you ever see him? Do you know him?

NAQIB:

The constitution stipulates that persecution is forbidden.

MUNIB:

People everywhere are talking of the king's scandals. Why do the political police let them talk? Why don't they forbid them to talk? And what use is talk anyway?

LABIB:

None. A waste of time. Instead of talking, they should work.

MUNIB:

Among them you'd find one who has nothing to eat, and yet he'd start telling you the king did this and the king did that. The king appropriated five thousand feddans or the king killed so-and-so. The king took so-and-so's wife, or put so-and-so in jail...

NAQIB:

Persecution, Mr. Farid, is forbidden. It's forbidden under the rule of the king.

MUNIB:

(Continuing) What's it to them. Let him do what he likes. He's a king!

NAQIB:

When the king of kings gives...

MUNIB:

Triviality and immorality. And what scandals? Is there such a thing as a scandal?

NAQIB:

God commands us to cover up.

LABIB:

People now devour each other's flesh...

AGIB:

No morals!

GHARIB:

I believe that Mr. Farid has committed a gross mistake. He covered up the defective piers.

FARID:
>Me? I covered up the piers?

GHARIB:
>You kept silent. For three months now, you've said nothing.

LABIB:
>Today black is white and white is black. The values are lost!

MUNIB:
>No values any more!

HASIB:
>It's anarchy!

GHARIB:
>Mr. Farid, I will ask you an important question. *(He stands up to convince those present of the importance of the question.)*

SHAKIB:
>*(To Habib)* Do you like basbousa?*

GHARIB:
>You say that as soon as you started on your job you reported to the Ministry that the piers were defective?

FARID:
>That is officially documented.

GHARIB:
>I know.

FARID:
>Well...

GHARIB:
>Wait. How did you know that the piers were defective when you'd just started on the job?

FARID:
>I examined them.

GHARIB:
>As soon as you started on the project?

FARID:
>Yes.

GHARIB:
>Why?

FARID:
>To make sure.

---

*An Egyptian pastry.

GHARIB:

Sure of what?

FARID:

Whether they were good or not.

GHARIB:

That means you were not sure that they were good?

FARID:

How could I be sure when I hadn't built them?

GHARIB:

(As if he has found a fault) So you had suspicions?

NAQIB:

Suspicion is sinful!

GHARIB:

Why are you silent. Are you afraid to admit that
you had suspicions?

FARID:

(Vexed) It's every engineer's duty to examine the
foundation on which he is going to build. How can
you say such things?

GHARIB:

I can't tolerate your speaking to me in this manner.
I am an engineer like you. No, I'm not like you. I'm
a senior engineer. I am Gharib Bey Gharib, Director
General, First Class. I have medals. I don't permit
you to speak at all... I...

CHAIRMAN:

Please don't be offended, Gharib Bey. Mr. Farid, before you speak, you should know to whom you are speaking!

CHARIB:

Mr. Chairman, what was I going to say? Let's go back
to our subject. The question now: How many days did
it take you to examine the piers?

FARID:

Two days.

GHARIB:

You examined twenty piers in two days.

FARID:

That's what happened.

GHARIB:

I know it happened. But it's an enthusiasm...

MUNIB:

Worthy of appreciation.

GHARIB:

> On the contrary, it's worthy of blame. Because it's suspicious enthusiasm.

NAQIB:

> Excessive interest calls for suspicion.

MUNIB:

> An evil intention is established.

NAQIB:

> Intention is what counts, not deeds.

GHARIB:

> If you'd had a sense of responsibility, you'd have waited.

FARID:

> Waited for what?

GHARIB:

> Waited until you'd consulted your superiors.

FARID:

> Kharboutli Bey said the piers were defective.

GHARIB:

> Yes, but he said they were good enough. Which means defective and not defective.

FARID:

> Is there such a thing as ""defective and not defective

GHARIB:

> That's what all young people are like today. No sense of responsibility.

CHAIRMAN:

> That's true!

HASIB:

> Then the country is lost! The country is lost!

MUNIB:

> They say the king has left the country and is having fun in Europe...

NAQIB:

> If the head of the family...

MUNIB:

> A young man in the prime of his youth. Shall we confine him? Have him stay here with us? What would he do? What would he do with people who have no sense of responsibility?

NAQIB:

> The sense of responsibility, fellow members, is a very serious issue, an impossible one. Because in order to have a sense of responsibility, we should

first know what responsibility is. Who can define
responsibility? Such a man would be a hero and deserves a decoration. The philosophers ask whether
man is responsible or not...

CHAIRMAN:

Naqib Bey, please!

NAQIB:

I beg your pardon. If philosophers...

CHAIRMAN:

Keep to the point, I say!

NAQIB:

The point is that Mr. Farid is responsible.

FARID:

Responsible for what?

NAQIB:

(Continuing) Responsible for public interest.
Public interest, fellow Members, should be above all
considerations. Private interests are this country's
bane. Nepotism and bribery everywhere! The only consideration is whether this man or that is a relative
or a friend. Anyone who tells the truth in this
country is branded a heretic. Here is Mr. Farid, a
living example...

FARID:

(Stands up calmly and shyly) Thank you.

NAQIB:

(Continuing) A living example of slyness. And slyness
is the current vogue. Slyness, fellow Members, consists in saying one thing and meaning another. Mr.
Farid says that the Piers are defective. Why? Because
they cannot support the bridge. This means that it's
for the public interest, a most beautiful sentiment,
and one that deserves our thanks. But who can believe
that anybody in this country cares for the public
interest? I ask your consciences, does anyone of us
think of the public interest?

CHAIRMAN:

What's that you're saying, Naqib Bey? If you can't
speak, shut up.

NAQIB:

(Furious) I can't speak? I speak Arabic, French and
English fluently. I studied at the *Ecole normale,
the Polytechnique,* and at the...

CHAIRMAN:
> Watch your words, then.

NAQIB:
> Wait, please. I was saying that since the public
> interest no longer interests anyone, which means
> that it's become an old-fashioned notion, why
> then does it interest Mr. Farid? Impossible! It
> follows then that the purpose behind this affair
> of the piers is not the public interest but pri-
> vate interest. This means that Mr. Farid has a
> stake in it. *(He takes out a pack of cigarettes
> and lights a cigarette.)*

SHAKIB:
> "There was a woman..." *(To Hasib)* Wake up, Man, is
> there anything better than women? *(He tickles him.)*

HABIB:
> *(Alarmed)* Where?

CHAIRMAN:
> *(To Naqib)* Where's this interest?

NAQIB:
> That is the secret I cannot unravel, but...

LABIB:
> *(Very stupidly)* A terrible secret!

MUNIB:
> Public interest; people say public interest...

AGIB:
> There's no secret to it. Farid wants to do Sherif
> harm.

HABIB:
> He doesn't like him. No, he doesn't like him.

LABIB:
> I too heard as much.

FARID:
> But I don't know him. I've never seen him in my life.

SHAKIB:
> Is it necessary that one dislike only those one
> knows? It doesn't follow.

MUNIB:
> Mr. Chairman, May I speak?

CHAIRMAN:
> Munib Bey has the floor. Go ahead please.

MUNIB:
> People say public interest is lost, gone; that is,

that everybody cares for his own interests only.
This is quite possible. When I was at Oxford...

CHAIRMAN:

No, please stick to the subject.

MUNIB:

Just a minute. Why shouldn't I speak? Everybody
else did. Is my voice unpleasant? Don't you like
me? Am I a bore? Anyway, bear with me. When I was
at Oxford, I was walking once down the street and
found people standing in a queue, a line, that is.
People in England stand in a queue when they want
to buy something or go to the movies. So I decided
to stand with them. An hour passed, two hours
passed, but the line did not move one step. So, I
told myself, "What am I going to do now? Shall I
go on standing till morning. I don't even know why
they are standing here." So I asked the man right
in front of me, "Why are you standing in the line?"
He told me, "I found the man in front of me standing and so I stood." I asked the man in front of
him and got the same answer, and the next man gave
me the same answer, and so on until I reached the
first one. When I asked him why he was standing,
he told me that he had found the man in front of
him standing, and so he had gotten in line. I asked
him, "Where's the man who was in front of you?" And
he answered that he had gotten bored and left. So I
asked him what he was standing there for. He said,
"I am waiting for my turn." So I said to myself,
"Oh what a people, the English people!"

LABIB:

An intelligent people. *(Seriously and very stupidly)*
I see from the story we've just heard that they're
intelligent, very intelligent!

SHAKIB:

Labib Bey, Labib Bey, do you like hazel nuts?

LABIB:

(With an idiotic smile) Yes. Do you have some?

SHAKIB:

No, I'm just asking.

NAQIB:

Colonialism! Colonialism, fellow Members, is a plague

Colonialism is a catastrophe...

CHAIRMAN:

Naqib Bey, what have we to do with colonialism
now?

NAQIB:

Colonialism is the root of all evil.

CHAIRMAN:

What evil?

NAQIB:

This present evil, the evil of the piers. Colonialism, as you may know, is not stupid, as you think.
Colonialism is intelligent...

CHAIRMAN:

What has it got to do with our present subject,
Man?

NAQIB:

Mr. Chairman, wait, if you please. With your leave,
colonialism is intelligent. It bluffed us. It made
us forget public interest. And here is Mr. Farid,
a living example, in front of us...

MUNIB:

People are walking barefoot and yet they don't
like the Barefoot Project.* They ask what the gov-
erment did with the money it collected in order
that the people might wear shoes. What do you think
the government would do with the money? Will it buy
shoes for the cabinet members? Impossible! It's a
sum of over a million pounds. It's true they collected the money three years ago, and it could have
innundated the whole country with shoes and slippers.
It's also true that the people are still barefoot,
but it doesn't matter. I mean it's nothing to be
ashamed of. It's possible that they can't make shoes.
It's possible they sent to England to get the shoes
but they haven't arrived yet. The shoes might have
arrived but could still be waiting for customs release. But the people are hard to please. They walk
barefoot and yet they don't like the Barefoot Project. Just like the Piaster Project...

*A charity project to combat bare feet by providing
shoes for the needy. A donations campaign was started
and money collected, but the project did not material-
ize.

CHAIRMAN:

Enough, Munib Bey, enough.

MUNIB:

I don't understand why you resent me so today. I didn't speak at all today.

CHAIRMAN:

To the point. To the point.

MUNIB:

Everything's to the point. Why aren't you with me today, Mr. Chairman?

CHAIRMAN:

O.K., go ahead!

MUNIB:

The Piaster Project, I say. They collected piasters without end from the people to build a fez factory. When the factory started production, people stopped wearing fezes. The factory closed down. And this is the story of our factories, one closed down and other hasn't opened yet. What can the government do for the people? Why did they take off their fezes? Why are they walking barefoot? Why don't they see the doctor? Why don't they go to school? When I was at Oxford...

LABIB:

(With enthusiasm) By God, it's reasonable, very reasonable, my Friends...

SHAKIB:

Labib Bey, Labib Bey, is your hand itching?

LABIB:

(Smiling stupidly) No, why do you ask?

SHAKIB:

Nothing. My hand's itching.

NAQIB:

(Encouraged) The poverty, the ignorance and the disease in which the people are wallowing, fellow ...

CHAIRMAN:

This can't go on, my Friends. We are meeting today to reach a decision about the bridge problem, not to review the problems of the country.

NAQIB:

Mr. Chairman, the bridge problem is part and parcel
of the country's problems. In order to understand
it for what it really is, we have to understand the
problems surrounding us.

FARID:

(Stands up calmly) Exactly, Naqib Bey. Today I understood why the bridge is a problem. I thought...

SHAKIB:

We don't care what you think.

FARID:

Yes, you do. You should know what you are. You don't
see yourselves and you don't know what you're doing.

NAQIB:

Mr. Chairman!

CHAIRMAN:

Sit down, Mr. Farid. You don't have permission to
speak.

FARID:

And you? Who gave you permission for the nonsense
you've been saying for hours?

CHAIRMAN:

Sit down, I tell you. One more word...

FARID:

Do what you like. I must speak. I must let you see
what you are. I thought it was a simple issue: the
piers are defective, so, we remove them. But before removing them, we have to remove whoever built
them. And that is not Sherif Sami alone. I often
have heard people speaking of the triviality,
corruption, and loss of values, and all the things
you spoke about like parrots. Today, and only today,
did I come to understand why we have to overcome all
these things. Not for the advancement of the country,
no! Only so that one might live without feeling that
the life of any street dog is cleaner than his own.

SHAKIB:

Out! Kick him out!

FARID:

Do you know what you are doing? You are telling all
engineers in Egypt, "Steal, cheat, build without
foundations," and they will. The result will be the
ruin of the country. And you are ruining the
country with your own hands. Why? Why? Who's to

gain by this ruin? If anyone were to write your
story people would say the writer was mad, hallucinating, and they have every right, because it's
really absurd.

SHAKIB:

Kick him out!

FARID:

Who would believe that treason has become so natural in your lives and that anyone who is not a
traitor is in your view a criminal who must be
executed.

(Loud murmurs from the members. Exit Farid.)

HASIB:

Fire him!

SHAKIB:

He must be fired!

LABIB:

He's dangerous!

HABIB:

My knees can't hold me!

MUNIB:

He's a traitor! When I was at Oxford...

HASIB:

Somebody is behind him!

AGIB:

He has no morals!

SHAKIB:

He's a political activist!

NAQIB:

Clandestine!

AGIB:

He's bitter against the palace.

LABIB:

What's his party?

NAQIB:

Who's his father?

SHAKIB:

Who's his mother?

MUNIB:

Who's his sister?

GHARIB:

None of this matters. What's important is that he

is not fit to be an engineer. Hence, he must be
fired.

SHAKIB:

O.K. Lets pass a decision giving him the sack and
send it to the Ministry.

GHARIB:

Dictate the phrasing of the decision, Shakib Bey.

CHAIRMAN:

Gharib Bey, Shakib Bey, respected Members, we cannot fire Farid.

SHAKIB:

After what he did? There was nothing else he could
have done but take off his shoes and beat us with
them.

GHARIB:

I'll resign if he isn't fired!

HASIB:

I'll do the same.

MUNIB:

It's an insult!

NAQIB:

It's treason!

MUGIB:

He must be confined!

SHAKIB:

In a cell!

HASIB:

In a madhouse!*

SHAKIB:

In a warehouse!

LABIB:

In a whorehouse!

NAQIB:

In an outhouse!

HASIB:

In a workhouse!

AGIB:

In a hothouse!

*This, and the following six lines, have been changed
to match the rhyme of the Arabic text, where the dialogue breaks down to almost meaningless, but rhyming
exchanges.

GHARIB:

In a cell!

CHAIRMAN:

Respected Members, I am obliged to disclose the secret to you. I have instructions from high up that Farid is not to be fired. Not only that, but he must go back to the job and build the bridge!

SHAKIB:

Really? Somebody must be backing him!

HABIB:

That's why he said what he said!

LABIB:

We're lost!

MUGIB:

It seems he comes from a good family!

AGIB:

He has good morals!

MUNIB:

He speaks...

NAQIB:

Everything he said is correct!

MUNIB:

He speaks like an upper-class person!

LABIB:

I didn't understand a thing!

SHAKIB:

We should call him back and conciliate him.

LABIB:

Yes, we could settle it with him!

HASIB:

He shouldn't say no.

HABIB:

He's one of us!

GHARIB:

He's an efficient engineer!

CHAIRMAN:

Respected Members, respected Members, Farid doesn't have any backing!

SHAKIB:

No backing? How come?

CHAIRMAN:

The evidence that Farid has that the piers are defective is the piers themselves. And these, of
course, are strong proof. If Farid were to be
fired, he wouldn't keep quiet. He'd go to the papers, stir up the opposition, and there'd be a
scandal!

NAQIB:

A scandal?

CHAIRMAN:

Yes, a scandal! And one scandal will bring about
another scandal, and it won't stop. And you know
the bloody rackets in this country, each worse
than the other. You also know that the country is
full of thieves, substantial thieves compared to
whom Sherif Sami looks innocent. In short, this
business can ruin a lot of people, people whom we
know, friends of ours, relatives, people among
ourselves. This is the situation. Do you understand now?

SHAKIB:

What then?

CHAIRMAN:

The Ministry has suspended Farid from his job to
intimidate him. Today a decision has been issued
reinstating him. Tomorrow morning, I'll notify
him and instruct him to build the bridge.

MUGIB:

Why, then, did you ask him to attend the council
meeting?

CHAIRMAN:

To teach him a lesson, that is, to intimidate
him. And I think he was.

LABIB:

He was terribly intimidated.

HABIB:

He went out frightened as a cat!

MUGIB:

Like a dog wagging his tail!

SHAKIB:

He retreated!

AGIB:

His morals are weak!

LABIB:

He has no personality.

NAQIB:

What happens when the bridge falls down?

CHAIRMAN:

When the bridge is built and falls down the cabinet
will have been changed.

GHARIB:

Quite reasonable. It will fall down during the next
administration!

SHAKIB:

A nice joke on the next administration. They deserve it!

CHAIRMAN:

Well, then, let's pass the resolution. Nasib Effendi,
call the names, without the titles, if there's no
objection. Please, those who agree should say, "I
agree." *(He taps the table with his pen.)* Attention.
Go ahead, Nasib Effendi, call the names.

NASIB:

(Calling the roll) Gharib

GHARIB:

I agree.

NASIB:

Agib

AGIB:

I agree.

NASIB:

Habib

HABIB:

I agree.

NASIB:

Shakib

SHAKIB:

I agree.

NASIB:

Mugib

MUGIB:

I agree.

NASIB:

Munib

MUNIB:
>   I agree.

NASIB:
>   Hasib

HASIB:
>   I agree.

NASIB:
>   Naqib

NAQIB:
>   I agree.

NASIB:
>   Muhib Bey

CHAIRMAN:
>   I agree. It's unanimous. Write it down, Nasib
>   Effendi: unanimous agreement.

NASIB:
>   *(Writes.)* Unanimous agreement. *(He asks.)* Unani-
>   mous agreement on what?

CHAIRMAN:
>   *(To Gharib)* Right! On what?

GHARIB:
>   *(To Agib)* On what?

AGIB:
>   *(To Labib)* On what?

LABIB:
>   *(To Habib)* On what?

HABIB:
>   *(To Shakib)* On what?

SHAKIB:
>   *(To Mugib)* On what?

MUGIB:
>   *(To Munib)* On what?

MUNIB:
>   *(To Hasib)* On what?

HASIB:
>   *(To Naqib)* On what?

NAQIB:
>   *(To Muhib)* On what?

CHAIRMAN:
>   (From this point until the end of the scene he
>   assumes the attitude of an elementary school-
>   teacher.) Well, then. He who agrees that the

piers are defective as the committee says, should
say "defective," just the word "defective." We
don't want anything more than that, understand?
Nasib Effendi will handle the roll-call. Go ahead.
*(The word "defective" rises higher and higher in a
musical scale in each row, i.e., twice.)*

NASIB:

Shakib

SHAKIB:

Defective!

NASIB:

Habib

HABIB:

Defective!

NASIB:

Labib

LABIB:

Defective!

NASIB:

Agib

AGIB:

Defective!

NASIB:

Gharib

GHARIB:

Defective!

CHAIRMAN:

And I...defective! All right. Now the other row;
let's finish.

NASIB:

Naqib

NAQIB:

Defective!

NASIB:

Hasib

HASIB:

Defective!

NASIB:

Munib

MUNIB:

Defective!

NASIB:
> Mugib

MUGIB:
> Defective!

CHAIRMAN:
> Great. Great. Very good. O.K., once more, and be
> good. He who agrees that the piers are not defec-
> tive, as the committee says, should say "not de-
> fective." Just these two words, "not defective."
> Understand? All right, Nasib Effendi.

NASIB:
> Shakib

SHAKIB:
> Not defective!

NASIB:
> Habib

HABIB:
> Not defective!

NASIB:
> Labib

LABIB:
> Not defective!

NASIB:
> Agib

AGIB:
> Not defective!

NASIB:
> Gharib

GHARIB:
> Not defective!

CHAIRMAN:
> And I...not defective! O.K., second row.

NASIB:
> Naqib

NAQIB:
> Not defective!

NASIB:
> Hasib

HASIB:
> Not defective!

NASIB:
> Munib

MUNIB:

Not defective!

NASIB:

- Mugib

MUGIB:

Not defective!

CHAIRMAN:

Great. The resolution is--write it down, Nasib
Effendi--"The piers are defective and not defective." I thank you, respected Members, for this
wise resolution and I congratulate you. The session is adjourned.

Quick Curtain

Act II   Scene III

*(Uncle Kamel's house. It is midnight. A dim light
comes from a small lantern at the entrance of the hall
near the garden. Abul Uyun's chair is empty. Shahira's
door is half-open on the garden side. Mahassen sits in
front of the door fully facing the audience. She is
wearing a red evening dress, with no sleeves and a low
neckline. On her head is a diamond crown and in her
hand a flower which she is plucking, one leaf after the
other.)*

MAHASSEN:
He loves me. He loves me not. He loves me. He loves
me not. He loves me. He loves me not. How come?
(Pause. She arranges the crown on her head.) He's
stupid. Where could he find a prettier girl? *(She
takes a mirror out of her purse and looks at herself.)*
My eyes are beautiful, my nose is fine, and everything about me is delicious. And I love him. I'm
dying for him, and he...*(She sees Farid coming from
the garden gate in her mirror. Scared)* Oh Mama, the
ghost! *(She runs to Shahira's room. Farid comes forward. She sees him. He stops. She runs to him and
throws herself into his arms. She puts her arm around
his neck, shaking.)* Farid. Oh how you scared me. I
I thought you were the ghost.
FARID:
(Pushing her away) What ghost?

MAHASSEN:
>*(Enthusiastically)* The ghost that appeared to Mrs.
>Sekina, Hagg Bassiouni's wife. Can you imagine
>that ghosts now appear in broad day light?

FARID:
>Nonsense! Impossible!

MAHASSEN:
>It's impossible, but it happened. The poor woman
>is in the hospital. Imagine his audacity in appear-
>ing to her right at noon! She was baking bread and
>found this thing, his face all hair, tall and black
>as coal, his eyes lengthwise and gleaming, standing
>over her head. She screamed. Her children, the
>servants, and the neighbors all came. They threw
>dust at him, but he wouldn't budge. He moved only
>when he heard the fire truck. He entered a very
>small hole in the oven, a tiny little hole. The
>firemen aimed their hoses at the oven, but the
>more water, the more the fire blazed. They were
>afraid they might set the house on fire, so they
>left. As soon as they left, the fire died out.
>Ismail says it's something in physics. Physics
>or chemistry, I can't remember.

FARID:
>Is Ismail in town?

MAHASSEN:
>Your hands are cold, Farid. Ismail is in Alexandria.
>He called me.

FARID:
>When?

MAHASSEN:
>At seven o'clock. Where were you all this time?
>I've been dressed up and waiting for you since ten
>o'clock. And here you come at one o'clock. Where
>do we go now?

FARID:
>Did we agree to go anywhere?

MAHASSEN:
>No, but if you'd come earlier we might have gone
>out.

FARID:
>Gone out where?

MAHASSEN:

Right, where could we have gone? Farid, you never take me out. It must be that you are not in love with me. Ismail will not be able to come before Saturday, and today is Wednesday.* Well, it doesn't matter. Every night I'll wear a different dress and stay here with you. It isn't necessary to go out. What a lovely car Ismail has! You should get your-self a car, Farid. Otherwise, how are we going to go out? You should see the dresses I bought in Alexandria. They are so beautiful! So lovely! How do you like this dress? Ismail says that I look like a model wearing it. Look! *(She displays the dress like a fashion model.)*

FARID:

Didn't you break up with Ismail?

MAHASSEN:

(Simply) We made up. Things change, you know.

FARID:

You said you wouldn't see him anymore.

MAHASSEN:

I can't Farid. As soon as I heard his voice over the telephone, it was as if nothing had happened. Tell me, and don't be a bad boy. Honestly, am I not like a queen?

FARID:

(Nodding approval slowly as he silently looks at her.)

MAHASSEN:

You think I'm crazy, right? But why shouldn't I be a queen? Is Nariman** better than I am? But I would not marry Farouk. He's fat and looks like a mule. He's exactly like a bull now. What does he eat, that man? *(She thinks a little.)* The king of England. No, I don't like the English. Do you remember? *Ya Aziz, ya Aziz, kubba takhud li-Ingiliz.**** (She*

---

*There is a slight contradiction here, since this is pre-
 sumably the same night on which the Council meeting of
 the previous scene was held, namely, Saturday.
 **King Farouk's second wife.
***A popular slogan meaning "May plague take the English."

makes a gesture with her closed fist.) You look so handsome when you're cross! I'm not going to marry anybody else but you. Don't be sad. *(She is really happy.)* With you I feel I'm really a queen, even without going out. Even here, at Uncle Kamel's house. Give me a kiss, Farid. *(She advances while he retreats.)*

FARID:

What about Ismail?

MAHASSEN:

Is Ismail with us now?

FARID:

Aren't you betraying him now?

MAHASSEN:

Betraying him? I never thought about that.
(Short pause, then she bursts out laughing.) Oh, Farid, don't be so meticulous. Go to Alexandria and see what the girls do there. Each one of them dates ten boys. Would such a girl be betraying them all?

FARID:

Does Ismail know that you...that there is anything between us?

MAHASSEN:

Oh my goodness, he'd kill me! He's so jealous. *(Pause)* But why are you asking? *(Perceptively)* Oh, so it's because he doesn't know that I'm betraying him? *(Playfully)* Well, you know everything between me and Ismail, so I'm not betraying you, my love. *(Truthfully and simply)* I can't betray you, Farid. I can never betray you.
(The horse neighs loudly.)

FARID:

Listen, Mahassen.

MAHASSEN:

Yes, Darling.

FARID:

I think you should marry Ismail.

MAHASSEN:

And you are able to say it? Is it over now? Do you hate me? What a pity. *(She cries.)* What a pity.

FARID:

I want you to be happy.

MASHASSEN:

> *(She raises her head and dries her tears.)* I am
> happy. I am happy, Darling, so long as you are with
> me. *(She kisses his hand.)* Tell me, why were you
> in the Council meeting so long? What did you do?
> *(Farid doesn't answer.)* He doesn't answer! *(Fondling
> him)* I know. I know that my Beloved is upset,
> wounded. And I'm the cause. Do you think I'm
> stupid? I understand everything. You...

FARID:

> There's no need...

MAHASSEN:

> Let me speak, Farid. I have to.

FARID:

> What do you want to say?

MAHASSEN:

> I want to say a lot of things that I haven't said
> to anyone. *(She looks at him silently for a moment.)*
> You've lost weight, my Darling, and become ex-
> tremely handsome. I missed you so in Alexandria.
> Sometimes I'd sit and cry for a long time and
> Ismail would ask me why I was crying, and I would
> tell him I didn't know. I was yearning for you
> to be by my side, to be able to reach out my hand
> and hold yours, to put my head on your shoulder,
> to kiss you, and to go on crying until I had washed
> away the immense sadness in my heart. And then I'd
> laugh, laugh at the least pretext. Ismail would tell
> me I was crazy, and I'd tell him he was crazy, too.
> When I felt I was leaving, coming back to you , my
> joy couldn't be contained by the world. The world
> becomes too small for my happiness when I feel
> that I'm still yours. Without you, my Beloved, I'm
> not worth a thing.

FARID:

> I...

MAHASSEN:

> *(Puts her hand over his mouth.)* Don't say anything.
> I know you don't believe me.

FARID:

> I believe you, but...

MAHASSEN:

> But you don't love me. I know. How could you love
> me after I had known another man, after I had be-
> trayed you, Farid. Didn't you say...

FARID:

> I didn't say...

MAHASSEN:

> Didn't you say I betrayed you with Ismail? Do you
> think I didn't understand what you meant. I wish
> I hadn't told you, Farid. *(Short pause.)* I
> couldn't have done it. I can cheat anybody else
> but you.

FARID:

> Enough, Mahassen, there's no need...

MAHASSEN:

> Let me speak, Farid. What are you going to lose
> if I do? You want me to marry Ismail, right?
> But I don't want to marry him. I want to marry
> the man I love. I want to marry you, but you
> don't want to marry me. Even if you agreed to
> marry me, you'd hate me. You won't forget that
> I betrayed you. And if I agreed to marry Ismail,
> he would hate me. He won't forget that I be-
> trayed him. Why are men so faithless, Farid?
> And women too. The world is full of faithless
> men and women. And they are living happily...

FARID:

> Nonsense!

MAHASSEN:

> No it's not nonsense. It's the truth. It's only
> because I'm an idiot, stupid and kind-hearted.
> And so are you, Farid, my Darling. You are kind.
> That's why we can't make it. It's a pity, Farid.
> It's a pity for both of us together. *(She
> cries. A very short pause. then she raises her
> head suddenly.)* How I wish I'd suddenly find
> myself transformed into a palm tree!

FARID:

> A palm tree?

MAHASSEN:

> Yes, a palm tree. Like these. (Pointing) But
> not in Uncle Kamel's house. Somewhere far away,

say in the desert. Standing there alone. And
you? What would you like to be, Farid?

FARID:

I don't know.

MAHASSEN:

A crow, Farid. A crow. The crow is beautiful.
It looks nice, minds its own business and never
harms anyone. You'd fly away and come at night
to sleep...on the palm tree. And I'd give forth
dates for you to eat, and we'd live happily.
(With a different, serious and sober tone) Farid,
send me off tomorrow morning on the first train.

FARID:

Where?

MAHASSEN:

Anywhere. Sneak me away, hide me. Listen, send
me off to Cairo. Put me somewhere that only
you would know about. And when Ismail comes on
Saturday, tell him I ran away or died or anything; and then, after a month, two months,
anytime you like, come and take me. I'll live
the rest of my life at your feet. I swear by God
I'd do it, Farid. If there were a train now, I'd
be gone.

FARID:

No, you must stay where you are.

MAHASSEN:

Stay for what, Farid? Wait for what?

FARID:

Wait for Ismail--to face him and face yourself.
Face reality.

MAHASSEN:

Then I'm lost. I'm finished.
(The horse neighs. Sundus enters hurriedly.)

SUNDUS:

(At the top of his voice, frantically) Master
Kamel, the horse jumped! The horse jumped!

KAMEL:

(Entering) Jumped? Where did it jump, Boy?
(Abul Uyun and Hamed enter.)

SUNDUS:

(Continuing) But we brought him back. We ran
after him.

KAMEL:

    The bastard!

SUNDUS:

    (Continuing) We brought him back, but he wants
to escape again. What shall we do?
*(The neighing of the horse continues for a short
while.)*

KAMEL:

    Kill him!

SUNDUS:

    Kill him?

KAMEL:

    Yes, kill him and eat his meat.

FARID:

    Impossible!

HAMED:

    He might mend his ways.

KAMEL:

    He's no good now that he's broken the fence.

MAHASSEN:

    Since he's crazy, death is better for him.

KAMEL:

    (To Sundus) What are you waiting for? Take the
watchman, take all the men and go kill him.

FARID:

    It's a crime!
(Sundus goes out.)

KAMEL:

    Kill him! *(He sees Said going out of the house.)*
Said! *(He calls. Said looks towards him, then
continues walking towards the door.)*

KAMEL:

    Where are you going, Boy?
(Said continues walking.)

KAMEL:

    (Scared. In a thundering voice.) Said!

SAID:

    (Stops) What do you want?
(Karima enters wearing a night gown.)

KAMEL:

    (Advances towards Said, grabs his hand and pulls

him to the center of the stage.) Come here.
Where are you going? I didn't think I'd be
able to find you.

SAID:

(Sarcastically) Why? Was I lost?

KAMEL:

(Regaining his dignity) What brought you here?
(Said doesn't answer.) Speak! Why did you come?

SAID:

I came to get my gun.

KAMEL:

(Scared again) What are you going to do with it?
Where are you going?

SAID:

I'll go where I want to go. I'm free.

KAMEL:

I know where you're going. I know everything
about you.

SAID:

So what? Are you threatening me?

KAMEL:

(Relenting a little) I'm trying to explain to
you, to warn you.

SAID:

I don't need your warnings.

KAMEL:

(Roughly) No, you do need them. *(He suddenly
relents and almost whispers.)* The police are
waiting for you tonight. They have set an ambush
for you. Do you understand?

SAID:

(Cruelly) And what do you want?

KAMEL:

(A little roughly) I want nothing. I want you
to give up this smuggling business. The law
won't leave you alone. It'll break you.

SAID:

The law? Ha! It is I who break it. I break it
every day and stomp on it with my shoes. For
three years now...

KAMEL:

You don't understand anything.

SAID:

I understand everything.

KAMEL:

If you faltered once, they'd have no mercy on
you. They'd kill you as they killed me.

SAID:

They killed you? They acquitted you.

KAMEL:

They acquitted me, but they killed me.

SAID:

(Sarcastically) Speak sensibly, Man! Is it that
you're innocent, and they killed you, or is
it that they couldn't kill you because there
was no evidence?

KAMEL:

(Furiously) Evidence? I have the evidence.

SAID:

Where is it?

KAMEL:

(Retracting) The truth. The truth is the evidence.

SAID:

That's an old one.

KAMEL:

You don't know the truth. Nobody knows it but
me.

SAID:

Any why are you concealing it? What do you fear?

KAMEL:

I don't fear anything. I'm afraid for you and
your sister. *(He pauses. Reluctantly)* But perhaps if you knew, you'd be better. *(As if de-
claring something new)* The kerosene stove did
not explode in front of Shahira as I said in
the investigation. *(Pause. Still reluctant)*

SAID:

(Sarcastically) That, too, is an old one. Ha,
ha, ha! *(He laughs.)*

KAMEL:

(Screaming) Your mother committed suicide,

Boy! She set fire to her bed. We found the kerosene can under her bed. Abul Uyun *(Pointing to him)* carried it in his arms while it was burning and threw it outside. He returned with his face burning and his eye-sight gone.

SAID:

The kerosene can is no evidence.

KAMEL:

(Furiously, screaming) You want the evidence? Here it is. *(He takes a letter out of his pocket and throws it on the floor.)* Your mother had written this before she committed suicide, asking me not to try to find out the reason. If only I could understand why?

HAMED:

(Picking up the letter) Strange!

MAHASSEN:

(Wiping tears from her eyes.) Why, Father? Why did you remain silent all these years? Why didn't you speak out the first day?

KAMEL:

What could I say? Sully her name? Bring shame upon you?

MAHASSEN:

But...

KAMEL:

But what? I didn't know that all this was going to happen, that you'd live in shame until you died, because your father was a criminal who killed your mother.

FARID:

But the truth should have come out.

KAMEL:

Of what use is that? If they'd known the truth, they would've had mercy neither on me nor on her. They'd have said, "She was in love. That is why she committed suicide." They'd have said, "He was tormenting her. That's why she killed herself." Of what use is the truth? They'd still have killed me. *(Soud of bullets. He screams.)* They killed him. They killed Shihab, my friend. *(He collapses, holding Abul*

Uyun's shoulder.) They killed him. *(Said goes out. Mahassen puts her hand on her eyes. Hamed stands still. Farid walks to the far left. Karima hurries towards Farid. The sound of another bullet. Kamel is still collapsed.)*

KARIMA:

(Holding Farid's hand, scared) Why did they kill him, Farid? Why did they kill him?

FARID:

Because be broke the fence. *(Slowly as if talking to himself. Facing the audience)* They tied his feet, covered his eyes and shot him. *(Short pause)* Nothing is easier than killing an animal.

Curtain

Act III   Scene I

*(Uncle Kamel's house. Fifteen days have passed
since the events of Act Two. It is 5 p.m. The house
of Sarhan Bey, one of the town's notables, where
several people are gathered, including Sha'lan, Dr.
Lam'i, Shekh Tannir, Zaki Effendi, Master Halawa. At
Uncle Kamel's house, Zakya and Sundus are seen eating.
Abul Uyun is in his chair.)*

YOUSSEF:
    In what way is Farid like his uncle?
SUNDUS:
    How could I eat his flesh? He was my friend.
SHA'LAN:
    Both are crooks.
ZAKYA:
    Your friend? Do you take horses for friends, now?
SHA'LAN:
    When Kamel found out that he had been caught,
    he gave up his portion of the estate and was
    thus acquitted.
ZAKYA:
    Take a man or a woman as a friend...
SHA'LAN:
    And when Farid found out that he was going to
    be caught, he attributed the piers to Sherif.

SUNDUS:

> He was better than a hundred men. He was strong enough to demolish a mountain.

SARHAN:

> So it's Farid who...

SUNDUS:

> Courageous.

SHA'LAN:

> Yes, it's Farid who built the piers.

ZAKYA:

> A lot of good his courage did him!

YOUSSEF:

> Where did you get all this?

ZAKYA:

> They killed him.

SHA'LAN:

> From higher sources.

SUNDUS:

> Why not? Death comes first to the courageous.

YOUSSEF:

> What sources?

SUNDUS:

> Ten men couldn't break him down.

YOUSSEF:

> I saw the piers with my own eyes before Farid even set foot here in this town.

SUNDUS:

> After jumping over the fence, he agreed to come back only with me.

SHA'LAN:

> You counted them?

YOUSSEF:

> No, of course I didn't.

SHA'LAN:

> Well then, shut up!

YOUSSEF:

> Shut up and let you speak this nonsense?

SUNDUS:

> I wish I'd let him go.

ZAKYA:

> Let him go where?

SHEIKH TANNIR:
Pray for the Prophet, Men!
SUNDUS:
Go wherever he wanted to go.
SHA'LAN:
Do you think I speak nonsense, Men?
SUNDUS:
God's earth is big enough.
SARHAN:
What you say is impossible, Sha'lan. Everyone
knows.
SHA'LAN:
People know nothing. They're just rumors.
SUNDUS:
I wish I'd let him go.
SKEIKH TANNIR:
The town is full of rumors.
DR. LAM'I:
And public opinion is influenced by rumors.
SHA'LAN:
You believe me now? The doctor himself says it's
a rumor.
YOUSSEF:
How could it be a rumor?
DR. LAM'I:
There's even a theory which says that public
opinion is made up of rumors.
SUNDUS:
He loved only me...
ZAKYA:
You're both crazy.
SHA'LAN:
Listen to this, Men! Sherif had built some
piers, three or four, then Farid came and com-
pleted them.
SARHAN:
It's possible.
SHA'LAN:
He completed them by building bad piers. That
is the story.
ZAKYA:
Aren't you going to come back to your senses,
Boy?

TANNIR:

    Everything is possible.

YOUSSEF:

    It's Farid who reported on the piers.

SHAHIRA:

    (Appears to Abul Uyun) What can we do now?

YOUSSEF:

    Then why did the committee come here?

SHA'LAN:

    They came to investigate.

ZAKYA:

    Aren't you coming, Boy?

YOUSSEF:

    Investigate?

ZAKYA:

    To the other side of the river?

SHA'LAN:

    Yes, to cross-examine Farid.

SUNDUS:

    I told you, it's no use.

SHAHIRA:

    What can we do?

YOUSSEF:

    Well, if Farid were wrong, why did they give
    him back his job?

ZAKYA:

    No use?

SHA'LAN:

    You know how it is with nepotism and all that!

SHAHIRA:

    What can we do?

SUNDUS:

    Yes, it's no use, no use. *(Exit Sundus)*

ZAKYA:

    (Going out, sadly) No use. It's no use.

YOUSSEF:

    Then why does Farid refuse to go back to work?

MAHASSEN:

    *(Mahassen enters, holding a picture of her mother
    in her hand)* If I only knew the reason.

YOUSSEF:

    Why is Farid refusing to build the bridge?

SHAHIRA:
　　Our love leads nowhere...
SHA'LAN:
　　In order to harm Sherif Sami. He wants to avenge
　　himself.
MAHASSEN:
　　Oh, my beloved mother. *(She kisses her mother's
　　picture.)*
SARHAN:
　　Why should he avenge himself?
TANNIR:
　　What did he do to him?
SHAHIRA:
　　What can we do?
SHA'LAN:
　　He deserted his sister.
SARHAN:
　　He divorced her?
SHAHIRA:
　　Our love must stay here *(She points to her heart.)*
　　forever...
YOUSSEF:
　　But Farid has no sisters.
HALAWA:
　　The town's business is dying!
SHAHIRA:
　　And be buried with us. *(Starts to go out.)*
MAHASSEN:
　　If only I knew who tormented you!
TANNIR:
　　You mean this is a rumor?
HALAWA:
　　Didn't we come here to write the petition?
SHAHIRA:
　　And be buried with us. *(She disappears.)*
HALAWA:
　　Why don't we write it? What are we waiting for?
MAHASSEN:
　　Why, Mother? Why?
YOUSSEF:
　　And the meeting?

HALAWA:
      Let's go to the meeting.
SARHAN:
      Let's go, Men. *(They go.)*
MAHASSEN:
      Why, Mother? Why?
      (Karima and Hamed enter.)
HAMED:
      (Fresh and happy) And that's how the miracle
      happened. Communication without contact.
KARIMA:
      Mahassen, didn't you go to Alexandria?
MAHASSEN:
      I changed my mind.
HAMED:
      My beloved ignored me, so I ignored her, too.
      And I wrote...
MAHASSEN:
      A letter? What did you say?
HAMED:
      What letter? I wrote a story...a story!
MAHASSEN:
      A story? What can she do with a story?
HAMED:
      She can read it, cultivate herself.
MAHASSEN:
      Do you write stories?
HAMED:
      (To Karima) She's not with us!
KARIMA:
      Don't you know that they published a story by
      Hamed?
MAHASSEN:
      I don't believe it!
HAMED:
      That was in the past, when the transmitter
      wasn't working, because the receiver wasn't
      working either. Now the transmitter is working.
MAHASSEN:
      What are you gibbering about?
HAMED:
      No. No. I won't permit you to speak like that
      to a respectable author. Don't you know that we

are the architects of the soul. We clear it
and clean it and build bridges on it. Where did
Farid go?

MAHASSEN:

You're hallucinating!

HAMED:

Well, go on. Go on and I will twist your psyche
around, efface it. *(Looks at his watch.)* It's
now ten and the meeting is at eleven. Could he
be with my uncle in the fields?

KARIMA:

I don't think so.

MAHASSEN:

Why not? Aren't they friends now? *(To herself)*
They're alike...

HAMED:

Indeed, they are alike, my brother and my uncle.
They both liberated me.

MAHASSEN:

From your beloved?

HAMED:

From myself. They made the transmitter work.
It's they who made the jinni of writing take
possession of me.

MAHASSEN:

(Sarcastically) Oh mama!

HAMED:

It is really frightening to hold the pen and
find that it writes all by itself, and it goes
on writing and writing. I become frightened.
Oh, my God! Where does it get all these
things? But it's a story that makes the rocks
speak, be it that of my uncle or that of my
brother. Where is that guy? Shouldn't he say
where he's going before he goes? What does he
think this house is?

KARIMA:

Do you think this meeting will do any good,
Hamed?

HAMED:

It must! We have nothing else. If the people
won't look after their own interests, who will?
The government has proved ineffectual, no good.

MAHASSEN:

And your beloved, did you leave her?

HAMED:

Leave her? Why? Have I gone crazy?

MAHASSEN:

Didn't you say she left you?

HAMED:

I said she's not aware of me. Leave her?
Impossible!

MAHASSEN:

Where is this beloved of yours?

HAMED:

My beloved is here *(Waving his hands)* and here
...and there. Everywhere!

MAHASSEN:

The unknown beloved!

HAMED:

Not likely! I know her very well. I could spot
her in the midst of a hundred thousand girls.
But she doesn't know me. *(To Karima, in an
attempt to change the subject)* Did I tell you
I was writing a play?

KARIMA:

Really? What's it called?

HAMED:

I don't know yet.

KARIMA:

What's it about?

HAMED:

It's about life...this world, society. The
scene is a large garden in which people are
living. When the curtain rises, we see a man
sitting in the middle of the garden, holding
some bricks and building...

MAHASSEN:

A house?

HAMED:

No, a wall. A high wall. In the second scene
the number of people building increases to two;
in the third scene, three; in the fourth, four;
in the fifth, five; and so on until everyone in
the garden is busy building the wall.

KARIMA:

> And then?

HAMED:

> And then what?

KARIMA:

> How are you going to end it?

HAMED:

> I don't know. All I can see is the wall rising,
> the darkness increasing, the air diminishing,
> and they are still building.
> *(Enter Kamel)*

HAMED:

> Uncle, have you seen Farid? *(Kamel shakes his
> head.)* Where could he have gone?

KAMEL:

> You haven't left, Karima?

KARIMA:

> I'm going to take the evening train.

KAMEL:

> Why don't you stay with us? *(Short pause)* On
> second thought, you'd better leave. Who knows
> when your husband is going to get out of jail.

MAHASSEN:

> How many years could he get?

KAMEL:

> At least five years. Oh, he's stupid!

MAHASSEN:

> *(Sarcastically)* And are you going to stay five
> years in Cairo, Karima? Won't you be bored?

KAMEL:

> Karima is going to spend some time with her
> folks and some with us.

KARIMA:

> Believe me, Uncle, I don't want to leave, but
> Mother insists. I also want to visit a friend
> of mine who is married to an influential man
> in the palace. He might do something.

MAHASSEN:

> To make them release Said? That would be wonder-
> ful of you!

KARIMA:

> Farid submitted a petition to the palace.

MAHASSEN:

    Oh.

KARIMA:

    (Changing the subject) How's farming, Uncle?

KAMEL:

    Very bad. I'm not going out there anymore.

KARIMA:

    But why? Your health's improved a lot since you went out there.

KAMEL:

    What good is that?

HAMED:

    The peasants don't work?

KAMEL:

    They work. They work even harder than before, but without uttering a single word. They're afraid, as if in a funeral.

HAMED:

    What do you care, so long as production is increasing?

KAMEL:

    I didn't go out to the fields in order to increase production. I went there to stand with the men, to be in touch with them. I thought I would be able to become the Kamel I once was. But it didn't work. The path is blocked and will remain so, and I must stay the Kamel they made, the monster who set fire to his wife, and sat watching her until she was dead. Uncle Kamel.

HAMED:

    You haven't gone out in the fields for ten years.

KARIMA:

    The peasants forgot you. They're not used to you.

KAMEL:

    (Furiously) And my children, are they also not used to me? Why did Said go out that night? If he'd believed me he wouldn't have gone out. And Mahassen? Mahassen only pretends in front of you, but she...

MAHASSEN:

    I believe you, but I'd like to know the reason. I want to know why she did that to herself.

KAMEL:

How should I know? How?

MAHASSEN:

(Simply and softly) Why did they accuse you?

KAMEL:

(Furiously) Didn't I just tell you? She still
suspects me...
(Enter Farid)

HAMED:

Where have you been, Brother?

FARID:

On the other side. This is for you. *(Gives
Karima a rose.)*

KARIMA:

(Joyfully) From the other side?

MAHASSEN:

None for me?

FARID:

I'm sorry, I brought only one.

KARIMA:

(Looking fixedly at the rose) It's so beautiful.
It has all the colors.

HAMED:

What made you go to the other side at this time
of day?

MAHASSEN:

(Sarcastically) He went to fetch Karima a rose.

FARID:

No, I went in order to see the other side, to live
there a while.

HAMED:

Haven't you seen it before? Or have you forgotten
it?

FARID:

Indeed, I had forgotten it.

KARIMA:

(Stunned) Impossible, Farid!

FARID:

It's impossible, but it happened. That night of
the Council meeting, I thought the other side
didn't exist, that it was an invented fable. So
I took the rowboat and went over there. The

waves were high and the water was full of
whirlpools. I could have lost my way. I kept
rowing until I reached it and put my feet on
the ground, and then I came back. But only after
I had made sure that the other side existed,
even though I couldn't see it. It was so dark.

HAMED:

Now that you have seen it and satisfied yourself,
let's go to the meeting.

KARIMA:

Farid, this time you shouldn't leave them without
convincing them. This is your last chance.

FARID:

I can't believe that in order to tell people in
this country that right is right and wrong is
wrong, one must expend all this effort. What
if one were lying or misleading them?

HAMED:

One need not exert any effort. He'll find the
road paved and nice for him. Did you see the
last issue of *The Hammer?*

FARID:

No.

HAMED:

(Produces a magazine from his pocket.) There you
are! Better still, let me read the part that's
of interest to you. It's a long article.

KARIMA:

About Farid?

HAMED:

(Searching in the magazine) About Farid and
Sherif Sami. Here it is. Listen, sir. *(Reads)*
"And that's how right vanquished wrong! The
Council of Engineers has unanimously adopted a
decision to the effect that the piers are good
after they had been shown to a commission of
foreign experts who testified that they were
excellent, unmatched even in the most advanced
countries of the world. It is expected, as a
result, that Engineer Farid Ezzat will be transferred to southernmost Egypt and that Engineer
Sherif Sami will be promoted to a higher post."

FARID:

But nothing of the sort happened!

KARIMA:

Are they going to transfer you, Farid?

MAHASSEN:

To southernmost Egypt!

HAMED:

And promote Sherif Sami?

FARID:

But nothing of all that happened. And no such
thing is going to happen. I was in the Ministry
yesterday. The Undersecretary understands the
whole affair well. It was he who advised me to
write a petition to the palace.

HAMED:

How about the commission of foreign experts who
said the piers were excellent?

FARID:

Nothing of the sort happened, Hamed. You know
that.

HAMED:

(Violently) I know it didn't, but as far as
people are concerned, it happened. And more will
happen. Tomorrow the other papers and magazines
will follow the example of *The Hammer* and write
about it. Are you sure of what they are going
to write?

KARIMA:

Send in a refutation.

HAMED:

Who will publish it? And suppose they did publish the refutation, who would believe it? And
suppose some people did believe it, many others
wouldn't. Sherif Sami would send a reply and the
whole thing would turn into a personal quarrel
between Farid Ezzat and Sherif Sami.

FARID:

But I don't know him!

HAMED:

Even if you climb the highest minaret and keep
shouting, nobody will believe that you don't know

him. Why do you say the piers are defective?
You must have a grudge against Sherif Sami. The
thinking of people here cannot go beyond that.

KARIMA:

But it's impossible that Farid should keep
silent.

FARID:

Is Selim coming here soon to visit his parents
or something?

HAMED:

Which Selim?

FARID:

Selim Ali, the journalist. Your friend.

HAMED:

What do you want from him?

FARID:

To write an article to answer these lies.

HAMED:

Selim Ali is the one who wrote this article and
signed it. Here it is. *(Gives him the magazine.)*

FARID:

But why did he do that? He knows Sherif Sami
well. They were friends...

HAMED:

They were friends and then they fell out with
each other, I know. Then Sherif probably visited
him and invited him for a drink or something of
the sort and they were reconciled. And here's
the result. *(Pointing to the magazine.)* I think
it's quite obvious.

KARIMA:

But what's to be done, Hamed? What's to be done?

HAMED:

What's to be done shall be done. Let's go to
the meeting.
(Farid and Hamed stand up.)

KAMEL:

Sit down, Farid. *(To Hamed)* And you too, sit
down. Sit down, I say. *(They both sit down.)*
Where are you going?

FARID:

I'm going to meet the people.

KAMEL:
    What do you want from them?
FARID:
    I want them to write a petition demanding that
    the piers be removed.
HAMED:
    Uncle, this isn't the time. The meeting is only
    fifteen minutes from now. *(Looks at his watch.)*
KAMEL:
    Farid is not going to the meeting.
FARID:
    Why?
KAMEL:
    Because what you are doing is wrong. Wrong!
FARID:
    Wrong?
KAMEL:
    Yes, wrong. You think you are doing your duty,
    right? I too thought I was doing my duty, but
    there is no such thing as duty. Your duty is
    that when you see something wrong, you should
    not try to correct it. You should keep away
    from it, run, escape!
MAHASSEN:
    Keep away from evil. Grandma used to say that
    all the time.
FARID:
    Do you want me to see them committing suicide
    and remain indifferent?
KAMEL:
    Yes, remain indifferent. Isn't it much better
    than acting the brave man and committing suicide
    yourself? What did my courage do for me? For
    ten years I've been imprisoned within four
    walls and will stay so for the rest of my life.
    Had I gone to jail, I'd have been better off.
    There'd have come the day when they'd have
    realized that an injustice was done to me, and
    so would be friends with me again. I wouldn't
    have lived and died a criminal, an outlaw in
    their view.

MAHASSEN:

    If I only knew why they accused you?

KAMEL:

    (Furiously) Did you hear? This is the second time she asks that question today and she's none else but my own daughter. Once they've accused you, whatever you say or do is of no consequence. When her mother died, her family wrote a petition accusing me. They said I wanted her money. I gave up my portion of the legacy. They said I was in love with another woman. It was proved in the investigations that I had no relationship with any woman. But what's the use? As soon as the investigation was over, the people began to avoid me. My clients started withdrawing their cases. I visited all my friends one after the other trying to explain. They'd say, "Look, he has a guilty conscience. He's defending himself. If he were innocent, he'd have said nothing." When I closed down my office and stayed home they said, "Look, he can't show his face to anyone after what he has done. He is surely a criminal." Once they accuse you...

KARIMA:

    But they haven't accused Farid, Uncle.

KAMEL:

    All that and they haven't accused him yet? Didn't they prove him wrong? Didn't they say the piers were defective but would do? Now aren't the defective piers excellent? Don't they want to promote Sherif Sami? Don't they want to punish Farid? Tomorrow they will say that Farid is a thief, that he was the one who built the piers.

FARID:

    I'll say it's not true.

KAMEL:

    See? You'll have to defend yourself. Once they've accused you, what can you do? And as soon as you start defending yourself, they'll say, "Aha! It is he who actually built them. He's trying

to cover the egg on his face." And how are you
going to defend yourself? Will you say they are
rumors? They'll say, "Where there is smoke,
there is fire." Except that the air is filled
with smoke, dirty, suffocating smoke and ashes
and no fire. Not one single blaze to purify
people's souls of the trivia and the filth in
which they live. Don't you understand yet, Farid?

HAMED:

(Looking at his watch) You're late, Farid.

KAMEL:

You think I'm hallucinating, Hamed. That's why
you haven't uttered a word and kept looking at
your watch. But you are wrong.

FARID:

Uncle...

KAMEL:

Turn back, my Son. You're still at the beginning.
Turn back before they close the loop around your
neck and have you trapped. Turn back before they
make you Uncle Farid. Ask to be transferred. Take
as much money as you like. Bribe them; bribe them
to transfer you.

FARID:

Before I met the Minister I was thinking of asking to be transferred. After I met him I changed
my mind.

KAMEL:

Why? What did the Minister tell you? What did he
promise you?

FARID:

He promised nothing.

KAMEL:

Then what did he tell you? Speak!

FARID:

He told me, "I've studied this subject very
well. It's an unpleasant subject which I don't
like to talk about." I asked him, "In what
sense is it unpleasant, your Excellency?"
He said, "Unpleasant... Don't you understand
what the word unpleasant means?" I said, "Does
it mean I was wrong in reporting that the piers

were defective?" He said, "No, you were not
wrong. The piers are indeed defective." I told
him I couldn't build a bridge on such piers,
because it would fall down, and he said, "It's
none of your business whether it falls down or
not. You can't guarantee anything, can you? Go,
Effendi, and do your job." By the time I went
out, I had decided that the piers must be removed.

KAMEL:

Who will remove them?

FARID:

The people. The people whose town it is. The
people who will use the bridge, who must know
that the bridge they want to be built for them
will collapse, will drown them, and will never
take them to the other side. That it's treason,
not a bridge.

MAHASSEN:

(Claps.) Bravo, Farid! Why don't you write
stories like Hamed?

KARIMA:

(Rebukingly) What's that, Mahassen? What does it
mean?

KAMEL:

Go apologize to the people, Hamed. Farid isn't
going to the meeting.

FARID:

(Stands up.) I told you I have made up my mind!

KAMEL:

(Interrupting) Made up your mind about what?
Killing yourself?
(Farid and Hamed go out.)

KAMEL:

Go, kill yourself! Commit suicide!
*(He walks to his room. Zakya enters hurriedly
and grabs Kamel's galabiya.)*

ZAKYA:

Did you see my ball?

KAMEL:

Go away, Girl! *(He pushes her away and goes
into his room.)*

ZAKYA:

(Addressing Karima and Mahassen from a distance as if there were nobody there.) My ball! They stole it from me. I'm going to tell my mother. *(She walks out, calling.)* Mother, Mama Zakya...

KARIMA:

I should go pack my suitcase. *(She walks to the door. When she gets close to it, Mahassen calls her.)*

MAHASSEN:

Karima!

KARIMA:

(Looking in her direction) Yes, Mahassen?

MAHASSEN:

Come here, I want to tell you something.

KARIMA:

(Walks over to her.) What do you want?

MAHASSEN:

Does it smell good?

KARIMA:

What's that?

MAHASSEN:

Have you already forgotten it? It's still in your hand.

KARIMA:

The rose?

MAHASSEN:

Yes, the rose that Farid brought you. Show it to me.

KARIMA:

What do you want to see it for? Here it is. *(She gives her the rose.)*

MAHASSEN:

I'm going to smell it. Why shouldn't I? *(She takes the rose and puts it beside her.)*

KARIMA:

You didn't smell it.

MAHASSEN:

I don't feel like it now.

KARIMA:

You're behaving strangely today.

MAHASSEN:
   Is it my behavior that is strange?
KARIMA:
   You mean mine? Actually I don't understand
   anything at all.
MAHASSEN:
   You understand everything. *(Pause)* Since when?
KARIMA:
   Since when what?
MAHASSEN:
   Since when did your relationship with Farid
   start? Since when have you been in love? Tell
   me.
KARIMA:
   Are you crazy?
MAHASSEN:
   You are the one who's crazy. A married woman...
KARIMA:
   Mahassen, one more word and I swear I won't
   speak to you the rest of my life.
MAHASSEN:
   Don't you try to pull that one on me. Not that
   ...
KARIMA:
   Enough, enough. *(She puts her hand on her head
   despondently and walks hurriedly toward the
   door.)*
MAHASSEN:
   *(Runs after her, grabs her and turns her
   around.)* So there's nothing? What about this
   rose, then?
KARIMA:
   Where is it. *(Walks eagerly to where the rose is,
   takes it and walks toward the door, looking at
   it lovingly.)*
MAHASSEN:
   See? All your life is in this rose. Why? Why?
   Isn't it because he brought it to you?
KARIMA:
   (Dreamily) Because it's from the other side.
   The side of salvation. Farid wants me to build

a house there in the midst of roses and live in
it with Said. Ha, ha, ha. *(Laughs hysterically
and long.)*

MAHASSEN:

(Shaking her) Karima, Karima! Are you crazy?

KARIMA:

(Continuing) Said hates roses and loves Karima.
There they are sitting in their beautiful
little house with jasmine all over the window.
(Suddenly scared) On the jasmine are snakes,
snakes, and Karima is in Said's arms. Where can
she escape from the snakes? Where can she go to
be away from the snakes? The snakes on the
jasmine...the snakes! *(She looks around as if
snakes are surrounding her. She doesn't know
where to go. Then she collapses on the nearest
chair, holding her neck with her hand as if
suffocating under a frightful nightmare.)*

MAHASSEN:

(Runs to her, pats her cheek and calls her.)
Karima, Karima. Wake up. Open your eyes, you're
here, in Uncle Kamel's house.

KARIMA:

(Opening her eyes) I know. *(Looks around.)*

MAHASSEN:

See. There are no snakes.

KARIMA:

(Longingly) If only they'd build the bridge.

MAHASSEN:

What would happen?

KARIMA:

I'd be saved from all this.

MAHASSEN:

You're silly. Is that why you're so interested
in the bridge? You think it'll change the
universe? Not even a hundred bridges...

KARIMA:

Don't say that, Mahassen. When the bridge is
built and you walk on it...

MAHASSEN:

Where to? Where can I go if the man who was
going to build the bridge has gone away. Until

this moment I thought he was still here, that
he was thinking of you, but would come back to
me. But no. He isn't coming back, Karima.

KARIMA:

Farid? *(As if she is learning this for the
first time)* What about Ismail?

MAHASSEN:

Ismail was rashness, idiocy, madness. Ismail
was suicide, suicide. *(She bursts out crying,
loudly.)*

KARIMA:

(Goes to her and takes her head on her shoulder.)
Dear Mahassen *(Pause)*

MAHASSEN:

*(Opens her eyes and raises her head as if she
were not crying, then kisses Karima in gratitude,
tenderly.)* Dear Karima. *(She lowers her head
again and starts crying.)* Beloved mother.

Curtain

Act III   Scene II

(Same day at 6 p.m. Uncle Kamel's house, the same as before. In Uncle Kamel's house, Abul Uyun in his place, Zakya playing with the ball. The courtyard of the town school, people gathering there.)

HALAWA:
    Stop talking everybody! The town's business is dying...
TANNIR:
    Let's drop this business about the petition, Mr. Farid.
FARID:
    No petition?
TANNIR:
    I meant we'd better be reconciled. Or, what do you think, Men?
CHORUS:
    Yeah...yeah...
FARID:
    Who's to be reconciled?
TANNIR:
    You and Mr. Sherif.
FARID:
    But we haven't quarreled!

TANNIR:
>Look Mister, everyone in this town knows what happened between you and Mr. Sherif.

FARID:
>Let's suppose that whoever built the piers is anonymous. What do we care who built them?

ZAKI:
>We're taking pity on the guy who built them.

YOUSSEF:
>You're taking pity on the guy who built them, but you care nothing about the bridge?

HALAWA:
>We want the bridge, Men. The town's business is dying.

CHORUS:
>Yeah...yeah...

SARHAN:
>Are we to blame if we're taking pity on Mr. Farid?

FARID:
>Taking pity on me? Why? Did I build the piers?

ZAKI:
>(Wickedly) You and Mr. Sherif are one and the same, after all...

DR. LAM'I:
>Look, Mr. Farid, are you sure all the piers are defective?

HALAWA:
>Mr. Doctor, what are the piers to us? The business is dying...

TANNIR:
>Let's get it over with, Master Farid. Let's finish it.

FARID:
>What do you mean "get it over with?"

TANNIR:
>I mean, let's build the bridge.

FARID:
>Please understand me. Anyone building a bridge on these piers will be committing a crime.

HALAWA:
>A crime? We're lost, Men. (He rolls a cigarette.)

CHORUS:
     Yeah...yeah...
FARID:
     If you are ready to assume responsibility for
     the people who are going to die...those who
     will drown... I am not.
ZAKI:
     Death and drowning?
SARHAN:
     To that extent?
YOUSSEF:
     And ruin and destruction and loss.
TANNIR:
     And the government, Men, are they condoning
     this? The government?
YOUSSEF:
     The government's left us in the lurch. That's
     why we must look after ourselves.
HALAWA:
     And the business?
FARID:
     We'll take care of it.
ZAKI:
     What's that you are saying, Mr. Farid? What can
     we do without the government?
TANNIR:
     We won't be worth anything.
CHORUS:
     Yeah...yeah...
DR. LAM'I:
     And don't forget that the government is more
     aware of the people's interests.
FARID:
     You must understand the situation precisely.
     The government does not now want to remove the
     piers.
SARHAN:
     And you want us to tell the government to remove
     them?
TANNIR:
     Do you want us to oppose the government, Mister?

ZAKI:
>
> You want to be the ruination of this town?

TANNIR:
>
> Do you know what would happen if we sent a
> petition saying the piers were defective?

ZAKI:
>
> They'd say someone was inciting them.

ZAKYA:
>
> One red...

SARHAN:
>
> They would neither remove the piers...

TANNIR:
>
> Nor would they ever build the bridge.

ZAKYA:
>
> And one green...

ZAKI:
>
> They'd say "let them drop dead."

TANNIR:
>
> They'd say "let them go to hell."

SARHAN:
>
> "They don't deserve it."

ZAKYA:
>
> *(Calling)* Mother!

TANNIR:
>
> You want us to oppose them now? Let's mind our
> own business.

ZAKI:
>
> Let's keep our peace.

SARHAN:
>
> Do no ill or good.

CHORUS:
>
> Yeah...yeah...

HALAWA:
>
> The business is dying...

CHORUS:
>
> Yeah...yeah...

DR. LAM'I:
>
> Then there's a falsification there, Mr. Farid.

HALAWA:
>
> Falsification? Where?

ZAKYA:

> One red...

FARID:

> What is the falsification, Dr. Lam'i?

DR. LAM'I:

> The Council says the piers are defective but
> not defective. What does that mean?

ZAKYA:

> *(Faster)* One red and one green...

ZAKI:

> *(Enthusiastically)* I'll explain to you why they
> said they were defective. I'll explain. *(Pause.
> He thinks hard.)*

SARHAN:

> Why did you stop, Zaki Effendi?

ZAKI:

> Patience, Sarhan Bey, patience. Well, it's
> quite obvious, quite obvious. The Council of
> Engineers says that the piers are defective.
> *(Thinking)* Why? Why? *(Loudly as if he had made
> a discovery)* Because they are defective. It's
> quite obvious.

CHORUS:

> Yeah...yeah...

DR. LAM'I:

> Not so obvious. The same Council says they are
> not defective. Why? There must be a reason.

CHORUS:

> Yeah...yeah...

ZAKI:

> I'll explain...

SARHAN:

> They may be in collusion with Sherif Sami.

TANNIR:

> Maybe he's their friend.

YOUSSEF:

> Sherif doesn't know any of the Council members.

DR. LAM'I:

> *(Pedantically)* Then why did they say that?
> There must be a reason.

TANNIR:

> And if you know the reason...

ZAKYA:

(Calling) Mother! Mother!

FARID:

I'll tell you the reason. The reason is that
there's no reason.

DR. LAM'I:

(Sarcastically) Is that right?

TANNIR:

Is that possible, Mister Farid?

ZAKI:

Does it make sense that the government should
build a bridge without a foundation for no
reason?

TANNIR:

This is quite unreasonable. The best engineers
in the country drowning people with their own
hands for no reason?

FARID:

And what is reasonable today? What thing has a
reason? The corruption which is such that nobody knows where it begins and where it ends?
What is its reason? Is it fate?

ZAKI:

(Eagerly) I know the reason. I know the reason
now. *(Pause.)*

CHORUS:

Yeah...yeah...

ZAKI:

You want to know why the Council says that the
piers are not defective, right?

TANNIR:

Right.

ZAKI:

Because the piers are really not defective,
that's why.

TANNIR:

Strange, Men! How did we miss that?

SARHAN:

It's very reasonable.

CHORUS:

Yeah...yeah...

YOUSSEF:

How reasonable, since the same Council said that
the piers were defective?

ZAKYA:

One red...

FARID:

And I say, and am ready to prove, that they are
defective.

ZAKYA:

And one green...

DR. LAM'I:

So you agree with the Council on this point only?

FARID:

Of course, because this is the truth.

DR. LAM'I:

What truth, Mr. Farid? Do you expect us to believe you and disbelieve the best engineers in
the land?

FARID:

What does that mean?

DR. LAM'I:

It means, of course, that the piers are not
defective, and if the Council has said otherwise,
it's just because they are being nice to you.

SHA'LAN:

(Jumps up victoriously.) You see now?

FARID:

The Council nice to me? Why?

DR. LAM'I:

Are you asking us? You should ask yourself.

ZAKYA:

(Loudly) Where are you, Mother?

TANNIR:

They're covering up for you!

SARHAN:

They don't want to give you the lie, so you
won't be harmed.

TANNIR:

You want to harm the man and jeopardize his
livelihood?

SARHAN:

God Almighty!

TANNIR:

>Is it really true that Sherif Sami built the piers, all of them?

FARID:

>What are you saying?

TANNIR:

>Did you go to the Minister to tell him that the piers were defective, or...?

ZAKI:

>Why did they suspend you from work?

LAM'I:

>Why don't you want to build the bridge?

TANNIR:

>What have they done to you?

ZAKI:

>Haven't they reinstated you?

SARHAN:

>The bridge for which we want to so much trouble until they agreed to build it.

ZAKI:

>What would you have done had you been a stranger to this town?

SARHAN:

>What would you have done?

HALAWA:

>The business is dying, Mister, dying. People...

CHORUS:

>Yeah...yeah...

YOUSSEF:

>(Walks over to where Farid and Hamed are standing. Addressing the rest) You're confusing everything, hallucinating...

ZAKYA:

>Red and green...

FARID:

>Forget it, Youssef, there's no need.

HALAWA:

>(Jumping to the center of the stage) No need? Get the petition, Man. Write! Write "We, the people...the people of this town..."

FARID:

>(Interrupting) The people of this town (Pause. Thinking)

HALAWA:
    (Joyfully to Farid) Great, you're on our side
    now. Stay with us.
CHORUS:
    Yeah...yeah...
FARID:
    The people of this town *(Very calmly and simply)*
    have betrayed their town.
HALAWA:
    *(Furiously. Shouting in Farid's face and at the
    audience.)* Oh people...people...
CHORUS:
    Yeah...yeah...yeah...
    *(The lights dim on the school courtyard, but
    stay on in Uncle Kamel's house. Then it dims
    gradually until the curtain falls in a near-
    blackout. Enter Sundus.)*
ZAKYA:
    Didn't you see my mother, Kid?
SUNDUS:
    Your mother? Who's your mother, Woman?
ZAKYA:
    My mother, Zakya. Didn't she pass by here?
SUNDUS:
    Come to your senses, Woman. Your mother, Zakya!
ZAKYA:
    (Taking the balls out her pocket) One green and
    one red...Mother gave them to me. Aren't they
    nice?
SUNDUS:
    Yes, they're nice.
ABUL UYUN:
    Sundus! Sundus!
SUNDUS:
    (Goes over to where he is) You want something?
ABUL UYUN:
    Did they say, Boy?
SUNDUS:
    (Quickly. He doesn't want to act.) They didn't
    say a thing.
ABUL UYUN:
    Are you sure they didn't, Boy?

SUNDUS:

    (Quickly) I told you they didn't. *(He goes over to Zakya, who is standing next to the wall in obvious fear.)* What's wrong, Girl? What are you afraid of?

ZAKYA:

    (Happy that Sundus is back) Yesterday he twisted my arm. He almost broke it. *(She points to Abul Uyun.)* When Mother comes, I'm going to tell her.

SUNDUS:

    Zakya!

ZAKYA:

    (Looking around) Did my mother come?

SUNDUS:

    Oh my God! What can you do with this girl?
    (Suddenly) Listen, Girl, do you want to marry me?

ZAKYA:

    Marry you? No, I'm too young. Let's play.

SUNDUS:

    (Dismayed) Play?

ZAKYA:

    Which would you like better, the green or the red?

SUNDUS:

    The red.

ZAKYA:

    No, take the green. *(She gives him the ball and starts playing.)* One red... Say...

SUNDUS:

    What do I say?

ZAKYA:

    I say "one red" and you say "one green." *(They play on their way out.)*
    (Enter Karima and Hamed.)

HAMED:

    What's upsetting you, now?

KARIMA:

    I'm not upset, Hamed.

HAMED:

    What are you reading?

KARIMA:

Stories from India.

HAMED:

Tell me one.

KARIMA:

Shall I tell you the story of the mouse?

HAMED:

The mouse, the cat, whichever one you like.

KARIMA:

An Indian wizard was once washing his face in
the river. As he put his hand in the water, he
caught a small she-mouse. He charmed her into
a pretty girl and as he had no children of his
own, he adopted her and brought her up as best
he could. When she grew up he wanted her to get
married. He got her the best suitors there were
in the world. The moon, she turned down; the
cloud, she didn't like; the mountain, she refused
because it was too high. When he gave up, he
asked her, "You tell me, who do you want to
marry?"

HAMED:

What a question! A human being like her, of couse.
A prince, a maharaja, not a mountain or a cloud.

KARIMA:

No, do you know what she said? She said she
wanted to marry a mouse.

HAMED:

A mouse! How stupid! And what did he do?

KARIMA:

He changed her into a she-mouse again and let
her look for her husband herself. I'll go up
and pack my suitcase.

HAMED:

I won't let you go before you tell me why you're
so upset.

KARIMA:

I don't know, Hamed. I told you.

HAMED:

Look, why should you be upset? Either because
you are leaving for Cairo, or because of the
bridge, or because of Said, or because of my
play...

KARIMA:

    What's wrong with your play?

HAMED:

    I can't find an end.

KARIMA:

    Where did it stop?

HAMED:

    The same spot. The wall is getting higher, the
    light diminishing... What's to be done?

FARID:

    (Entering) A very gloomy vision, Hamed.

HAMED:

    It's reality, my Brother. I invented nothing.

FARID:

    Reality must be changed.

HAMED:

    Go ahead, at least I'll find an end for my play.

KARIMA:

    What's the latest, Farid?

FARID:

    Lots of things. People have nothing to talk
    about now but Farid.

HAMED:

    They want to trap him, but Farid is not a mouse.

FARID:

    The latest they're saying is that I can't build
    the bridge.

KARIMA:

    And of course you were upset. I know you, any
    little thing...

FARID:

    That was in the past, Karima. But now it's
    different. I know they resent me. They hate me.
    But even if they were to put me in jail today,
    I wouldn't be upset.

HAMED:

    Naturally!

FARID:

    No, not as natural as you think. In the beginning,
    the world before me was like fly-paper in which
    one becomes entangled in dirt and filth with each
    step. For some time I couldn't get rid of that

feeling. Then, after the Council's decision, I
saw the people around me as if they were monsters
whom I should fight. Evil was everywhere, strong
and obstinate like tongues of flame which will
obliterate you and destroy everything you love
if you don't put them out. Today, after the meeting with the people, after the rumors and the
accusations...

HAMED:

You think all the people are crazy?

FARID:

No, they're pitiable, drowning without being
aware of it. That's why the bridge must be built.
It's not going to be as easy as I thought. On
the contrary, it will be quite difficult and
will require effort and sacrifice, but it must
be built, and on solid foundations, otherwise
we'll all sink up to here. (Points to his neck.)
I see everything clearly now. The world has
never been more clear to me.

KARIMA:

You mean there is hope for the bridge, Farid?

FARID:

Of course, there is hope.

KARIMA:

And I will see the other side and set my feet
on it?

FARID:

And live there, if you wish.

KARIMA:

When, Farid? When?

FARID:

One of these days. After a year or two or three;
I don't know.

HAMED:

May God preserve you, my Brother. The wall is
getting taller and the light dimmer. Tell me
how to end my play.

KARIMA:

(Enthusiastically) Let someone break the wall
and get it over with.

FARID:

A single person will not do, not even Samson.

HAMED:

He must have twenty or thirty workers, at least, each with a shovel and basket. The stage will be too crowded.

FARID:

No, Hamed. I mean that those who made the wall should be the ones to demolish it. Everyone should remove with his own hands the part that he built. That is the only way.

SUNDUS:

(Entering) Youssef Bey is waiting outside.

KARIMA:

Let him come in. *(To Farid)* I must go now.

FARID:

No, we are going out. Tell him I'll be right there.

KARIMA:

Let's say goodbye now, Farid.

FARID:

No, I'll take you to the station. I won't be long. We have an appointment with the representative. Not more than fifteen minutes.

KARIMA:

Good. You meet the representative now, and tomorrow morning I'll see my friend from the palace. There's still hope.

HAMED:

In the party? The place? You must have gone back to your dreams.

KARIMA:

Don't be such a pessimist, Hamed!

FARID:

Hamed's right. *(Tenderly, almost whispering)* Nobody else but the people themselves will build the bridge.

KARIMA:

The people? After what they did today?

FARID:

Have you forgotten that you're one of the people of this town, and I and Hamed and Youssef?

344 Modern Egyptian Drama

There are at least a hundred like us. Tomorrow
this hundred will be a thousand, and the thousand will be ten thousands, until the day comes
when everyone in this town can build the bridge.
I'll leave you now.

HAMED:

(Standing up) I'll come with you to look for
inspiration. I'll roam the streets until I find
it.

FARID:

I won't be late.

KARIMA:

Bye.
*(Farid and Hamed go out. Karima walks toward
the stairs and goes out. Meanwhile, Shahira
appears.)*

SHAHIRA:

I can't, my Beloved. This life is destroying me.

ZAKYA:

(Entering) One red...

SHAHIRA:

I can't...

ZAKYA:

And one green...

SHAHIRA:

I can't...

ZAKYA:

Red and green...*(She sees Kamel pulling
Mahassen by the hands.)* Mother! Mother! *(She
runs out, scared.)*

KAMEL:

Are you crazy? Have you gone mad? Explain it to
me. *(Pulls her by the hand.)* Explain!

MAHASSEN:

(Calmly, in a subdued voice) What do you want
me to explain?

KAMEL:

Tell me why you did that to yourself?

MAHASSEN:

I didn't do anything.

KAMEL:

Why did you want to kill yourself?

MAHASSEN:

    I didn't. Here I am, alive.

KAMEL:

    Good heavens! Come, sit down.

SHAHIRA:

    Kamel loves me.

KAMEL:

    (Tenderly) Tell me what's bothering you.

SHAHIRA:

    I can't leave him.

KAMEL:

    Mahassen, answer me, my Daughter. What's wrong?
Why did you do that?

MAHASSEN:

    I want to get over it.

    (Abul Uyun lights a cigarette.)

KAMEL:

    You want to get over what?

MAHASSEN:

    What she got over.

KAMEL:

    Your mother?

MAHASSEN:

    I want to rest.

KAMEL:

    Rest from what?

MAHASSEN:

    From what she rested from.

KAMEL:

    How do you know why she was tired?

MAHASSEN:

    I know.

KAMEL:

    What do you know? What is it that you know?

SHAHIRA:

    I wish he hated me!

MAHASSEN:

    I know why she killed herself.

KAMEL:

    Why? Why?

MAHASSEN:

    You were the cause.

KAMEL:

>I was the cause? You must be mad. I sacrificed
>my life for her, my whole life.

MAHASSEN:

>Because of your sense of guilt.

KAMEL:

>What sense of guilt? What have I done?

MAHASSEN:

>You tormented her.

KAMEL:

>Why should I torment her?

MAHASSEN:

>You couldn't forget.

KAMEL:

>Forget? Forget what?

MAHASSEN:

>Forget that she was in love with someone else.

KAMEL:

>*(Shouting)* Shut up! *(Pause)* Shahira? Shahira,
>who was like a white lily, and as pure? Shahira
>never knew another man but me, me, me...

MAHASSEN:

>Then why did she kill herself?

KAMEL:

>How should I know? How could I?

MAHASSEN:

>You must have suspected her.

KAMEL:

>*(To Abul Uyun)* Did you hear, my Friend?

ABUL UYUN:

>I heard.

MAHASSEN:

>You must have taunted her.

SHAHIRA:

>He cherishes me.

MAHASSEN:

>Annoyed her...

SHAHIRA:

>He's doing all he can to make me comfortable.

KAMEL:

>Did you hear?

MAHASSEN:
> You made her desperate.

SHAHIRA:
> He loves me.

MAHASSEN:
> You made her lose her mind.

KAMEL:
> Did you hear?

ABUL UYUN:
> *(Nervously)* I heard. I heard.

MAHASSEN:
> You hated her.

KAMEL:
> I hated Shahira? I?

SHAHIRA:
> I wish he'd hate me.

MAHASSEN:
> What could she do? She killed herself.

KAMEL:
> Did you hear? Did you hear? Tell her! Tell her!

MAHASSEN:
> You killed her. *(She cries.)*

KAMEL:
> *(Continuing)* You were living with us. Tell her!
> Tell her!

MAHASSEN:
> *(Still crying)* You killed her. You hated her.

ABUL UYUN:
> *(Loudly, as he stands up)* Mahassen, your mother
> killed herself because your father loved her.
> *(Warmly)* He loved her. *(Collapsing)* I wish he'd
> hated her. I wish to God he had. *(Almost break-
> ing down)* I wish he had.

KAMEL:
> *(Mildly surprised)* Why should I have hated her,
> my Friend? Why?

ABUL UYUN:
> *(Comes to)* What am I talking about? *(Hysterically)*
> Sundus! *(Controlling himself)* Did you say, Boy?
> *(Enter Said, in a hurry)*

KAMEL:

>Said! *(Goes to him and embraces him.)* My Son!
>*(Mahassen kisses Said, holds his hand and tenderly
>seats him beside her.)*

ABUL UYUN:

>Welcome back, Said.

SAID:

>How are you?

KAMEL:

>How did you get here, Said? Did you escape?

SAID:

>Escape? Jump over the fence and run away? Ha, ha,
>ha. No, I am not Shihab.

KAMEL:

>Then how did you get out?

SAID:

>They let me go.

KAMEL:

>On bail?

SAID:

>They let me go for nothing. They were mistaken.

KAMEL:

>Mistaken?

SAID:

>Yes.

KAMEL:

>They make mistakes and throw people in jail? I
>thought you were lost for good.

SAID:

>If one understands them, one never gets lost.

KAMEL:

>Even after what happened?

SAID:

>What happened? The five hundred pounds they got?

KAMEL:

>And they acquitted you?

SAID:

>Who spoke of acquittal? They realized they were
>mistaken. They even apologized and were ready
>to kiss my boots. Ha, ha, ha, ha...
>*(Enter Hamed in a hurry)*

HAMED:

    Did Farid come back, Said?

SAID:

    How's it going, Hamed?

HAMED:

    Where's Farid?

MAHASSEN:

    What's the matter, Hamed?

HAMED:

    Farid was fired on instructions from the palace.

MAHASSEN:

    Impossible! *(She cries.)*

KAMEL:

    When did these instructions arrive?

HAMED:

    Nasib Effendi received the telephone message
    this afternoon.
    (Karima enters, carrying a suitcase and the rose.)

KARIMA:

    Said! *(She goes over to him and kisses him on the
    cheek.)*

SAID:

    Are you leaving?

KARIMA:

    I was leaving for Cairo.

SAID:

    To visit me? And you brought me a rose, huh?
    Merci (He snatches the rose from her hand.)

KARIMA:

    (Screaming) Said!

SAID:

    What's the matter?

KARIMA:

    (Reaching out her hand) Give me the rose!

SAID:

    Didn't you get it for me?

KARIMA:

    Said, please. It's not like other roses.

SAID:

    Really? Let's see. *(He pulls the leaves off the
    rose and throws them one by one on the floor.)*

KARIMA:

    Said, leave this rose alone.

SAID:

>You don't say! Here it is. *(He throws it on the floor.)*

KARIMA:

>*(Goes over to it.)* It's from the other side.

SAID:

>*(Goes over to the rose and stamps on it with his shoes.)* O.K., here's to your other side.

KARIMA:

>*(Advances toward him and stares at him. Short pause, then she says calmly)* Do you think that because you stamped on it that it's dead? That you killed it? That it no longer exists? No. No. *(As if in a dream)* I see it in front of me, there, alive and shining and full of color. And I see the other side, large and wide and full of light and people. The people are holding hands and walking. Along the road are roses, roses everywhere. And there I am, walking on the bridge. I crossed the bridge and now I am walking with the people, my hands in their hands. And there's my home, in the middle of the roses. I opened the door and entered. I sat near the window. The jasmine is all over the window...white, yes, white! I don't see any snakes. There are no snakes in the jasmine.

Curtain

THE FARFOORS

A Play in Two Acts

by

Yusuf Idris

Cast of Characters

Author

Farfoor

Master

Lady (Master's Wife)

Second Lady

Woman (Farfoor's Wife)

Man

Woman from Audience

People of Funeral Procession

Corpse

Spectator I

Spectator II

Spectator III

Spectator IV

Spectator V

Spectator VI

Woman Spectator (Liberty)

Young Spectator

Woman Spectator

Voices

Curtain Operator

Audience

Act I

*(The stage is completely empty except for a rostrum
on which are microphones, a water pitcher and a glass.
At the rostrum stands a very elegantly dressed man who
looks very much the "intellectual." He is tall and wears
a pair of impressive eyeglasses that makes him look even
more respectable. He has on a tuxedo jacket, white shirt
and a bow-tie. When the play starts, or when the curtain
rises, he clears his throat, covering his mouth with his
hand, and says:)*

AUTHOR:
Ladies and Gentlemen, good evening. Please have
no fear. I am not going to make a speech or anything of the sort. I am the author of this play.
Now, we could have started at once and each one
of you could have gone ahead and watched it alone,
in the dark, as you do when you go to the movies.
However, we are in a theatre, and a theatre is a
celebration, a big meeting, a festival. It is
a lot of people, human beings who have left
their troubles outside and have come here to
live together for two or three hours. It's a big
family having a reunion and celebrating first,
the reunion itself, and second, the fact that
in the course of this reunion, it will dramatize,
philosophize and ridicule itself frankly, im-
pudently, and without any inhibitions. That is

why in my play there are no distinctions between
actors and spectators. You will do some acting,
and the actors will do some spectating. Why not?
If you know how to watch, you must know how to
act. You say you don't know how to act? Come on,
now! You act all the time! Who among you did not
act to get his boss to give him a few days off?
Who didn't put on a show to get a loan? Who
didn't play the very happy woman before her husband when his mother came to visit? What professional actress can produce the sigh that any
of you does when she sees a dress in a store
window? You've even come here tonight to play at
being spectators. For all these reasons, we've
decided tonight to give your suppressed talents
a chance. So, instead of playing the respectable spectator who wipes his mouth after every
laugh so that it won't be seen by anyone...Why?
Don't be shy or embarrassed. We're all human
beings, brothers and sisters. Why are you afraid
of each other? Why are you as stiff as wood?
Why are you so far apart from each other? Your
shoulder is touching your neighbor's, and yet
a thousand miles separate you. Why? Look at him,
my Friend. Bid him "good evening." Offer him a
cigarette. He speaks Arabic just as you do, and
I swear, he has no fangs. On my part, I'll also
eliminate the usual distance between author and
public, the distance that makes each suspicious
and afraid of the other. Allow me to come closer
to you. *(He leaves the rostrum and approaches
the front of the stage. The audience discovers
that despite the elegance of his upper half, he
has on very short pants showing his long, wiry
legs and shoes with no socks. When everyone
laughs:)* With all appreciation for your noble
feelings and your boundless joy that I've come
closer to you, I see no reason for your laughter.
The play hasn't begun yet...*(Laughter)* Come on,
have you never seen an author so close before?
(Laughter) Please, ladies and gentlemen, please.
My whole intention was to eliminate the distance

between us and to raise the curtains hiding each of us from the others, and to live for an hour or two or three, till the morning if you like, playing, composing and spectating together. *(Loud music, indicating the entrance of an actor, is heard. The Author points to where it comes from.)* Wait there, Farfoor. Nobody should enter yet. I haven't quite finished. *(Addressing the audience again)* Tonight, brothers and sisters, I'd like to introduce to you the biggest, greatest, most splendid, most important and most solid...*(Music again. The Author turns furiously towards the entrance, shaking his thin, long legs very nervously. He remains silent for a moment as if rebuking everybody by his sulky manner. As soon as he turns around and tries to open his mouth, music is heard again. He turns quickly towards the door and says in despair:)* Well then...no way...Find another author. I'm not going to do any more authoring. You think you're teasing me? O.K., I won't write anything.

VOICES FROM THE WINGS:

We won't do it again. Go ahead, write. Please do.

AUTHOR:

Brothers and Sisters, I'd like to present to you tonight the biggest, the greatest and the most solid Farfoor on this earth. But before I do that, we have to look for his master.

(Music starts again, but the Author goes on talking insistently while Farfoor, making a lot of noise and commotion, enters. Farfoor wears a very old and peculiar suit which is a combination of the apparel of acrobats, circus clowns and puppets. He is dark or darkish in color and has white powder or flour on his face (or a special mask). On his head he has an old fez or a pointed hat that looks like a fez. It is essential that the actor playing Farfoor should have in his own private life a talent for making fun of people or making them laugh. He enters like a tempest, whirling around, causing a great commotion in the front seats, forcing the people there to fall back

*and make a wider circle, using a maqra'a, which
is a piece of hard board or thin wood which makes
a loud sound but causes no pain. Farfoor strikes
the people in the front rows. He finds the Author
standing there, still talking about the most
splendid, most fantastic, biggest, etc., and
strikes him on the head.*

AUTHOR:
> *(Turning around, sharply)* How dare you enter be-
> fore I'm through, Farfoor? Who told you to enter?
> Now, as you came on, go off!

FARFOOR:
> Not likely, Smartie. You go off!

AUTHOR:
> Me?

FARFOOR:
> Of course, you! You're an author. You write out
> there. I am Farfoor, so I stay here.

AUTHOR:
> Shouldn't you wait until I introduce your Master
> to the audience?

FARFOOR:
> Never mind. I'll do that.

AUTHOR:
> Well, at least let me introduce you.

FARFOOR:
> You can't even introduce yourself! So how can
> you introduce me? And, by the way, what's that?
> *(Looking the Author over)* What's that you did to
> yourself?

AUTHOR:
> What is it you don't like?

FARFOOR:
> Well, your pants. What's this, anyway?

AUTHOR:
> What's wrong with my pants, huh? These are
> author's pants.

FARFOOR:
> Do authors usually do that?

AUTHOR:
> But of course! How else can they be authors? They
> must author everything. I authored this for myself.
> An original outfit. What's wrong with that?

FARFOOR:

It's fantastic! If you'd only shorten them a
little, add a short act on the side and a few
words as foreword...Also there's no harm in
adding an afterword. It'd be even more fantastic!

AUTHOR:

Oh heavens! Stars! Isn't it enough that you
entered before you're supposed to? Do you also
have to come and interrupt me, slowing down our
business here? We'd better look for that snotty
Master of yours. Where could he have gone? He
was in my hand one second ago. *(He looks in his
pockets, bends to look under the seats, then
turns to Farfoor and tells him sharply:)* Instead
of cavorting around, join me in the search!

FARFOOR:

It's none of my business. If you produce a
master, I'll work. If you don't, shall I work
with you?

AUTHOR:

I forgot what he looks like. As you know, Farfoor,
I always forget. Could it be this one? *(As he says
this he pulls out one of those seated in the
front seats and takes him to the center of the
stage.)* Is it this one, Farfoor?

FARFOOR:

This one? *(He looks at him in disgust, walks
around him, raises his jacket and taps on his
chest with his fingers as if it were a wooden
board. The man's chest produces a hollow sound
like that of wood.)* What's that? What did you do
to yourself, man? *(Taps on his back. The same
hollow sound.)* Have you been celebrating All
Hollows lately? *(He puts his hand in the man's
pocket and searches, then takes it out holding
half a loaf of dark bread.)* Goodness gracious!
*(He puts his hand in the man's other pocket,
this time producing a quarter of a loaf of dry
white bread. He goes on searching all of the man's
pockets and the folds of his clothes until he
empties them of their contents of breads of
different kinds and shapes.)* What do you do,

Uncle? Are you a food inspector? *(He eats a piece of bread but spits it out at once.)* I'll cut my arm off if this bread hasn't been eaten before. And why are you so scared? *(The man looks even more scared.)* Steady, Boy, steady! *(Farfoor hits him on his right side and he bends to the left. Farfoor hits him on the other side, and he bends to the right.)* A very elastic Master, huh? *(He hits him from the front, the back and the two sides. The man always bends in the opposite direction.)* He must have been conceived in the spring! You!

AUTHOR:

I don't have time, Farfoor. I am very busy and have all kinds of appointments.

FARFOOR:

Busy or not, it's not my business. It was you who lost him.

AUTHOR:

Farfoor, my friend. I have a radio series that I haven't finished yet. You look for him.

FARFOOR:

I look for him? I'll stay here and cross my legs until you find a master for me. *(He sits in the air as if in a seat and crosses his legs.)*

AUTHOR:

(Selecting another spectator) Now what do you think of this one? I don't think you can find a better one.

FARFOOR:

I told you I want a Master. A Master, a Master, A MASTER! Someone big and respectable! One that makes you want to serve him. Say someone like Hussein Riad* in his robe and his respectability.

But this one! What happened to him anyway? Why is he so tall? Wait there, you! *(He rushes at him and raises his right hand to the front and*

---

*An Egyptian actor at the National Theater who, during the 1950's and 1960's, often played the role of the old, middle-class father or uncle.

his left to the back.) Wait. Let me remember
where I saw him before. Oh, I see now! He's
either the T.V. antenna or its spitting image.

AUTHOR:

Well, there you are, Farfoor. I found him.
*(He points to the Master who is fast asleep in
his seat.)*

FARFOOR:

Why is he...?

AUTHOR:

He fell asleep while you were talking. Now it's
four-thirty and I haven't even written it!

FARFOOR:

Either you deliver him awake or I disclaim all
responsibility.

AUTHOR:

Please, Farfoor! The series will be on the air at
nine. I'm in a hurry. If I waited one more minute,
it would be lost. There you are. Wake him up and
work. But I am warning you, Farfoor! O.K., I'll
go now.

FARFOOR:

Wait there. Here's the Master. Where's the
Mistress?

AUTHOR:

Oh, Mistress! My foot!

FARFOOR:

Have you forgotten that too? I swear by God the
Almighty, I won't touch the play. No mistress?!
You can't do that to me. I've been looking for a
mistress since the last play. Lose anything but
that!

AUTHOR:

She's not lost or anything. I've just forgotten
all about her.

FARFOOR:

I'll not work before she arrives!

AUTHOR:

Upon my honor, Farfoor, I'll send her in a cab
immediately.

FARFOOR:

Your Honor, a cab. Cab of your honor!

AUTHOR:

    My honor, Farfoor!

FARFOOR:

    It's up to you. An author's honor is like today's matches, you strike 'em ten times and in the end they don't light.[*] It's up to you.

AUTHOR:

    Excuse me now.

FARFOOR:

    Bye now. Take care lest a policeman should see you and plagiarize you.

AUTHOR:

    Farfoor, the play!

FARFOOR:

    Have no fear. You just send me my Mistress and you can count on me doing things you never dreamt about!

AUTHOR:

    Farfoor! The play! I want it to be a big hit.

FARFOOR:

    Leave it to me. It'll be such a smash that at the very least we'll have one case of concussion.

AUTHOR:

    Farfoor, my reputation. The audience, the critics, the glory. The seventh scene in the tenth act will either raise me skyhigh...

FARFOOR:

    Or land you under the ground, God willing. Have no fear on that account. You'll end down on the ground if God wills.

AUTHOR:

    Farfoor! I...

FARFOOR:

    Go away! *(He runs toward him, intending to hit him. Author exits.)*

AUTHOR:

    (From offstage) Farfoor, the scene.

[*]This is a play on a saying popular in the theatre of the 1930's and 1940's in Egypt: "A girl's honor is like a match; it lights only once."

FARFOOR:

    Number seven in act ten. Smash...audience...
concussion...critics...radio...glory...series...
(Changing his tone) hot cakes...coke...*(Turning
to the audience)* An author, hah! As if there's
such a thing. *(Turning to the Master)* Uncle, wake
up. The Author's gone and things are working out
at last. Wake up, Man. *(He lifts the Master's
head up then lets it go and it drops to his chest
again. The Master snores.)* We haven't even started
and you're snoring already! Wake up! Does any of
you have a hammer? Wake up, Man. *(He hits him on
the head with the slapstick.)*

MASTER:

    (Waking up with a start) Heh, hop, hum...Eh,
what? who? where? Where are we?

FARFOOR:

    You never can tell. *(Looks out toward the
audience)* Where are we, really?

MASTER:

    Is it you?

FARFOOR:

    You thought I was Christine Keeler?[*]

MASTER:

    God forgive you. You've interrupted such a dream.

FARFOOR:

    What did you dream about?

MASTER:

    (Dreamily) I was dreaming, may God protect us...

FARFOOR:

    Yes, what were you dreaming about? You must
have been dreaming that you were asleep.

MASTER:

    (Same tone) No, no, no! I was dreaming that I
was dreaming.

FARFOOR:

    What were you dreaming that you were dreaming
about?

---

[*]The reference is to a "call girl" involved in the so-
called "Profumo Affair," a sex scandel in which
British government officials were implicated.

MASTER:

I was dreaming that I was dreaming that I was dreaming.

FARFOOR:

And that very last time...that last "I was dreaming...," what were you dreaming about?

MASTER:

That I was dreaming!

FARFOOR:

(Now impatient) And you were dreaming that you were dreaming of what?

MASTER:

I was dreaming that I was dreaming that I was dreaming that I was dreaming.

FARFOOR:

Oh, what a dream! Don't worry, it's for the good. You know its interpretation, Master?

MASTER:

What is it?

FARFOOR:

That you're still asleep and that you won't wake up until someone like me wakes up with the wish that he wishes that he wishes to give you such a beating! *(He starts hitting him. The Master protests.)* It's not your fault. It's the fault of that loose-kneed Author who made you a Master and left you dreaming, while the fleas have eaten me up outside.

MASTER:

Stop this impertinence, Boy! Who are you to beat me?

FARFOOR:

I'm your servant, Farfoor.

MASTER:

Does that give you the right to beat me?

FARFOOR:

Why not? Democracy, you know!

MASTER:

And why did you wake me up, Boy?

FARFOOR:

What? To start working on the first act!

MASTER:

    How do we do it?

FARFOOR:

    You're my Master and I'm Farfoor and I'm Farfoor
    and you're my Master.

MASTER:

    I am your Master?

FARFOOR:

    Yes.

MASTER:

    And is there such a thing as a Master without the
    appurtenances, Boy? Where's the palace, the
    servants, the retainers, the valets, the gardens,
    the sable steeds, the senoritas, the harem, the
    pomp, the splendor and the glory?

FARFOOR:

    Here they are. *(Pointing to himself)* I am all
    thy pomp and greatness, thine all!

MASTER:

    You? A louse like you?

FARFOOR:

    Now, look here Master. Don't you dare. The play
    hasn't started yet and I haven't gotten under
    the skin of the role. When I do and become
    Farfoor, call me as many names as you like.

MASTER:

    O.K., then get under the skin a little so I can
    show you. Have you?

FARFOOR:

    Not yet.

MASTER:

    Ready now?

FARFOOR:

    Ready.

MASTER:

    (Bursting out) You bastard! *(He receives a very
    sharp hit on the head from Farfoor and is scared.)*
    What happened, Boy?

FARFOOR:

    Your pardon, sir. I hadn't quite gotten under the
    skin of the role.

MASTER:
>And now?

FARFOOR:
>No, now I am ready. Go ahead.

MASTER:
>Now, look here, last time I had the fright of my
>life and I really can't stand too much of that.
>Are you ready now?

FARFOOR:
>Go ahead, Man.

MASTER:
>Are you really good and ready?

FARFOOR:
>Really good and ready!

MASTER:
>You're Farfoor and I am your Master?

FARFOOR:
>Exactly. You're Farfoor and I am his Master. I
>am Farfoor and you're his Master. I am his
>Master Farfoor and you're his Master's Farfoor.
>All is good.

MASTER:
>Well, don't you have a cigarette, Boy. My flesh
>has been craving a smoke since morning.

FARFOOR:
>Why don't you smoke, if your flesh is craving it?

MASTER:
>And what prevents people from smoking, Smartie,
>when their flesh craves it?

FARFOOR:
>It must be the cough.

MASTER:
>Yes, the cough. Have you got a cigarette?

FARFOOR:
>I have.

MASTER:
>O.K., give it.

FARFOOR:
>O.K. Give it so I can give it.

MASTER:
>Where do you get it from?

FARFOOR:

   The store.

MASTER:

   Didn't you say you had it?

FARFOOR:

   I have it in the store, but it needs ten piasters
   or something to come with me.

MASTER:

   What if I don't have any money?

FARFOOR:

   So, you don't have any money tonight again? We've
   done five hundred plays together, and in none of
   them do you make the mistake of being a true
   master or take a piaster out of your pocket and
   say, "Take it, Farfoor. Go have fun." What
   Masters are these?

MASTER:

   I swear I don't have any, Farfoor.

FARFOOR:

   O.K., show me your tongue.

MASTER:

   Here it is. *(He shows his tongue.)*

FARFOOR:

   If you've lied, it won't go back in your mouth.
   *(The Master tries to draw his tongue back in
   but cannot. He points to Farfoor and his tongue,
   but Farfoor is not interested.)*

FARFOOR:

   It's no business of mine. You brought it on
   yourself. Why did you lie?
   *(The Master is very nervous and is trying hard
   to put his tongue back in his mouth, pointing
   to Farfoor.)*

FARFOOR:

   I've nothing to do with it. I can't intervene
   between you and your tongue. *(The Master's face
   grows very red; he is almost suffocating. He
   begs Farfoor with his hand.)*

FARFOOR:

   You won't do it again?
   (Master nods.)

FARFOOR:

You have money?

(Master nods.)

FARFOOR:

How much?

(Master makes sign of "three.")

FARFOOR:

Three pounds?

(Master shakes his head.)

FARFOOR:

Three piasters?

(Master shakes his head.)

FARFOOR:

Three milliemes?

(Master shakes his head.)

FARFOOR:

Three what, then?

(Master insists vexedly and pleadingly that it's three.)

FARFOOR:

O.K. Let's have him put his tongue in again, then we'll know three what. O.K., you can put your tongue in.

MASTER:

(Puts his tongue in, feels his face and head and neck. Breathes in relief.)

FARFOOR:

Tell me three what now.

MASTER:

Three half-piasters.

FARFOOR:

What a Master!

MASTER:

Don't you have a cigarette?

FARFOOR:

No, I don't. Now, let's get started. Wake up and concentrate and empathize so we can begin. If the Author should come and see us playing around we'll be lost.

MASTER:

I am a Master, right?

FARFOOR:

 Yes, so what?

MASTER:

 O.K., at least we have established that. But what about me? What's my name?

FARFOOR:

 How should I know?! Ask the man who wrote you.

MASTER:

 I know only you. What's my name?

FARFOOR:

 Your name's Master, period.

MASTER:

 No, no. It doesn't make sense. Is there a Master without a name? Listen, Farfoor, give me a name, Boy.

FARFOOR:

 So the Master wants a name now?

MASTER:

 Yes. Give me a name that suits a Master like me.

FARFOOR:

 That's not my line. I ordered one with a built-in name.

MASTER:

 Boy, I am ordering you to find me a respectable name.

FARFOOR:

 O.K., we'll call you the Jackass.

MASTER:

 You're impolite. Is this a name, Boy?

FARFOOR:

 I didn't invent it. All respectable people have names like that. And none of them will please you.

MASTER:

 Who said so?

FARFOOR:

 O.K. We'll call you the Rat.

MASTER:

 Boy!

FARFOOR:

 O.K., don't be angry. The Cat. What do you think? Well, how about the Animal?

MASTER:

 Boy!

FARFOOR:

You think I'm making it up. I swear by God these
are real names. The Sot. The Fool. I swear by
God our landlord is called Ustaz Hamed, the Fool.
It's all like that. The Camel family, the She-
camel, the Sheep-man, the Goat-man, the Raven,
the Bald family, the Blind, the One-eyes, the
Nasal. And why should you be an exception? The
Deaf. The Basket. The Tub-man, the Fly Whisk-
man, the Short-tailed man, the Fleece-man, the
Hunchbacked-man, the Hashish-man. Haven't you
heard of Mamdouh Bey who writes his name on his
cards as Mr. Mamdouh Hassan. Do you know his
family name? Mamdouh Hassan the Thief, that's his
family name.

MASTER:

But there are good names, Boy.

FARFOOR:

Like what? Tell me.

MASTER:

Abaza, for instance.

FARFOOR:

You want to be fat and walk in installments?
No, Sir!

MASTER:

Dous, for instance. How about Dous?

FARFOOR:

You want to be from Assiut? No, Sir.

MASTER:

How about Fouda, Boy?

FARFOOR:

No, no. Fouda, Lehaita, Ahour, Abou Samra. These
names don't suit you. You better stay like you
are, a respectable Master without a name.

MASTER:

O.L. We'll do without a name. How about a job?

FARFOOR:

What about it?

MASTER:

What do I do, Farfoor?

FARFOOR:

You're my Master. What more do you want?

MASTER:

    No. If I am a Master, I must have a job. Listen, Farfoor, choose a very respectable job for me, Boy. Something modern.

FARFOOR:

    How about being a national capitalist?*

MASTER:

    Don't you have anything better?

FARFOOR:

    I do. Would you like to be an intellectual?

MASTER:

    What do your intellectuals do?

FARFOOR:

    They do nothing,

MASTER:

    How come?

FARFOOR:

    This question clearly proves that you are not an intellectual.

MASTER:

    What else is there?

FARFOOR:

    Would you like to be an artist?

MASTER:

    Artist in what? What do I do?

FARFOOR:

    An artist with no art.

MASTER:

    Is there such a thing?

FARFOOR:

    Ohoo...We have a lot of those. They're all over. *(He reaches inside his clothes and takes out his hand closed.)* Would you like a handful? How about being a singer?

MASTER:

    What do I do as a singer?

FARFOOR:

    You say ""Ah'' for thirty or forty years.

*The private sector in Egypt.

MASTER:

    Just that?

FARFOOR:

    No, no. Melodious "Ahs" of course; sometimes it's Ah Aha... Sometimes Ohohoo and occasionally Eheehee...

MASTER:

    (Disgusted) And would you like to see your Master doing that Farfoor?

FARFOOR:

    How about writing songs?

MASTER:

    How?

FARFOOR:

    That is the simplest of all. Look, you go to the druggist and fill one of your pockets with the "envious eye," the second with the "censurers' talk," the third with "staying up all night," and the fourth with "doctor's wound" and if you can't find that, let it be a doctor without wounds. In your small pocket, get some "eyelids," and one whole kilogram of "dark complexion" and some "fair complexion."*

MASTER:

    And what do I do with all that?

FARFOOR:

    You go from one singer to another and give them assortments, God will take care of the rest.

MASTER:

    God forbid! Find me a respectable job, I tell you.

FARFOOR:

    Well, be an author like the one we have.

MASTER:

    Farfoor!

FARFOOR:

    No offense! How about being a lawyer?

MASTER:

    What do they do?

---

*These are some of the most common themes in Arabic songs.

FARFOOR:

>You beg the court's justice to judge in your favor.

MASTER:

>And if the court doesn't?

FARFOOR:

>We'll have the advance fees, anyway.

MASTER:

>No. I prefer to be a prosecutor.

FARFOOR:

>That man who hates everybody for no reason? No, Uncle. A judge is better.

MASTER:

>What does he do?

FARFOOR:

>You keep studying the case intently and prepare the summations and then when you go to the court, you postpone it. Don't you like it? Well, you can work as a physician.

MASTER:

>No, I don't know anything about medicine.

FARFOOR:

>You think physicians do?

MASTER:

>Please, Farfoor.

FARFOOR:

>O.K., you can work as an accountant. You save people tax money and take it yourself.

MASTER:

>Stop it.

FARFOOR:

>I've found it! A fantastic job. Be a football player!

MASTER:

>That requires qualifications.

FARFOOR:

>No qualifications. Go play in the street.

MASTER:

>Farfoor, stop this impudence.

FARFOOR:

>These are the qualifications. You throw your books away and play in the street for two or

three years until you're a cub of sixteen
or seventeen. In time they'll discover you and
you become a star and then Captain Latif* will
look at you and say "What a boy... Bravo Sido..."
And all the people in the stadium will shout
"Sido! Sido!"**

MASTER:
No, no. Football is a children's game.

FARFOOR:
Why not? We're all children, but some are small
and some big.

MASTER:
You mean all these people are children?

FARFOOR:
Big children, upon your life. I mean the biggies.

MASTER:
Then how does one know a big child from a little
child?

FARFOOR:
By their mustaches. Those that have mustaches...

MASTER:
...are the big ones.

FARFOOR:
No, you Fool, the little ones. Because when they
grow up, they shave their mustaches off.

MASTER:
But how do you tell one from the other?

FARFOOR:
I'll tell you. You can always tell that the
child is big when he has a family.

MASTER:
A family that is big like him?

FARFOOR:
No, you Fool. A small family.

MASTER:
The way I figure it is that the big one will
have a big family.

*A T.V. and radio sports commentator, who is famous
in Egypt for his histrionics in play-by-play
commentaries.
**A play on the word for "master" in Arabic.

FARFOOR:
>No, a big one has a small family.

MASTER:
>And the big family?

FARFOOR:
>That you always find with a little child.

MASTER:
>It's very confusing!

FARFOOR:
>No, it's very comic: the little ones want to be
>big ones and the big ones want to be little
>ones and when these become big they become small
>and when they become small they like to get big
>but they get smaller. It's very comic. See how I
>laugh. *(He stretches his mouth and bares his
>teeth without smiling.)* I've found it. I've
>found you a very good job!

MASTER:
>What?

FARFOOR:
>How about being an announcer?

MASTER:
>No, Sir, no. I know that one. Isn't he that
>very talkative guy who, when he doesn't find
>somebody to talk to, locks himself up and talks
>to himself thinking that nobody can hear him?

FARFOOR:
>How about a traffic policeman?

MASTER:
>What does he do?

FARFOOR:
>He's a poor man like the rest of us who don't have
>cars, yet all day long he orders around those
>that do have cars. How about this one? Work as a
>doorman at the Hilton. With this outfit of yours,
>they'll accept you at once and will even give
>you a clothing allowance.

MASTER:
>What do I do there?

FARFOOR:
>You'll be a European-style beggar. You stand
>there in all your elegance and those going in
>and out will give you...

MASTER:

    Don't you know of any job where one can work?

FARFOOR:

    There's one. Work as a thief.

MASTER:

    O.K. I am ready to do that.

FARFOOR:

    Now, would you like to be a big thief, a medium thief or a regular-sized one?

MASTER:

    Does it require any thinking? A big one of course.

FARFOOR:

    Well, then work in import and export trade.

MASTER:

    And the medium one?

FARFOOR:

    Start a co-op.

MASTER:

    Anything but that. How about a regular one?

FARFOOR:

    That's a really poor one who sweats doing it, climbs pipes to get into a house, or picks a wallet that turns out to be empty...something like that.

MASTER:

    No, I'll be a grave-digger.

FARFOOR:

    Fie, oh fie! You want to work on the edge of the world? If your foot slips or something, you'll find yourself in the other world.

MASTER:

    At least it's better than being a thief.

FARFOOR:

    No, by God, stealing is much better.

MASTER:

    Well, I guess I'll work as a police detective.

FARFOOR:

    You mean that guy whom everyone knows to be a detective, yet who is the only one that doesn't know it? I tell you, an engineer is better.

MASTER:

    No, I don't have the strength.

FARFOOR:

> Then they'll make you a senior engineer. *(Changes his tone)* How about forgetting all that and working for the government? You have all the qualifications.

MASTER:

> How so?

FARFOOR:

> Don't you want a place where you can sleep and dream that you're dreaming? You'll have from one pay day to the next, a whole month of dreaming.

MASTER:

> I have a mind to work as a cab-driver.

FARFOOR:

> Is your eyesight good?

MASTER:

> Of course!

FARFOOR:

> Do you know the streets of Cairo?

MASTER:

> I know them all.

FARFOOR:

> Can you sit for an hour without cursing everybody's religion?

MASTER:

> Yes.

FARFOOR:

> Then you don't qualify as a cab-driver.

MASTER:

> How about a conductor? Please, a conductor.

FARFOOR:

> Do you know how to swim?

MASTER:

> Swim where?

FARFOOR:

> In your sweat.

MASTER:

> Is that necessary?

FARFOOR:

> Very much so. If you don't know how to swim in your own sweat, you must learn how to swim in others' sweat. If you know neither, you'd be no good.

MASTER:
>What exactly is the matter? Don't you like any-
>thing at all? Are you a critic or something?
>None of these occupations pleases you. How are
>these people living? Everyone of them must have
>a job and is quite happy doing it, God be praised.

FARFOOR:
>Who told you they are happy? If they were, they
>wouldn't be here.

MASTER:
>And who told you they're not happy?

FARFOOR:
>And why should we quarrel over it when they're
>here? We can ask them. You, People, everyone
>here. You that are happy with their jobs raise
>your hands. *(Short pause.)* There, did you see?
>None of them raised their hands.

MASTER:
>You're such a liar! There's a guy who's been
>raising his hand for quite sometime.

FARFOOR:
>That one over there? Did you raise your hand? Well,
>please stand up so we can see you. *(The spectator
>stands up, still raising his hand.)* Are you happy
>with your job?

SPECTATOR:
>Very, very much.

FARFOOR:
>What do you do?

SPECTATOR:
>I'm looking for a job.

FARFOOR:
>See?

MASTER:
>If they don't like their jobs, then why do they
>work?

FARFOOR:
>Out of disgust!

MASTER:
>Out of disgust, they work?

FARFOOR:
>But then, how do you like the result of their
>work? Isn't it also disgusting?

MASTER:

So, if one wants to find a good job...

FARFOOR:

One must choose the most disgusting one.

MASTER:

So the best job is the most disgusting job. Very well then, I'll be a grave digger. O.K., let's go.

FARFOOR:

Where are you going?

MASTER:

I'm going to work.

FARFOOR:

What are you going to do?

MASTER:

Well, pass the time by digging one or two graves to help the day pass.

FARFOOR:

You're quite a Master! Everything in the world can be ready-made except graves, these must be made to measure. Where's that dead man for whom you'll be digging?

MASTER:

He's there.

FARFOOR:

Where?

MASTER:

He's there. He must be crossing a street, or on a ferry boat, or driving a truck after a nice fix and going to the Demerdash hospital. He'll be here in an hour.

FARFOOR:

Are you sure?

MASTER:

Of course I am sure, especially that guy of the Demerdash. He's a certain fatality.

FARFOOR:

Why Demerdash? Isn't Qasr el-Eini* a good one?

*Cairo's biggest hospital.

MASTER:

    No. It isn't a matter of Qasr el-Eini. The Patients die before they are admitted.

FARFOOR:

    You mean you are sure you're getting a corpse today?

MASTER:

    I am dead sure of that. Nothing is easier than death now. The other day a guy wanted to shave and he died.

FARFOOR:

    I know a better one. He wanted to be born and he died.

MASTER:

    The poor thing didn't have time to live.

FARFOOR:

    You mean he didn't have time to die.

MASTER:

    I mean to live.

FARFOOR:

    Is this a life for people to live in order to die?

MASTER:

    Is that a joke?

FARFOOR:

    Yes, and a bad one too.

MASTER:

    It seems it is, but we don't know it.

FARFOOR:

    Then the best thing would be to turn it around.

MASTER:

    Turn it around into what?

FARFOOR:

    At least into a good joke?

MASTER:

    How?

FARFOOR:

    Instead of living in order to die, we should die in order to live.

MASTER:

    How do we die in order to live?

FARFOOR:

> I tell you, it'd be a good joke if, instead of
> planning to live and then worrying lest we
> should die, we should plan to die so we'd rejoice
> whenever we live a day through. And if we die,
> that'd be nothing new.

MASTER:

> In this case the best thing one can do is to be
> gravediggers.

FARFOOR:

> The only problem would be: for whom? To bury
> whom?

MASTER:

> Each other.

FARFOOR:

> What's so original about that? Isn't that what
> they do all the time?

MASTER:

> Farfoor, you're talking like a philosopher.

FARFOOR:

> Me? Never. You want me to do like those people?
> I wasted my life reading the philosophers and in
> the end they proved that I exist.

MASTER:

> Where you fond of philosophy, Farfoor?

FARFOOR:

> No, I was looking for a job and was reading to
> find out what work was best and why. The result
> was that I wasted my life reading ugly things
> like: *The Tragedy of Man, Being and Nothingness,
> The Moment of Choice, Free Will* and *The First
> Thrust*. What's all this to me? I want a philosophy
> which tells me what to do. Me! Me! Farfoor, that
> human being whom, if I were to pinch now, would
> feel it. What should I do? And why? Nobody told
> me. And the result is that I am working as a
> Farfoor.

MASTER:

> Two more lines like that and you'd be a poet.

FARFOOR:

> You mean those people who when they're full up
> sing of hunger and when hungry sing of satisfac-
> tion, and when they suffer write poetry, and when

they're pleased call it loss, and when they fall
in love, curse love and when they stop loving
curse those that don't love. No, no. Please
keep them away from me, for God's sake.

MASTER:

Sour grapes! They express the things that hurt
people.

FARFOOR:

Is that smart?

MASTER:

Is it smart to bear your sufferings in silence?

FARFOOR:

Neither this nor that is smart, neither those
who are patient nor those who cry out.

MASTER:

Who is smart then?

FARFOOR:

Do you want the truth? The truly smart?

MASTER:

Yes.

FARFOOR:

The one-hundred percent smart ones?

MASTER:

Those that commit suicide?

FARFOOR:

That's silly.

MASTER:

They mystics?

FARFOOR:

That's helplessness.

MASTER:

Those that live no matter what?

FARFOOR:

That wouldn't be a life. That'd be death-in-
life.

MASTER:

Who, then, are the smart ones?

FARFOOR:

I don't know them. See, I fooled you.

MASTER:

Then you're a smart one.

FARFOOR:

> No, nobody is smart. Let's start working. We've
> just given you a name and a job. Get going,
> time is flying.

MASTER:

> Did we decide on anything?

FARFOOR:

> What shall we do? We human beings are like this:
> when we fail to choose and find only one solu-
> tion we call it the solution of our choice. Go
> ahead and work. Let's get it over with.

MASTER:

> You mean digging?

FARFOOR:

> Yes, of course, go ahead!

MASTER:

> Without a corpse?

FARFOOR:

> Wasn't it your idea?

MASTER:

> Yes. O.K., let's work. But, I'll have you know
> that all laws pertaining to individual work
> contracts must apply to me. Yes. No arbitrary
> firing, no punishment without investigation and
> no nonsense.

FARFOOR:

> You haven't even started yet!

MASTER:

> I like to know my rights. And we have our rights,
> as you know. Yes. One hand by itself cannot clap.
> Don't you agree, Men? (Looking toward the audience)
> Since we are the ones who toil, we should get
> the fruits of our toil. Right, Men?

FARFOOR:

> How about working just enough to justify these
> words?

MASTER:

> No. Conditions must be clear. And conditions
> agree upon in advance will help when it's time
> to be fired. I don't like to be unfair to any-
> body nor anybody to be unfair to me. Is that
> clear or not?

FARFOOR:
    It's clear.
MASTER:
    Agreed, then?
FARFOOR:
    Agreed.
MASTER:
    O.K., here's the shovel. You work.
FARFOOR:
    Me? Work?
MASTER:
    But of course! Who do you think should work?
FARFOOR:
    You.
MASTER:
    No. I am your Master. So, you work for me.
FARFOOR:
    Then what was that about the contract, the
    the unfairness and the firing?
MASTER:
    All is in effect.
FARFOOR:
    For me?
MASTER:
    No, for me.
FARFOOR:
    Why for you, if I am the one who's going to
    work?
MASTER:
    I'll also work.
FARFOOR:
    What are you going to do?
MASTER:
    I'll be your Master.
FARFOOR:
    Yes, but what does it entail?
MASTER:
    That I master you.
FARFOOR:
    That you master me? What kind of job is that?
    No, that won't do. What do you mean master me?
    Where are we? I'll do nothing.

MASTER:

> That's your role, Boy, Don't you know it? Are
> we playing games? Don't you know the play?

FARFOOR:

> Does the play say that I do everything and you're
> just a Master?

MASTER:

> Don't start that!

FARFOOR:

> Who would write such a silly play? Are you sure
> you didn't write it yourself?

MASTER:

> It seems you haven't written before...Mr. Author!
> (The Author appears.)

AUTHOR:

> What is it? What happened? Was there any deviation
> from the text of my play?

MASTER:

> He doesn't like the play.

AUTHOR:

> How so? Is it any of his business? What's he got
> to do with it? When it says you're a Master, it
> means you're a Master. A Farfoor is a Farfoor
> with his feet over his head. Do you hear?

FARFOOR:

> (His feet over his head) I hear! I hear!

author:

> And next time you disturb me like this, you'll
> be out at once. Understand?

FARFOOR:

> If only you wouldn't be so nervous.

AUTHOR:

> And don't you say one syllable on your own.
> "Do that." "Yes, sir." "Speak." "Yes, sir."
> "Go." "Yes, sir." "Come." "Yes, sir."

FARFOOR:

> Yes, sir. You can go now, if you like. We got
> the message. *(To the Master)* Was it really
> necessary to let us hear all that? Wait until
> he's gone.

AUTHOR:

> I am leaving now, next time...

FARFOOR:

    (Interrupting) There'll be no next time. We won't
do it again, ever.

AUTHOR:

    I am warning you!

FARFOOR:

    I am warning you not to forget the Mistress.

AUTHOR:

    I swear...

FARFOOR:

    No need. No need. Goodbye. *(Author exits.)*

FARFOOR:

    (Continuing) O.K. You Master of misfortune.
You'll regret it.

MASTER:

    Get going, Farfoor, don't waste our time. Carry
the shovel and work.

FARFOOR:

    God is my witness. Let's work. *(He raises the
shovel and is about to dig.)*

MASTER:

    Stop. Don't dig here.

FARFOOR:

    Where should I dig?

MASTER:

    (Pointing to another place) Here.

FARFOOR:

    Why here and not here?

MASTER:

    Because since you want to dig here and I want
you to dig here then my here is better than
your here.

FARFOOR:

    What book is that in?

MASTER:

    Since I am your Master, my opinion will always
be better than your opinion.

FARFOOR:

    Even if my opinion is right and yours is wrong?

MASTER:

    There's no such thing as a right or a wrong

opinion. The right opinion is mine and the wrong one is yours.

FARFOOR:

But I say otherwise.

MASTER:

Then you're wrong. Without discussion you're wrong.

FARFOOR:

(Looking at him and breathing hard) You mean I should dig here?

MASTER:

Did I say here?

FARFOOR:

Where, then?

MASTER:

There, you Dummy. *(Pointing at another place)*

FARFOOR:

Here?

MASTER:

Is here like there?

FARFOOR:

Just as you want. O.K. Here?

MASTER:

What eternal stupidity is that? I told you here, *(Pointing to the right)* which means, here *(Pointing to the left)*. Don't you understand what here means? *(Pointing in front of him)*

FARFOOR:

(Stupidly) What does here mean?

MASTER:

(Points behind him) It means here.

FARFOOR:

To tell you the truth. I don't understand. Do you understand?

MASTER:

All that I understand well is that I am your Master.

FARFOOR:

Master, my Master. Tell me, my Master.

MASTER:

What do you want?

FARFOOR:

Why are you my Master?

MASTER:

Don't you know why I am your Master, Boy?

FARFOOR:

(Pointing to the shovel on the ground) May I be
turned into one like that if I knew.

MASTER:

You're such a dumb Farfoor! Don't you know why
I am your Master?

FARFOOR:

I don't know. Do you know?

MASTER:

It's part of my work, Boy, that I don't. Why
are you my Farfoor then? You're my Farfoor, so
you must know for me.

FARFOOR:

On this point in particular, I don't know.

MASTER:

And I don't know. So my "I don't know" super-
sedes your "I don't know."

FARFOOR:

So?

MASTER:

Why are you asking me? This is the thousandth
play that we've been in together.

FARFOOR:

Is it sinful to ask?

MASTER:

I don't know. Why don't you ask the Author? It's
none of my business. He's the one who wrote you,
and he should know. Don't give me a headache.

FARFOOR:

Let's look at it rationally. It doesn't really
need an Author. Now, are you not a human being
exactly like myself? Even if we followed Darwin,
you developed from an ape and I developed from
an ape like you.

MASTER:

Who knows? Your grandfather, the ape, may have
been my grandfather, the ape's Farfoor.

FARFOOR:
    Among the apes there's no such thing as Masters
    and Farfoors.
MASTER:
    Then you agree with me that only human beings
    could be Masters and Farfoors?
FARFOOR:
    Who said that?
MASTER:
    That is what I think. If you don't like it, ask
    the Author.
FARFOOR:
    He left a long time ago.
MASTER:
    Call him.
FARFOOR:
    (Calling) You, there! Author!
MASTER:
    Be polite, Boy. You know these authors like to
    be respected and flattered.
FARFOOR:
    Mr. Author, your Excellency the Author.
    Greatest, biggest, most solid and splendid
    Author.
    *(The Author enters. He is now a dward or a
    child who is half as tall as he was earlier.
    He is still wearing the short pants.)*
AUTHOR:
    What do you want, Farfoor?
FARFOOR:
    Are you the Author?
AUTHOR:
    Who else could I be? Do you have dealings with
    another author?
FARFOOR:
    God forbid. I'm not one of those, Mister. It
    just seems to me that you're a little smaller.
MASTER:
    If you please, Mr. Author, could you tell
    Farfoor why I am a Master?
FARFOOR:
    Yes, why?

AUTHOR:

>Does that require any questions? It's as
>obvious as the day. I hope your next question
>is not why I am the Author. In my play, there's
>no such thing as "why?" There's only "Yes, sir."
>Understand?

FARFOOR:

>Why? *(Quickly correcting himself)* Yes, sir.

AUTHOR:

>Farfoor, I know your tricks. You'll probably
>come to your senses only when you find your-
>self thrown out in the street. Listen, this is
>your Master without any whys or what fors. And
>you are Farfoor without any fuss. Whatever he
>tells you to do, you should do. Otherwise...
>*(He makes a gesture with his hand. Two terrible
>giants appear, with a terrifying, menacing
>look in their eyes.)* I'll have them throw you
>out. Did you hear?

MASTER:

>Did you hear, Farfoor?

FARFOOR:

>I heard. I heard. I heard. One for him and one
>for you and one for these people. Go now. Bye.

AUTHOR:

>*(Turns to go out, walks a few steps then turns
>again to give Farfoor a final, wordless warning.)*

FARFOOR:

>I know. The play, the series, the seventh scene
>in the tenth act, the smash, the concussion. I
>know it all. But don't forget to send the
>mistress.

AUTHOR:

>I swear by...

FARFOOR:

>Go now, my God bless you.
>*(Exit the Author. The two giants withdraw.)*

MASTER:

>Did you hear him, Farfoor?

FARFOOR:

>Whether I heard or not, it doesn't matter.
>Where were we? *(He takes the shovel.)* Let's work.

MASTER:

No, I can't work anymore. I'm exhausted.

FARFOOR:

From what?

MASTER:

From work.

FARFOOR:

To tell the truth, may God help you, you
must rest immediately.

MASTER:

I don't want to rest.

FARFOOR:

What do you want to do?

MASTER:

I want to marry.

FARFOOR:

What?

MASTER:

Marry. Don't you understand what that is?

FARFOOR:

Well, why don't you go ahead, nobody is holding
you back. Unless you want me to marry for you.

MASTER:

What's wrong with that? Am I not your Master and
you my Farfoor?

FARFOOR:

No, please, Master. Ask me to break rocks, or
grind gravel. I'll do anything. But please forget this thing about marriage.

MASTER:

What's that to you? Are you marrying for yourself? You're marrying for me.

FARFOOR:

Who knows. I might get stuck with it, and then
I'll be finished.

MASTER:

Farfoor, don't argue.

FARFOOR:

Please, Master. You're a healthy man, you have
your peace of mind. Why should you court misfortune?

MASTER:

> None of us can do without marriage.

FARFOOR:

> Does that mean one should do without his life
> and money?

MASTER:

> Boy!

FARFOOR:

> Brrm... What does he mean, marry for him? And
> whom do I marry for you?

MASTER:

> How should I know? It's your job, or do you
> want me to do a Farfoor's job?

FARFOOR:

> Do you mean I should look for the bride, find
> her, propose to her, have the contract con-
> cluded, and...

MASTER:

> And you stop right there and stay where you are.

FARFOOR:

> You mean you leave me all the thorns and the
> muck and you take just the rose, ready and
> clean? What a pig of a master!

MASTER:

> That's how it goes with all Masters. Attend to
> your job now.

FARFOOR:

> (Yielding, shakes his head.) May God be my
> witness. We'll look for a bride. Gentlemen,
> ladies, mademoiselles, old maids... A man of
> good family, who has a good position, tends to
> be quiet and loves sleep, wants a wife. Did
> anybody say yes? Is there among you a bride
> who's an excellent housekeeper, fair of com-
> plexion, is devoted to the sacredness of
> matrimony, and likes rope-skipping and reading
> love stories? Nobody?

MASTER:

> Why did you stop. Go ahead, move!

FARFOOR:

> Move where, Master? Did the door bell ring?

MASTER:
>Didn't it?

FARFOOR:
>No, it didn't.

MASTER:
>So?

FARFOOR:
>So what? I asked him especially for that, the respectable Author whose only concern is to scare me. I asked him to send her over. He must have forgotten. Who knows what part of the series or in what radio station...The transmission in Abu Za'abal must be over, while he's sitting in the Anglo Bar.

MASTER:
>Wasn't she supposed to ring the bell?

FARFOOR:
>Only I do what's supposed to be done! As for others, you've heard for yourself.

MASTER:
>Listen.

FARFOOR:
>(*Listening in a funny manner*) It seems this knocking is only in your head, Master.

MASTER:
>What's to be done now? How do you like waiting for her in front of all these people like wet wash on a winter day?

FARFOOR:
>I don't like it. But let me tell you this. How about if we forget about the Author and the Lady he's sending and have you marry one of the people here.

MASTER:
>What nonsense! These are spectators, boy! They came here to watch, not to get married.

FARFOOR:
>That's how it all starts. You go to watch and you find yourself stuck in a marriage. Here they are in front of you. Choose the one you like.

MASTER:

> You mean I should really go ahead and select?
> May God guide our steps. *(He searches the
> auditorium.)* What do you think of that one,
> Farfoor? Or that? She looks quite nice. No, no
> wait. What do you think of the one sitting over
> there? She's quite fantastic.

FARFOOR:

> The one sitting over there?

MASTER:

> Yes.

FARFOOR:

> *(Hits him on the head.)* She's my mother, Boy!

MASTER:

> Well, how about that one?

FARFOOR:

> Which?

MASTER:

> The one with the red scarf around her neck.

FARFOOR:

> That one?

MASTER:

> Yes, that red thing is driving me crazy.

FARFOOR:

> It's a necktie worn by a man.

MASTER:

> O.K., how about that other one?

FARFOOR:

> That one over there? She's married, Master
> Boy.

MASTER:

> How did you know?

FARFOOR:

> Don't you see the two men with her?

MASTER:

> Well, what do you think of the one wearing
> that large black hat?

FARFOOR:

> That one?

MASTER:

> Yes.

FARFOOR:
>Are you blind? That's Dr. Mandour.*

MASTER:
>I give up, Farfoor. You choose for me.

FARFOOR:
>On one condition.

MASTER:
>What?

FARFOOR:
>*(Thinking it over)* Well, now. *(He surveys the auditorium quckly, then his eyes stop at the front of the left box.)* I've found her.

MASTER:
>Where?

FARFOOR:
>The one sitting over there in the box to the right.

MASTER:
>I don't see her. Where is the right box?

FARFOOR:
>Do you see the seed** that respectable man sitting over there is eating?

MASTER:
>Yes, I see it.

FARFOOR:
>After you leave it turn right, then go straight ahead. Do you see her, now?

MASTER:
>To tell the truth, I don't. But I agree to marry her.

FARFOOR:
>Just like that, without seeing her?

MASTER:
>It's enough that she's in a box. She must be well off.

*The late Dr. Mohammad Mandour, a famous literary critic and university professor.
**Seeds similar to sunflower seeds with shells on, a source of annoyance to actors in theaters, especially when everything is quiet.

FARFOOR:

> Do you hear, girls in the pit? Ten piasters'
> difference fetched a husband. *(Then he addresses
> the box to the right.)* You, Lady sitting in the
> box next to us. Please look at us here. Here.

LADY:

> Are you speaking to me?

FARFOOR:

> Not really, I am speaking to the moon.*

LADY:

> Poison.**

FARFOOR:

> I could take three handfuls of that daily like
> Omo*** for the sake of your eyes.

LADY:

> What vulger words! What do you want?

FARFOOR:

> Would you marry my Master, soul of the heart of
> the Master's Farfoor?

MASTER:

> *(Interfering)* What are you saying, Farfoor?
> Do you want to scare her away? You stand aside
> now. Allow me, Lady.

FARFOOR:

> You go away. Sit over there; it's none of your
> business. This is my job, didn't you say so?
> Do you want to be a Farfoor, now? Have some
> self-respect; try to be a Master. *(He addresses
> the Lady again.)* Would you marry my Master,
> soul of the heart and apple of the eye of the
> Master's Farfoor?

LADY:

> What's your Master?

FARFOOR:

> About one hundred kilograms.

---

  *The moon has long stood for beauty in women in
  Arabic poetry and folklore.
 **A literal translation of the word in Arabic used
  by women, not always very sincerely, to express
  lack of interest in advances made by males.
***A reference to a detergent commercial.

LADY:

What does he do?

FARFOOR:

Now, we'll be embarrassed. Well, would you
please come over here a minute.

LADY:

I won't budge one inch before I know what he
does.

FARFOOR:

Well, it's something...let's say...the opposite
of obstetrician.

LADY:

I don't care what he does. Does he have money?

FARFOOR:

Sacks. Sacks and sacks.

LADY:

Then, tentatively, I'll come. *(She leaves her
seat and goes to the stage.)* What's his name,
this Master of yours?

FARFOOR:

As for names, you can give him any that you like.

LADY:

Why? What family does he come from? I hope he
doesn't have a bad name.

FARFOOR:

It's neither good nor bad; he comes from the
family of the Unnamable.

LADY:

A very vulgar name, that. Anyway I am ready to
give him my family name.

FARFOOR:

What family is that?

LADY:

The Sillies, it's a very famous family. Haven't
you heard of it?

FARFOOR:

Of course I have. It has branches everywhere.
None are more abundant than the Silly ones.

LADY:

Listen! What's your name?

FARFOOR:

    Farfoor.

LADY:

    Listen, *garçon* Farfoor, my freedom is very
    important to me. I don't like anybody to re-
    strict it. Is your Master a reactionary man?

FARFOOR:

    I don't understand what "reactionary" means.

LADY:

    If he'd let me come home at 2 a.m. or later,
    he'd be progressive. Any time earlier than
    that, he'd be reactionary.

FARFOOR:

    Have no worry on that account, Lady. He sleeps
    all the time.

LADY:

    Would he allow me to keep my friends, the men,
    I mean?

FARFOOR:

    I'd be lying to you if I said I knew that.

LADY:

    It's such a modest request. My friend Kaki
    Qulqas insisted that she and her husband have
    her boy friend stay with them on the honeymoon.

FARFOOR:

    Well, she's right. What's a boy friend between
    friends? And whatever he does, he's just a boy.
    O.K. Lady, would you marry my Master?

LADY:

    I don't mind having him for a month on trial.
    If it doesn't work out, we'll get a divorce.

FARFOOR:

    My Lady, even employees are kept on trial, for
    three months. How can you be divorced after one
    month? What if something or another had happened
    in the course of the month?

LADY:

    So what? One can always have an appendectomy
    or a tonsilectomy.

FARFOOR:

    I meant...

LADY:

That's also what I meant.

FARFOOR:

Well, what's the relation between the appendix or the tonsils and that thing which you meant? I don't understand.

LADY:

That's what we call it when we go to the hospital--appendix or sometimes we say the tonsils. That's what I always say.

FARFOOR:

Do you always...

LADY:

What can I do? They once wrote in the papers that I had two tonsil operations in one month.

FARFOOR:

Does that also get published?

LADY:

We don't like to do anything secretly. Everything is open.

FARFOOR:

How many times did you remove your appendix?

LADY:

I don't remember...seven or eight...

FARFOOR:

And the tonsils?

LADY:

Oh, I didn't keep track. Oh, especially that last, last time...

FARFOOR:

Was it the tonsils or the appendix?

LADY:

Appendix! He had such a pair of eyes, I had to go back to the hospital after one week for another operation.

FARFOOR:

(Loudly) Listen, Master, Master! Did you fall asleep again?

MASTER:

What? Where are we? What happened? Who are you?

FARFOOR:

Here's the bride, Master. Just what you had in mind! Pretty! Comes from one of the biggest families in Egypt, the Sillies, and very clean, neither tonsils nor appendix, nor tooth cavities. She's removed everything. And if you'd like, she can remove them again and again. What do you think?

MASTER:

Do you like her, Farfoor?

FARFOOR:

In front of these people, I don't mind being a patch on her shoes. But it's a matter of taste.

MASTER:

Farfoor, see if my taste likes this lady or not.

FARFOOR:

(Turning to the other side) Do you like her, his taste? *(As a ventriloquist)* Very, very much. *(To the Master)* Did you hear?

MASTER:

Yes, I heard. O.K., go ahead. Marry us, Farfoor.

FARFOOR:

You want me to work as a ma'zoon* also? Well, why not? Your hand, Lady. *(His hands shake before he holds her hand.)* Your hand, Master. You, my Master, whose name is my Master, do you take this woman for... *(A Knock on the door.)*

MASTER:

What's that, Farfoor? *(A woman's voice.)*

THE VOICE:

You people who are doing a play...

FARFOOR:

How perfect! It seems she's the lady sent over by the Author. *(Knocking continues.)* Shall I open the door or leave her out there?

MASTER:

Do you want her to cause a commotion? Open the door.

---

*A ma'zoon is a man who performs marriage ceremonies.

FARFOOR:
>   And this one?

MASTER:
>   Don't worry, we'll explain everything, and
>   all will be settled.

FARFOOR:
>   *(Goes over to an imaginary door, turns an
>   imaginary knob. Makes indistinct sounds, then
>   mimics the sound produced by the opening of a
>   door.)* The Door is open. *(A Lady enters wear-
>   ing a belly-dancer's outfit.)* My!

SECOND LADY:
>   What's that? Are you deaf or something?

FARFOOR:
>   *(Is busy watching her, striking out his tongue
>   in excitement.)* Holy bananas! What's that?
>   *(He sniffles.)*

SECOND LADY:
>   Why don't you stand straight so I can talk to
>   you. Aren't you the folks who are doing a play?
>   *(Farfoor is very busy inspecting her.)* Are you
>   an idiot, or is it only the way you look?

FARFOOR:
>   It seems so.

SECOND LADY:
>   Your Author met me and we had a drink at
>   Groppi's* and he sent me over with my role.
>   *(She discovers the other Lady.)* What's that?
>   Did I come all this way to find she's stolen
>   my role?

MASTER:
>   Please, Lady. This Lady there is only watching
>   the play and has done nothing.

SECOND LADY:
>   Watching? Then what's she doing here? If she
>   wants to watch, she can go sit over there with
>   the spectators. This is our place. Let her go
>   to hers.

*A cafe and cocktail lounge in downtown Cairo.

LADY:

    I wouldn't let someone like you kick me out of
my place here.

SECOND LADY:

    But what are you waiting here for? Do you want
to act with us?

LADY:

    I'll wait for my husband. We've just been engaged
and we were about to write the contract.

SECOND LADY:

    God damn the day! What do you think I came here
for? It's my role: to marry him. Don't kid
yourself into thinking you can swipe him from
me. Now, do you want to leave here in peace or
would you rather I break your head?

LADY:

    Are you going to stand there while she says
that to me?

MASTER:

    What can I do? Farfoor, you rascal, think of a
solution.

FARFOOR:

    The only solution, Master...The only solution,
my Master, is that this one marries you and
that one marries me. This way we'll come out
even.

SECOND LADY:

    Me marry you? Why? You think jobs are that
scarce or that I've fallen so low? My role is
to marry that guy and I'll play it. Anybody
who wants to stop me will have to deal with my
slippers. My slippers, by the head of my father.

LADY:

    Don't get carried away. I won't demean myself
and go back to my place empty-handed just because of someone like you. And mind you, I take
judo lessons every day at the club.

SECOND LADY:

    *(Tries to attack the Lady. Farfoor intervenes
and holds her back.)* And I'll show you what your
judo is worth.

FARFOOR:

> *(To Second Lady)* One that's as beautiful as you
> are shouldn't wrestle with that marionette-like
> thing over there, really.

LADY:

> Listen, I have delicate nerves, I can't stand
> this. Now I'll have my fit! *(She tries to attack
> the Second Lady. The Master holds her back.)*

SECOND LADY:

> *(Tries to extricate herself from Farfoor. The
> more she tries, the stronger Farfoor holds her
> and also the more his whole body shakes because
> her exciting body is in his arms.)* Let me get
> her, that bitch!

FARFOOR:

> *(Sweating and shaking)* She's a Silly!

LADY:

> *Laissez-moi,* leave me. Let go of me, *Monsieur!*
> Did you hear what she called me?

MASTER:

> *(Looks behind him while still holding her and
> calls Farfoor who answers him by turning his
> head, while keeping his body in the same
> position.)* Why don't you think of something?

FARFOOR:

> Have mercy on me, Man. I am shaking all over.
> Even my brain is shaking. How can I think?

MASTER:

> Listen to me! *(Very loudly)* I have a very good
> solution for everybody. Now, if you'll stop
> quarrelling, we'll all be happy.

SECOND LADY:

> Are you going to marry me?

LADY:

> Are you going to marry me?

MASTER:

> I'll marry whichever is better. *(He notices
> that Farfoor, although the fight is over, is
> still holding the Second Lady.)* What are you
> doing there? The fight is over.

LADY:

> Of course, he'll marry me. I am the better one.

SECOND LADY:

One toenail of mine is better than the whole of you. You and your Silly family.

MASTER:

No, no, no! It won't do like that. Now, instead of fighting, I want each of you to demonstrate to me how she's better. *(A knock on the door.)* Who is it knocking on that door, now?

SECOND LADY:

It must be the woman who's going to marry Farfoor. The Author had sent her with me, but I left her at the door and came in to make sure...Only to find this sweetie pie here.

FARFOOR:

Somebody to marry me? Oh, he's a good Author after all. What does she look like? Is she pretty like you?

MASTER:

This is not the time, Farfoor. *(More knocking on the door)* Go answer the door first.

FARFOOR:

No, I'm shy.

MASTER:

Go open it, Boy.

FARFOOR:

Well, I'll open it but I'll be very shy; I'll keep my eyes on the ground all the time. *(In exaggerated shyness, Farfoor goes to the door looking at his feet all the time. When he opens the door, a tall, thin man enters, wearing a long black dress, with a black scarf covering his hair and a veil with red beads covering his face.)* Please come in. Welcome! *(Still looking at his feet.)*

WOMAN:

(She (He) is also very shy and speaks in a suppressed tone.) You see, I'm too shy. You're Farfoor, right?

FARFOOR:

And I, too, am too shy. How about if we both stop being shy and look at each other, come what may?

WOMAN:

O.K. *(She lifts the veil and raises her face
at the same time Farfoor is raising his. He
sees her face.)*

FARFOOR:

Good heavens, no! *(He runs away, trying to hide
behind his Master.)*

WOMAN:

(Advancing toward him, still shy.) Bah! Are you
still shy, Farfoor? Are you one of those or what?
The man told me you're quite a devil and I love
devils like you. Come here! *(She tries to pull
him, but he moves away.)*

FARFOOR:

Please, Master I beg you! Keep this hag away
from me.

WOMAN:

Not even the chief of police can keep you
away from me. I loved you at first sight and
it's over now. If only you wouldn't slip through
my hands like that!

FARFOOR:

(Very scared, evading her) Help! Help!

WOMAN:

Say what you like and do what you like. Nothing can save you from me once I get hold
of your hand.

FARFOOR:

I'll cut it off. By the holy saints, I'll
cut it off!

WOMAN:

Is that so? Oh, come now. *(She finally manages
to catch him.)*

FARFOOR:

(Shouting) Police! Rescue squad! Ambulance!
Health people! D.D.T. *(He tries to escape.)*

WOMAN:

Do you think you can run away? Not in this
world!

FARFOOR:

I'd rather leave it than see you...*(She forces*

him to look at her face. He closes his eyes.)
What a day! What a day! God have mercy on us.
What are you?

WOMAN:

I am a woman, Farfoor, and a coquette too!

FARFOOR:

No, no. I am the woman. I renounce all manhood
if women are like you. Please, I am a woman.
*(The heated discussion between the two ladies
and the Master is now resolved by the decision
declared by the Master.)*

MASTER:

Are we agreed then? I'll marry whoever proves
better than the other.

SECOND LADY:

I'll show you how much better I am. Give us
some music there. *(Belly-dancing music. The
Second Lady starts dancing, trying her best to
excite the Master. Whenever Farfoor tries to
look at her or come closer to her, the Woman
checks him violently. When the Second Lady's
dance is over, the Master starts moving toward
her involuntarily. The Lady, however, grabs him
by the hand.)*

LADY:

This is vulgar dancing that you shouldn't be
watching. You should be dancing with me. *(In a
commanding voice)* Maestro! *(Music for the twist
is played. The Lady dances with the Master in
an exciting manner. He forgets his previous
excitement and when the dance is over, he is
still holding the Lady in his arms.)*

WOMAN:

Don't you pay any attention to this lewdness,
Farfoor. Let's both play stick-fencing. *(They
start playing. During the game Farfoor receives
several blows on his sides, back and stomach.
When the match is over, Farfoor faints in the
Woman's arms.)* See how I made you swoon?

FARFOOR:

(Panting) It's my broken bones.

SECOND LADY:
> *(Pulling the Master)* Don't you like my figure, which is like a branch of ben?*

LADY:
> *(Pulling the Master toward her)* How about my figure which is like that of a mannequin?

WOMAN:
> As for that, they can't stand the competition. I am the ben itself.

FARFOOR:
> It must be Ben Franklin!

SECOND LADY:
> Do you see my eyes, like a gazelle's?

LADY:
> How about mine, prettier than Ann Sheridan's?

WOMAN:
> Don't worry, my eyes are bigger than a cup!

FARFOOR:
> Yes, camel's eyes!

SECOND LADY:
> Do you see my mouth, like Solomon's ring?

LADY:
> Mine is almost like a shirt's button hole!

WOMAN:
> What shall I say, I, whose mouth is like a thimble?

FARFOOR:
> An elephant's thimble, upon your life!

LADY:
> Do you see my hair, smooth as natural silk?

SECOND LADY:
> Can it compare with mine, smoother than ostrich plumes?

WOMAN:
> And my hair, isn't it truly *nu'man*** tresses?

---

*The ben is an Asiatic tree of the genus *Moringa*.
**I have kept the word in Arabic so that Farfoor's pun in the next line would make sense. The word refers to the anemone.

FARFOOR:

> You must mean Nu'man Ashour!***

MASTER:

> Enough! Enough! I'm really too confused to
> choose one of you. For this reason, I'll marry
> you both. Now, what do you think?

SECOND LADY:

> Think? You rake, you lewd...You!

LADY:

> Libertine! Polygamist!

MASTER:

> *(Addressing the Second Lady)* You mean you don't
> want to marry me?

SECOND LADY:

> Who mentioned such a thing?

MASTER:

> *(Addressing the Lady)* What about you?

LADY:

> Who said I'd accept defeat?

FARFOOR:

> Congratulations, Uncle. May you live to enjoy it!
> *(The Master takes each of the Ladies in one
> arm and walks over to right exit. Meanwhile, the
> two Ladies' hands are fighting behind his neck.
> Farfoor tries to steal away from the stage, but
> the Woman grabs him and keeps him there.)*

WOMAN:

> And you, my Farfoor, what did you say?

FARFOOR:

> We are all mortal. Dust to dust!

WOMAN:

> Heaven protect us! Did somebody you know die?

FARFOOR:

> Yes, me.

WOMAN:

> You? God preserve you! So long as I am with you,
> death will not dare come near you.

FARFOOR:

> But you are death!

WOMAN:

> Come, my Darling! Come on. *(When he resists,*

***An Egyptian Playwright.

the Woman hauls him over her shoulder and carries him to the left exit.)

FARFOOR:

(To the audience) We are all...*(Pointing to his new wife behind her back.)* mortal! *(The Master enters from the door to the right massaging his face with eau de cologne after a warm bath.)*

MASTER:

Oh! Marriage is such fun. It's a million times better than celibacy!

(Enter Farfoor from left door, his head covered with a huge bandage on which large stains of blood can be seen.)

MASTER:

How are you faring in marriage, Farfoor?

FARFOOR:

It's given me ten stitches so far.

MASTER:

That's because you people don't understand the art of life. You don't know how to handle her, fondle her, pat her, embrace her, play games and make jokes.

FARFOOR:

That's exactly what I did.

MASTER:

How come you're injured, then?

FARFOOR:

She returned my play a little too roughly and broke my head.

MASTER:

I'm so happy that I don't feel anything.

FARFOOR:

I don't feel anything either, because of my swollen head.

MASTER:

Women are the most beautiful things in the world.

FARFOOR:

When they are women!

MASTER:

Imagine how I feel knowing I'll be two fathers today. I am so happy, I could fly.

FARFOOR:

Two fathers at the same time?

MASTER:

Yes, at the same time.

FARFOOR:

Congratulations!

MASTER:

And you, aren't you going to have a child?

FARFOOR:

That I might have a child is very possible, but
that she will have a child is quite unlikely.
Do you imagine that she's like a woman, capable
of such a thing. Personally, I can't imagine that.

LADY:

(Enters, carrying a baby.) Congratulations,
Husband. It's a boy. Look!

SECOND LADY:

(Enters, carrying a baby.) Congratulations,
Hubby, it's a girl, a beauty!

WOMAN:

(From outside) Congratulations, Boy! Congratulations, Farfoor, it's a boy. *(Farfoor's wife enters
carrying on her shoulders a man who cries like
a baby and asks for food. She gives him a loaf
of bread and an onion which he breaks on her
head with his fist and gobbles up with the loaf.)*
See your son, Farfoor? Come, play with him a
little. Come on. *(Farfoor, reluctantly, tries
to carry the son but the latter pushes him,
causing him to fall on his back.)*

LADY:

Excuse me, Darling. The baby has to be fed now.

SECOND LADY:

And I have to change her diapers.

LADY:

But please don't forget to get the things I
told you about. *(She goes out.)*

SECOND LADY:

And remember the money I told you about today.
(She goes out.)

WOMAN:

> Listen, Farfoor. My son needs an amulet to ward
> off the evil eye, and you know how people can
> envy him.

FARFOOR:

> What evil eye, Woman? What could they envy about
> him? I only wish they could envy him a little.

WOMAN:

> It's none of my business. He wants an amulet
> and the amulet has to be made by the sheikh and
> the sheikh wants ten piasters. If you don't pro-
> duce ten piasters by noon, your time will be up.
> (She goes out.)

FARFOOR:

> May a jet plane take your life! My time will be
> up! For ten piasters? Why? Is my life worth no
> more than an empty sack?

MASTER:

> What's to be done, Farfoor?

FARFOOR:

> I don't know why it's so damn tough. For several
> days now we've been doing nothing. No corpses to
> bury. It seems it's the holiday season and no-
> body goes to hospitals.

MASTER:

> Don't you worry, death never takes a holiday.

FARFOOR:

> What do you mean, "Don't you worry"? If I don't
> get her some money today she might really kill
> me. Find a way.

MASTER:

> Me find a way? Then what's your job?

FARFOOR:

> What do you want me to do?

MASTER:

> Get us a corpse to work on.

FARFOOR:

> Where can I get one now? Borrow it. You, Mister,
> over there. Can't you spare a corpse until next
> pay day?

MASTER:

> Stop that, Farfoor. Find us a corpse.

FARFOOR:

> *(Searching with his eyes among the audience.)*
> I can't find any. They're all, praise be to God,
> one hundred percent hale and sound.

MASTER:

> Well then, here's an easy solution. Kill somebody.

FARFOOR:

> Kill somebody! Has the man gone mad? Kill somebody
> to bury him for fifty piasters?

MASTER:

> And for less than that. And if I had to, I'd kill
> you. We want money. We want work. Either you kill
> someone or I will kill you.

FARFOOR:

> Has it come to this?

MASTER:

> Yes.

FARFOOR:

> Are you serious?

MASTER:

> Serious.

FARFOOR:

> You're not kidding?

MASTER:

> When I tell you I'm serious, then I'm serious.

FARFOOR:

> It seems he's goddamn serious. No, sir. I'd be
> better off killing someone.
> *(Voice from the audience calling, "You who want
> to kill someone! Murderers! Someone wants to die,
> who's interested?")*

MASTER:

> What's that, Farfoor?

FARFOOR:

> I don't really know. It's somebody offering
> himself.

MASTER:

> Just what we wanted. Call him.

FARFOOR:

> You there. You who are looking for a death!

MAN:

> Yes, someone calling?

FARFOOR:

    Yes, here! Come on up!

MAN:

    Where? Where are you?

FARFOOR:

    Third floor.

MAN:

    Listen, I am not going to come up and then go
down again. I've been doing nothing else all
day. My feet can't stand it any more. If you
really mean it, I'll come. If you don't, God's
earth is wide.

FARFOOR:

    Why is he such a troublemaker? No, Uncle. We
really mean it. Come on up.

MAN:

    Here I am. Go ahead, please. I don't have much
time. Would you like me to die here or shall I
sit on that chair or would you rather I slept
on the floor?

FARFOOR:

    Easy. Cool it, Man.

MAN:

    I tell you I am in a hurry. Your weapon ready?
You have a gun or do you prefer a knife in such
cases?

FARFOOR:

    What's that? Cool it, Man.

MAN:

    Now, look here Mister, I don't like this
fastidiousness. Do you intend to kill me or not?

FARFOOR:

    I do.

MAN:

    What are you waiting for?

MASTER:

    What's this hurry all about, Man? The world's
not going to run away. Easy, Man. Let's discuss
it.

MAN:

    Discuss what?

MASTER:

> This man is going to drive us crazy. What are
> you? Do you want to commit suicide or something?

MAN:

> Commit suicide? Who said such a thing?

MASTER:

> Then why do you want to die so fast?

MAN:

> What's wrong with that? I'm kind of overactive
> and whenever I have to do something, I like
> to do it real quick. I won't have any rest
> until I'm finished.

MASTER:

> This enthusiasm is commendable when it involves
> work, but this is not work; it's no joke either.
> It's death.

MAN:

> For you, it's death. For me, it's work.

MASTER:

> Work?

MAN:

> Yes, any objections?

MASTER:

> It's not a matter of objections or no objec-
> tions. The whole thing is, I never heard of such
> a job before.

FARFOOR:

> Nor me either. I swear by God and may I lose my
> eyesight!

MAN:

> It's possible, but this is my job.

MASTER:

> Your job is to die?

MAN:

> Yes.

MASTER:

> Strange! What kind of job is that? Who'd want
> to do it?

MAN:

> Oh, millions. The other day our employer announced
> that more help was wanted and more than a thousand
> persons applied, with all kinds of recommendations
> from influential people.

MASTER:

> Your employer?

MAN:

> We're a group of people working for a man who supports us, financially, you know. Now this man has enemies, so whenever they want to kill him, he sends one of us to die for him.

MASTER:

> And how's it going? The business, I mean.

MAN:

> It's very slow, right now. Jobs are very scarce.

MASTER:

> That's too bad, indeed. But why is that?

MAN:

> Well, it goes by supply and demand. We're too many and those that want to kill are too few. Would you believe it, people are no good anymore. Everybody is scared to kill now. Some go to courts, some go to the Security Council. It's so bad it makes you sick.

MASTER:

> Are you disgusted, too?

MAN:

> Very much so. I was so disgusted, I resigned.

MASTER:

> Why did you do that?

MAN:

> So that I could work for myself. Nothing's better than being independent, your own Master, you know.

MASTER:

> How so?

MAN:

> Well, it means I offer myself for killing. Who knows? With a bit of luck I might find somebody willing to do me in.

MASTER:

> How full of wonders is this life! Really, a grave digger comes across many wonders!

MAN:

> No, there's really no wonder about that; it's nothing new. Or is it because I am a small

dealer? Haven't you heard of our colleagues,
the Foreign Legion or something of the sort?
Or is it because they're Europeans?

MASTER:

But, really, I mean...with all respect for your
opinion...Personally, I couldn't accept such a
job.

MAN:

Why's that?

MASTER:

Is that a job? It's suicide, Man. I never heard
of a man who seeks death just for the heck of it.

MAN:

There you're wrong! It's the best job there is.
A job that you do once in your life and it's
over. Not one that you'd have to keep doing
everyday and still die in the end. Let's put it
this way: I want to go to Alexandria and so do
you. I'd like to close my eyes and open them and
find myself there. But you want to take a camel.
It most probably will die before even reaching
the Rest House.*

MASTER:

I hope you haven't come from Abbasia** to go to
Alexandria.

MAN:

Me? It seems it's you who comes from there. Which
of us is insane? The one who wants to go to
Alexandria on a camel or he who wants to take a
plane? But really, Mister, I don't have much time
for all this. I don't like talking too much.
Here's my neck at your disposal. And my soul is
waiting for you to take it.

MASTER:

How about the wages. Who do we pay?

MAN:

Don't worry about that. Tomorrow or the day
after, my wife will come to collect from you.

*A wayside cafe between Cairo and Alexandria.
**Abbasia is the site of a lunatic asylum in Cairo.

MASTER:
>This is really something else. Now, suppose
>she doesn't believe me and they lock me up?

MAN:
>In that case you'd be an idiot who didn't do his
>job well.

FARFOOR:
>Master, please let's forget about this job.

MASTER:
>You shut up! This is not the business of Farfoors
>like you. *(To the Man)* O.K., then. I know how to
>handle that.

MASTER:
>Now it's your turn, Farfoor, to do your job.
>Did you hear? Here's his neck.

FARFOOR:
>So?

MASTER:
>Who's going to work for me?

FARFOOR:
>Anything but that! I am just a Farfoor and not
>really qualified.

MASTER:
>Farfoor, as I told you this morning, either you
>kill him or I kill you. No need for this
>disobedience.

FARFOOR:
>Oh, no? On that, I'll be disobedient as much as
>I like, and you do whatever you can. Get the
>Author, the director, I don't care. I shall not
>kill. Anything but that!

MASTER:
>It's up to you. Mr. Author! Greatest of all
>Authors! Farfoor is disobedient again.

AUTHOR'S VOICE:
>*(From off stage)* Are you defying me, Farfoor?
>I'll blow you up. I'll burn you. I'll send the
>giants for you. *(The shadows of the two giants
>appear close to the door.)*

FARFOOR:
>*(Looking alternately at the two shadows and the
>Man offering his head to be cut off)* What do I
>do?

MASTER:
   Heh?
FARFOOR:
   What do we do now?
MAN:
   Why don't you finish me off? What sort of job
   is this that forces us to accept these disgust-
   ing conditions?
MASTER:
   Farfoor! Do your job. *(Makes a gesture that
   Farfoor must kill the Man)*
FARFOOR:
   Well, I submit everything to God and the Author.
   O.K., but how can I kill him? How can I kill
   you, Man? What's he doing bending over like that?
   Are you looking for a lost shilling or something?
   How do I kill him, Master?
MASTER:
   With this pick.
FARFOOR:
   But this is for digging, for earning our living!
MASTER:
   This also is earning our living.
FARFOOR:
   It's not fair, really. How can I dig a man's
   head so early. Well, I submit all to God. Heh!
   *(He raises the pick and tries to land it down
   on the man's neck, but he shakes and gives
   up trying.)*
MASTER:
   Where's your courage, Farfoor? Strike, Boy.
FARFOOR:
   Where's your courage? Why don't you strike?
MASTER:
   Hate him and strike.
FARFOOR:
   Why should I hate him? He did nothing to me.
   Well, I hate you. I can't stand you. You make me
   sick! Heh! *(He raises the pick, but his hand
   shakes.)*

MASTER:

No, no, not like that. You should hate him more.
He's your enemy. He's against your livlihood.

FARFOOR:

Is he my livelihood or against it? Which should
I believe? You, there! You're my enemy. Your
father is my father's enemy and your grandfather is my grandfather's enemy. I'll take
vengeance. *(He raises the pick, but he's still
shaking. The Master gets furious, rushes at him,
takes the pick from his hand and pushes him
away.)*

MASTER:

Farfoors like you are slaves and cowards. Does
this require a Master to do it? Get out of my way.

MAN:

Either you finish the job and kill me or I'll go
and find somebody else to do it. I'm late already.

MASTER:

Listen, Fellow. I'll make it easier for you. No
need for picks or anything. I'll strangle you.
But I don't want any screaming or cries for help,
understand? Otherwise, I won't kill you.

MAN:

Have no fear, Mister. I'll die with a smile on
my face.

MASTER:

Close your eyes. They have a look which I don't
particularly care for.

MAN:

O.K., here are the eyes.

MASTER:

In the name of God... *(His hands get close to the
Man's neck.)*

FARFOOR:

Keep your hands off!

MASTER:

(Turning around, scared) What's that, Boy. You
scared me. What do you want?

FARFOOR:

So, you're scared of me but not of what you're
doing. Aren't you ashamed of yourself, killing

the man without blessing him? Are you an
atheist or something?

MASTER:

God bless you. Heh! *(He grabs the Man's neck.)*

FARFOOR:

(Jumping up and down, hysterically scared) Oh
Cain, why do you kill thy brother? The first
sin. Have mercy on those on earth so He in
Heaven may have mercy on you!

MASTER:

Listen, Boy. If you don't shut up, I'll kill you
first. Go away. *(He grabs the Man's neck.)*

FARFOOR:

(Calling loudly) People! Humanity! Men! Aren't
you ashamed? Help, Brothers! How can you sit back
and watch your brother in humanity being killed?
Where are your values? Where's justice? Where's
the law?

MASTER:

(Rushing at him with open fists) Wait until I
get you!

FARFOOR:

(Running away) Help! The man's changed into a
monster!

MAN:

(Very much dismayed) This is no way to make a
living! Damn independent business! These amateurs
are very difficult to get along with. I should've
gone to a professional and been done a long time
ago.

MASTER:

We'll finish you! *(He starts squeezing the Man's
neck and whenever he's about to strangle him
Farfoor starts shouting, "Keep your hands off!"
or "Holy saints," or "Police," or "God," etc.,
while circling hysterically around the Master.
He looks at the Man's face and finds his tongue
hanging down and his eyes protruding.)*

FARFOOR:

Oh, God! He killed him for real! Help! Murderer!
Arrest him!

MASTER:
>   *(Approaching him after stretching the Man on
>   the floor. He is still in the frenzy of killing.)*
>   Are you going to shut up or...?

FARFOOR:
>   I'm shutting up. I won't utter a word. I'll be
>   silent forever! Even if I speak, I'll do that
>   silently. Oh, my God, how can you kill him in
>   cold blood like that and in front of these
>   people. *(The Master gives him the same look as
>   before.)* Sh! I am shutting up. Everybody shut
>   up, his appetite is awakened. Look at his eyes.

MASTER:
>   *(Returning to normal)* Listen, Farfoor?

FARFOOR:
>   *(Doesn't answer.)*

MASTER:
>   Farfoor!

FARFOOR:
>   I am silent.

MASTER:
>   Speak.

FARFOOR:
>   I am silent, period.

MASTER:
>   *(Angrily)* Are you going to answer or...?

FARFOOR:
>   I am. No need for that "or."

MASTER:
>   Listen, Boy.

FARFOOR:
>   Yes, Master.

MASTER:
>   Bury this man.

FARFOOR:
>   Why? The one who killed him should bury him.

MASTER:
>   Either you bury him or I bury you.

FARFOOR:
>   Isn't it easier to bury him? *(He notices that
>   the Master's look is beginning to change.)* Any-
>   way, I can't sit and see you getting exhausted.
>   I'll bury him. *(He digs a grave and buries the
>   Man.)*

MASTER:

Did you bury him?

FARFOOR:

I even made the angels settle his score and
prove him wrong, too.

MASTER:

Bravo, Farfoor! That's the right spirit for
Farfoors. But I am upset, Farfoor.

FARFOOR:

Are you mad at me? I did...

MASTER:

(Angrily) Not at you. At myself. *(Changing his
tone)* My conscience is giving me a bad time.

FARFOOR:

Do you have such a thing, Master?

MASTER:

Yes and a very sensitive one, too. What shall I
do?

FARFOOR:

Take a purgative!

MASTER:

I am serious, Farfoor. I'm not kidding. Anyway,
take this fifty piaster note, this job's wages,
and give it to those at home to get some
vegetables and meat.

FARFOOR:

Why get met from the store if we have it here
fresh? *(The Master gives Farfoor a note which
he takes and walks over to the door and gives
to the air saying...)* Go eat meat, but make sure
it's fresh. *(He goes back to his Master and finds
him still sad.)* How are you now, Master? Is your
conscience still aching?

MASTER:

Yes, it is, Farfoor!

FARFOOR:

You should have taken a purgative like I told
you! But now, what are you going to do?

MASTER:

Do you know, Farfoor, what I should do to have
some peace with my conscience?

FARFOOR:
> What?

MASTER:
> You should get me another man to kill.

FARFOOR:
> *(Suddenly shouting very loudly)* No! He's
> becoming a vampire! Nobody will be safe with him
> again. Next time he'll kill me. Listen, damn your
> Author. I am leaving you, giants or no giants.
> I can take a beating. I am going.

MASTER:
> Are you crazy, Farfoor? I am ordering you to stay,
> Boy.

FARFOOR:
> Why are you ordering me?

MASTER:
> I am the Master.

FARFOOR:
> Why are you a Master? And whose Master? And
> why should you be a Master? Why? I don't know
> you, nor do I have any Masters. I am leaving.
> *(He leaves the stage, passing through the
> audience.)*

MASTER:
> Boy! Farfoor!

FARFOOR:
> I've already left.

MASTER:
> What about the second act?

FARFOOR:
> It's your problem. You and whoever made you a
> Master. Bye.

Curtain

Act II

MASTER:

What's to be done now? Now I am completely stuck.
Imagine a Farfoor like that standing me up? What
shall I do? Where do I find him? Where do I look
for him? Did any of you see Farfoor? How do you
like the situation in which Farfoor's left me?

FARFOOR:

*(Enters from the auditorium door into the aisle
between the rows of seats, pushing a cart loaded
with surrealistic figures representing Europe
and America, parts of cannons, planes and gallows,
etc. Calling)* Junk! Junk! Any antiques for sale!
Old glory for sale! Old greatness for sale! Old
Masters for sale! Old cannons for sale! Old
A-bombs for sale! Does anyone have any H-bombs
for sale? Magazines! Books! Philosophy! Newspapers!
Plays! Theaters! Ancient Authors for sale!

A WOMEN FROM THE AUDIENCE:

Junk dealer, we have an old torpedo. Would you like
to buy it?

FARFOOR:

It must be her husband. No, Lady. That's obsolete
now. Now we're interested in at least H-bombs.
Come on, before the show starts. Cobalt! Heavy
water! Nuclear radiation! Dill pickles! All
antiques for sale! Old glory for sale! Greatness!
Old ideas for sale! Junk!

MASTER:

It must be him. It is him. I'd know him among a million people. Farfoor!

FARFOOR:

(Has come very close to the stage now) Master, Boy!

MASTER:

Where have you been, Farfoor?

FARFOOR:

Where have you been, Master?

MASTER:

Help me, Farfoor.

FARFOOR:

Your hand, Master.

(The Master reaches out his hand and pulls Farfoor up on the stage. They embrace and kiss several times.)

MASTER:

Now, really, Farfoor. I've been looking for you for the last thousand years. No, not one thousand, say five thousand years.

FARFOOR:

This man's such an incurable liar! It's not five minutes since we left each other in front of everybody.

MASTER:

And where were you, Farfoor? Where did you go? What did you do?

FARFOOR:

I was in the big, wide world. What could I do?

MASTER:

Did you work for other Masters?

FARFOOR:

Lots and lots of them, and each worse than the other.

MASTER:

And what's that junk thing?

FARFOOR:

It's the job given me by my Master.

MASTER:

Who's your Master?

FARFOOR:

    That's his name, a soccer player, a goal keeper or something and he is sending me all over the place looking for second hand glory and greatness. Now I can't take it anymore. And how are you faring, Master?

MASTER:

    I am contented. God be praised.

FARFOOR:

    Is your conscience still itching?

MASTER:

    Well, no. The kids are seeing to that...

FARFOOR:

    Are they grown up now?

MASTER:

    Oh, and married and their sons and daughters are married. Some died and others are coming.

FARFOOR:

    This man is such a liar! All this in five minutes! *(Then to the Master)* So now you don't bury anybody with your hands?

MASTER:

    I told you the kids are seeing to that.

FARFOOR:

    Did they take the same trade?

MASTER:

    They took it and developed it to such ingenious dimensions!

FARFOOR:

    How so?

MASTER:

    Remember how you and I had such trouble burying one person? Each of them used bury ten or twenty thousands a day without much effort. Take my son, Alexander. He alone buried over a hundred thousand. Thutmosis, who was a little older, buried an even greater number.

FARFOOR:

    Thutmosis and Alexander? Why did you call them that?

MASTER:
>I've given them the names of history's heroes, each his own name. Take Napoleon, for instance, he buried over three million.

FARFOOR:
>Which Napoleon? Yours or history's?

MASTER:
>Mine, Farfoor. They're all my sons.

FARFOOR:
>And are they all a million-and-upward grave diggers?

MASTER:
>Yes.

FARFOOR:
>Bravo! They're sure legitimate sons!

MASTER:
>You know my son, Mussolini?

FARFOOR:
>How many millions?

MASTER:
>No, this one never went to work without his elder brother who gave him courage.

FARFOOR:
>Which brother?

MASTER:
>Hitler. In one season they grossed more than eight million corpses.

FARFOOR:
>What season was that? Was there cholera or something?

MASTER:
>What cholera, Man? Eight million in the good old way. Did you forget when we'd run out of corpses, when we'd kill a man and bury him?

FARFOOR:
>No, I didn't but according to your own account their season must have lasted a hundred thousand years to do all this work.

MASTER:
>No! Your knowledge is very backward. Didn't I tell you they were geniuses at it. They invented all kinds of things and never worked with their hands. They'd kill a thousand in a second.

FARFOOR:

 Suppose they did kill a thousand every second.
 Doesn't each need a grave dug to measure?

MASTER:

 I see now how behind the times you are! I told
 you they were geniuses. They invented things
 that'd kill and bury automatically, with no shovels
 or digging.

FARFOOR:

 That's how a progeny should be! They're all
 taking after you! You must have made a very huge
 fortune!

MASTER:

 Yes, I did, but I also spent a lot. The result
 is as you see--broke as a newborn babe. How
 about you? How did your wife and son do?

FARFOOR:

 You should say wives and sons!

MASTER:

 Are they many?

FARFOOR:

 So many you couldn't count them. Heard of the
 Hyksos?

MASTER:

 Them?

FARFOOR:

 Do you know Spartacus and his comrades?

MASTER:

 Of course, of course. My Roman woman's sons
 buried quite a few of those.

FARFOOR:

 These are all mine. Do you know Kafur the
 Ikhshidi, Antar ibn Shaddad, Abu Zeid? I
 couldn't really start to count them.

MASTER:

 No need, Farfoor. Nothing is like the good old
 days.

FARFOOR:

 You mean when you and I were...

MASTER:

 Yes, yes, we had no children, no women, no
 money, no crowds, no nothing.

FARFOOR:
So you remember?
MASTER:
And now I've found you, Farfoor.
FARFOOR:
And I've also found you, Master.
MASTER:
What do you think? How about if we forgot all
that has happened?
FARFOOR:
O.K., it never happened.
MASTER:
And have a brand new beginning?
FARFOOR:
A brand new beginning or beginning new brand.
Whatever you say.
MASTER:
And get under the skin of the role.
FARFOOR:
And get under the skin of the role.
MASTER:
Are you ready?
FARFOOR:
Go ahead.
MASTER:
Listen, you Boy...
FARFOOR:
What? What? What? What did you say?
MASTER:
I said, "Listen, you Boy," didn't we agree to
start all over?
FARFOOR:
Start what?
MASTER:
The play.
FARFOOR:
What play?
MASTER:
Our play. (*Holds a huge book and brandishes it in
Farfoor's face.*) *Farfoor and His Master*, have you
forgotten?

FARFOOR:
>No, I haven't, but how do we start?

MASTER:
>Like every time. You are Farfoor and I am the
>Master. O.K.? Let's begin. Listen you B...

FARFOOR:
>*(Loudly and strongly)* Stop! Stop right where you
>are!

MASTER:
>What's the matter?

FARFOOR:
>I don't have any role to play in that play.
>Farfoor! Again? Over my dead body...or somebody's
>body, anyway. Forget it, Man! That was a long
>time ago!

MASTER:
>What kind of talk is this, Farfoor? Have you
>gone crazy or something? Am I inventing anything?
>*(Holding the play)* It's all in the play.

FARFOOR:
>Don't you give me that crap again, neither the
>play nor any nonsense. What play is that you're
>blackmailing me with? Whenever I open my mouth
>to speak you say, "the play, the play." God
>damn the play! For a thousand years, a hundred
>thousand years, you've been holding that play
>over my head. "Dig, Farfoor. Fill, Farfoor.
>Build, Farfoor. Fall ill, Farfoor. Go lame,
>Farfoor. Scratch my back, Farfoor." God damn
>all such Farfoors.

MASTER:
>Behave yourself, Farfoor. Don't use such strong
>language in my presence.

FARFOOR:
>God damn you and your fathers too!

MASTER:
>Well, in that case, I'll let the Author...

FARFOOR:
>Goddamn the bastard Author too. What Author is
>that who has authored everything against me?
>Did I kill his father or marry his mother? He's
>worse than a landlord with his tenants. What

play, man, and what Author? No, no, no, in all
scripts and languages. No!

MASTER:

What's the matter? What's come over you, Boy? You
must certainly be possessed by a fiend or something! You were like an innocent and blind
kitten. What happened?

FARFOOR:

I am starting to open my eyes.

MASTER:

You're starting to be an impudent jackass, and
very soon you'll start to kick. You'll ultimately
try to make me a Farfoor and yourself a Master.

FARFOOR:

So what if I do? Will the sky fall down? Will
Judgment Day come now? Will a millieme buy a
cigarette?

MASTER:

That the sky should fall down is quite reasonable; that Judgment Day come now is not improbable,
but for a millieme to buy a cigarette or five
half-piasters a pound of beef or you become a
Master and I a Farfoor, that's impossible!

FARFOOR:

(Mimicking him) That's impossible! *(Angrily)* Why
is it impossible?

MASTER:

That'd be another play which you might want to
write.

FARFOOR:

Yes, I'll write it. So what? I'll write it. Is
that so difficult?

MASTER:

You're out of your blooming mind. Wake up, Boy!
Aren't you afraid someone might overhear you?
You write the play? How on this earth can you
imagine...? You, you undernourished worm, you
skunk, you mouse with no tail, you want to
write a play and be an Author?

FARFOOR:

Why not? If it is the pants, I sure can cut them
shorter or raise them higher or even take them

off completely. And if it is the play, what
could happen? Screw things up? So what? Whatever
I screw up won't be any worse than your screwed
up Author of the third scene of the tenth act,
the series, etc. etc.

MASTER:

Never in my life have I seen the likes of your
impudence. Don't you like what he writes, Boy?

FARFOOR:

Am I alone in that? Does anybody like it? Ask
anybody here if they know of any author on earth
who does what he does or screws things up worse
than him, the one who makes one person forever
Farfoor and another forever Master! Why? Is he
blind? Doesn't he have any taste? Are there no
critics? At least for the sake of change. People
are bored. Do you see that guy over there? (He
points at a spectator.) I hear him getting bored
with my own ears. He's been very busy getting
bored for the last hour.

MASTER:

Almighty Lord. Isn't he the same Author you've
raised to heaven, Farfoor? Is he not the same
person you knelt down to whenever you saw him?
Is that over now? You've changed so much
Farfoor. What has changed you?

FARFOOR:

What changes people has changed me.

MASTER:

And what changes people?

FARFOOR:

People.

MASTER:

Are you changed?

FARFOOR:

Yes, completely.

MASTER:

Then what's to be done?

FARFOOR:

Nothing. Nothing will do now.

Master:
    Do you intend to work or don't you?
FARFOOR:
    If it's a matter of work, I'd work till the
    morning. But never as a Farfoor.
MASTER:
    It seems you are bent on upsetting me. What's
    wrong with you? Must you make all this fuss all
    the time? Why don't you let it be?
FARFOOR:
    No!
MASTER:
    You know our Author is neurotic and gets mad
    very easily.
FARFOOR:
    No!
MASTER:
    And his giants, have you forgotten them? Just
    look at your eye, you almost lost it.
FARFOOR:
    No!
MASTER:
    What do you mean, "No"? Why "no"?
FARFOOR:
    No particular reason. I can stand beating,
    humiliation, disgrace, a black eye, a broken
    hand and still, NO!
MASTER:
    Why are you so stubborn?
FARFOOR:
    I'm not being stubborn; he's the one who is
    stubborn. I have done absolutely nothing. All I
    want is simply to understand.
MASTER:
    What do you want to understand?
FARFOOR:
    I'd like to understand why I am a Farfoor and
    why you are a Master.
MASTER:
    Is that a joke?
FARFOOR:
    Nothing could be more serious. I tell you I'd
    like to understand.

MASTER:
Understanding is not our line, Son. We're actors.
FARFOOR:
Well, I've decided not to act unless I under-
stand. I must know why I am a Farfoor and why
you are a Master.
MASTER:
You're so funny! Didn't the Author tell you
that the play's like that? Why should you argue?
FARFOOR:
That doesn't satisfy me. I'd like to understand.
I've nothing against plays nor against Authors
for that matter. I want a play that I can under-
stand and an Author who convinces me.
MASTER:
Convinces you of what?
FARFOOR:
Of everything. And the first thing is you, Your
Excellency, Your Highness, Your Lordship, you,
you. Why are you a Master? And I, who am I?
Why am I a Farfoor?
MASTER:
Didn't he tell you that every Master should have
a Farfoor?
FARFOOR:
Why?
MASTER:
Because every Farfoor must have a Master.
FARFOOR:
Why?
MASTER:
He must, period. He must.
FARFOOR:
You mean in the play?
MASTER:
In the play and elsewhere. Everywhere. Everyone
must. Everyone's either a Master or a Farfoor
and every Farfoor has a Master and every Master
a Farfoor. And that's the way it is.
FARFOOR:
That's the way what is?
MASTER:
The play.

FARFOOR:

    Then it is wrong.

MASTER:

    Wrong or not, we haven't come here to correct
things; we've come to work. We shouldn't concern ourselves with whys and wherefores, or why
the Author said this or that. For an hour we've
been chattering away, neglecting the play. Now
we don't have much time. We're just starting and
we have a lot to cover yet. Now, we've talked a
lot, and beaten around the bush. Do you want to
work or would you rather I called the Author to
handle you?

FARFOOR:

    No!

MASTER:

    Farfoor!

FARFOOR:

    No!

MASTER:

    It's up to you, then. Mr. Author! Greatest Author!
Most splendid, most magnificent, grandest Author!

VOICES:

    (From offstage) Don't waste your time. He left
a long time ago. *(Farfoor laughs.)*

MASTER:

    Left? Where did he go?

VOICE:

    We don't know.

MASTER:

    (Gesturing vexedly to Farfoor to remain silent)
When is he coming back?

VOICES:

    We don't know. Maybe tomorrow, or the day after
or after a year, a thousand years. Maybe he'll never
come back. We don't know.

MASTER:

    Then what do we do?

VOICES:

    Do it whatever way you like.

MASTER:

    How?

VOICES:

> We don't know.

FARFOOR:

> Hurray! Lovely!

MASTER:

> What nonsense is that? How can he desert us
> like that? How can he write us and leave us like
> this? What do we do now? *(Meanwhile, Farfoor
> is busy expressing joy and relief by means of
> all kinds of acrobatics.)* What do we do now,
> Dummy. Speak, stupid! Tell us what we're going to
> do.

FARFOOR:

> Stop right there! That's past now. If you call
> me Dummy I'll call you sixty thousand million
> times Dummy. If you say anything, I'll stick my
> fingers into your eyes.

MASTER:

> You were sensible, Boy, just a moment ago! What's
> come over you?

FARFOOR:

> Well, I was afraid, but now I am free! I am no
> longer a human being, I am a free agent. God
> be praised! I no longer have an Author. Oh boy!
> Being written is so ugly it's almost obscene! The
> most beautiful thing on earth is feeling that
> you're your own Author, that you can do it any
> way you like!

MASTER:

> Wait a minute! What do you mean "your own
> Author?" That's anarchy! If the Author's left,
> the play's still there! What do you think of
> that?

FARFOOR:

> What play, Man? That was before the war! A play
> without an Author and giants is not worth anything.

MASTER:

> Don't be impolite, Boy? When he was still here,
> you were obedient as a dog. Now it's different,
> heh? What a base race! A cowardly race that
> fears only what it sees! Now, the Author, as you

know, is a very busy man. He must have gone here
or there. Or is it "when the cat's away" now?
Wake up! Up with you, let's do our job.

MASTER:

FARFOOR:

Do it yourself. I'm comfortable like this.

MASTER:

Farfoor!

FARFOOR:

I am not Farfoor.

MASTER:

Shame on you. I am your Master.

FARFOOR:

Nor are you my Master. Now, we're both men like
each other.

MASTER:

Yes, you are a man. Nobody's denying that. But
you're playing Farfoor in this play.

FARFOOR:

Then I have nothing to do with the play. You can
play it alone.

MASTER:

That's exactly the problem: that I can't play it
alone. If it were possible, I wouldn't have asked
you. We have to do it together, the two of us.

FARFOOR:

Why?

MASTER:

Because that's the way it is. And not only this
play; any play requires at least two.

FARFOOR:

You're referring to old plays. Nowadays authors
write plays to be played by one actor only.
There are plays that are even more modern, plays
where nobody at all acts. The world has advanced
so much, and so have people. Only you are stuck
with that Author's play. But even he has left
it behind.

MASTER:

Say whatever you like about it, but you must
know that we have nothing else. And here we've kept
the people waiting and must start working immediately, otherwise that which happened in Ismailia
might happen to us.

FARFOOR:

No, please. Anything but that Ismailia thing.
Please.

MASTER:

O.K. Let's get to work.

FARFOOR:

Did I ever refuse to work?

MASTER:

God be praised! Is it all right then?

FARFOOR:

All right what?

MASTER:

That you play the role and that we begin?

FARFOOR:

And be a Farfoor?

MASTER:

I don't think you want to play Snow White.

FARFOOR:

No, sir. Thanks.

MASTER:

Listen, Farfoor. I'm fed up now. I can't say
anything anymore. I swear by God I might smite
you down dead.

FARFOOR:

You're capable of doing it, really you are! Who
knows but that you might take after your sons
and do it. By God, you might!

MASTER:

(Looking at him in great exasperation) Listen,
on my part, I'm going to work. I'll ease my conscience and play my part.

FARFOOR:

You know Uncle Master what's wrong with you?
It's true they're many, but your biggest weakness
is that you're always like that, as if your
conscience is sort of oversized. Why don't you
remove it and give us a break, Man? I swear by
our village saint that they have surgical
operations in America where they remove the
conscience. They discovered it shortens one's
life.

MASTER:
>I'm going to start working.

FARFOOR:
>I don't know why this man reminds me of my aunt, Nabawiyya. She was very fat and had more than eighteen kids. And all day long she sat there scowling and grumbling and whenever I saw her face I almost died laughing. I'd ask myself, how can she be so serious when she's given birth to all that regiment? Did she do it scowling and gloomy as she looks now? Ever since then whenever I see somebody who looks very serious and gloomy, I can't help laughing.

MASTER:
>For the last time, Farfoor! I tell you I'm going to begin.Here I am sitting down, crossing my legs and starting. Listen, Farfoor...

FARFOOR:
>*(To the audience, meowing like a cat)* Meow, does anybody have a cat? I hear a cat meowing.

MASTER:
>I say, listen. Listen, Farfoor.

FARFOOR:
>Did any of you hear anything? Personally I don't hear anything.

MASTER:
>*(Bursting out)* Do you want to drive me mad, Boy? Do you want to be my death? You want me to be paralyzed? Answer me!

FARFOOR:
>Yes, sir. What is it? What can I do for you?

MASTER:
>Are you working or aren't you?

FARFOOR:
>I am ready to do anything. But if it is Farfoor and Master, I am not ready.

MASTER:
>How so?

FARFOOR:
>I'm on strike. It's my right, after all. I am striking. I am on strike until the play is changed. Until such time, I wish you very happy times. Goodnight.

MASTER:

> You think you're annnoying me? Go ahead, go on
> strike. It's up to you. You think I'll mind. On
> the contrary, I am also on strike. Even if you
> were to say to me "Let's work," I won't. Let's
> see who'll suffer the most. You know very well
> that no work means no pay. I'll leave you like
> that until you become a begger. Go ahead,
> strike. You think I'll be intimidated? I don't
> care. You think you're working for me? It's up
> to you. *(Farfoor is busy trying to twist his*
> *body into different shapes like those of*
> *Indian fakirs, into the most painful positions.)*

MASTER:

> Sleep on axes' edges, on nails, or eat lizards,
> I don't care. I'll keep after you until you're
> as desperate as a church mouse. Either you or
> I...

FARFOOR:

> *(To himself)* If only I weren't so hungry! I'd have
> torn him to pieces. Yet, never! Even if I had
> to tie a stone on my stomach.

MASTER:

> Why are you silent, Farfoor? Are you hungry or
> are you out of cigarettes or are you sad because
> you're broke? Would you like me to lend you some
> money? *(He takes out a huge wallet from his*
> *pocket.)* Good Heavens! I have only ten pounds
> left. It doesn't matter. Before I start feeling
> hungry, they'll be issuing a death certificate
> for him.

VOICE OF MASTER'S WIFE:

> Darling, today's the fifth! *(In a polite voice*
> *from behind the curtain)* You haven't given me the
> household money. Don't you know that the seam-
> stress's money is due this month. I hope you
> realize that I'm beginning to be cross. If you
> don't get the money by tomorrow, I can't tell
> what I'm going to do.

VOICE OF FARFOOR'S WIFE:

> Aren't you ashamed of yourself? You sent me two
> piasters with the boy? What can I do with two

piasters? You think I could change them and pay
the rent? Whenever I talk to you, you say
tomorrow might be better. I swear by the Prophet
and all kinds of saints that if you don't get
the money tomorrow, you and your children are
going to eat nothing but mud. And I'll do it too.

VOICE OF MASTER'S WIFE:

No. I think we've gone too far. I can't stand it
anymore. We said we'd put off winter clothes
until the summer. We decided not to go to
Alexandria, saying we could go to the swimming
pool in Mena House.* But has it finally come to
this? Now we have to eat dark bread? That's
impossible! I never ate or tasted it. Find
another way, Hubby. I can't stand it another minute.
*(She enters, followed by four girls, one carrying
a baby, the second wearing a maid's clothes, the
third those of a chambermaid, the fourth those of
a nurse.)*

LADY:

Where's the money?

MASTER:

There's no money.

LADY:

Why? Do you spend it on someone else?

MASTER:

No. There's no money because there's no work.

LADY:

Why's there no work? Did people give up dying?
Did the germs go on vacation?

MASTER:

No, his Highness is on strike.

LADY:

Why?

MASTER:

He doesn't like to be a Farfoor.

LADY:

Why doesn't he?

MASTER:

I don't know. Ask him.

*A hotel close to the Pyramids in Giza.

LADY:
>   I'm asking you. And when I do, you are supposed
>   to answer. Why doesn't he like that?

VOICE OF FARFOOR'S WIFE'S:
>   Where's that son of a bitch? So he sleeps out
>   now? *(She enters followed by an army of boys in
>   tattered clothes and bare feet.)* If he's a man,
>   he wouldn't do that. All he can do is act like
>   a cock rooster and have ten sons a year! When
>   they go hungry, what do I feed them? How do I
>   feed them? Where is he, the son of...*(She dis-
>   covers him lying down.)* Oh, help me God, you
>   Son of a bitch! So you're sleeping here with
>   nothing on your mind? *(She screams.)* Oh, my
>   ill luck! How unfortunate I am!

FARFOOR:
>   *(Waking up from his "strike" mood)* What happened,
>   Woman? Did somebody die?

WOMAN:
>   You!

FARFOOR:
>   I'm still alive, Woman!

WOMAN:
>   I'm going to kill you right away! So you leave
>   us and come to sleep here?

FARFOOR:
>   I'm not sleeping, Woman. I am on strike.

WOMAN:
>   May you, by the Grace of God, be struck in the
>   eyes. Who did you strike? And why did you strike
>   him? And when did he strike you?

FARFOOR:
>   On strike means that I'm not working. And also
>   try to be more thrifty with your prayers because
>   you're tall and close to heaven and your voice
>   is faster than lightening. They might be answered!

WOMAN:
>   Why are you not working?

FARFOOR:
>   Because this man wants to employ me as a Farfoor
>   all the time.

WOMAN:

Why not?

FARFOOR:

Before anything, take these boys away from here.
Go away boys. Get out of here! Dismissed! Don't
you have a bottle of insecticide? Go away, Boys!
Why are they like that? Is it possible that I
am the father of all these? My heart tells me
that at least three or four of these boys are
here by mistake. Go away. Order them to go,
Woman.

WOMAN:

They take after their father. Gentleness won't
do. You, Bastards, go away. *(The kids run out.)*

FARFOOR:

(Under his breath) Bastards, you Bitch!

WOMAN:

You say he wants to employ you as a Farfoor,
so what?

FARFOOR:

There are lots of things you don't understand.
There is...

LADY:

(To the Master) He has every right.

WOMAN:

(To Farfoor) Did you ever hear of an eye being
over the eyebrows? *(From now on, each woman will
be addressing her husband.)*

LADY:

That was in the past. What's that nonsense
about a Master and a Farfoor?

WOMAN:

Even your fingers are not equal!

LADY:

Why do you enslave people, Hubby, when their
mamas have given them birth as free men.
Wake up, Hubby.

WOMAN:

There are Masters and then there are people like
you who can be nothing but Farfoors.

LADY:

The world has changed and developed.

WOMAN:
    There are men and then there are men's Masters.
LADY:
    Even the king of France was beheaded. *Liberté!*
    Fraternité! Égalité! Wake up!
WOMAN:
    There are gold men and there are copper men and
    then there are tin men, half rusty as you are.
LADY:
    It's not a universal law or anything. That's
    just talk they invented a long time ago. But
    we're children of today! Nobody's superior or
    inferior. I am like you and you're like me.
WOMAN:
    The bull is stronger than the man like you and
    works more. But who puts the other to work? Man!
LADY:
    You're a human being and he is a human being! The
    concept of Master and Farfoor exists only in
    some people's heads, people who think of them-
    selves as better than others or smarter than
    others.
WOMAN:
    It's true you do all the work. But he also uses
    his head to put you to work. The guy who uses
    his head is a Master and he who uses his body
    is a Farfoor!
LADY:
    Even if you're smarter, who said this gives you
    the right to control?
WOMAN:
    It's just as you've seen. Wherever you go, you'll
    be the Farfoor!
LADY:
    Be as much of an excellent man as you like,
    but is it my fault that I'm not excellent?
WOMAN:
    In which case, a Master we know is better than
    one we don't. And a living Farfoor, Master
    Farfoor, is better than a thousand starving
    Masters.

LADY:

> You don't know how to work, Hubby. We're
> living off him.

WOMAN:

> Any any work is like any other work. If you
> don't work, we'll die of hunger.

LADY:

> Go conciliate him.

WOMAN:

> They have this world, and we have the next.

LADY:

> See what he wants to do and let him do it. If
> there are no roles, find another play.

WOMAN:

> In the other world, we'll be the Masters and
> they'll be the Farfoors. All it takes is a little
> patience. God's on the side of those that are
> patient and we are the patient ones. This
> world's Farfoors and the next world's Masters.
> We...

LADY:

> Don't be obstinate or we'll all be ruined. Go
> conciliate him. I don't have time. I have an
> appointment with the seamstress.

WOMAN:

> Go, Farfoor. Have some guts and go. Why are
> you so stiff as if you are going to drink
> castor oil? Go, Farfoor.

LADY:

> O.K. Hubby, take the initiative. Go, my sweetie
> Darling.

WOMAN:

> If you need something from the dog, Farfoor,
> what do you say to him?* Don't forget.

MASTER:

> *(Facing Farfoor)* I don't know what to say.

FARFOOR:

> I also don't know what to say.

MASTER:

> I am embarrassed, Farfoor.

*The old popular saying is, "If you need something
from the dog, call him 'Master'."

FARFOOR:

> And so am I. How about if we both stop being
> embarrassed and look at each other and let
> come what may?

MASTER:

> O.K.

FARFOOR AND MASTER:

> *(Together, as they turn)* I am ready to do all
> you want me to do.

FARFOOR:

> That way we'll never get done. Listen, Master
> Boy, do you insist that I work as a Farfoor?

MASTER:

> No, no. No need for a Farfoor at all. No need
> for the whole play if you like.

FARFOOR:

> Hard luck, Master.

MASTER:

> Why, Farfoor?

FARFOOR:

> Because if you'd waited one more second, I'd
> have succumbed and told you that I am ready to
> work as your Farfoor all my life. But now it's
> over. You've conceded to me, and since you said
> it, it is irrevocable!

MASTER:

> So you cheated me into saying it? Well, I take
> back my word.

FARFOOR:

> No, no, no. How can you say that? How can some-
> one like you, who's been a Master for I don't
> know how many thousands of years, as you say,
> take back his word. That won't do.

MASTER:

> Isn't that better than allowing his word to take
> his masterhood away?

FARFOOR:

> If you take it back, your masterhood will be
> gone and if you stand by it, you will be giving
> it up. And whichever way you like, it will be
> gone. So would you rather lose it or give it
> up of your own accord?

MASTER:

    Don't push it like that. Anyway, everything can
    be made up. So now we've left the play behind,
    no Master and no Farfoor.

FARFOOR:

    Goodbye *(He throws the book aside.)* Bye!

MASTER:

    Does this mean we'll stay like this without a
    play?

FARFOOR:

    Who said so?

MASTER:

    Is there another play? Do you have one?

FARFOOR:

    No, I don't.

MASTER:

    Then where's the other play?

FARFOOR:

    The one we're going to write.

MASTER:

    That's just like you, Farfoor. You like to make
    jokes when it's time for serious things. What
    do you mean, write? Can we write even one
    sentence, even a word? How can we write a play?
    And when? Now, in front of these people? Can
    we write it, live in it and act it all at the
    same time? Why? Did anyone tell you we were
    geniuses?

FARFOOR:

    You're complicating it too much. It's a very
    simple thing, and needs no genius. You'll find
    it very easy.

MASTER:

    What do you mean easy? And how can two people
    sit and write a play together?

FARFOOR:

    We'll divide it.

MASTER:

    How divide it?

FARFOOR:

    One of us could write the roles and the other
    could choose. Now, would you rather write and
    I choose or I write and you choose?

MASTER:

> *(To himself)* What an idiot? I'll choose the
> easier job, of course. *(To Farfoor)* Go ahead,
> you write and I'll choose.

FARFOOR:

> *(To himself)* What an idiot! He doesn't know that
> there's not any choice in what I'm going to write.
> Listen, Master. No, no, that won't do. That
> was just a slip of the tongue. From now on, as
> we agreed, there's going to be neither Master
> nor Farfoor. Are you following? Now, we won't do
> as authors do. We'll neither dream nor say
> things that are not true. We'll start from
> reality, with what we have right here.

MASTER:

> What do we have?

FARFOOR:

> Me and you.

MASTER:

> You mean a Farfoor and a Master!

FARFOOR:

> Are you kidding? I am a man and you're a man.
> What does that mean. Two men, right? And we
> are both equal.

MASTER:

> Very well. So?

FARFOOR:

> So we both work equally, neither I nor you as
> a Master.

MASTER:

> You mean we both are Farfoors?

FARFOOR:

> Why don't we forget these old names? Or, I mean,
> if that would make you happy, you can suppose
> that we're both Farfoors.

MASTER:

> Very well then and who's the Master?

FARFOOR:

> What Master? There are no Masters. Each of us
> is his own Master and each his own Farfoor.

MASTER:

> But...

FARFOOR:

> No buts. Here we are, starting all over, right
> from the beginning. No Author, no play, no
> nothing. Let's work.

MASTER:

> What do we do?

FARFOOR:

> Our old trade, as grave diggers. O.K., my back
> to your back, your shovel in your hand and mine
> in mine. In the name of God. *(They raise their
> shovels and they collide.)*

FARFOOR:

> What are you doing, Man? Pay attention.

MASTER:

> Didn't we agree that none of us has the say over
> the other, that each of us is his own Master.
> Work then, Mr. Your-Own-Master! *(They start
> working. Farfoor drops his shovel and is about
> to speak, but one look from the Master
> makes him continue work. The Master stops work-
> ing; Farfoor looks at him accusingly and the
> Master indicates that he wants to scratch a
> certain point in his back but cannot reach it.
> He asks Farfoor and Farfoor refuses vehemently.
> The Master seizes his opportunity when both are
> rising and scratches his back against Farfoor's
> back. Farfoor is exasperated when this continues,
> so he bends down and stops there. The Master
> rises and pushes himself backward to scratch
> his back against Farfoor's and falls down on
> Farfoor's back. Farfoor rises, with the Master
> still sticking to his back, expecting him to
> leave, but he doesn't. Farfoor bends down to
> dig with the Master still clinging with his back
> to Farfoor's. When the latter realizes that,
> he rises very quickly, pushing the Master to
> force him to bend. Lightly he rises, leaving
> the Master bending down. Then he bends down
> and waits for the Master to rise, while the
> Master waits for Farfoor to rise. Farfoor rises
> very quickly and is soon followed by the Master,
> but Farfoor had bent down again.)*

MASTER:
　　Listen, Farfoor.
FARFOOR:
　　Not one word, Work.
MASTER:
　　I want to talk with you.
FARFOOR:
　　Do it while working.
MASTER:
　　(Looks vexedly at him and goes back to work.)
　　What, then, Farfoor? Are we going to go on like
　　this?
FARFOOR:
　　Yes, we will.
MASTER:
　　Do you like this?
FARFOOR:
　　I prefer this a million times to working alone
　　and to having you as a Master.
MASTER:
　　But we have to have a Master, Brother.
FARFOOR:
　　Why do we have to? No necessity.
MASTER:
　　At least someone to tell us when to work and
　　when to stop.
FARFOOR:
　　Each of us can tell himself.
MASTER:
　　Well, I am telling myself, stop. I stopped.
FARFOOR:
　　What's so heroic about that? Work, Man, like
　　you should.
MASTER:
　　It's not for you to tell me. Each his own
　　Master.
FARFOOR:
　　Listen, if you don't work, you don't eat.
MASTER:
　　And where's that food? Are the customers crowding
　　in on us? We've been working for a whole day for
　　nothing.

FARFOOR:

Never mind. They must be on their way. I see a
crowd approaching and some women screaming. It
must be a respectable corpse. Go ahead and work.

MASTER:

How would they know that we're here? Shouldn't
one of us work and the other go and meet them?

FARFOOR:

Nothing of the sort. We both work. And so that
they know where we are, we'll have a sign saying,
"Grave digging by Farfoor and Farfoor."
(*A funeral procession enters. Three men carrying
a corpse in a shroud without a coffin; two of
them carry it at the head and the third at the
feet. The corpse is the same man who was looking
for somebody to kill him in the first part.
Behind the funeral comes the widow, wearing black
with dust all over her face and a black head
cover. She's holding a black scarf.*)

FUNERAL PEOPLE:

Hello.

FARFOOR AND MASTER:

Hello.

FARFOOR:

It seems to me we've seen this guy before.

MASTER:

Where could we have seen him?

FARFOOR:

Don't you remember? It seems we've already
rendered him some services before. Don't you
remember the fifty piasters?

MASTER:

What fifty piasters?

FARFOOR:

When we were very broke, once.

MASTER:

Which time?

FARFOOR:

When we were looking for a corpse.

MASTER:

Which corpse?

FARFOOR:

> Yes, you're right. There were quite a few of
> them. It's hard to remember.

CORPSE:

> *(Bending his head a little, addressing Farfoor
> and the Master)*
> Are you the grave diggers?

FARFOOR AND MASTER:

> Yes, sir. Can we help you?

CORPSE:

> I need a good burial.

FARFOOR AND MASTER:

> By all means, the best burial in town.

FARFOOR:

> Would you like a first floor site.

MASTER:

> How about basement burial? The lower the better.

FARFOOR:

> Would you like a summer burial place?

MASTER:

> Or would you rather have a cover for winter?

FARFOOR:

> A northward site?

MASTER:

> Or a southward one?

CORPSE:

> What's that? Where's your employer?

FARFOOR AND MASTER:

> We're both employers.

CORPSE:

> Well, where are your employees?

FARFOOR AND MASTER:

> We're also the employees.

CORPSE:

> What nonsense is that? Is the other world as
> confused as this one? And by the way, are you of
> this world or the other?

FARFOOR AND MASTER:

> We're in between.

CORPSE:

> I can't take that. *(To his bearers)* Put me on
> the ground, Boys.

WIDOW:
Oh, apple of my eye! This was not your day, my
Beloved!

CORPSE:
Shut up, woman! Why do you insist on nagging in
both worlds? Let's see the problem of these
people here. Now, you both are employers and
employees, heh? But what you're doing is really
neither this nor that!

FARFOOR AND MASTER:
What is it then?

CORPSE:
It's child's play! Agree on one with whom I can
talk.

MASTER:
(To Farfoor) Didn't I tell you? One of us should
work and the other negotiate.

FARFOOR:
Nothing of the sort! We both work and we both
negotiate.

MASTER:
But he wants to talk with one person.

FARFOOR:
It's not up to him. It's up to us.

CORPSE:
Have you agreed?

FARFOOR AND MASTER:
Yes.

CORPSE:
Who do I talk with?

FARFOOR AND MASTER:
With both of us.

CORPSE:
I want one.

FARFOOR AND MASTER:
Two.

CORPSE:
One.

FARFOOR AND MASTER:
Two.

CORPSE:
Either you decide on one person or I'll find
someone else.

MASTER:
> See?

FARFOOR:
> Let him go wherever he likes.

MASTER:
> How can we let him go? What about the whole day's work?

FARFOOR:
> So?

MASTER:
> We should agree and I should talk with him.

FARFOOR:
> Never.

MASTER:
> He'll go.

FARFOOR:
> Let him go. It's better than letting him have the last say.

MASTER:
> We have to.

FARFOOR:
> Then we'll take turns talking with him.

CORPSE:
> Have you agreed?

FARFOOR AND MASTER:
> Yes.

CORPSE:
> Who am I going to talk with?

FARFOOR:
> With whoever has the turn to talk.

CORPSE:
> Woman, didn't I tell you to bury me in el-Ghafir? Now, you've brought me to El-Khanka.* O.K., let's see what graves you have.

FARFOOR:
> We have such a beautiful grave that even the living would love to be buried in it.

*El-Ghafir is the name of a burial ground in Cairo. El-Khanka is the district where a lunatic asylum is located.

CORPSE:
> Who did you make it for?

MASTER:
> For a very respectable pasha, like those of
> the old days.

CORPSE:
> Why wasn't he buried in it?

FARFOOR:
> It was too tight at the waist.

CORPSE:
> We'll see it.

MASTER:
> Please try it.
> *(The corpse tries the grave.)*

CORPSE:
> Is that a grave? It can accommodate neither a
> pasha nor even his chin.* It's a rat hole; it
> wouldn't even please a cockroach. How disgusting!

FARFOOR:
> What gives you the right to say all these things
> to us. Do you think we're your servants?

CORPSE:
> Of course you are. The guy who digs my grave and
> the one who prepares my shroud and the one who
> shines my shoes, all are working for me.

FARFOOR:
> No, we don't...

MASTER:
> *(Interrupting Farfoor)* This is my turn. No,
> sir. We work for ourselves.

CORPSE:
> No. You work for yourselves when you dig graves
> for yourselves. But so long as you are digging
> them for me and for others, then you are working
> for me and for the others. And really, whatever
> the case, your work is disgusting. Listen,
> either you find me a grave that's a little wider
> and at least half a meter shorter or else I'll
> fire you and find someone else. What do you say
> to that?

*A play on the words *"dhaqn el pasha"* in Arabic which
refers to a kind of flower.

MASTER:

>What do you say, you big mouth?

FARFOOR:

>You mean we're going to be Farfoors for such a
>sickly man?

MASTER:

>That's work. So long as you're working, you'll be
>working for others and these others are going to
>be your Masters.

FARFOOR:

>Really?

MASTER:

>Yes, really.

CORPSE:

>Have you decided?

MASTER AND FARFOOR:

>Yes.

CORPSE:

>On what?

FARFOOR AND MASTER:

>We'd rather be fired.

CORPSE:

>I knew right from the beginning that you're no
>good. Carry me, Boys. *(The funeral procession
>moves away as it has entered.)*

FARFOOR:

>Go, may a grave take you!

MASTER:

>Which was that?

FARFOOR:

>That was the tenth corpse to fire us. Or is
>it the eleventh? Well, it doesn't matter. See, I
>refused to work as a Farfoor for you; and now
>this corpse wants both of us to be his
>Farfoors! What kind of luck is that? We should
>have found another job.

MASTER:

>All jobs are the same.

FARFOOR:

>Then it's better not to do anything.

MASTER:

>Yes. *(After a pause.)* Now, do you see where your
>authorial creativity landed us. Your play is no
>good.

FARFOOR:
>And was your play any better?

MASTER:
>*(Mockingly)* Each his own Farfoor and each his
>own Master!

FARFOOR:
>Isn't it better than *(Mocking)*, "You're Farfoor
>and I'm your Master. Listen, Farfoor."
>*(Suddenly)* Listen, Master Boy, I have a great
>idea!

MASTER:
>Another authorial idea?

FARFOOR:
>No, it's divine inspiration. Something that no-
>body can write. It just came by itself. What do
>you think?

MASTER:
>What do I think about what? I've seen nothing.

FARFOOR:
>What do you think of this solution? You've worked
>as a Master and I as a Farfoor, and it didn't
>work. We both worked as Farfoors, and it didn't
>work. How about if we invert it?

MASTER:
>How?

FARFOOR:
>I do the Master and you the Farfoor!

MASTER:
>No, think of something else. What's new there?
>There will be a Master and a Farfoor.

FARFOOR:
>Let's try it. It might be different, how do we
>know? Let's try it once. Do Farfoor once in
>your life.

MASTER:
>O.K., let's try. But remember, I'm doing it only
>for your sake. Believe me, I am. O.K.

FARFOOR:
>Are you ready?

MASTER:
>Go ahead.

FARFOOR:

> Listen, you Master. *(Realizing his mistake)* No, no, I didn't mean that. Again. Are you ready?

MASTER:

> Go ahead.

FARFOOR:

> Listen, you Farfoor!

MASTER:

> Yes.

FARFOOR:

> What kind of "yes" is that? How can it stand by itself? Give it some life, Boy, some glow, you Dummy!

MASTER:

> Yes, Master!

FARFOOR:

> That's better. That's how you Farfoors operate, by being insulted. I know your kind very well, a base, mean kind. I've known you very well, ever since my late dad was living. He had bought me a Farfoor just like you to practice on.

MASTER:

> Practice what? Walking?

FARFOOR:

> No, dummy, to practice masterhood. In our family, before we learn how to walk, we learn how to be Masters.

MASTER:

> Are you going to write your memoirs or what? Let's not lose sight of our subject.

FARFOOR:

> Yes, let's stick to the subject. Listen, you Farfoor, what am I?

MASTER:

> You're my Master.

FARFOOR:

> And what are you?

MASTER:

> I am a grave digger.

FARFOOR:

> Don't you have anything worse?

MASTER:
   No, I don't.
FARFOOR:
   O.K., go ahead and work.
MASTER:
   All right. *(He starts working.)*
FARFOOR:
   (After a pause) Listen, you Farfoor. I have an
   idea. Instead of making graves all over the
   ground, dig them vertically, so we can save
   on the land.
MASTER:
   Vertical?
FARFOOR:
   Yes, like pop bottles in the case.
MASTER:
   O.K.
FARFOOR:
   Listen, Boy. I have another idea. Why do you dig
   the graves on one level only? That won't do. Dig
   them several stories; make them sky scrapers
   underground; let them scrape against the water.
MASTER:
   Yes, sir.
FARFOOR:
   Listen, you Farfoor.
MASTER:
   Yes, sir?
FARFOOR:
   I have a very progressive idea. I'd like you to
   dig the graves above the ground.
MASTER:
   How do I dig a grave above the ground?
FARFOOR:
   That's none of my business. All I have to do
   is give you the orders. Otherwise, what's your
   job? You have to think.
MASTER:
   Think? Think yourself!
FARFOOR:
   Think? Do you want me to give up my masterhood,
   Boy?

MASTER:

> But how do you expect me to think about that?
> What can I do? How do I dig a grave above the
> ground?

FARFOOR:

> It was said and done before.

MASTER:

> By whom?

FARFOOR:

> Cheops, you Stupid! Didn't they dig a grave
> above the ground for him?

MASTER:

> You mean a pyramid? Why didn't you say that
> right from the beginning?

FARFOOR:

> What do you mean, "...say that..."? If I did
> that, I wouldn't be a Master. A true master is
> one who says a grave above the ground when he
> wants a pyramid. And when he wants to fire
> somebody he tells him, "I think you should have
> some rest." When he wants to tell you that
> you're blind, he tells you to open your eyes a
> little. And when he wants to tell you that
> you're a thief, he'll tell you to count again.
> And when he wants to tell you to shut up, he'll
> say, "Allow me to finish what I was saying." This
> is true masterhood, not like yours. It's an
> art. I don't know how you became a Master. How
> did you become a Master, Boy?

MASTER:

> Wasn't it your wish?

FARFOOR:

> Are you insulting me?

MASTER:

> How?

FARFOOR:

> Don't you know that Farfoors like you, and my-
> self--formerly, of course--have their own
> language which they use for insulting their
> Masters. When they want to tell the Master that
> he's stupid, they tell him, "What intelligence!"

And if he tells you, "Pardon," it means "I
spit on you." "At your service" means "over your
dead body"; "Surely" means "never," and "I am your
servant" means "I come before you," etc., etc.,
or aren't you following?

MASTER:

I am at your service!

FARFOOR:

Over your dead body yourself!

MASTER:

Pardon, Master!

FARFOOR:

It's I who spit on you and whoever made you a
Farfoor!

MASTER:

I am your servant.

FARFOOR:

Well, I see you're learning fast; you're becoming quite a Farfoor.

MASTER:

And I see that you're getting to be a boor of a
Master.

FARFOOR:

(Yawning, with real boorishness) You don't say!

MASTER:

Tell me, Master. Why are you a Master?

FARFOOR:

Why a Master? There's no such thing as why. I am
your Master, period. Every Master must have a
Farfoor and every Farfoor must have a Master
or else confusion and anarchy will prevail.

MASTER:

I see you have changed, Farfoor.

FARFOOR:

(Has completely lost himself in his role) What do
you mean "Farfoor,"? I am your Master!

MASTER:

Nonsense! You're just forgotten yourself and
forgotten that we haven't yet found a solution.

FARFOOR:

What solution? Does anything need a solution?
I personally don't think a solution is needed.

MASTER:

> You're right. You forgot that it's divine
> inspiration which gave you the idea which we are
> trying. Now we have tried it and it's very
> clear it's not working.

FARFOOR:

> Let's wait a little; it might work.

MASTER:

> You've got used to sitting, it seems. *(Sharply)*
> Get up!

FARFOOR:

> Get up you...You just reminded me of my wife.
> O.K., I am getting up, but I'm telling you...

MASTER:

> I am telling you, either you find a solution
> or we'll go back to the play *(Points to where
> the book is.)*

FARFOOR:

> No, no, please. We must find a solution. There
> must be one. It doesn't make sense. Don't they
> say that there are a thousand solutions for
> every problem? I need just one. Does any of you
> have a solution? My brain's stopped, good people.
> It's disconnected. *(To audience)* Does anybody
> have a brain that is still working? Don't you
> have an author among you? Even a bad one...

SPECTATOR I:

> *(From the audience)* I have a solution.

FARFOOR:

> What did you say? You have a solution! Great!
> That's how it should be! I was sure I'd find
> at least one person whose brain's still working!
> Tell us what your solution is, tell us what to do.
> But mind you, it's no Master and Farfoor, is it?

SPECTATOR I:

> No, it's not.

FARFOOR:

> Then how did you solve it?

SPECTATOR I:

> That you both be Masters.

FARFOOR:

> That we both be Masters?

SPECATOR I:

    Yes.

FARFOOR:

    You mean that we, both of us, do not work?

SPECTATOR I:

    Yes.

MASTER:

    Then who works?

SPECATOR I:

    The state.

FARFOOR:

    The what?

SPECTATOR I:

    The state.

FARFOOR:

    What state? I don't understand a thing. Please
come over here and explain. *(The Spectator
moves to the stage.)*

SPECTATOR I:

    Yes, the state. The two of you can form a state
in which each citizen is his own Master and you
all become Masters and the state works.

FARFOOR:

    Oh, what a solution! You must be a genius. It's
very nice, this state business.

SPECTATOR I:

    But can you make it?

FARFOOR:

    Of course. It's very simple, nothing's more
simple. We can even make it an empire! How
come we never thought of this solution before?
(To the Spectator) O.K., thanks a lot, sir,
leave the rest to us. We've been honored.
Don't forget to say hello from us. *(Then to the
Master)* O.K., let's make a state.

MASTER:

    Do you think we can fabricate a state just like
this?

FARFOOR:

    Nothing is easier. Didn't they fabricate Israel
in one hour? It's very simple.

FARFOOR:
    Well, it needs a name.
FARFOOR:
    We'll give it one.
MASTER:
    We'll give it my name: The Masterly Empire.
FARFOOR:
    What do you mean "masterly"? That, at best,
    would be just good enough for a sausage plant.
    No, no, we'll go like Czechoslovakia or Malaysia,
    one syllable from your name and one from mine.
MASTER:
    Then it'd be the Masfoor Empire.
FARFOOR:
    Listen, there. You have nothing to do with it,
    you have no imagination at all, so, shut up!
    We'll call it The Great Empire of Farfoorea.
MASTER:
    What kind of name is that?
FARFOOR:
    What's wrong with Farfoorea? Isn't it better
    than Korea or Manchuria?
MASTER:
    But it doesn't have any letters from my name.
FARFOOR:
    What about the "a" at the end, or the "e"?
MASTER:
    You take two letters from my name and all the
    rest from yours?
FARFOOR:
    So what? You know states require sacrifices,
    and so I have sacrificed seven to your two.
MASTER:
    O.K. What happens after the sacrifices and the
    name?
FARFOOR:
    Now we are a state, a whole empire, the Great
    Empire of Farfoorea.
MASTER:
    Who's the emperor?

FARFOOR:

    No, no. It's very old-fashioned to have one
emperor to an empire. The latest vogue in
empires is that each citizen is an emperor. So,
you'll be an emperor and I, an emperor.

MASTER:

    (Shaking his head) But I still don't feel that
we're a state or an empire or anything.

FARFOOR:

    You're right there. We really need some
accessories, that's all. We need a radio station.
*(He runs to the door and comes back with the
speaker of an old gramaphone.)* Here's our
radio.

MASTER:

    How about the press?

FARFOOR:

    There you are. *(Takes an old newspaper from his
pocket.)*

MASTER:

    That's only one newspaper!

FARFOOR:

    So?

MASTER:

    And what date is it? It's very old. We need
papers that come out every day.

FARFOOR:

    That's an everyday paper.

MASTER:

    Every day the same paper?

FARFOOR:

    Why should we change it and have a press and
editors and vendors and headache? Is there anything new everyday that's worth a newspaper?
What happened yesterday is like what's happening
today and what will happen tomorrow. So, this
is yesterday's, today's and tomorrow's paper.
There's the radio, the press and the name.
What else?

MASTER:

    The constitution?

FARFOOR:
>Each his own constitution, really. You can write
>whatever you like there and change it in any
>way you like. O.K., ready now?

MASTER:
>Ready.

FARFOOR:
>Now we're Masters. Work, state! We broadcast
>over the radio. *(He holds the speaker.)* And
>open the papers. *(He opens the paper.)* And
>here we are, the whole state at our disposal,
>and each of us an emperor. Go ahead and work,
>state! *(Pause. They wait for something to
>happen but nothing does.)*

MASTER:
>It didn't work.

FARFOOR:
>Wait a little. There must be something wrong.
>*(He examines the speaker and turns the paper,
>listening and feeling.)* I don't know why it doesn't
>work.

SPECTATOR I:
>Somebody must operate it. It doesn't work by it-
>self.

MASTER:
>And I am volunteering to operate it for you,
>Brother Emperor.

FARFOOR:
>Thank you.

MASTER:
>*(Holds the speaker and speaks through it.)* I am
>the Great Empire of Farfoorea, at the disposal
>of its citizen-emperors and ready to perform any
>services they require of it.

FARFOOR:
>That's how it should be! This is an ingenious
>solution, not that dumb play!

MASTER:
>And in order to best serve my Masters, the
>Emperors, I have a modest request to make of
>them.

FARFOOR:

Modest or immodest, so long as you'll work, we
agree.

MASTER:

My modest request is that each Emperor should
place himself for some time at the disposal of
the Empire.

FARFOOR:

That's easy. I thought you'd request something
substantial. Here I am my dear Empire, at your
disposal. What do I do?

MASTER:

Emperor Farfoor should go to the burial sites
immediately and hold the shovel and dig.

FARFOOR:

That's easy also. Here we are digging.

MASTER:

Emperor Farfoor, dig faster.

FARFOOR:

Faster and stronger and harder, whatever you
like.

MASTER:

Emperor Farfoor, stop digging.

FARFOOR:

We stop digging, my Empire.

MASTER:

The Empire requires increasing your effort in
digging graves a hundred-fold.

FARFOOR:

Sure, a thousand-fold!

MASTER:

No. A hundred-fold means just a hundred-fold.

FARFOOR:

By all means. Don't be cross.

MASTER:

Reduce speed to one grave a month.

FARFOOR:

We have reduced the speed.

MASTER:

The Empire's honor requires that you dig with
one hand.

FARFOOR:

By all means.

MASTER:

And her dignity requires that you dig without using your hands.

FARFOOR:

By all means. *(He realizes the meaning.)* But how can I do that?

MASTER:

You dare argue with your Empire?

FARFOOR:

No, God forbid. *(Holds the shovel with his teeth and puts his hands behind his back and digs.)*

MASTER:

And considering the fact that graves outnumber corpses by a great margin, the Empire's interests require increasing the production of corpses. We want corpses. We want corpses for the ready-made graves at the rate of a thousand corpses per month. If you don't find a corpse, kill someone.

FARFOOR:

I think I...that voice is not unfamiliar. I've heard it before. I also know very well the point of view it advocates. *(He moves stealthily and surprises the Master from behind.)* So you're tampering with the Empire's machinery.

MASTER:

Tampering? I was operating it.

FARFOOR:

That was not our agreement. With all good intentions, I worked for it and you went and operated it. Which means that you used the Empire to make me work for you.

MASTER:

But what did you think? That's the way with empires.

FARFOOR:

I worked for it, not for you.

SPECTATOR II:

(Stands up to settle the dispute. Approaching the stage.) Emperor Farfoor, your job is to work for it. His job is to operate it.

FARFOOR:

No, stop that. *(To the Master)* Are you in collu-
sion with that man or what? Did you get him as
your attorney? Stop that. I am one full half of
the Empire. I will use my right according to my
constitution and fire you. *(Turning to the
Spectator)* And you too, although you haven't been
appointed yet. You are fired.

MASTER:

But my constitution doesn't give you the right
to do that.

FARFOOR:

My consitution or yours; I'll apply whichever
can fire you.

SPECTATOR II:

What's bothering you about this solution?

FARFOOR:

Is that a solution, Man? It's the same old
story. We have a state and it turns out to be
Farfoor and Master.

SPECTATOR II:

For any work to get done, there must be some
who work and some who set them to work.

FARFOOR:

Then what did we accomplish? Nothing. We're in the
same old rut of Master and Farfoor.

SPECTATOR II:

No, Farfoor and his employer.

FARFOOR:

Employer, Master, it's all the same. This
employer of mine, can he fire me?

SPECTATOR II:

If you don't do your job as it should be done,
he must fire you.

FARFOOR:

Then he's my Master. Take it as a rule, in any
place, at any time and with any people:
Whoever can fire me is my Master. Anybody who
loses his Master and wishes to know who that
is, should ask himself: Who can fire me? In
ninety percent of the cases, that one will be
the Master.

SPECTATOR II:

In order to live, we must work. And in order to work, there must be some that employ and some that work.

FARFOOR:

Farfoors and Masters.

SPECATOR II:

Farfoors and Masters, or privates and sergeants, group and leader, so long as there's no exploitation, what harm is there? If he is employing you for your own good, what's wrong?

FARFOOR:

What do you mean, there's no harm? The biggest problem is that we are human beings and a human being has dignity. Any control by one human being of another takes away some of the latter's dignity. And one's dignity is not so big that it can afford to be fragmented like that.

SPECTATOR II:

Would you rather have your dignity or your livelihood?

FARFOOR:

My dignity. Please, my dignity. My dignity is me. When it's lost, I am lost.

SPECTATOR II:

O.K., would you rather have your dignity and your livelihood or your dignity by itself?

FARFOOR:

If one must, then dignity by itself. The money could come later.

SPECTATOR II:

That's society's system, Farfoor. Any human society is like that. That's the human law, and we must all submit to it. Do you know any other law to which man can submit?

FARFOOR:

I know at least one law, one very basic human law and also a very simple one: the law that says that you are like me and that we must have our relationship not as one of employee and employer or group and leader or Farfoor and Master

or learned and ignorant or strong and weak. The
law of human beings. The law of the nine months
and the milk that we all sucked as babies. The
law which made us all wet our diapers when we
were little. The law which makes children all
brothers who recognize neither Master nor Farfoor.
The law of nature, the law of animals among
which you won't find a lion Master over lions
or a crow another crow's Farfoor.

WOMAN SPECTATOR:

(Cheers and shouts) Bravo, Farfoor. Your words
are all true. (Turning to Spectator II) This
empire of yours, Mister, is based on domination
and slavery and is no good for human beings.

MASTER:

(To the Woman Specator) What you're saying is
absolutely wrong.

FARFOOR:

Even if it's wrong, it's much better than a
million of your rights. Please go on, Lady.
Oh, Boy, if only you'd come closer.

WOMAN SPECTATOR:

I have to prove to him that he's wrong first.

FARFOOR:

Never mind about him. Prove to me. Please, I
want to be convinced. I am dying to be convinced
by you immediately on the spot.

WOMAN SPECTATOR:

I'll convince you in a practical way.

FARFOOR:

Great! I love practical ways. What do you say
to that, you Master Boy? What's that practical
way, Lady? If only you'd come a little closer.

WOMAN SPECTATOR:

I have another solution, another empire.

FARFOOR:

No, no, please forget about empires.

WOMAN SPECTATOR:

Just listen, it's a completely different empire,
in which everybody is free to do whatever he
likes. If he wants to be a Master, by all means;
if he wants to be a Farfoor, he can go ahead and
do it.

FARFOOR:

    If he wants to do nothing...

WOMAN SPECTATOR:

    He can go ahead and do it.

FARFOOR:

    Hurray! That's how empires should be! And
    what's the name of that empire, Lady?

WOMAN SPECTATOR:

    Liberty, The Empire of Liberty. Everyone there
    is free; no state orders you around, nobody
    interferes with your likes and dislikes, nobody
    impinges on your dignity.
    (During the preceding, the Woman Spectator has
    gone onto the stage and climbed a wooden block
    resembling the base of the Statue of Liberty.
    She now assumes the posture of said statue.)

FARFOOR:

    (Contemplating her with adoration) Holy Heavens!
    Lady, what's your name?

WOMAN SPECTATOR:

    Mrs. Liberty.

FARFOOR:

    And your man, what's his name? What's the
    masculine for liberty?

LIBERTY:

    No, I don't have a man. I'm not married.

FARFOOR:

    Divorced?

LIBERTY:

    Nor divorced.

FARFOOR:

    Widow?

LIBERTY:

    Nor a widow.

FARFOOR:

    Then how come you're a Mrs., when you're neither
    married nor divorced nor widowed?

LIBERTY:

    Just Mrs. What's wrong with that? Is it necessary
    for one to be widowed, divorced or married to be
    a Mrs.?

FARFOOR:

    No, of course not. No necessity at all! Why

should she? There are easier ways by far. Listen,
Mrs. Liberty, you are very liberty, very, very
much so. Long live liberty, brothers! I am
dying for liberty! Dear Liberty, my body shakes
when I think of thee! Listen, Mrs. Liberty,
I'd like to work for you. Would you employ me?

LIBERTY:

Yes, indeed.

FARFOOR:

My! What would you have me do?

LIBERTY:

What would you like to do?

FARFOOR:

What do I like to do? Is it really ncessary that
I do anything? How about if I just pretend that
I work?

LIBERTY:

No, seriously. What would you like to do?

FARFOOR:

Anything that doesn't have a Master! Do you
have such a job?

LIBERTY:

We don't call him Master, we call him Boss. And
any job that we have has a Boss. The best you
can do is to find a job where the Boss is good.

FARFOOR:

So that is liberty? That I am free to choose my
Boss?

LIBERTY:

What more could you want?

FARFOOR:

Now suppose I want to be above all Bosses. The
Bosses! Boss! Do you have such a thing?

LIBERTY:

We do, but that job doesn't have one Boss; it
has a whole council of Bosses, a thousand
Bosses.

FARFOOR:

Can they fire me?

LIBERTY:

According to the consitution...

FARFOOR:

    Then I don't want it. I want you to be my Boss,
to work beside you, to stand up there behind you.
If you get tired, you lean a bit on me; and if
you stand for too long, I'll be your seat. What
do you think?

LIBERTY:

    You mean one like you standing next to me?
That'll be infringing upon liberty which might
end in your hanging. Yesterday they hanged a
Farfoor like you who looked at me, and you
want to stand beside me?

FARFOOR:

    They hanged him because he looked at you?

LIBERTY:

    That's their opinion. We have freedom of opinion,
you know. He thinks he can look at me and they
think they should hang him for that look. What's
so strange?

FARFOOR:

    You mean one look cost a guy his head?

LIBERTY:

    Isn't it better than arrogance and dictatorship
and suppressing the freedom of speech?

FARFOOR:

    Oh, yes, much better. Let's go, Master. Let's
go, Brother!

MASTER:

    Where to?

FARFOOR:

    Let's leave this place where she is.

MASTER:

    Why doesn't she leave?

FARFOOR:

    No, let us leave. We should leave this country
of liberty and roam the earth until we come
upon a place where there's not one spot of
liberty. We don't want any of that, do we,
Brother? Let's dissolve the empire. We can offer
the radio station at auction and close down the
newspapers. (He folds the paper.) Let's go, Man.
What I'm really going to miss is her eyes. She
has such a pair of eyes! Anyway, where did we stop?

MASTER:

    We're back where we started. What's to be done
now, Farfoor? The state solution is also out.
What do we do now?

FARFOOR:

    Find another solution.

MASTER:

    Are there any remaining? The Master-Farfoor thing,
you didn't like. Both of us as Farfoors, it
didn't work. We reversed it and you were Master
and I a Farfoor, back where we started. We both
of us became Masters and tried all empires,
nothing worked. What more is left?

FARFOOR:

    Are you asking me? Ask them. Or are they only
good at watching us in this mess? Isn't there a
good guy among you who'd propose a solution?

SPECTATOR III:

    (Stands up.) Why don't you part company and each
work alone?
    (The lights in the auditorium are turned on making
it look like a convention. Lights on stage are
dimmed.)

FARFOOR:

    We did that, Smartie, in the first act and it
didn't work. I guess you were taking a nap.

YOUNG SPECATOR:

    I have a solution. I think you should get
some kind of machine and make it a Farfoor.

MASTER:

    Farfoors?

YOUNG SPECTATOR:

    Yes, each should get one of those machines and
operate it; he'd then be a Master.

MASTER:

    If we operate the machine, who operates us?

YOUNG SPECTATOR:

    Is it necessary that someone operate you?

MASTER:

    Anything that works, Son, must be operated by
somebody or something.

YOUNG SPECTATOR:

    Even man?

MASTER:

    Even man.

SPECTATOR IV:

    Make it an existentialism* then.

SPECTATOR V:

    Well, for people to exist, they have to eat
    first. And in order to eat, they have to work,
    and in order to work there must be a Master and
    a Farfoor.

SPECTATOR VI:

    That's absurd, and since it is so, let's have
    an absurd solution. What do you think?

A WOMAN SPECTATOR:

    What do you think they should do, for instance?

SPECTATOR VI:

    One of two things: either tie each Farfoor to
    each Master or divide each Farfoor by each
    Master and each Master by each Farfoor. In this
    way, instead of having thought and work each by
    itself, we'll be adding one-half thought to one-
    half work and one-half work to one-half thought.
    The only danger here is that thinking for work
    might turn into thinking about work because
    thinking for work is quite superior to thinking
    about work. Because work resulting from
    thinking for work is very superior to work
    resulting from thinking about work. What do you
    think of this solution?

FARFOOR:

    Frankly speaking, it's a very sensible solution!

SPECTATOR VI:

    Sensible! How so, Man? I've been racking my
    brain to make it absurd!

*Here is reflected the popular belief that associates
the Arabic word for "existentialism" with a kind of
anarchist arrangement where everybody can do
whatever he likes, and where there are no taboos
or restrictions.

FARFOOR:

O.K., then it's absurd. No offense meant, Brother.

SPECTATOR VI:

What do you mean "absurd"? That which people call "absurd" is in fact what I call sensible and that which they call sensible, I call absurd.

FARFOOR:

What sort of pest is this? He neither likes the sensible nor the absurd! How shall I answer him? Shall I tell him, "Exactly, this is sensibly absurd and absurdly sensible and the best part about it is that it contradicts the absurdity of the sensible because it is itself the sensible-ness of the absurd which is different from both the sensible and the absurd in the same way that the absurd and the absurd are different"? Do you understand, sir?

SPECTATOR VI:

It's as clear as day!

FARFOOR:

Didn't somebody think of a solution?

SPECTATOR V:

Why don't you apply equationalism*?

MASTER:

What do you mean by equationalism?

SPECTATOR V:

Equationalism! Don't you know what equationalism means? This is utter ignorance!

MASTER:

Please enlighten us, then, and God will reward you.

SPECTATOR V:

Equationalism means that this equates that. See how simple it is? You equate Farfoor.

MASTER:

How do I equate him?

SPECTATOR V:

You both work as grave diggers, don't you? It's really simple: one of you digs and the other fills in.

*A concept advanced by Tawfik al-Hakim.

MASTER:
> Then which is the Farfoor and which the Master?

SPECTATOR V:
> Whoever works ahead of the other.

MASTER:
> Would that one be the Master?

SPECTATOR V:
> No, he'd be the Farfoor because then he'd be working better.

MASTER:
> That way each will try to lag behind.

SPECTATOR V:
> Then whichever works ahead in lagging behind, which means, he who lags behind more would be...

MASTER:
> *(Interrupting)* The Master?

SPECTATOR V:
> No, the Farfoor, because in this case he'd be lagging behind better, because you see, the one who's best at work is also the one best at lagging. *(The Voices of the Master's and Farfoor's Wives, mixed up, impatiently)* I am fed up. I am absolutely sick and tired. I swear by the Prophet and by Him who made him Prophet, I'll make him the laughing stock of every good-for nothing son of a bitch. They're crazy idiots. Nothing will restore their minds but a good beating, nothing but a beating, absolutely nothing.

MASTER'S WIFE:
> *(Entering)* What's that, you lunatic?

FARFOOR'S WIFE:
> *(Entering)* I swear by all that's good, I will not let you off.

MASTER'S WIFE:
> Aren't you ashamed of yourself? Is this a way to behave? Is this what Masters do?

FARFOOR'S WIFE:
> I swear by God Almighty that had it not been for the shame of it, I'd have given you a spanking in front of all these people here and would have made it difficult to distinguish your fore from your aft.

MASTER:
     What's the matter, eh? What's wrong?
MASTER'S WIFE:
     What do you think you are, eh? Angels living in
     heaven? Ascetics? Mystics?
FARFOOR:
     Why? What's happened?
MASTER'S WIFE:
     Nothing! Except that you've left us all messed
     up and confused and helpless and stayed away
     from it all as if nothing's the matter. And
     what were you doing? Looking for a solution!
     A solution for what? And why? Why the hurry? What
     could be puzzling you so that you forgot about
     food and subsistence, about living and life?
FARFOOR:
     Why not, if it's important?
MASTER'S WIFE:
     What's more important than food? Than survival?
FARFOOR:
     More important than living is knowing why we
     live. And even more important than knowing why is
     to know how we're going to live.
MASTER'S WIFE:
     Like everybody else, that's how.
FARFOOR:
     And you know how everybody else is living?
MASTER'S WIFE:
     As they always have.
FARFOOR:
     And do you know how they've been doing it always?
     On top of each other, vertically, each carrying
     the other. Each Master has a Master above him
     and each Farfoor a Farfoor below him. Your
     husband, this Master, or this husband, your
     Master, is below another Master, which means
     that he's as much of a Farfoor as I am. And I
     have a Farfoor below me, which means that I,
     believe it or not, am also a Master. Three
     thousand six hundred million human beings form-
     ing a vertical pole, each carrying another, and
     each wanting to knock down the person he's
     carrying and at the same time to remain nailed

down to the one carrying him. I swear by the life
of my aunt, Nabawiyya, that we have been like
that ever since the time of creation.

FARFOOR'S WIFE:

And what's wrong with that? What's wrong,
Smartie?

FARFOOR:

What's wrong is that we're squeezed and tired
and sad and we don't know the reason. What's
wrong is that each of us feels that he's not
living in this world, but merely carrying the
world on his shoulders. What's wrong is that we
are irritable, ever since the time of Adam and
Eve, resentful, the carried want to strangle the
carrier and the carrier would love to chew up
the carried. What's wrong is that it's such a
ridiculous sight that if we were to look at it
in a mirror we'd have died laughing at ourselves.
But where's that mirror that would show people
themselves? Where's the mirror that would show
the four of us our exact postures as they
really are? Do you know what we really are? A
pole, your highness riding his eminence and his
eminence riding me and we're all piled on top
of that hag over there. And none of us really
sees, but we're all irritated and tired to
death. And listen to her wishing to make my
fore indistinguishable from my aft. Even our
love is unnatural, a love in which we don't meet,
but merely ride each other. Is there any other
species on earth living like that besides man?
Each distinguished person is referred to as a
Master, Master of his district, Master of his
country, Master of his homeland, Master of his
world, Master of history. Even our history forms
a pole, our states, our civilization, each state
wants to be Mistress over all states and each
civilization would love to subdue all civilizations.
And the result? Cudgel fights that develop into
rifle fights that develop into fights between
armies with bombs. Ten, twenty, thirty millions

fall from the pole and the next day fights start
all over again. Then we give them funny names:
The fall of Greek civilization and the rise of
Roman civilization! The cold war between the
East and the West! The conflict between Russia
and China and France and America! And everywhere
it is Master and Farfoor: Who is to be Master and
who Farfoor, and why should I be Farfoor and you
Master? Ever since life began it's been like that,
thinking that that's the way it is and that
people cannot live otherwise. But, in all
honesty, is that a life? Is that a way? I
swear by my Aunt Nabawiyya that we accept it for
one reason only, because we don't see it. If
we see it, we cannot go on accepting it. But,
after all, it's not our fault. It's the fault of
those who see for us, our philosophers and
thinkers, according to whom thinking must con-
sist in thinking for thinking, and true thinking
is that which thinks of what thinks of what
thinks. But here we have the problem of our whole
life. Couldn't someone think of a solution for
that?

MASTER'S WIFE:
What's that gibberish, Farfoor? Do you want to
reorganize the universe? You must be crazy!

FARFOOR:
You're right. Anyone who tries to order this
chaotic universe must be crazy. Those who
accept the chaos and let it be are the sane ones!

MASTER'S WIFE:
What's the universe to us? Let's stay here.

FARFOOR:
We are here, I swear we are. Everywhere in the
world and here and now, and every moment, the
fight is going on and has never ceased for a
second, here or elsewhere. Listen, isn't that
a bus conductor's whistle? The conductor must be
telling the bus-driver, "Don't start moving before I whistle," and the driver is answering, "I
am not your Farfoor, my salary is bigger than

yours." Isn't there some system that'd arrange
us next to each other, horizontally? Not one
single system?

FARFOOR'S WIFE:

That' all you're good at, blabbering. But
whatever you say, the kids are hungry. What do
I give them to eat? Words? I'm dizzy from the
lack of money and you're fainting from the lack
of lunch. How are you going to cure that,
Philosopher?

MASTER'S WIFE:

I've never seen anything like that in my life!
How can anybody leave his work, himself and his
family and sit there doing nothing until he finds
a solution for this Master-Farfoor problem?
Suppose he didn't find a solution? Suppose it
takes too long?

FARFOOR'S WIFE:

Suppose the solution refused to come. Suppose
it didn't come at all, what do we do?

MASTER'S WIFE:

Do you want us to die and be mummified next to
you?

FARFOOR'S WIFE:

Hold out our hands and beg?

BOTH WIVES:

Whether you find it or not, we don't care. We
must survive.

MASTER'S WIFE:

Think as much as you like. Only work and provide for our food.

FARFOOR'S WIFE:

And you too can eat, in the bargain.

MASTER'S WIFE:

Support us and also live and then think as much
as you like.

FARFOOR'S WIFE:

Off to work with you, and leave off this Master-
Farfoor stuff!

MASTER'S WIFE:

>And you too, Hubby. The whole world is moving;
>only you are at a standstill. Move or else you'll
>die. Life must go on, Darling.

MASTER:

>What do you think of that, Farfoor?

FARFOOR:

>What do I think? What brought this mess about
>is that "life must go on" business. The buffalo
>must go on being tied to the water wheel, and
>to do so they must put a blind over its eyes
>and this "providing" business is our blind,
>Master. So long as it's on, we'll never, never
>be ourselves nor know why we're going in circles.
>They are right! Life must go on! Carry your
>load and get up, Beast! Put the blind on and move.
>Because life must continue. *(Stretching out his
>hand to the audience)* A solution, quick, please,
>a system, a play, anything!

MASTER:

>It's no use, Farfoor! If you leave your old way
>behind, you lose your way. Let's go back to our
>play. *(Picks up the book.)* Where were we?

FARFOOR:

>Wait a minute! Why are you in such a hurry?
>Or are you afraid of your wife? Aren't you
>ashamed? A man like you afraid of his wife?

MASTER:

>Only a man can be afraid of his wife, Boy.
>Let's get on...

FARFOOR:

>We should call the Author.

MASTER:

>Didn't you hear with your own ears that he'd left
>a long while ago?

FARFOOR:

>Who knows? He may be back. Mr. Author! Our
>Savior! Our Hope!

VOICES:

>*(Offstage)* Who do you want?

FARFOOR:

>Good God! We want our Author. Is he back?

VOICES:
   Yes, he came back a short while ago.
FARFOOR:
   Praised be the Lord. Please send him here
   quick!
VOICES:
   You come and get him.
FARFOOR:
   By all means.
   *(Farfoor darts outside and back in again,
   carrying a bundle like swaddling clothes.)*
MASTER:
   Is this the Author?
FARFOOR:
   Why not? Don't judge by size!
MASTER:
   And this is going to give us the solution?
   Give it, here. *(He takes the bundle, unwraps it,
   discovers that there is another bundle, which
   he unwraps and finds another one.)* Where's the
   Author?
FARFOOR:
   He must be inside that one.
   *(The Master unwraps the bundle and discovers
   smaller bundles which he keeps unwrapping until
   it's the size of a hazel nut, then it gets too
   small to be seen.)*
MASTER:
   I hope you don't tell me he's inside this one!
FARFOOR:
   Who knows? Unwrap this one, too.
MASTER:
   Sorry about that. It's an atom.
FARFOOR:
   We must open it if the Author's inside.
MASTER:
   What do you mean inside? A big Author like
   that inside this?
FARFOOR:
   It's not impossible. He's an Author and capable
   of anything. Let's open it.

MASTER:

Can we? It requires a contract with Einstein,
and even if we could afford Einstein, and he
opened it, how do we know what's in there?
Do you guarantee that you'll find him there?
That, even if you did, you can speak with him
and ask for the solution? This bundle is a
million times more difficult than the solution.

FARFOOR:

But the solution is not difficult, it's
impossible.

MASTER:

And what you're saying is the most impossible
of them all. It seems that you're starting to
hallucinate. Are you, Boy?

FARFOOR:

What else can I do? We've nothing left but
hallucination.

MASTER:

But why should we hallucinate, Sonny Boy. We
have our play and everything's written down;
we haven't even started. Enough delay now.

FARFOOR:

*(Searching with his eyes among the audience,
appealing and pleading. Then closes his eyes and
goes over to where the Master is sitting, in a
Master-posture.)* I leave everything in God's
hands.

MASTER:

Ready?

FARFOOR:

(In a voice of fear, hopelessness and disgust)
Ready!

MASTER:

Are you sure?

FARFOOR:

Sure.

MASTER:

Listen, you Farfoor!

FARFOOR:

(Same tone of voice) I'm listening.

MASTER:

> I would like you, Farfoor, to choose for me.
> (*Suddenly throws the play aside and rises.*) You
> know what, Farfoor? This play's become so
> insipid, I personally don't feel like playing
> the Master. I've lost interest.

FARFOOR:

> And so did I, I swear. In all honesty...

MASTER:

> I know. I know what you're going to say. Even if
> we wanted to go back to the old play, we won't be
> able to do it. Wasn't that what you wanted to
> say?

FARFOOR:

> What I like about you is that occasionally you
> can be human and understand.

VOICES OF THE TWO WIVES:

> (*From offstage*) We don't hear you working.
> (*They peep in from the entrance.*) Why did you
> stop?

MASTER'S WIFE:

> If we don't hear you working right away, we'll
> bring everything down on your heads!
> (*Farfoor and the Master look toward them in
> terror and involuntarily back up to the
> forestage. When two Spectators shout, they jump
> in terror.*)

SPECTATORS IV AND V:

> What's that you've done?

SPECTATOR IV:

> You've created the problem and had us rack our
> brains over it.

SPECTATOR V:

> And now you want to run away?

SPECTATOR IV:

> I swear we won't let you off if you don't find
> a solution.

ENTIRE AUDIENCE:

> We want a solution.

TWO WIVES:

> We want work.

AUDIENCE:
    A solution!
WIVES:
    An eternal solution!
WIVES:
    Eternal work!
FARFOOR:
    Suppose we can't do either, good People? You
    mean to tell us that five or six hundred
    brains, with so many thousands of ideas per second
    cannot find one that will help us out?
MASTER:
    Don'd kid yourself, Farfoor. They're just like
    us, hopeless cases. Ever since human life began,
    people have been searching for a solution. Do
    you want these people now to provide a solution
    from their pockets as a magician would?
    *(The Curtain Operator, huge and bald, rushes
    in from the wing.)*
CURTAIN OPERATOR:
    Just what do you think you're doing, Pals.
    you think it's one of those private theaters with
    no laws or regulations. Your time's been up for
    ages now and the rope of the curtain is ruining
    my hand, waiting for you to end it, but it's no
    use! Can't you see? Don't you have any feeling?
    Frankly speaking, my wife is delivering tonight
    and I must run to be on time, at least to know
    what she's got there. I want it to be crystal
    clear that the mother and the baby are a
    thousand thousand times more important to me
    than your damned play. I have to let the curtain
    down now and run to see what happened.
FARFOOR'S WIFE:
    Farfoor!
MASTER'S WIFE:
    Hubby! Either you finish it...
FARFOOR'S WIFE:
    Or we'll finish you off.
AUDIENCE:
    We want the solution. The solution first!

FARFOOR:

O.K., O.K. All your demands are well taken. *(To Curtain Operator)* We're at your disposal, Brother. What should we do to satisfy you?

CURTAIN OPERATOR:

End it in any way.

FARFOOR:

How do you think we should do that?

CURTAIN OPERATOR:

If you can't find a solution at all, commit suicide. In more than a hundred plays I have let the curtain down on the hero committing suicide. So, you too go ahead and get it over with. You think you're better than Juliet or Cleopatra or Youssef Wahbi?*

FARFOOR:

(With gleaming eyes) What do you think Master?

MASTER:

It's not a bad idea.

FARFOOR:

It's a devilish idea! We've tried everything but nothing worked. Let's also try death. Don't we want absolute equality, with no Masters and Farfoors? You deserve a silver coin for this idea, Pal. I'll pay you at eight a.m. on Dooms-day!

MASTER:

But how do we commit suicide, Farfoor?

FARFOOR:

That's very simple. Get us two chairs, Pal. *(The Curtain Operator brings two chairs. The Master takes one and puts it in front of him to one side of the stage. Farfoor does the same on the other side.)* And the ropes! Drop us two ropes. *(A rope descends over each chair, tied in the form of a noose. When Farfoor sees the rope he shouts, "Mother!")*

*A veteran Egyptian actor famous for melodramatic acting.

MASTER:
> What does one do now, Farfoor?

FARFOOR:
> Stand on top of the chair, place your neck in the noose, then push the chair away with your foot and that'll do the trick.

MASTER:
> We might be strangled for real and die?

FARFOOR:
> Did you think we were kidding? Don't we want to try death?

MASTER:
> Yes, but not really try it.

FARFOOR:
> In death, there's no such thing as not really trying it; it's either death or no death.

MASTER:
> In that case, thanks a lot! What a day! Do you want me to take my own life? That's impossible!

FARFOOR:
> Don't be such a sissy. I'm just kidding. What do you mean death? We're going to act as if we are going to die.

MASTER:
> So it's just acting?

FARFOOR:
> Yes, just acting.

MASTER:
> Still, I'm afraid.

FARFOOR:
> If you want the truth, so am I.

MASTER:
> You go first.

FARFOOR:
> Yes, by all means. *(When he sees the rope, he gets down immediately.)* Try and go first, Master.

MASTER:
> Me first? No, it can't be. It's not done.

FARFOOR:
> That's impossible! I couldn't dream of such rudeness!

CURTAIN OPERATOR:

>Did I get you the chairs to die or to have a symposium.

FARFOOR:

>What a mean guy. May your wife deliver four babies and may they be as mean as you are.

MASTER:

>Shall we use one noose, Farfoor? At least we'll keep each other company.

FARFOOR:

>Oh, your mind's starting to work and come up with brilliant ideas. Death is great! Let's go.

MASTER:

>Impossible. Farfoors first.

FARFOOR:

>Did democracy also reach you lately? *(Farfoor stands on top of the chair and so does the Master. The Master points to the noose, inviting Farfoor to place his neck there.)*

MASTER:

>Go ahead, please!

FARFOOR:

>That's not done. Here, Masters go first. Go ahead, please. What's the matter? Stop shaking like that, Man. I'm telling you it's just a mock-death. Don't be such a softy!

MASTER:

>Death is death, even if it's just acting, Farfoor!

FARFOOR:

>So you want it done dramatically? Shall we say our last goodbyes?

MASTER:

>I think we should. Who know? It might be just that.

FARFOOR:

>Well, all right, see you at the Hour of Meeting. You know, your way isn't mine.

MASTER:

>Why? Aren't you coming to Paradise with us?

FARFOOR:

>Really? Have you forgotten Abel whom you've killed in this very spot?

MASTER:
>Why this unpleasantness now at the end? Didn't we agree to say goodbye with some nice words?

FARFOOR:
>Well, yes! What a life? Do you remember the beginning of the play, Master?

MASTER:
>Do you remember when you married for me, Farfoor?

FARFOOR:
>You mean the appendix Lady? Those were the days.

MASTER:
>Goodbye now, Farfoor!

FARFOOR:
>*(Embracing him)* Goodbye, Master! I'm even going to miss your stupidity!

MASTER:
>And where can I find your saucy, sharp tongue to which I'm now accustomed?

FARFOOR:
>Put your head in, Man. *(Master puts his head in.)* Leave some space for me. *(Farfoor puts his head in.)* Go to the side a little! He's so fat!

MASTER:
>Listen, Farfoor-Boy! I don't agree to this death experiment. It's never just an experiment, but always an end and we're just beginning the play, so how can we end it like this? And suppose we did find out that it's the great leveller we're told it is. What solution is that which solves but brings to an end; that which brings about equality and stoppage? Life without a solution is a million times better than death with a solution. Life itself is the solution, Boy. It's probably incomplete, but it's smart to complete it, not cancel it out.

FARFOOR:
>But we didn't know how!

MASTER:
>We ultimately will, and if we didn't, someone will come along who will. Take your head out, Boy.

FARFOOR:
> It seems you've been transformed into a human
> being for good. You deserve a kiss for your
> thoughts.

CURTAIN OPERATOR:
> A kiss? You think kissing will end it? It's up
> to you anyway, I'll end it.

(Complete Blackout)

MASTER:
> It seems he's going to strangle us.

FARFOOR:
> Keep back, Pal!
> *(Sound of bodies dropping on the floor and gasps.
> The lights come back on gradually. Farfoor and
> the Master, with their necks in the noose which
> is now wider, lie next to each other on the
> floor.)*

FARFOOR:
> Master!

MASTER:
> Farfoor! Where are we?

FARFOOR:
> This problem requires "Where are we?" and "Who
> are we?" and "Where were we?" and "Where are we
> going?"

MASTER:
> Do you think he killed us?

FARFOOR:
> He had an evil look in his eye, anyway!

MASTER:
> Now we have become like your bad joke: When we
> started to live, we died.

FARFOOR:
> Are you going to start wailing now? Didn't we
> want to try death? Now we've tried it; let's hope
> it works.

MASTER:
> You mean we died? Are we buried yet or not?

FARFOOR:
> A month ago now. And to reassure you, they've
> also stolen our shrouds.

MASTER:

What are we now? Worms?

FARFOOR:

Less.

MASTER:

Dust?

FARFOOR:

Less. We're atoms. I'm an atom and you're an
atom like the rest of us and now your term of
Mastery is gone for good. Here you'll find a
nucleus, a neutron, a bonbon, but no Master
and Farfoor. You'll tell me it's an end and a
beginning and life and death with or without my
will, but I don't care. The most important thing
now for me is that we're exactly alike.

MASTER:

What do you mean alike? Can't you see that each
thing revolves around another, and we will do
the same?

FARFOOR:

We?

MASTER:

You particularly will revolve around me.

FARFOOR:

Why me particularly? Because I'm a Farfoor?

MASTER:

No, because you're lighter. The law here is that
the lighter shall revolve around the heavier. So
you will revolve around me.

FARFOOR:

Do you always have to produce a law wherever we
go? What misfortune is that? Do you work for
these laws or what? Tell me what these laws are?
What do we have to do with them? Are you a master
or a collection of laws? Could it be that you're
just a collection of laws? No, sir. I'm not
going to revolve, not even once. Is that the
solution we're trying? I won't revolve.

MASTER:

You must! It's not a matter of your will.

FARFOOR:

> *(Moving in a circle as if a secret hand is pull-*
> *ing him and forcing him to move and revolve*
> *around the Master)* What? What? Not like that!
> Well, do you want me to revolve alone? Why
> don't you get up and revolve with me?

MASTER:

> It's not in my power. Against my will I'll be
> motionless and against your will you'll revolve.

FARFOOR:

> Are we going to stay like that?

MASTER:

> So long as you're like that I must remain like
> that.

FARFOOR:

> And so long as you're like that I swear I'll go
> on being like that.

MASTER:

> I'm like that.

FARFOOR:

> And I'm like that.

MASTER:

> Revolve, Farfoor.

FARFOOR:

> You mean I'll be the one to revolve? O.K., I'll
> revolve some for your sake.

MASTER:

> In this again you're mistaken. It's not "some."
> You will revolve forever.

FARFOOR:

> What do you mean forever, eh?

MASTER:

> I mean forever. For the next million million
> years, until we find a solution.

FARFOOR:

> What are you saying? What terrifying things are
> you saying? I don't believe you and yet I am
> terrified.

MASTER:

> Revolve, Farfoor!

FARFOOR:

> I'm doing it on humanitarian grounds, mind you.
> How many revolutions are these now?

MASTER:

Six.

FARFOOR:

Well, I've a short way to go. When they are ten,
tell me.

MASTER:

By that time, I won't be able to tell you. By
that time, I'll have become a system, incommunicado.

FARFOOR:

What system?

MASTER:

Your system.

FARFOOR:

And what's so original about that? You've always
been my system and always incommunicado!

MASTER:

It's over, Farfoor. *(He swallows his breath with
difficulty.)* It's over, I'm... *(He is completely
silent.)*

FARFOOR:

I'm beginning to get tired. How many are these
now, Master? *(Master doesn't answer.)* How many are
these, I say? *(Master doesn't answer.)* Stop this
silly joke and answer me! *(He goes on revolving
and gradually strange hollow sounds are heard
and they get clearer and nearer, as if they were
the drum boats to which the universe moves. The
lighting, meanwhile, is getting more and more dim.)*
Seventeen now. *(The beats go faster and so does
he.)* Speak, Man, don't be so mean. What a day! I
hope you're not really silent for good or have
become a system. Answer me, Man! *(Beats go
faster and so does he)* No, it's not going to work
this way. I'm extremely tired. Just a minute,
let me tie my belt. You there, standing like a
wooden block, say something, keep me company.
Even if you'd clear your throat or cough. *(He
hits at him with his maqra'ah, but as soon as
it touches the Master, Farfoor pulls back his
hand, shocked as if a very high electric current
had thrown it away and thrown him upward. He*

cries in pain, holding his arm. All this without ceasing to run or revolve.) Oh my God, it's almost a decillion volts. *(Speed increases)* What's that? I've revolved about a thousand times already. I'm afraid of the dark. It seems it's really death. No, no. Not like that, Mr. System, please. May God systematize you even more! Please, not like that, Uncle. Please, I'm tired. Author! *(The speed increases and the circles grow bigger.)* Any Author! You of the Absurd group. *(The speed, having reached its maximum, is steady there from now on.)* Good people! Farfoors! Save your brother. I am beginning to lose my voice! Find us a solution! A solution, good folks! Help! There must be a solution. Some solution somewhere, your brother is finished. Please, a solution NOT for me: FOR YOU! I'm just acting. *(His voice shakes.)* It's YOU who are revolving. *(He cries. The words die in his mouth and he opens and closes it without a sound. He goes on revolving in silence under the influence of the cosmic beat for one minute, then the curtain comes down slowly, while he is revolving. When it rises again for the curtain calls, Farfoor will still be revolving, yet with a final loud beat from the drum, he stops and turns to bow to the Audience.)*

End